I0824165

HISTORIC PHOTOS OF
DELAWARE

TEXT AND CAPTIONS BY ELLEN RENDLE

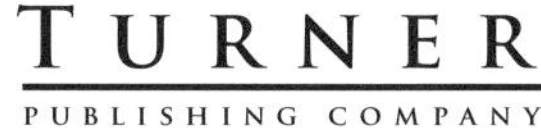

The tugboat *John J. Hagan* and the canal boat *Bloomington* travel along the busy Delaware River around 1901. The United States government undertook what it called the "Project of 1885" to deepen and widen the shipping lanes of the Delaware River from Philadelphia to the Delaware Bay, making the channel 26 feet deep and 600 feet wide.

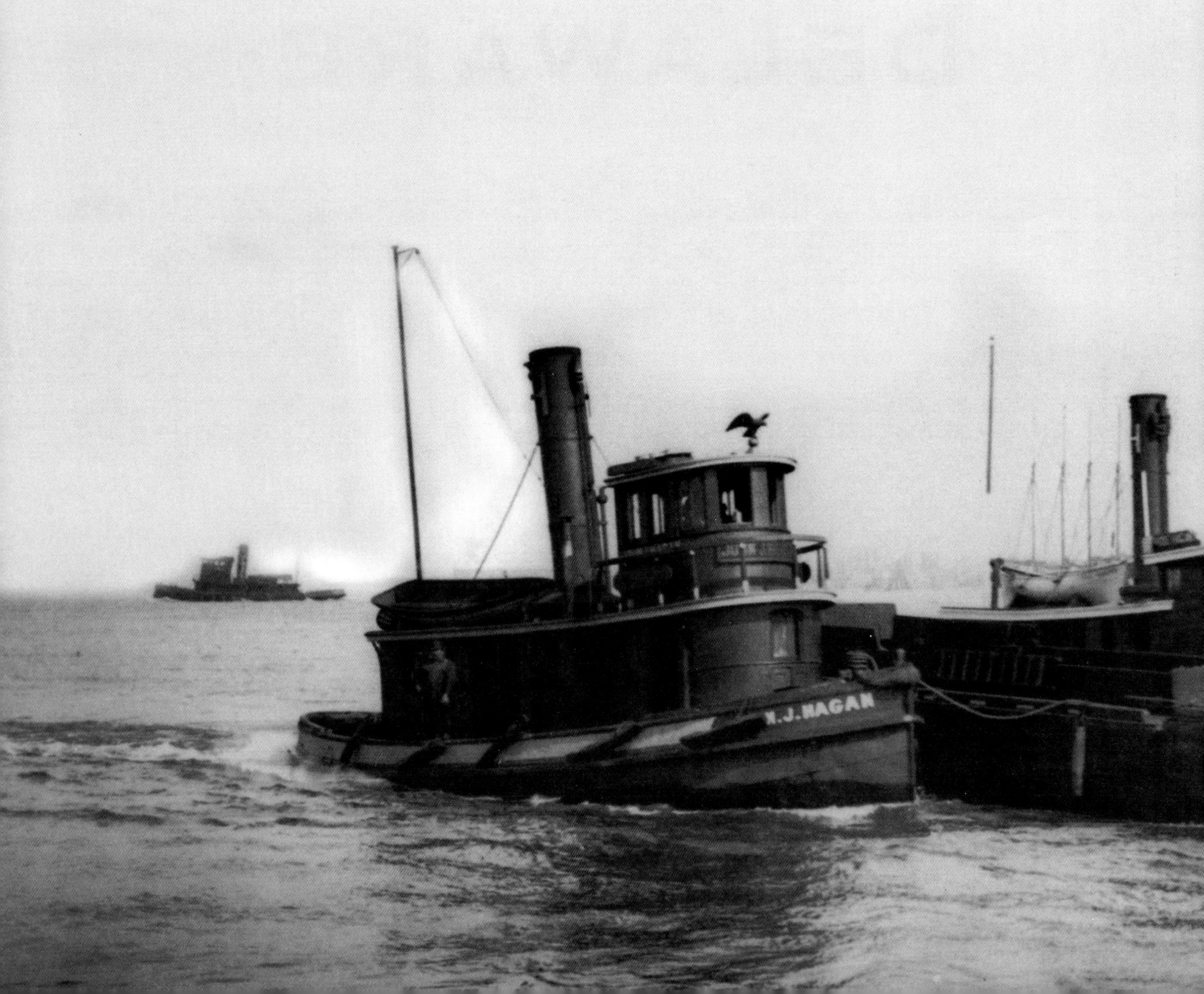

HISTORIC PHOTOS OF
DELAWARE

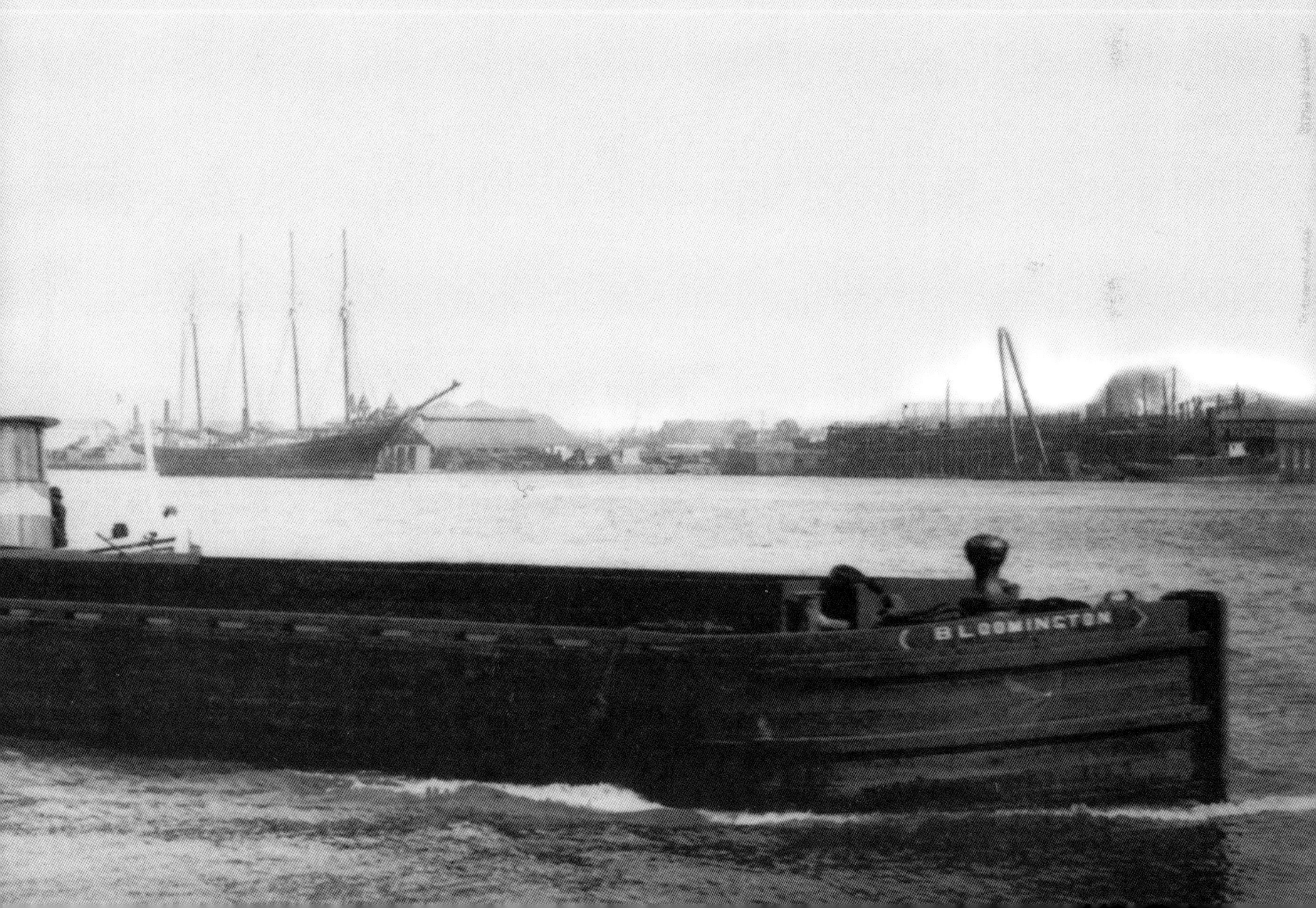

Turner Publishing Company
200 4th Avenue North • Suite 950
Nashville, Tennessee 37219
(615) 255-2665

www.turnerpublishing.com

Historic Photos of Delaware

Library of Congress Control Number: 2008901713

ISBN-13: 978-1-59652-440-8

Printed in China

08 09 10 11 12 13 14 15—0 9 8 7 6 5 4 3 2 1

Contents

Acknowledgments vii

Preface viii

The Railroads Bring Industry
(1860s–1899) 1

A New Century
(1900–1919) 45

Influences from Beyond the Border
(1920–1945) 103

Delaware in the Postwar Era
(1946–1970s) 165

Notes on the Photographs 200

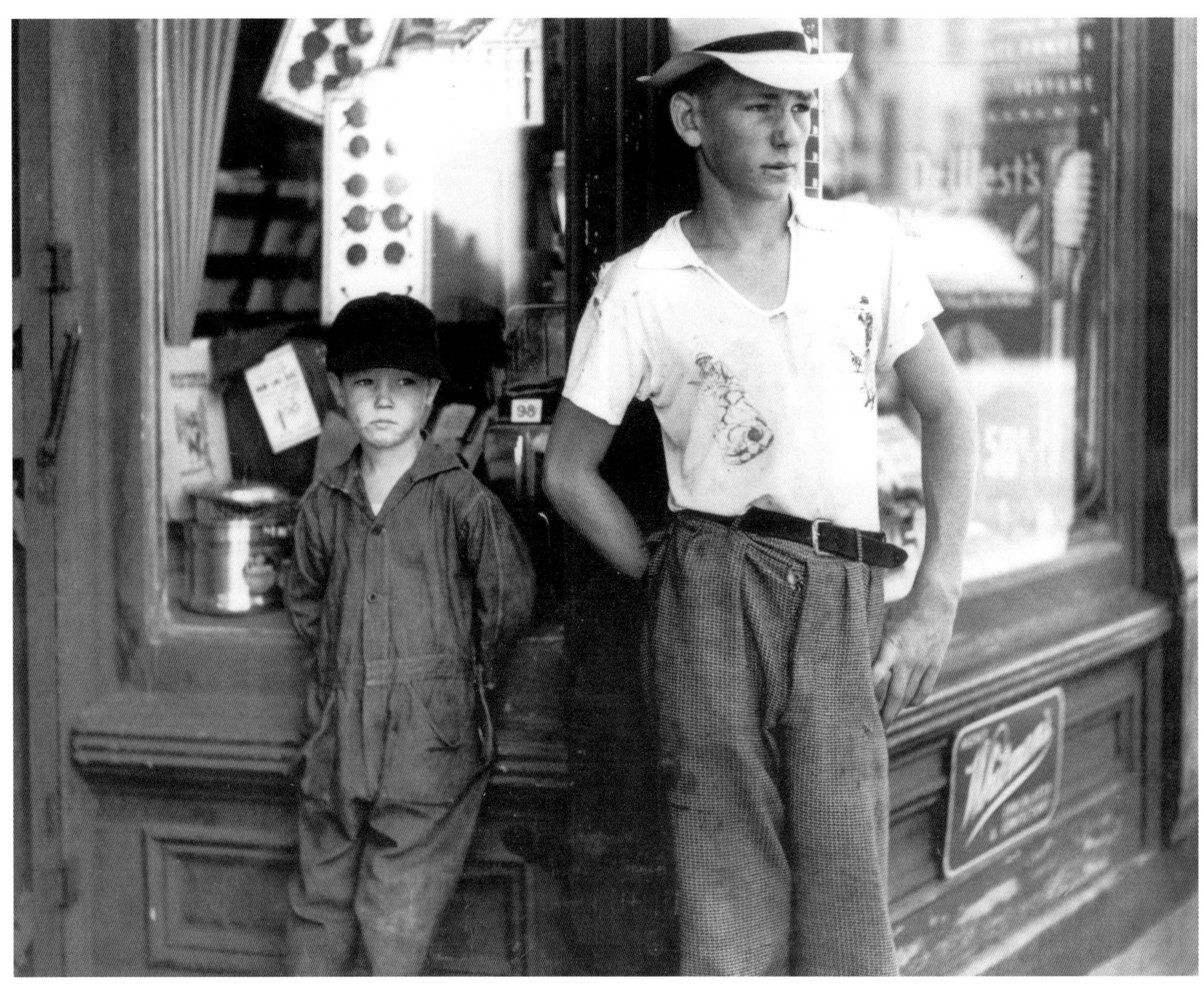

Photographer John Vachon traveling through Dover captured this moment of time in July 1938. Years of suffering through the Great Depression seem to be written on the boys' faces.

Acknowledgments

This volume, *Historic Photos of Delaware,* is the result of the cooperation and efforts of many individuals and organizations. It is with great thanks that we acknowledge the valuable contribution of the Delaware Historical Society and the Library of Congress for their generous support.

The author would like to thank her parents for introducing her to history and allowing her to study what she wanted to study, where she wanted to study it—even 900 miles from home. She would also like to thank her husband, John, for his continuing support. Finally, thanks to countless Delawareans who have worked to build the photograph collections at the Delaware Historical Society through the years. They are rich with historical moments, private memories, and enlightening depictions of the state's history.

PREFACE

The history of Delaware has been captured in thousands of photographs that reside in archives, both locally and nationally. This book began with the observation that, while those photographs are of great interest to many, they are not easily accessible. The area today is home to many residents, new and old, who are curious about the local history, especially as the streetscapes and individual buildings associated with that history sometimes seem to be in the way of progress. Many people are asking how to treat these remnants of the past. The decisions made affect every aspect of the urban environment—architecture, public spaces, commerce, infrastructure—and these, in turn, affect the ways that people live their lives. This book seeks to provide decision makers—citizens and officials—a valuable, objective look into the history of Delaware's towns, cities, and rural areas through photographs of the state.

Although the photographer can make decisions regarding subject matter and how to capture and present it, photographs, unlike words, seldom interpret history subjectively. This lends them an authority that textual histories sometimes fail to achieve, and offers the viewer an original, untainted perspective from which to draw his own conclusions, interpretations, and insights.

This project represents countless hours of research. The editors and writer have reviewed thousands of photographs in numerous archives. We greatly appreciate the generous assistance of the organizations listed in the acknowledgments, without whom this project could not have been completed.

The goal in publishing this work is to provide broader access to these extraordinary images, to inspire, furnish perspective, and evoke insight that might assist those who are responsible for determining the future of the great state of Delaware. In addition, we hope that the book will encourage the preservation of the past with adequate respect and reverence.

With the exception of cropping images where needed and touching up imperfections that have accrued over time, no other changes have been made. The caliber and clarity of many photographs are limited by the technology of the day and the ability of the photographer at the time they were made.

The book is divided into four eras. The selection begins with images from the nineteenth century. The second section spans the first decades of the twentieth century, when the region grew as both an industrial and a vacation center. Section

Three covers the period between the end of World War I to the end of World War II. Section Four continues the story from the postwar years to the early 1970s.

In each of these sections we have made an effort to capture various aspects of life through our selection of photographs. People, commerce, industry, recreation, transportation, infrastructure, and religious and educational institutions have been included to provide a broad perspective.

We encourage readers to reflect as they visit Delaware's many historic sites, enjoy the beaches and parks, and experience the amenities of this bustling state fronting the Atlantic Coast. It is the publisher's hope that in utilizing this work, longtime residents will learn something new and that new residents will gain a perspective on where the state has been, so that each can contribute effectively to its future.

—Todd Bottorff, Publisher

This unusual view, probably recorded around 1865, shows Old Swedes Church in Wilmington as seen from the southeast. Old Swedes is the nation's oldest church building still standing as originally built. It is still in regular use for worship.

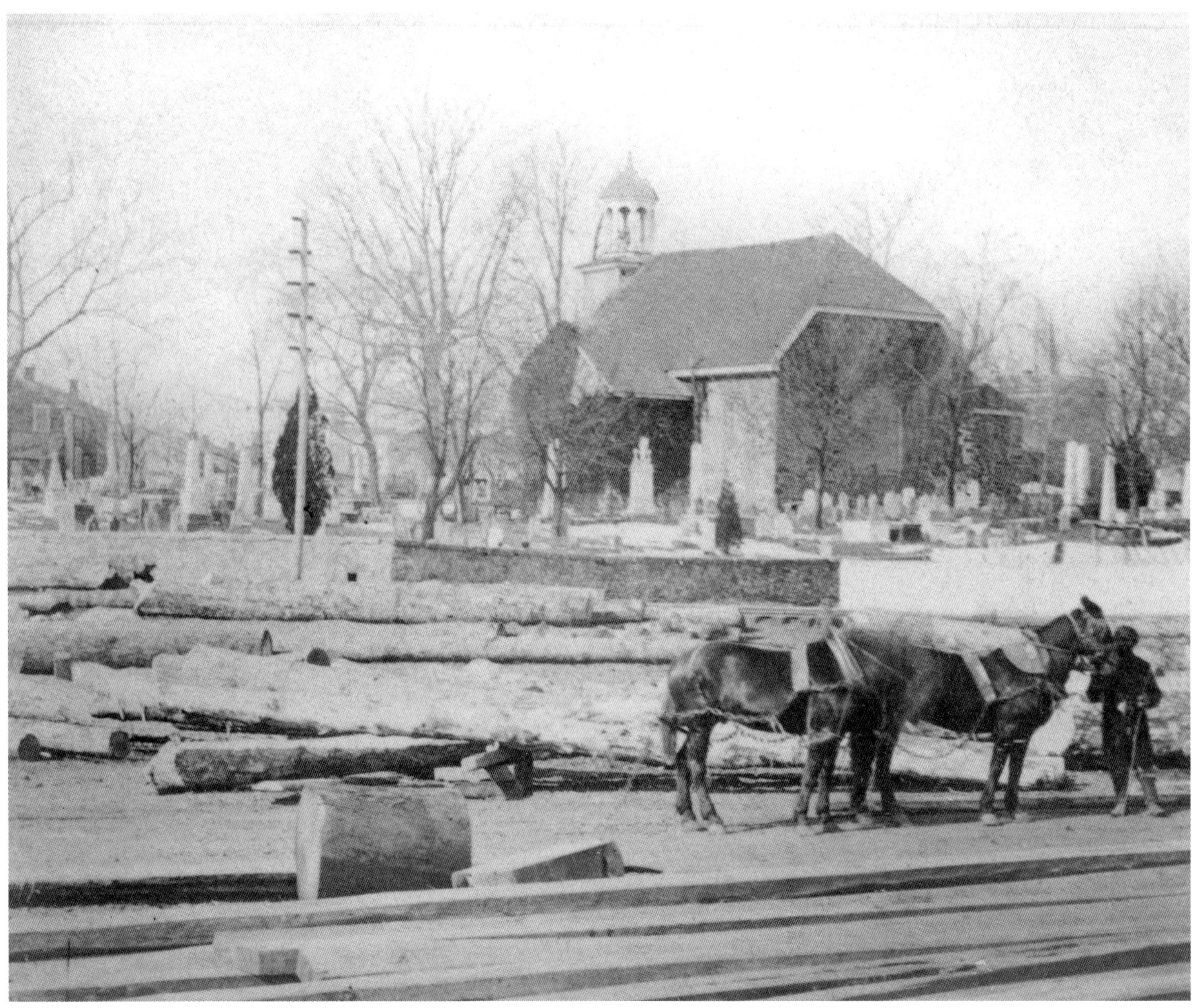

The Railroads Bring Industry
(1860s–1899)

Delawareans could not have foreseen all the changes to come as the Industrial Revolution (1820–1870) took hold of the nation. Throughout its early history, Delaware remained predominantly rural, but a system of railroads and canals connected the state to Philadelphia, Pennsylvania, as the nineteenth century advanced. Quick, affordable access to markets by way of the Chesapeake and Delaware Canal, completed in 1829, and the Philadelphia, Wilmington and Baltimore Railroad, completed in 1838, excited businessmen and brought new opportunities. Barge transportation was cheap and convenient for the Wilmington-based shipping firms making daily trips to Philadelphia. Manufacturing expanded along the Christina and Brandywine rivers. By 1890, Wilmington was a factory town.

Wilmington's skilled work force had built and maintained the Brandywine mills, and its businessmen had accumulated considerable venture capital. Well positioned to accept new opportunity, capitalists used new technologies to build an industrial, urban culture. Of the state's total population of 78,085, Wilmington accounted for 8,367. In the decades from 1840 to 1890, Wilmington's population increased by a factor of seven while the state's population doubled.

Railroad car construction and shipbuilding became Wilmington's largest industries. By 1865, Delaware's four biggest companies—Harlan and Hollingsworth, Pusey and Jones, the Lobdell Car Wheel Company, and Jackson and Sharp—manufactured railroad equipment. Carriage-making and tanneries also employed large work forces. Before the Civil War there were seven times as many farm workers as factory workers, but by 1900 more men worked in manufacturing than on farms. The new work force included farm boys who moved to the city, an increasing number of African Americans, and a steady influx of immigrants.

In 1856, the Delaware Railroad connected Seaford and Wilmington, and soon Kent County acreage under cultivation increased by 25 percent as farmers switched from raising grains to perishable foodstuffs. For the first time, towns located along the railroad grew faster than port towns.

Politically, the national division over slavery and the secession of Southern states from the Union divided Delawareans geographically and emotionally. In 1860, the state's slave population was under 1,800, but slavery was legal and the governor contemplated joining the Confederacy. In the end, Delaware became a border state. Twelve thousand Delaware men joined the Union army, about 500 Delawareans fought for the Confederacy, and federal records estimate that more than 900 blacks joined out-of-state Union forces.

Scaffolding surrounds Grace Methodist Church at 9th and West streets in Wilmington. The steeple is shown in the foreground before it was raised into position. The congregation intended to celebrate two things upon the church's completion in 1865: it was a memorial to the centenary of Methodism in the city, and it served as an offering of thanks to God for sparing the city from attack during the Civil War.

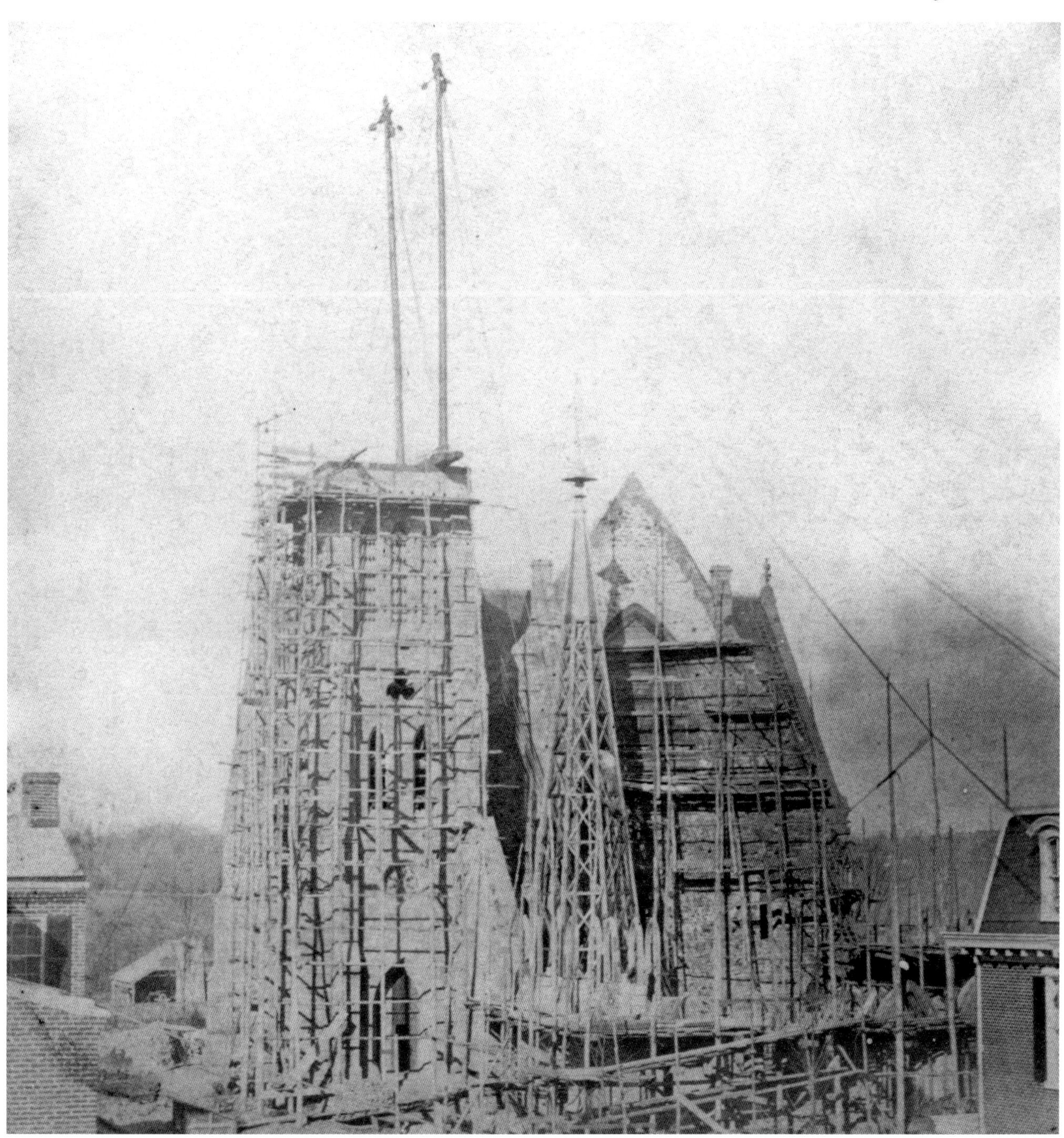

Photographers Gihon and Jones of Philadelphia captured this view of Fort Delaware in the 1870s. Built to protect the Delaware River, and ports of Wilmington and Philadelphia, it served instead as a prisoner-of-war camp for Confederate soldiers during the Civil War. Overcrowding and other adverse conditions caused it to be a place of suffering and disease. Seen here after the war it appears quiet and nearly empty.

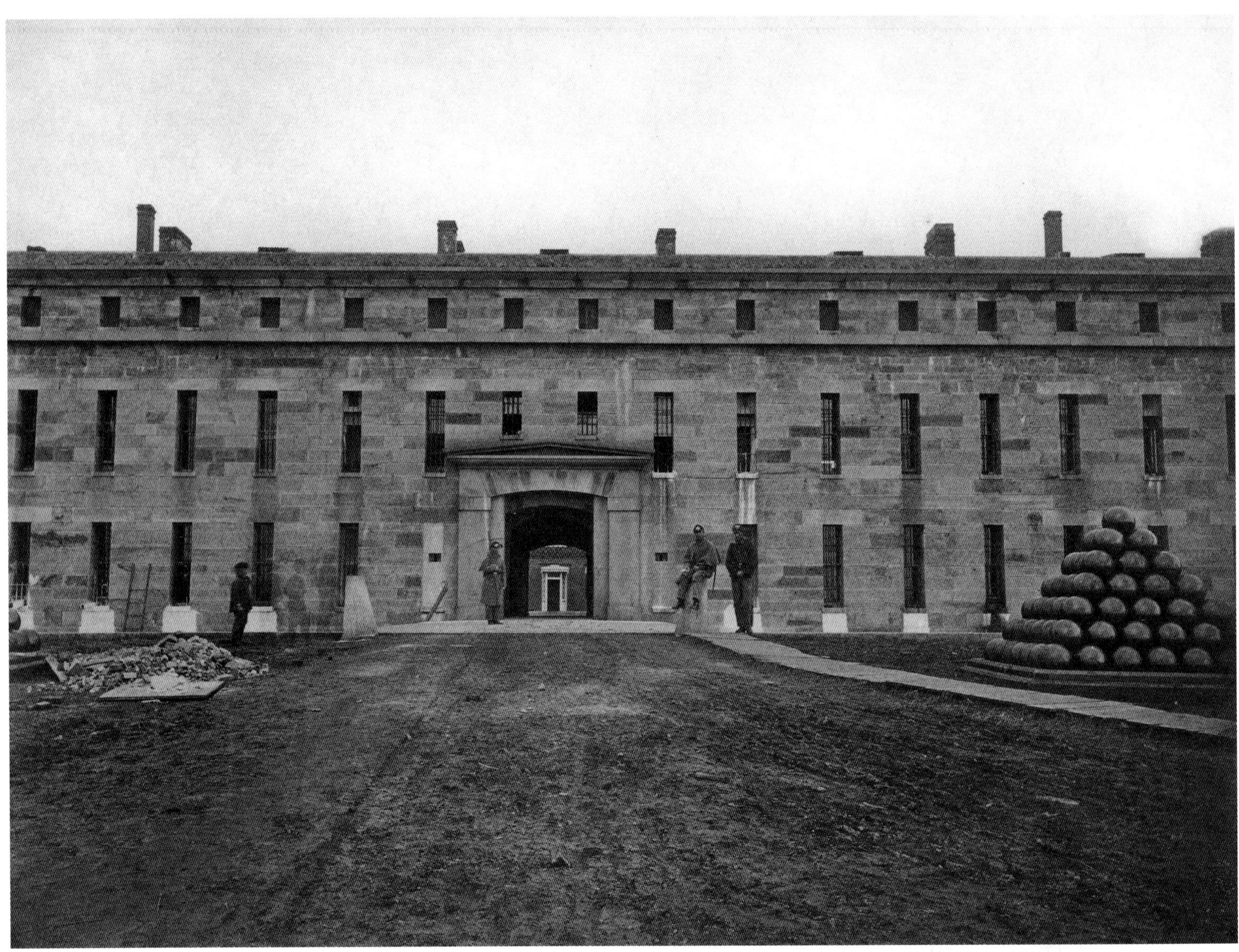

Market Street in Wilmington is shown on a bustling market day around 1863. This view, recorded from an upstairs window facing north, shows trucks lined up along the sides of the street to sell produce. A horse-drawn trolley approaches at lower center.

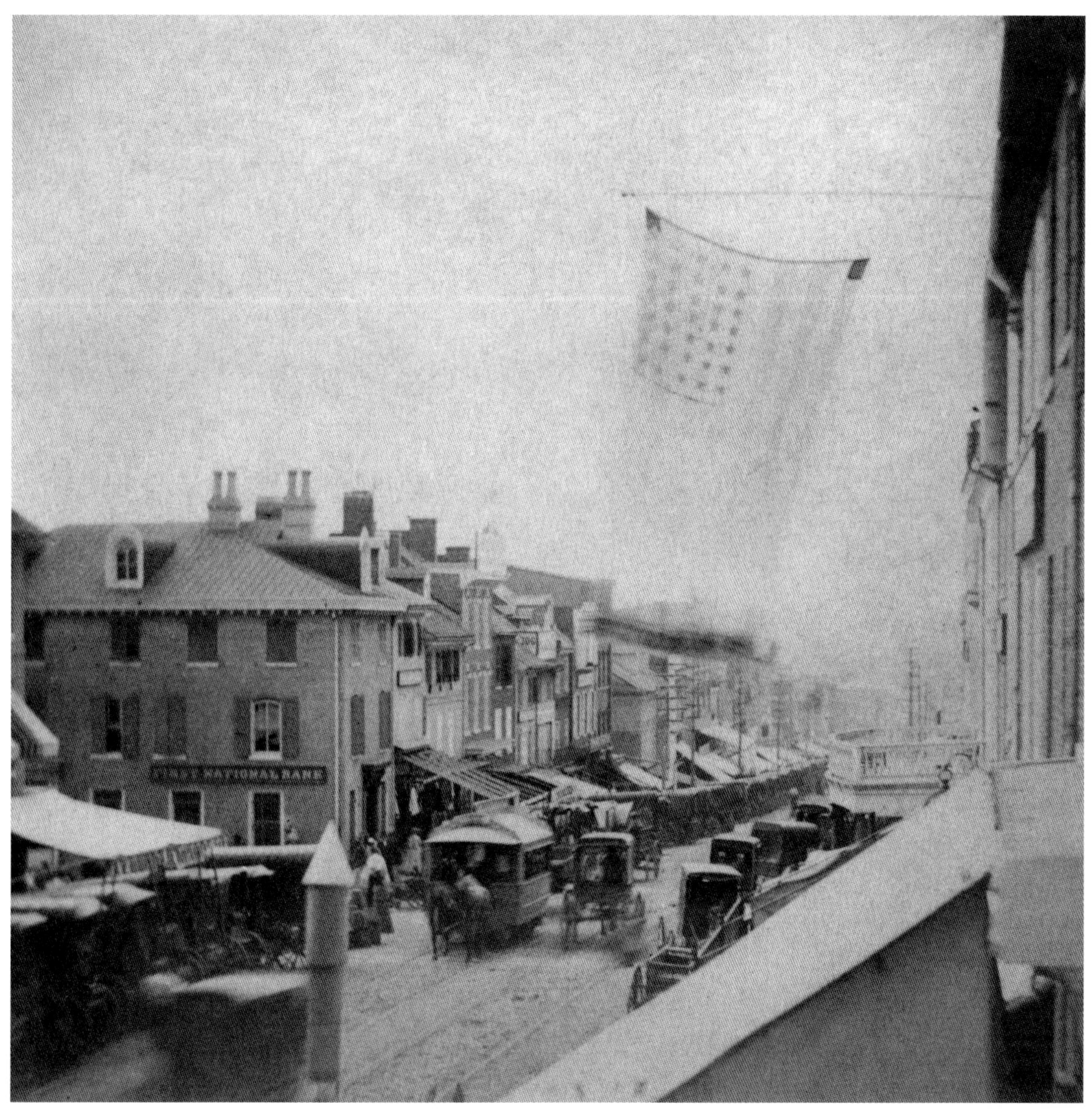

Photographer John E. Torbert took this photograph of Tilton Hospital. The hospital, built in 1863 at 9th and Tatnall streets, was torn down shortly after the Civil War ended. It was named for Dr. James E. Tilton (1745–1822), a native of Kent County. Tilton was in the first graduating medical class of the College of Philadelphia (1768), served in the Revolutionary War, and was appointed Surgeon General of the Army in 1813.

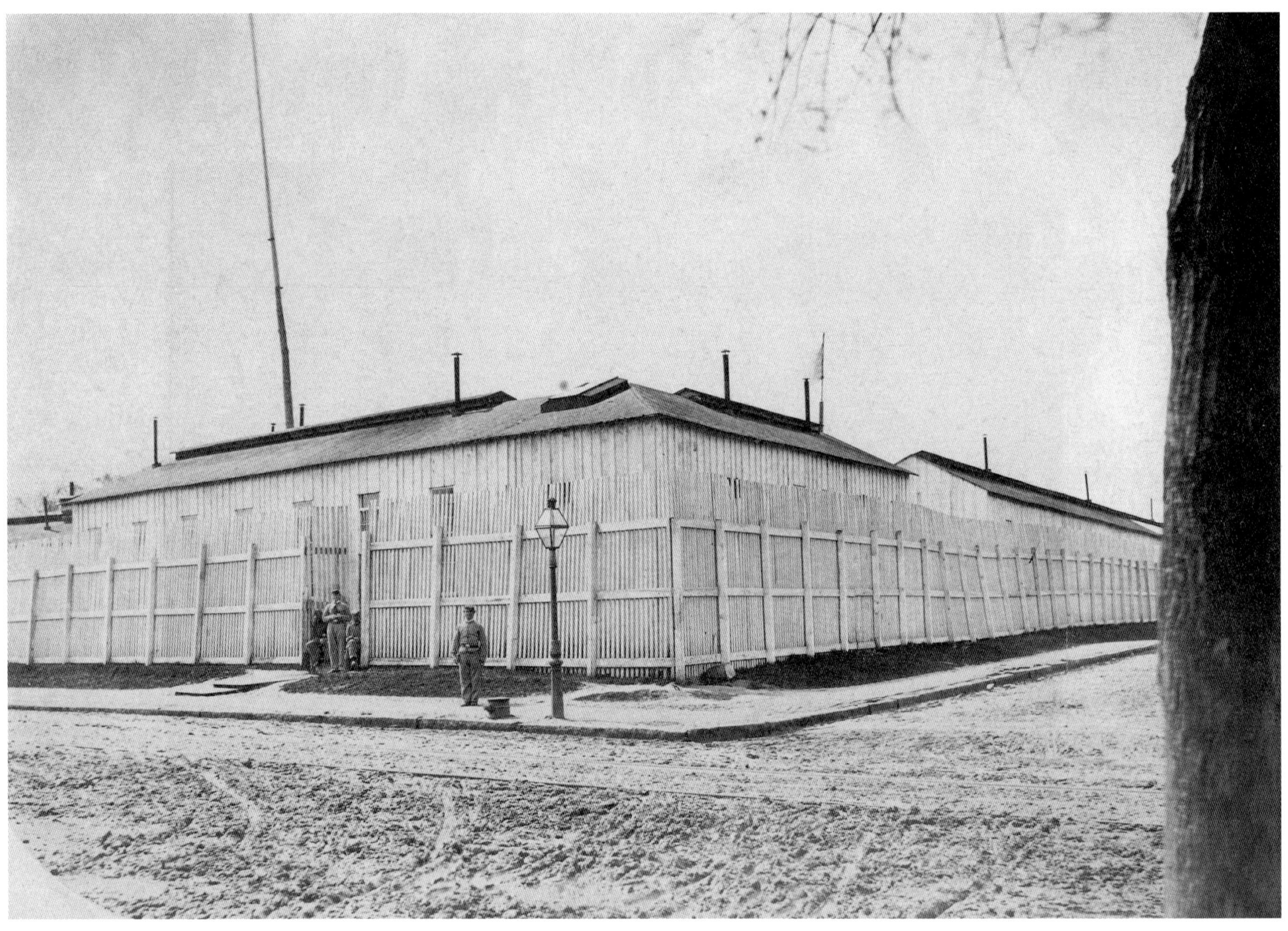

This group of six soldiers served in the First Delaware Regiment and Guard. Though the soldiers appear young, their flag shows that they have seen battle. Organized in April 1861, the regiment saw action at Antietam, Fredericksburg, Chancellorsville, Gettysburg, Petersburg, and Deep Bottom and was present at the surrender of General Robert E. Lee.

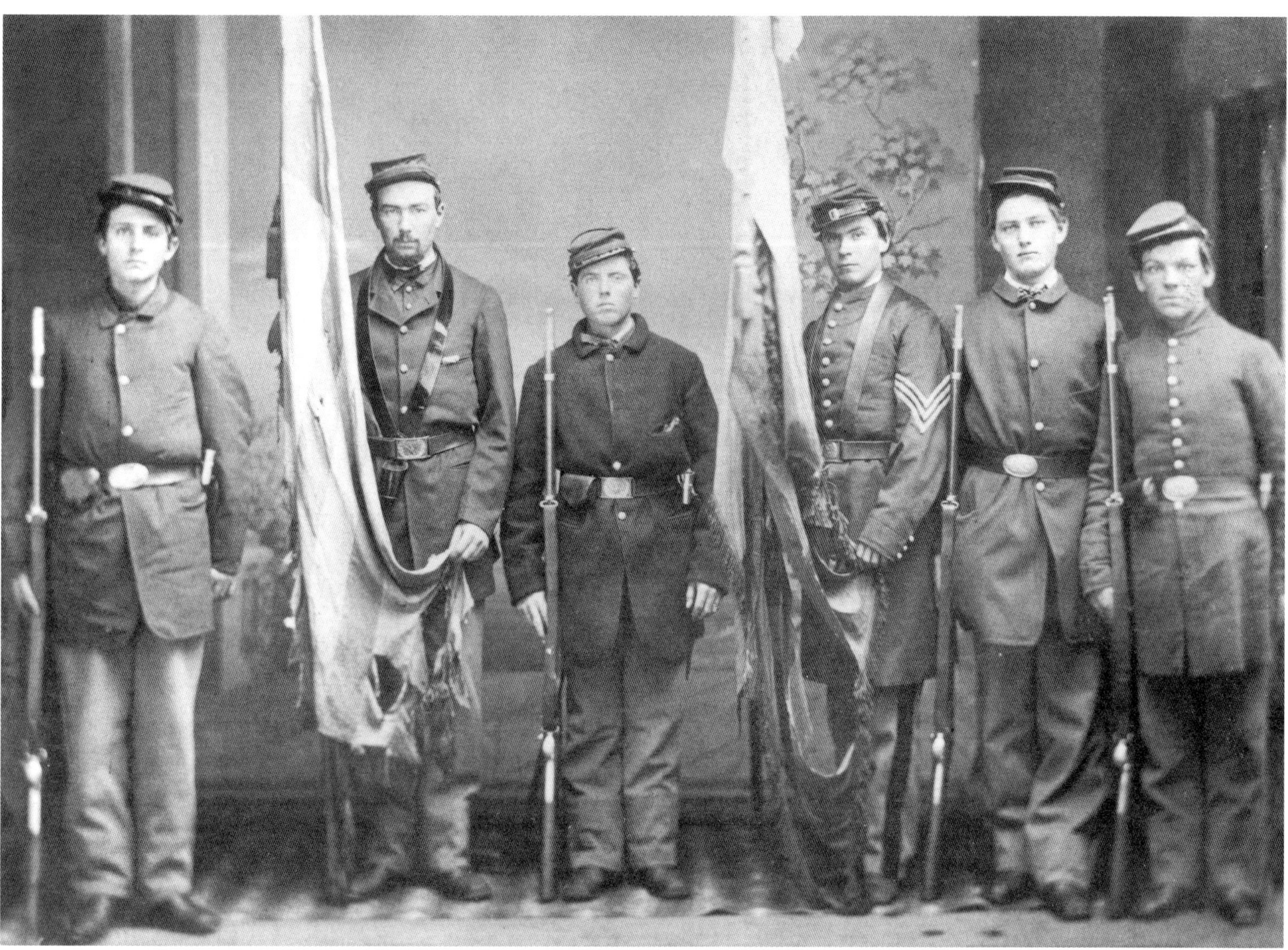

Locomotive No. 1 of the Philadelphia, Wilmington and Baltimore Railroad passes the shipyard of the Harlan and Hollingsworth Company at the foot of West Street in Wilmington in the 1860s.

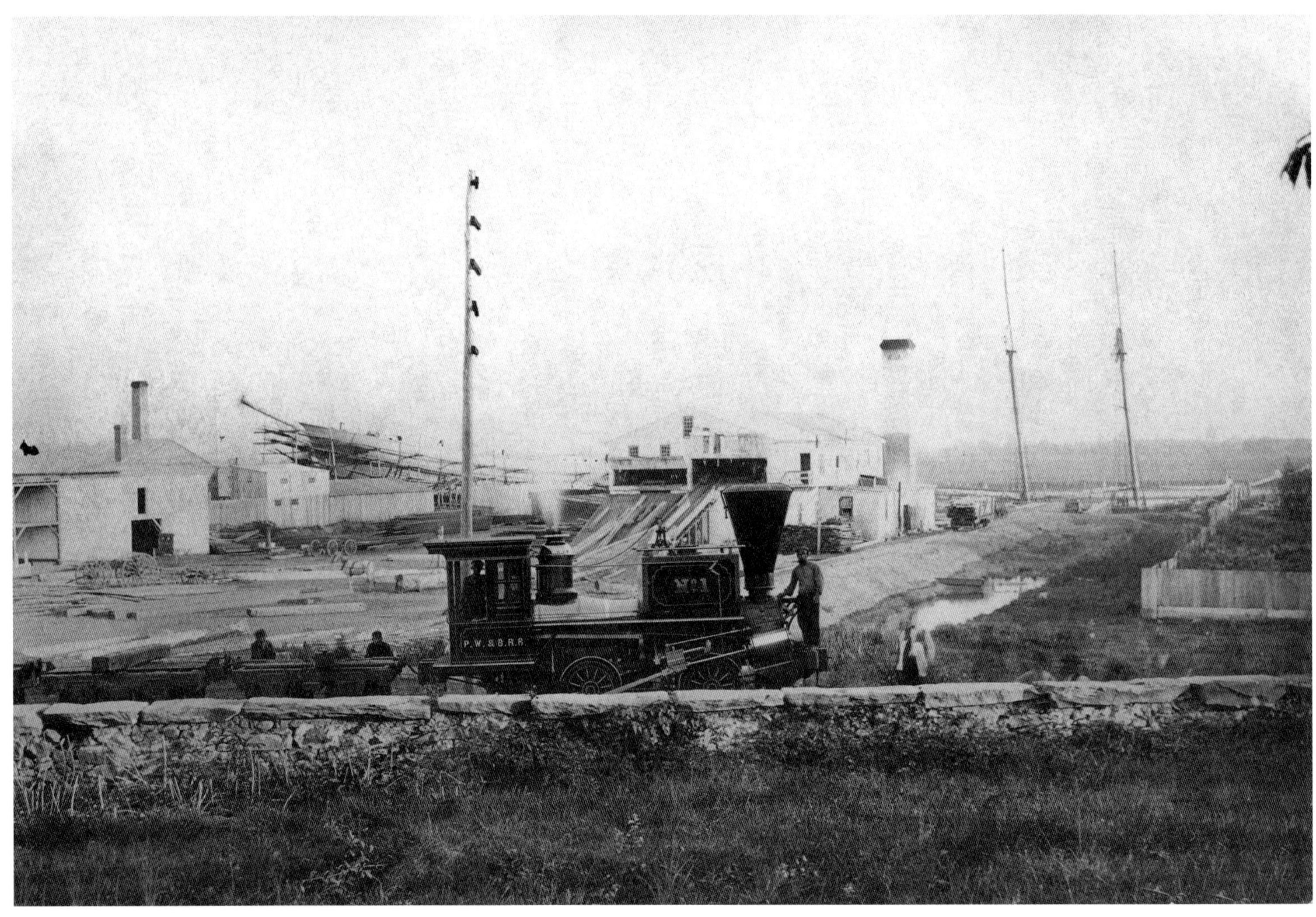

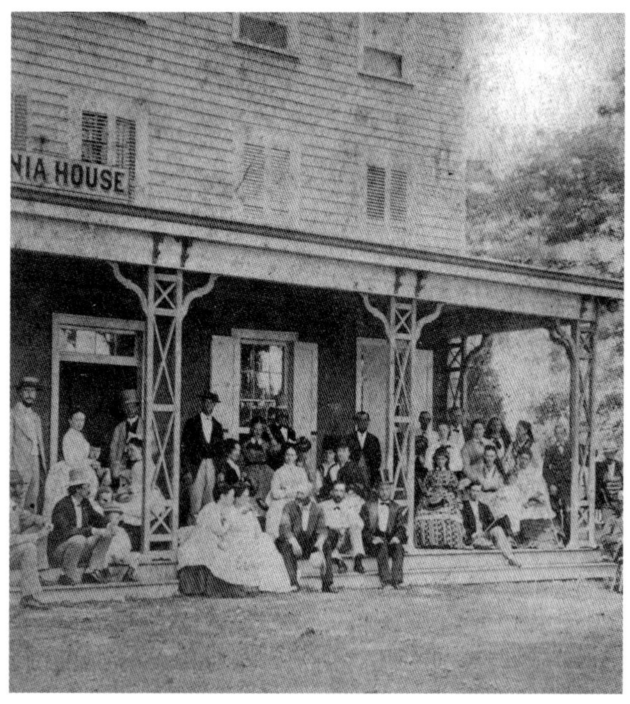

Delawareans enjoying leisure pose for the photographer in 1871. Among Delaware's popular summer resorts in the 1870s was Collins Beach, located midway between Odessa and Smyrna on the Delaware River. It was a regular stop on the excursion route of the steam-powered side-wheelers serving Philadelphia and Wilmington. In 1878, a tidal wave from a hurricane destroyed the pier, buildings, roads, and the allure of the resort.

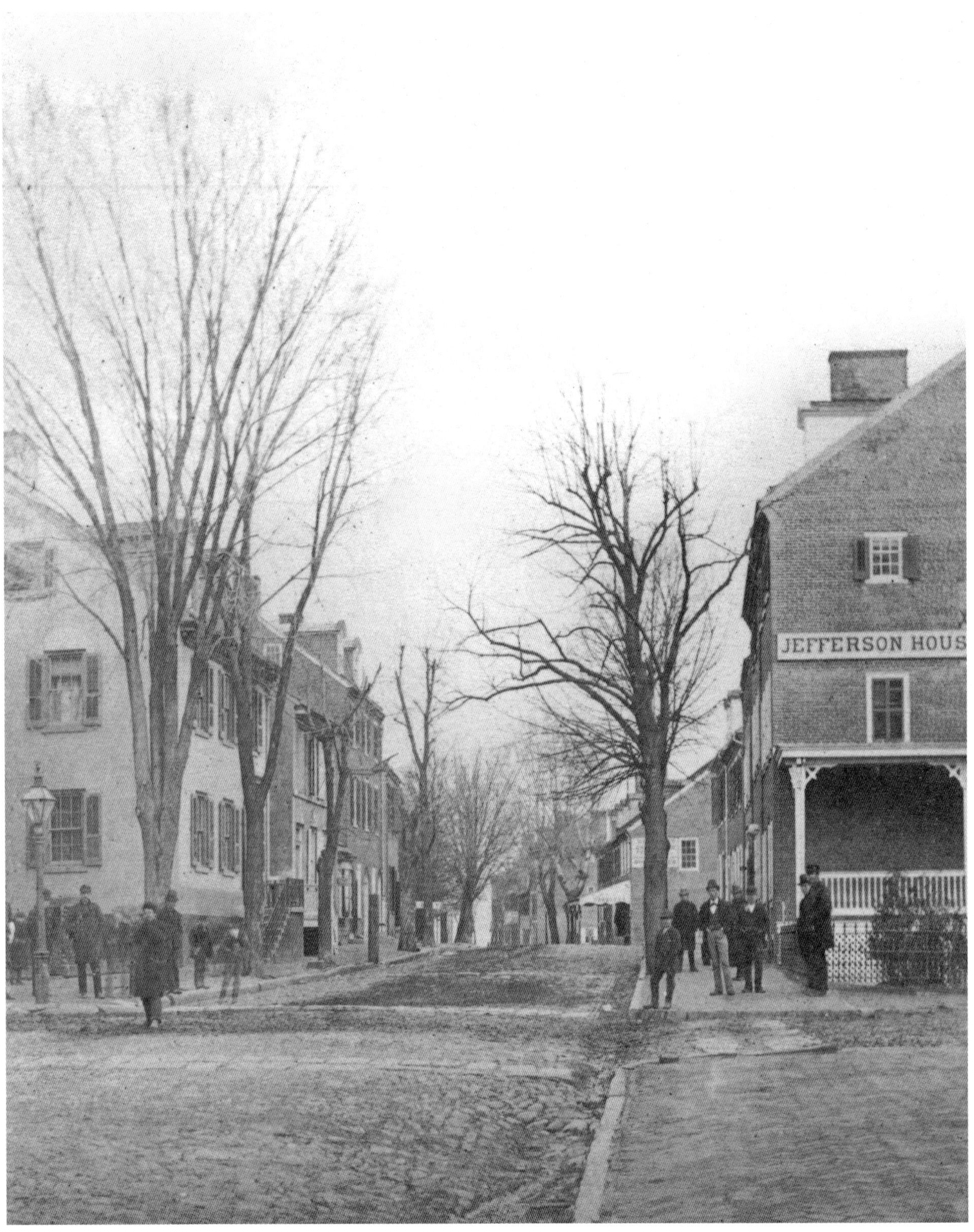

This photograph of the Strand in New Castle was recorded at an intersection of Delaware Street in the 1870s. The large number of gentlemen posing along the street is an indice of the enthusiasm photography could generate.

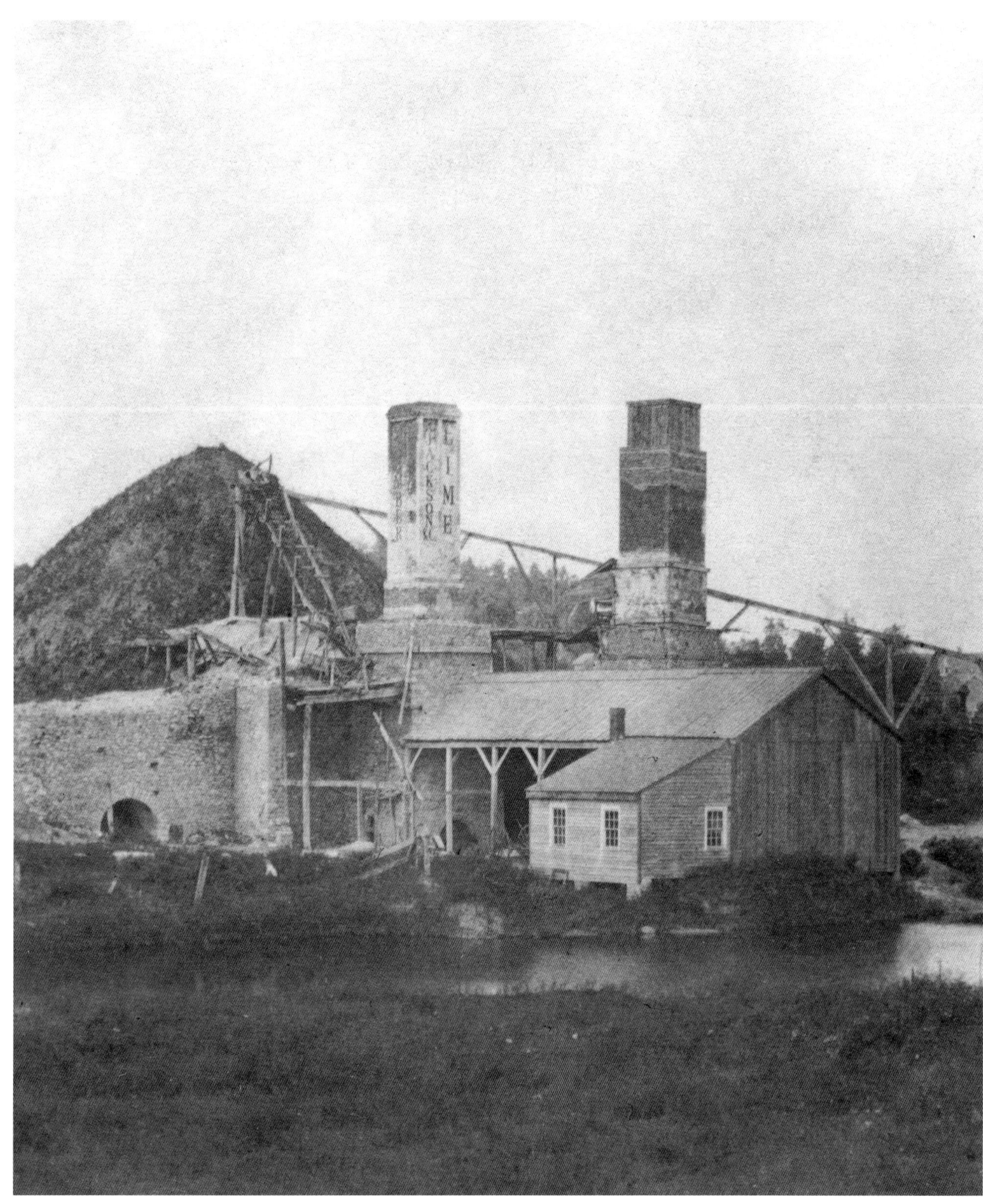

Jackson's limestone kiln, shown here in the 1870s, was located in Hockessin. John G. Jackson, born in Hockessin in 1818, bought a farm intending to be a farmer and writer, but business opportunities took him in other directions. He played an important role in the development of limestone quarries and kilns, served as chief engineer during the building of the Wilmington and Western Railroad, and even served a few terms as a state senator.

Harlan and Hollingsworth Company gathered its impressive work force for a company photograph at the yards. At the time, Harlan and Hollingsworth was Wilmington's largest firm and played a key role in Wilmington's rise to becoming the nation's largest producer of iron-hulled ships. Founded in 1836, the yards expanded to occupy 43 acres along the Christina River at the foot of West Street.

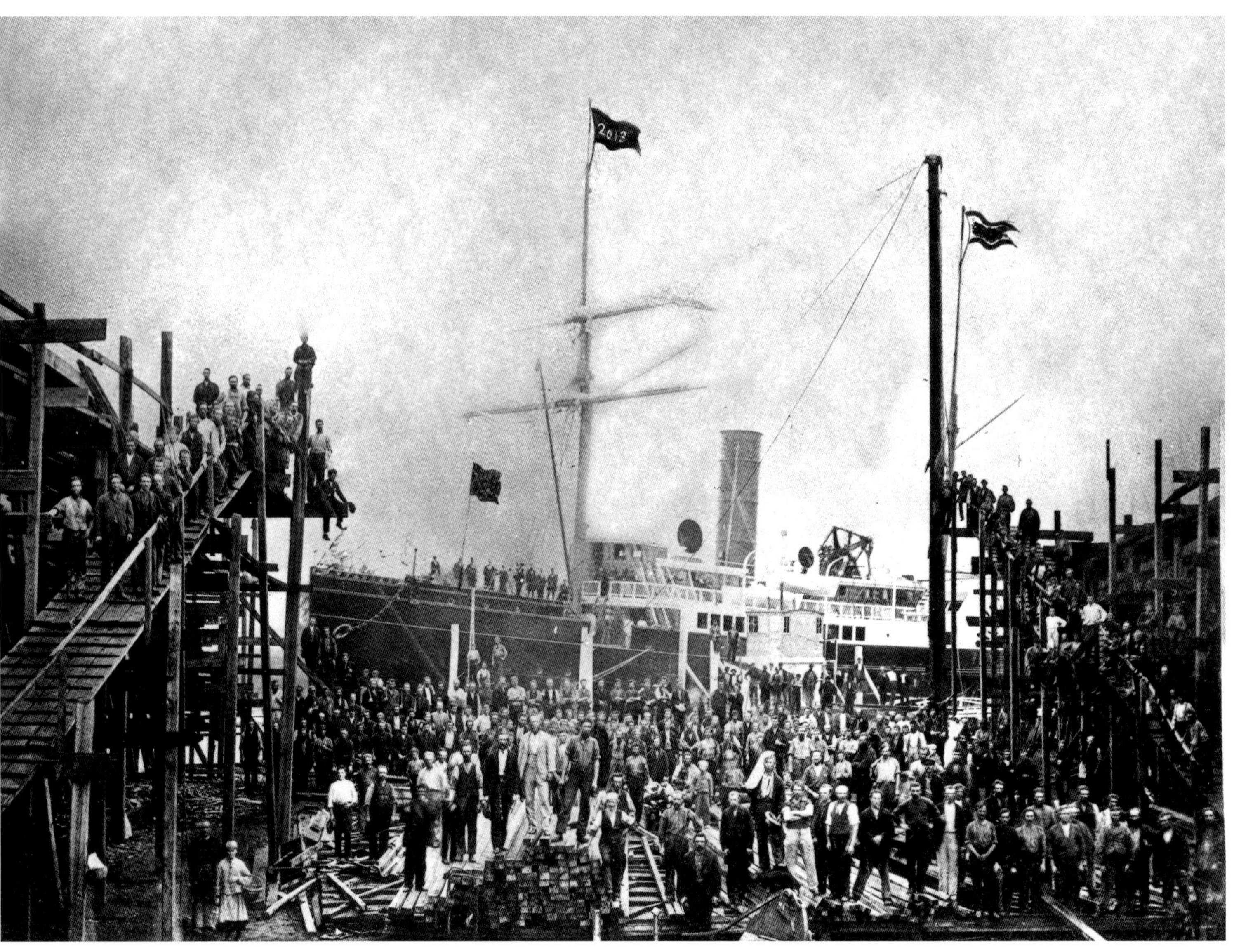

The Philadelphia, Wilmington and Baltimore Railroad car shops along Water Street at Walnut in Wilmington are shown here. The P.W. and B. was purchased by the Pennsylvania Railroad shortly after this photograph was taken.

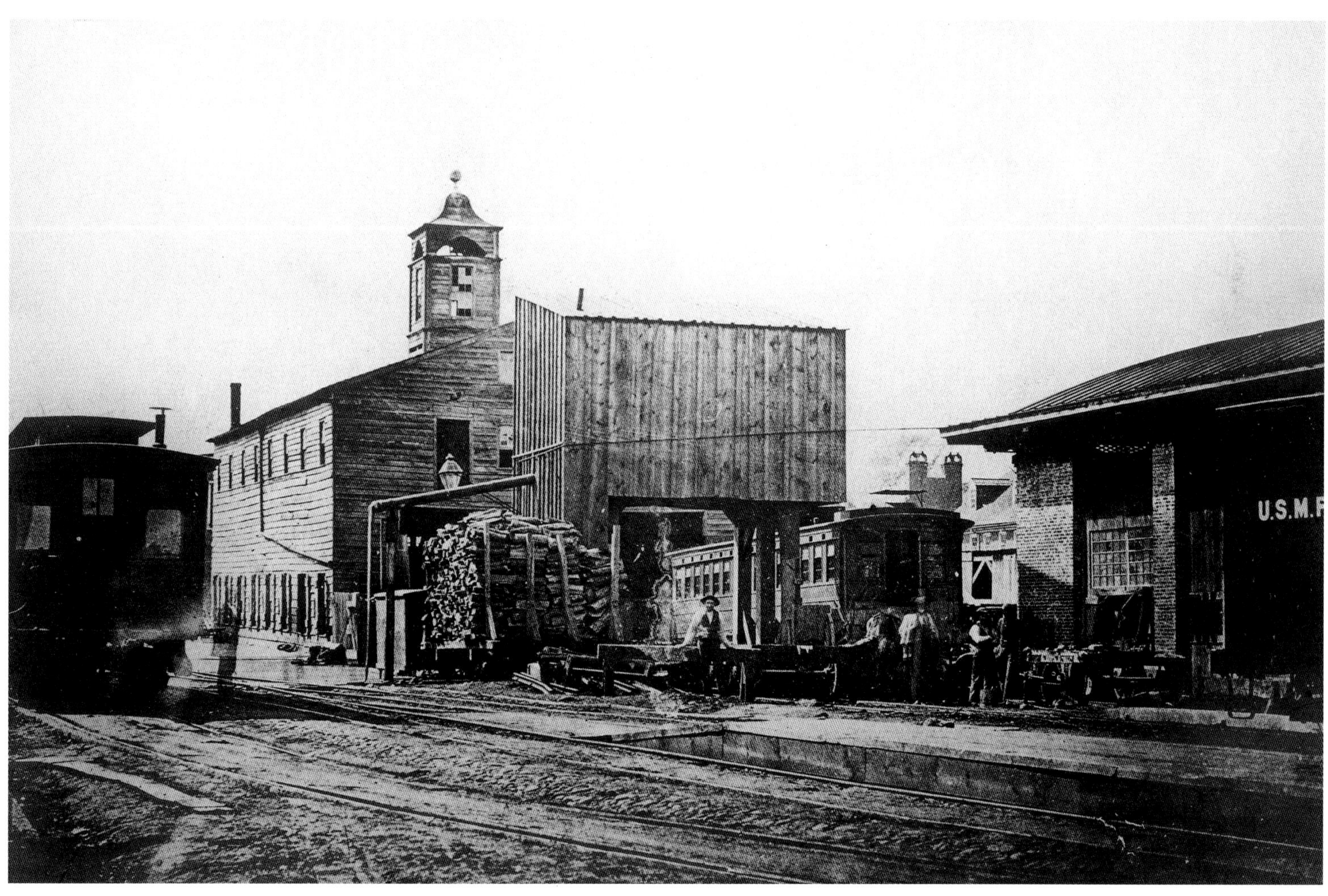

The Holly Tree Inn was organized by the local temperance group as a no-liquor lunchroom for workingmen. The inn opened January 14, 1875, located at Water and Market streets. It closed on September 10, 1877, for the purpose of erecting "a more inviting and commodious one on the same site." At the time this inn was in business, the blocks along the Christina River were crammed with industrial sites and warehouses.

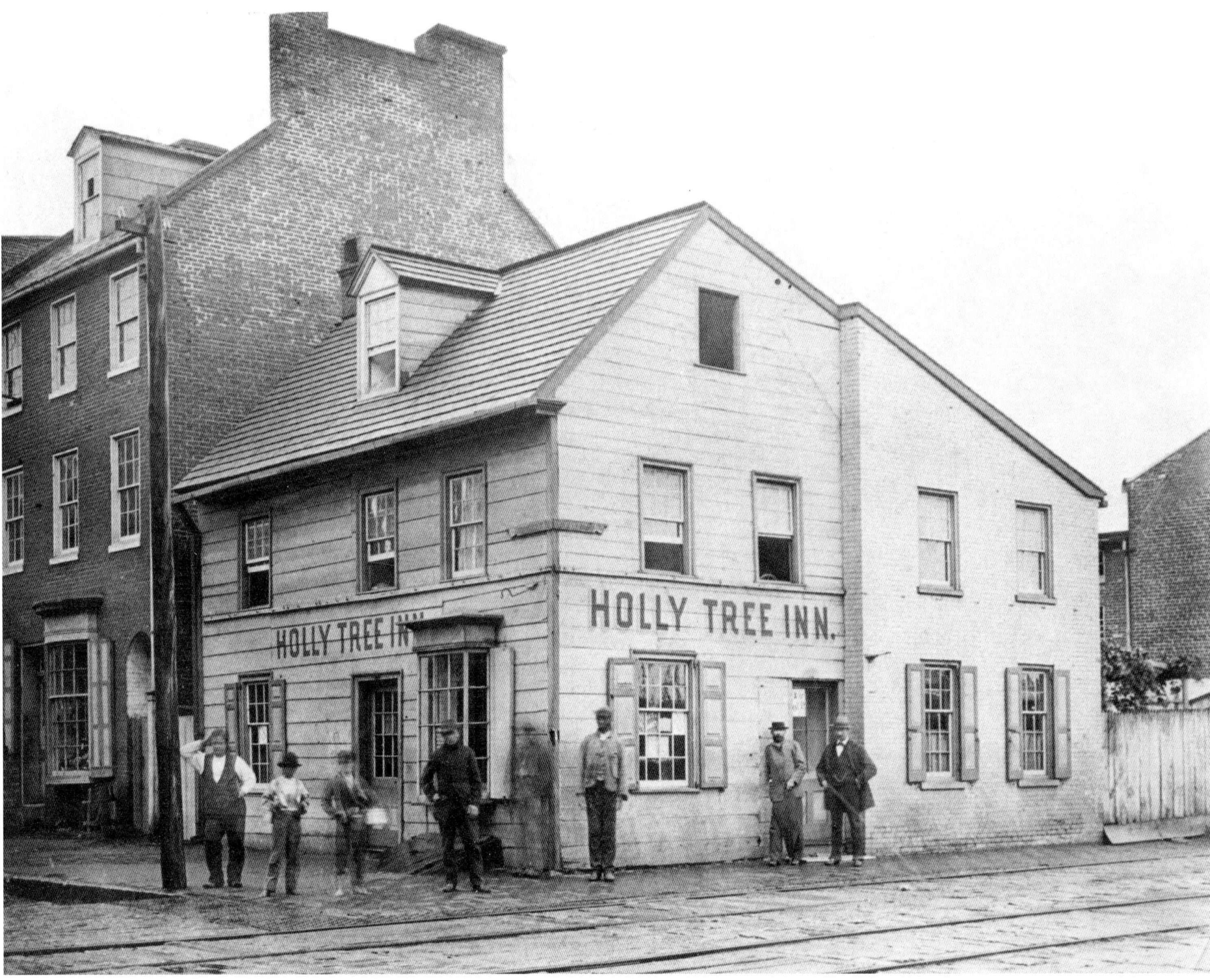

Members of the Wilmington Fire Department demonstrate their new Daniel Hayes Aerial Truck between 1872 and 1875. The firemen on the ladder seem to be acrobats as much as they are fire fighters. Questionable is whether water pressure at such heights sufficed to drench a fire.

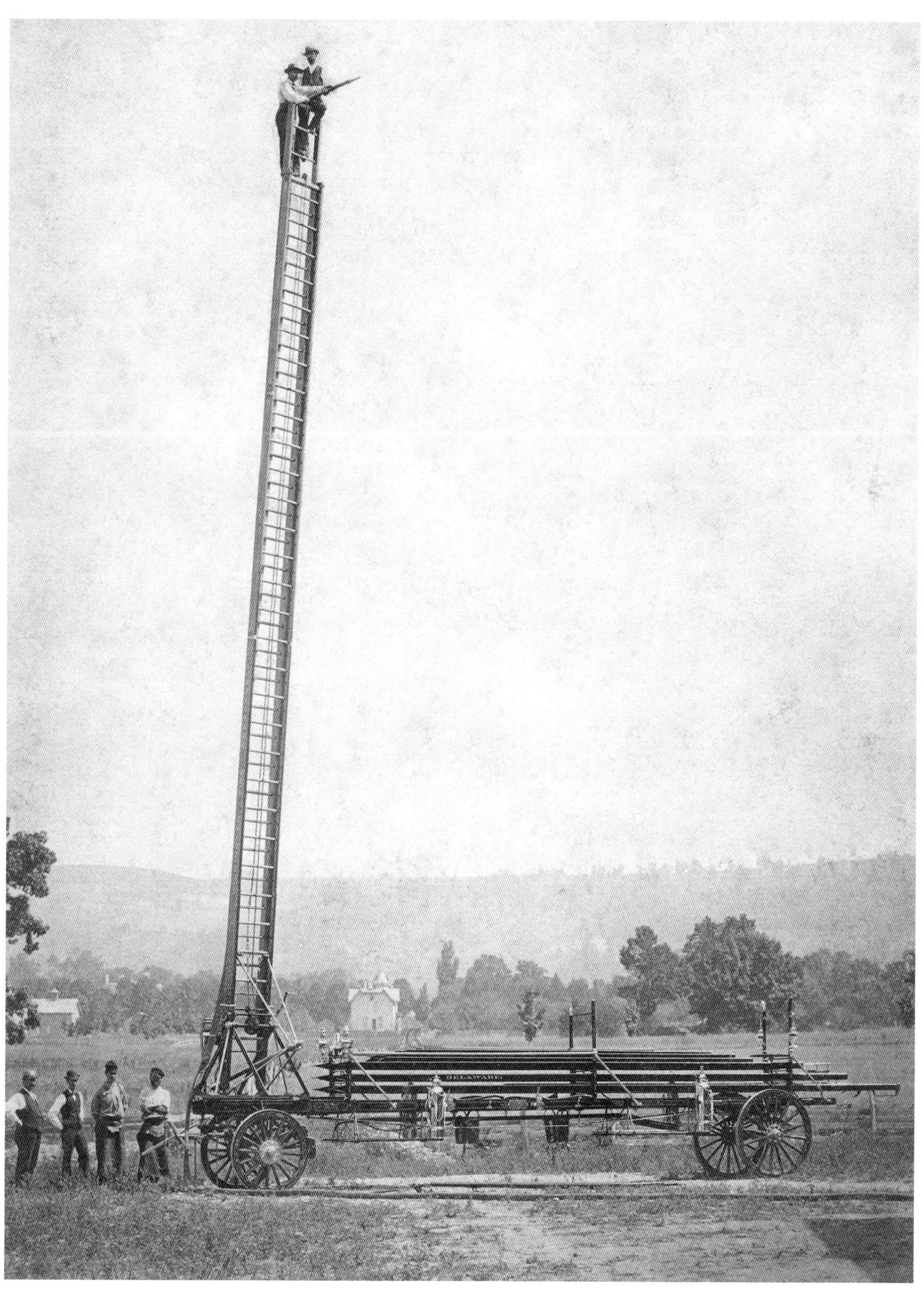

Built in 1881, the Pennsylvania Railroad Station at Water Street in Wilmington was an imposing structure. This station was not in use very long; it was replaced with the Frank Furness station in 1907.

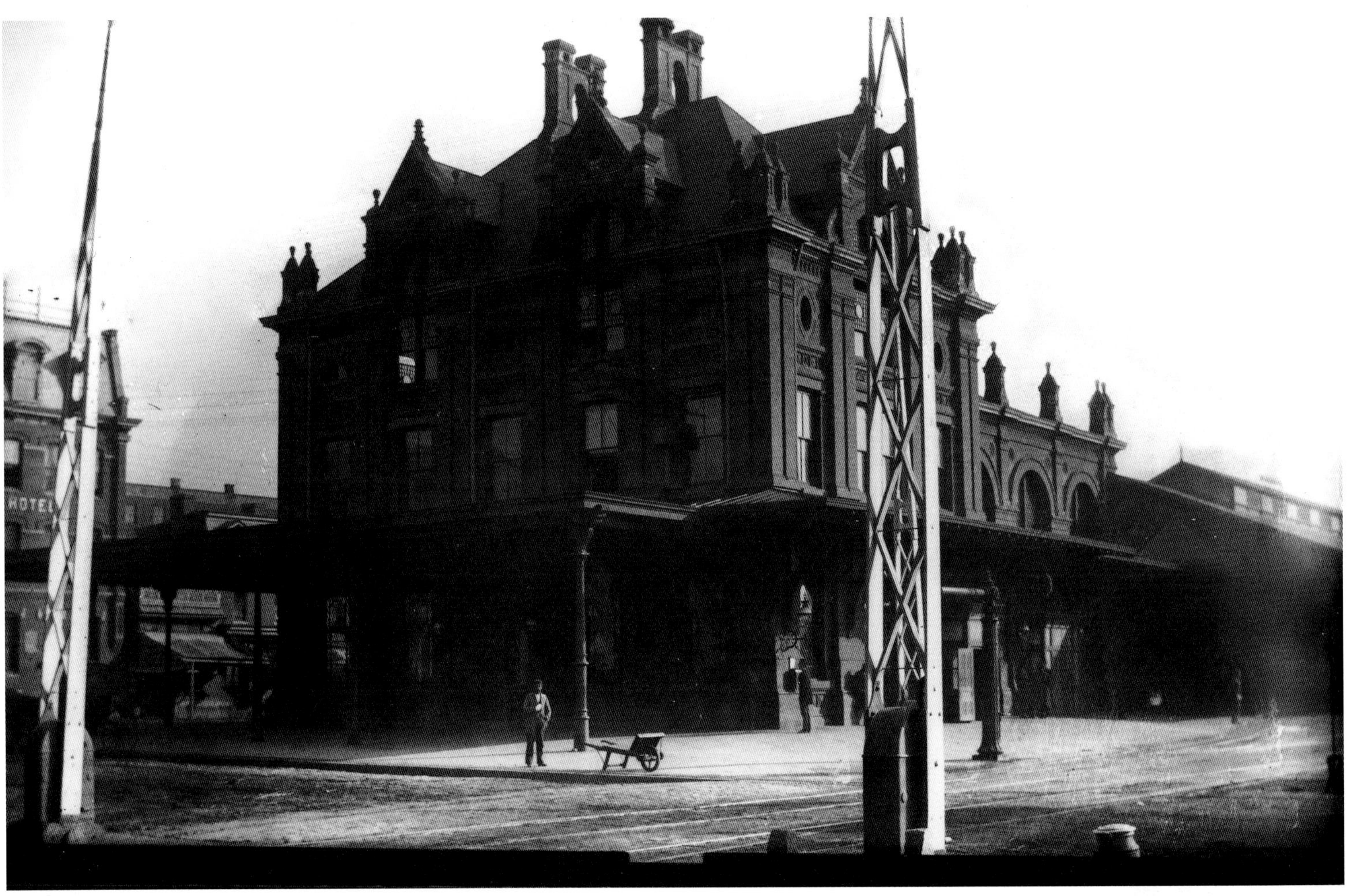

Here workmen are seen building a large wooden ship at the Jackson and Sharp Company around 1880. Located on Railroad Avenue at East 8th Street in Wilmington and founded in 1863, Jackson and Sharp also built railroad and trolley cars for customers throughout the United States, Europe, South America, and even Manchuria. The company was purchased by American Car and Foundry Company in 1901.

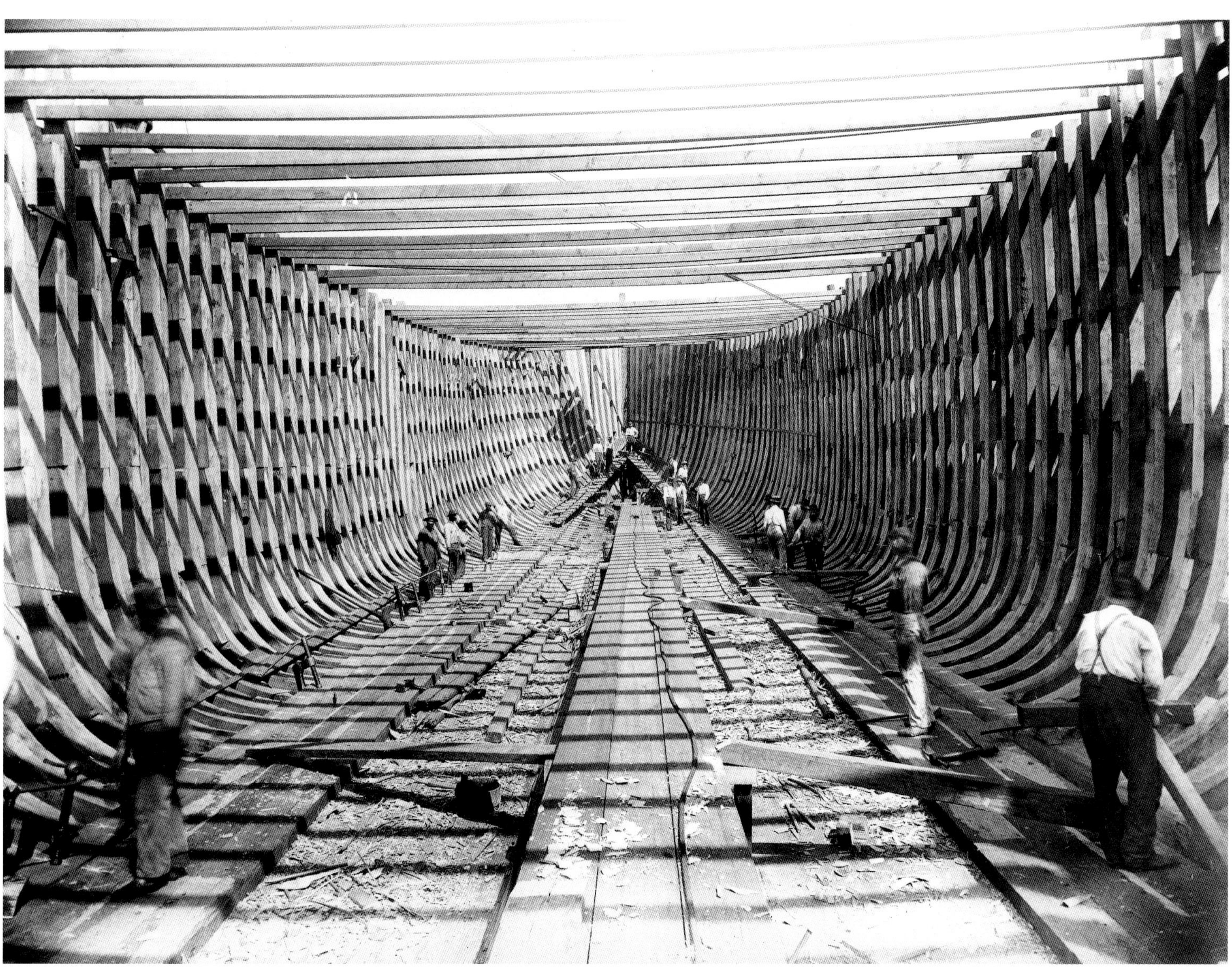

Brothers Edward A. and Warden R. Humphries pose outside the front door to their haberdashery at 216 Market Street in Wilmington. Nattily attired, they gave the same attention to displaying their wares. The shop closed in 1887.

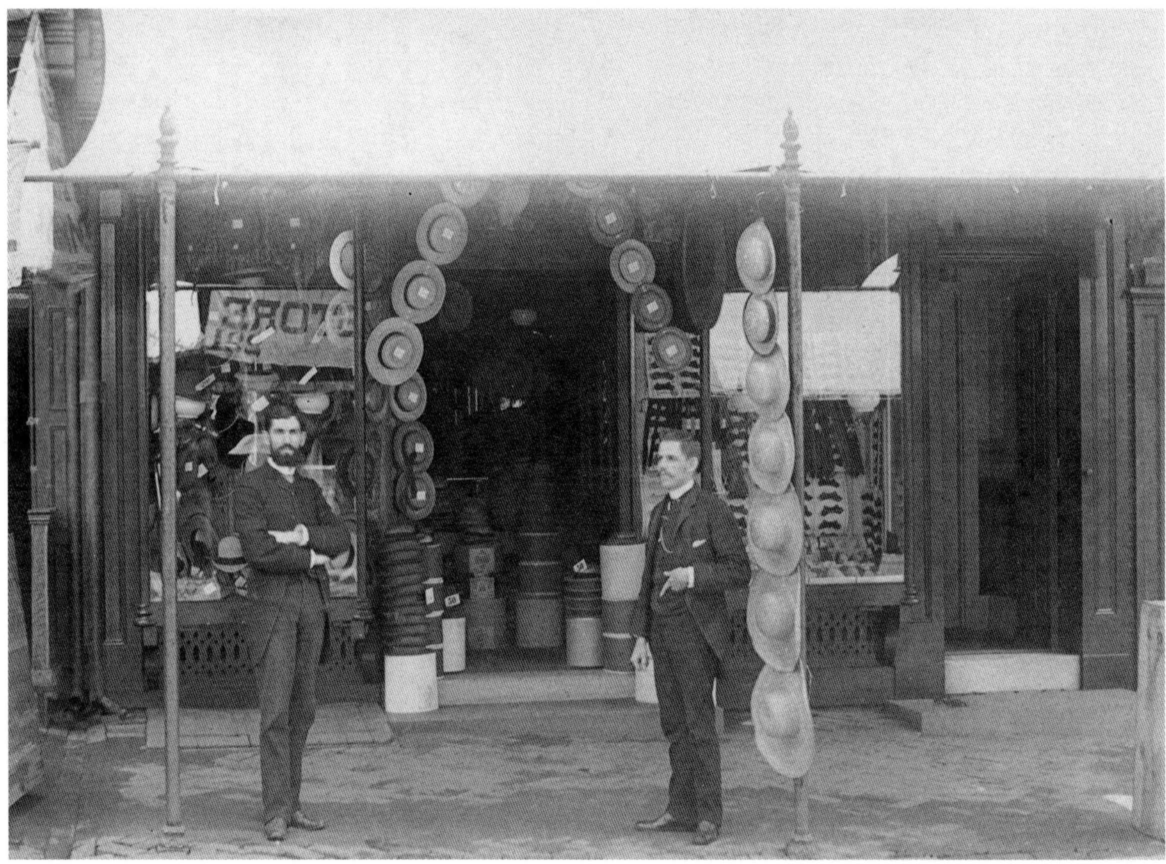

Employees of the Baltimore and Ohio Railroad stand next to a grasshopper engine, so named because it resembled a grasshopper in motion.

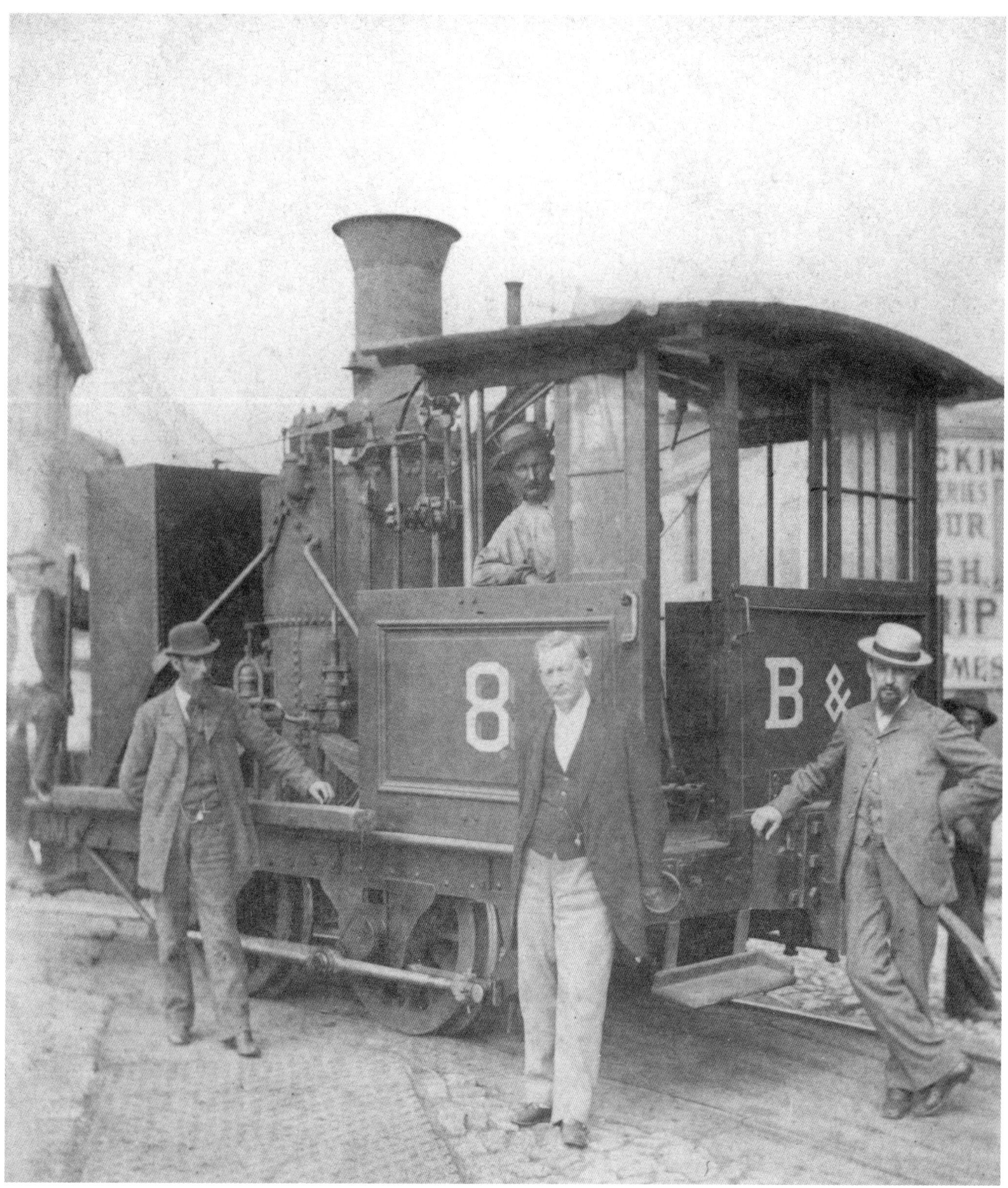

The Philadelphia, Wilmington and Baltimore Railroad connected Philadelphia and Baltimore by way of Wilmington and Newark in 1838. The station, shown here in the 1890s, can be seen today while crossing the railroad overpass just north of the sports arena and agricultural buildings on the University of Delaware campus.

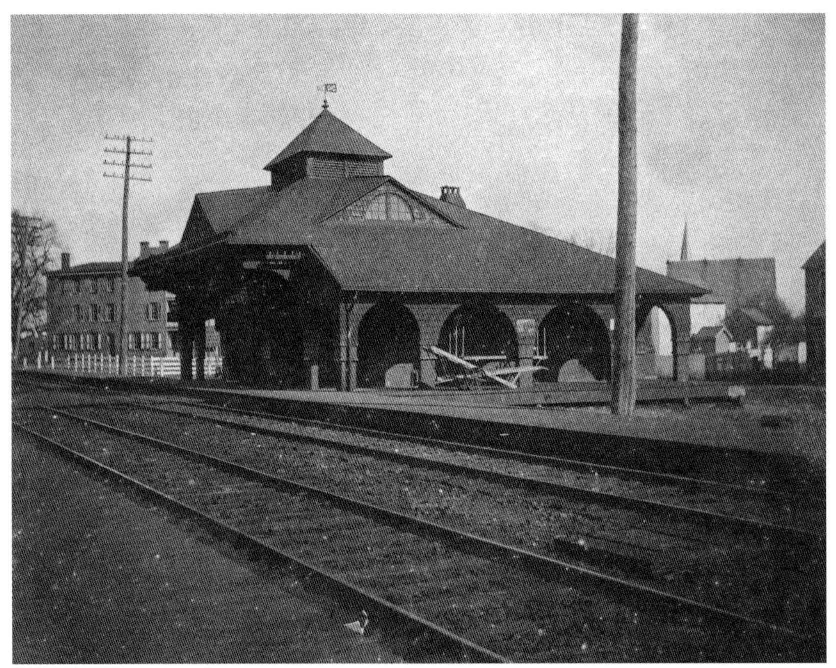

In 1886, Mary, E. Ruth, and Elizabeth Penn Hebb of Baltimore built a school on Pennsylvania Avenue at the southwest corner of Franklin Street. Founded in 1874 as a day and boarding school, the Hebbs' school taught Delaware's most privileged girls. These girls from the class of 1889 were among 36 girls to graduate that year. Six girls in the class were from Wilmington, one was from Dover, and the rest were from nearby states and England.

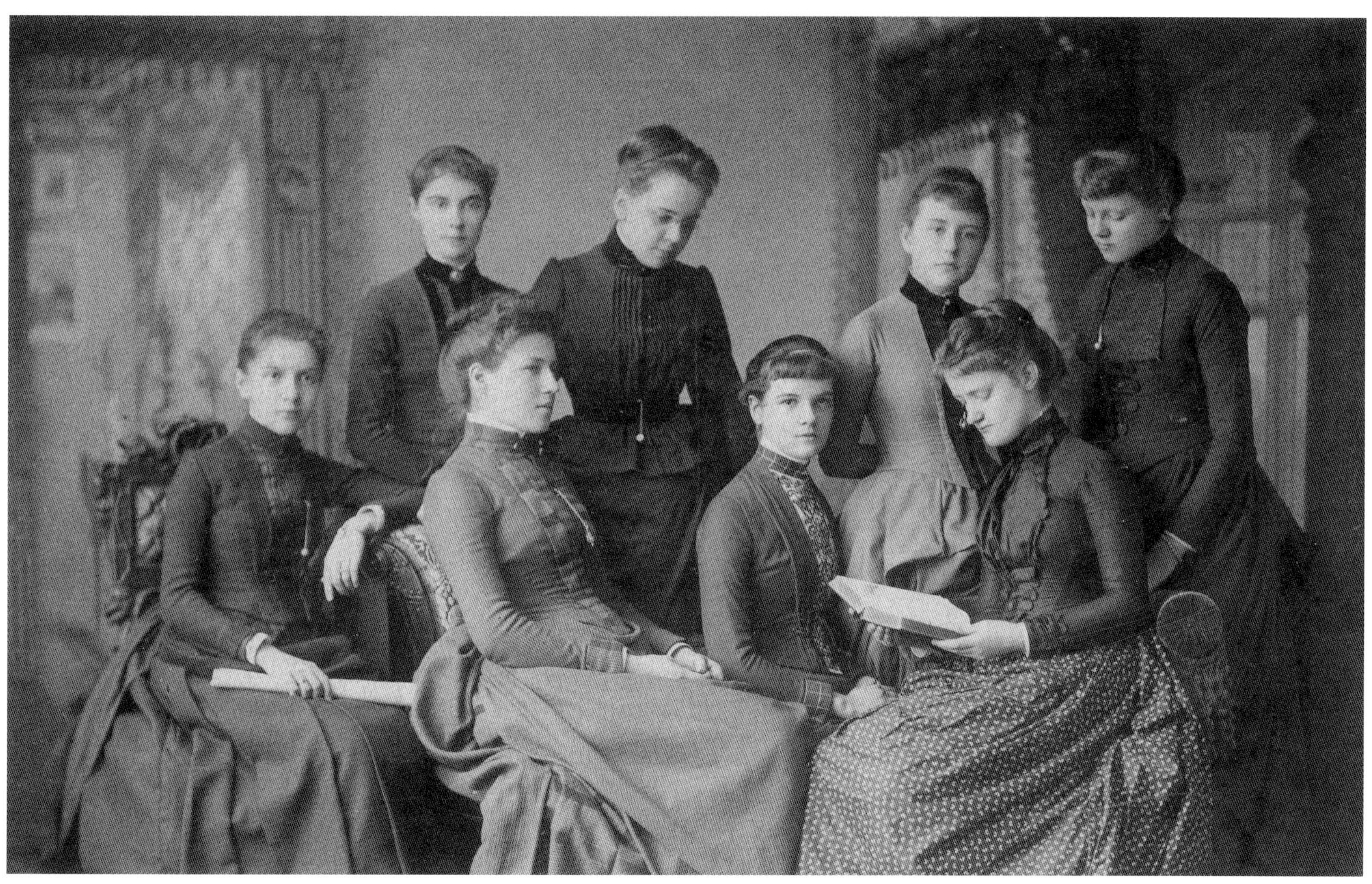

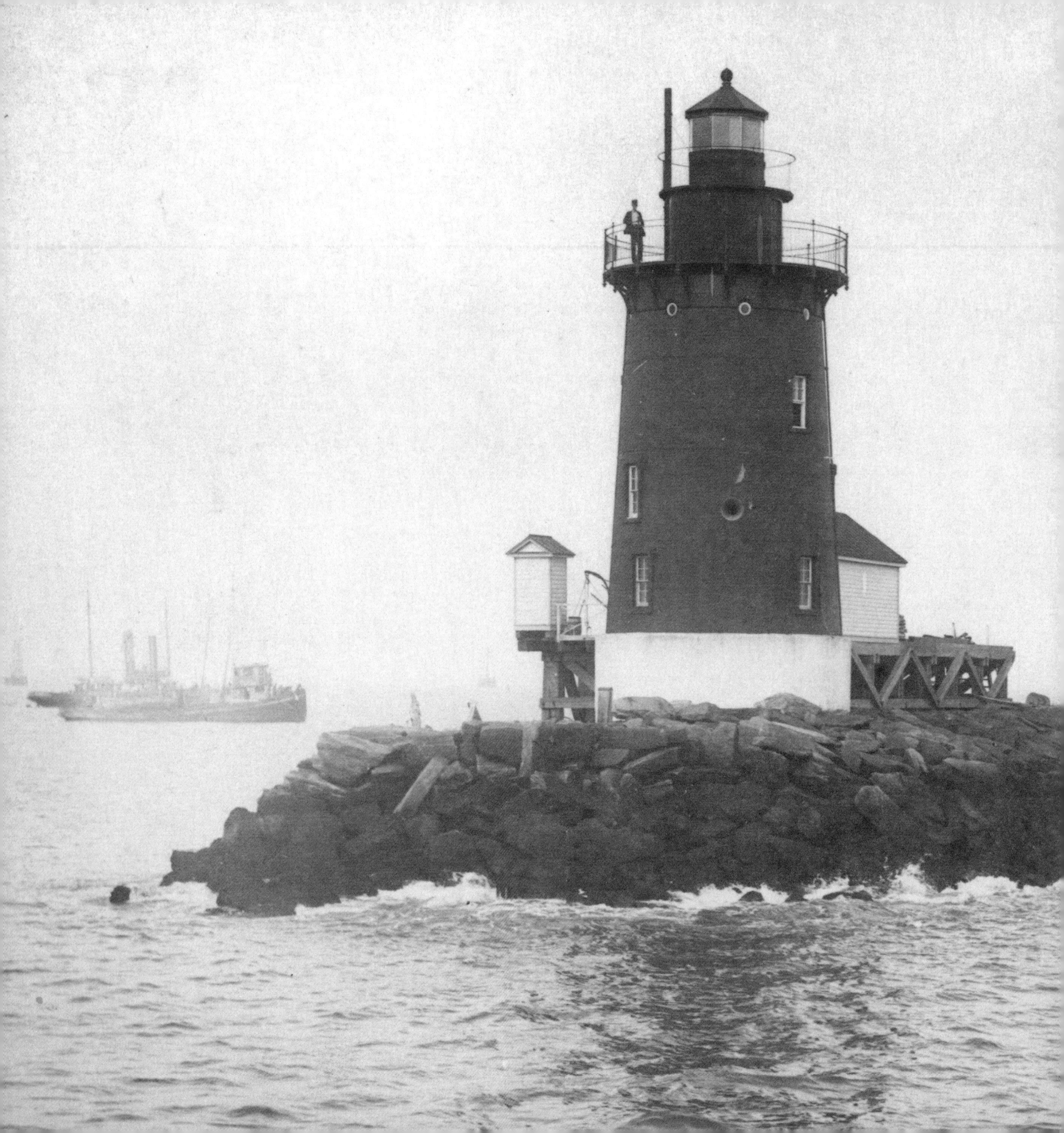

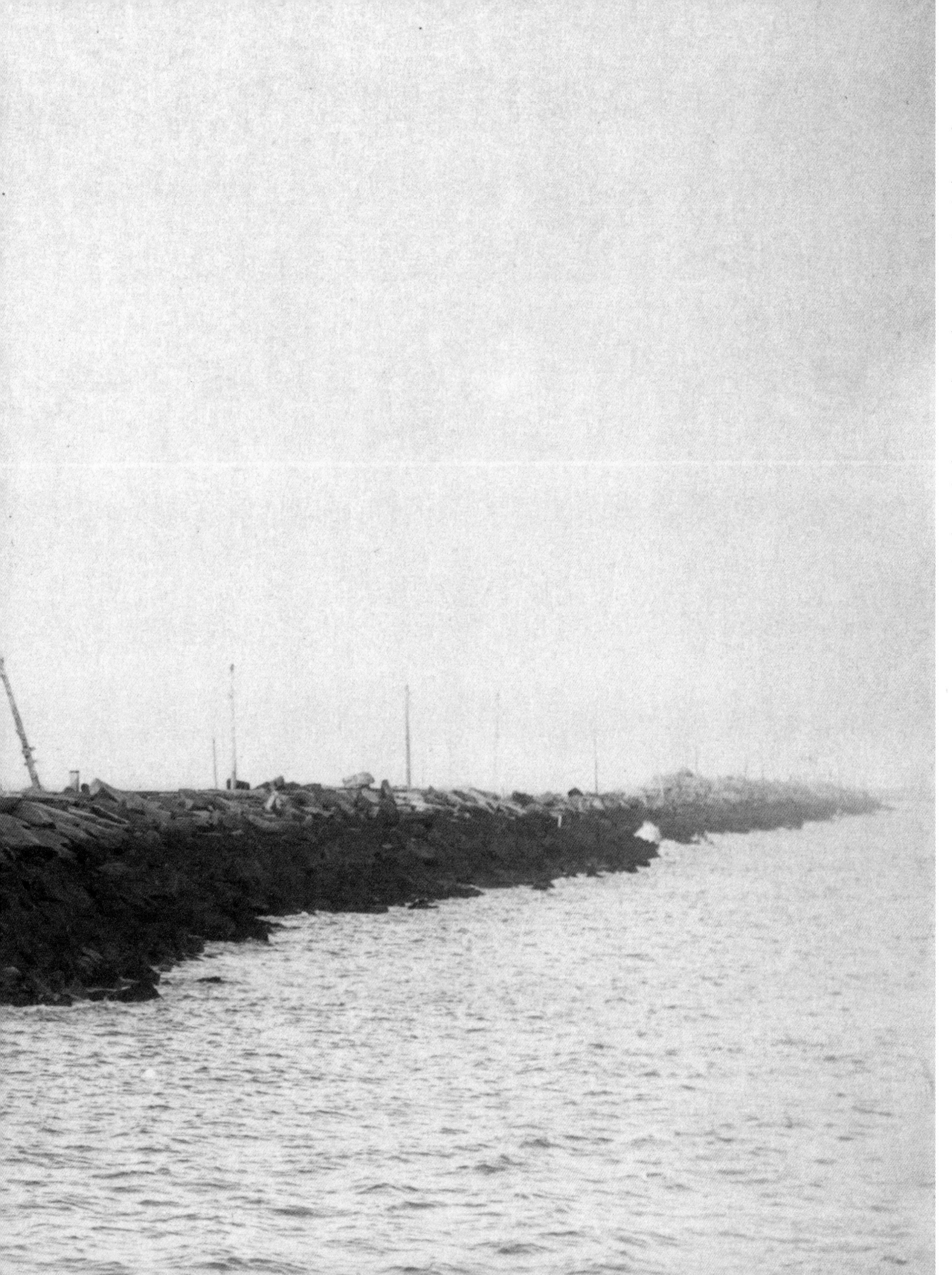

This view of the Delaware Breakwater was photographed by M. L. Stebbins around 1891. Construction of the Breakwater began in 1818, but the outer works, known as the Harbor of Refuge, was not completed until the late 1890s. It was an important safety tool for ship captains—in 1889, in one terrific storm 43 vessels had run aground in Lewes.

Major John R. Brinkle leads the Fifth Artillery Company on a practice march in 1889. The company camped at the Highlands, an area still known by that name.

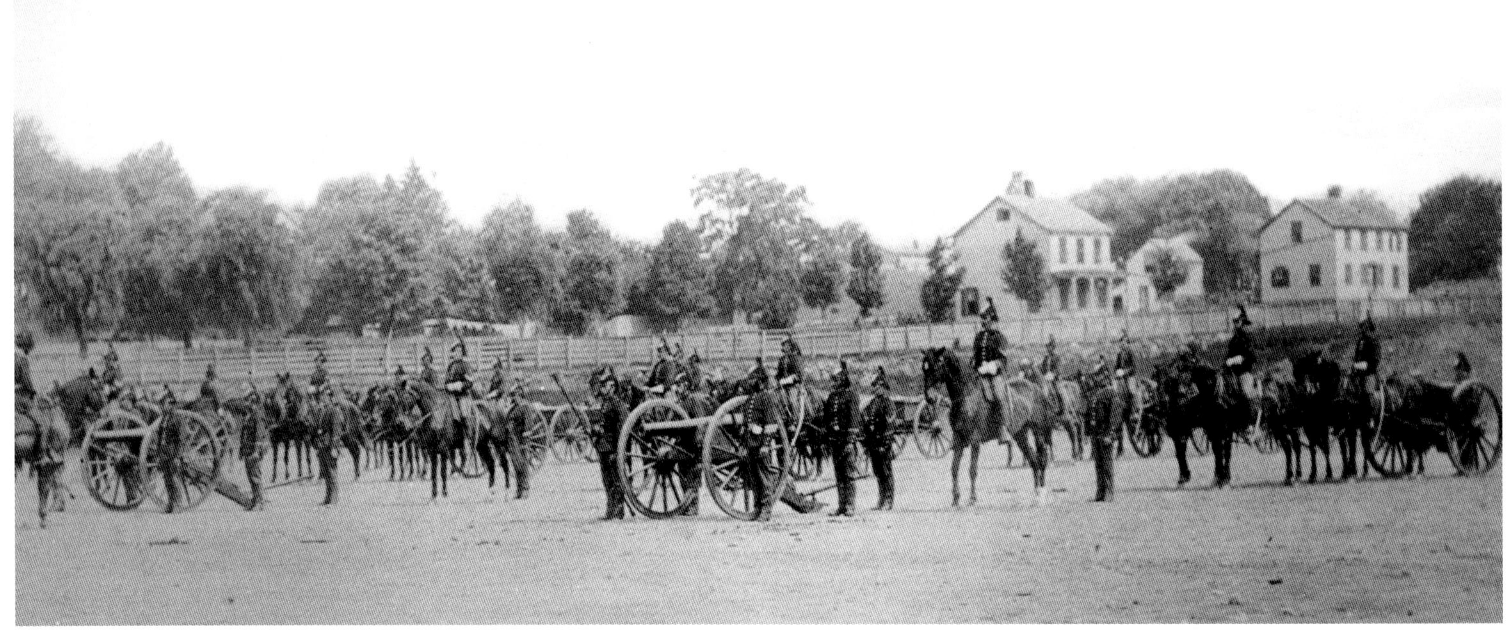

Delaware Bicycle Club members pose on a hillside with their penny-farthings. During the bicycle craze of the late 1890s and early 1900s, club members met and raced regularly in Delaware, Maryland, and Pennsylvania. One of the club's racers was Washington Seeds, the son of a Wilmington home builder. Seeds once held the world record for traveling 100 miles—a record that lasted less than 24 hours.

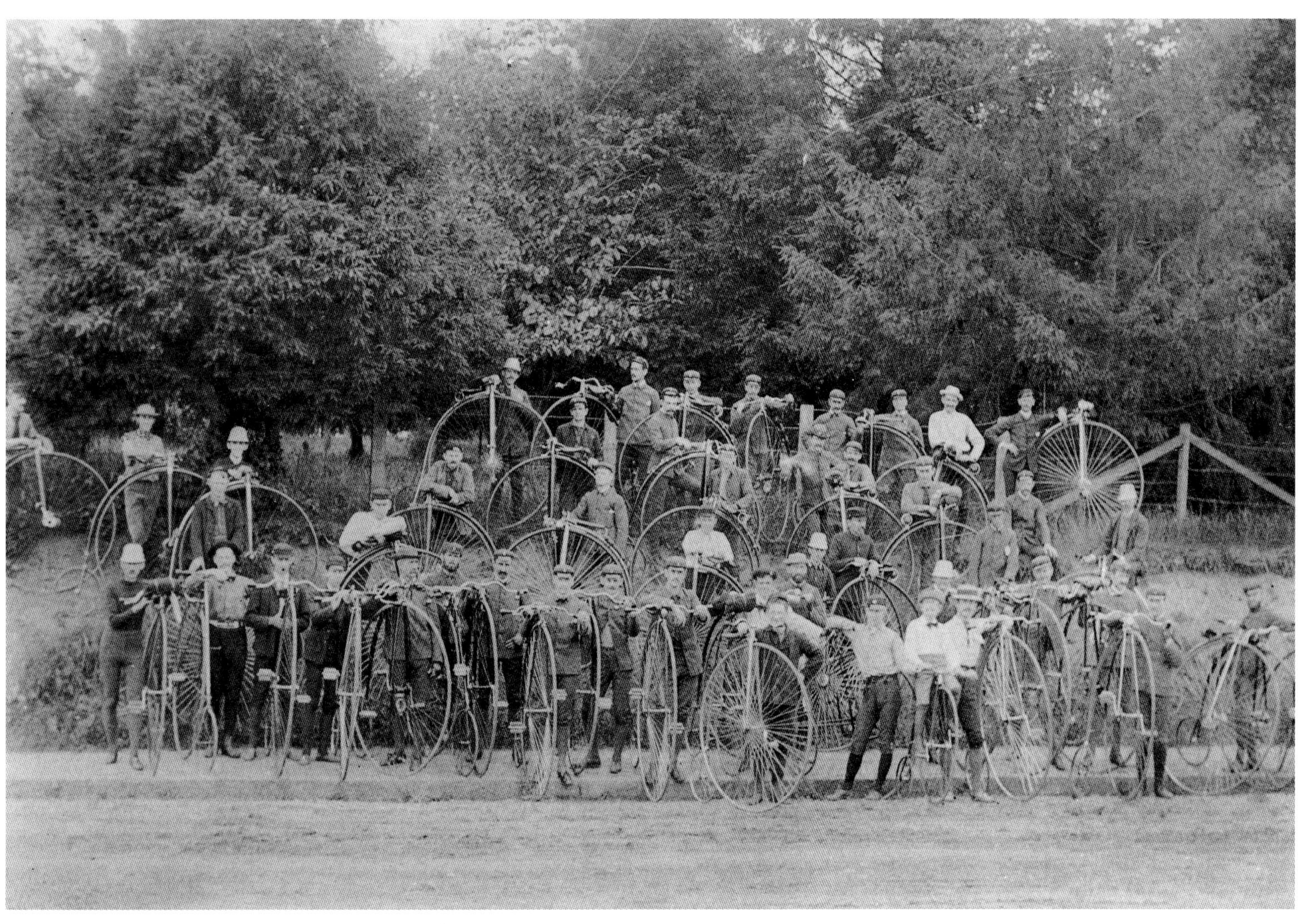

Lutton's Covered Wagon Team was recorded by Pierre S. Gentieu, photographer for the DuPont Company. Wagons carrying up to two tons of powder in barrels traveled through Wilmington to the Christina River. On May 31, 1854, three wagons did not keep the required quarter-mile distance from one another and collided. One wagon exploded, detonating the others. The teamsters, their horses, and two Wilmington citizens were killed, and Market Street buildings sustained severe damage.

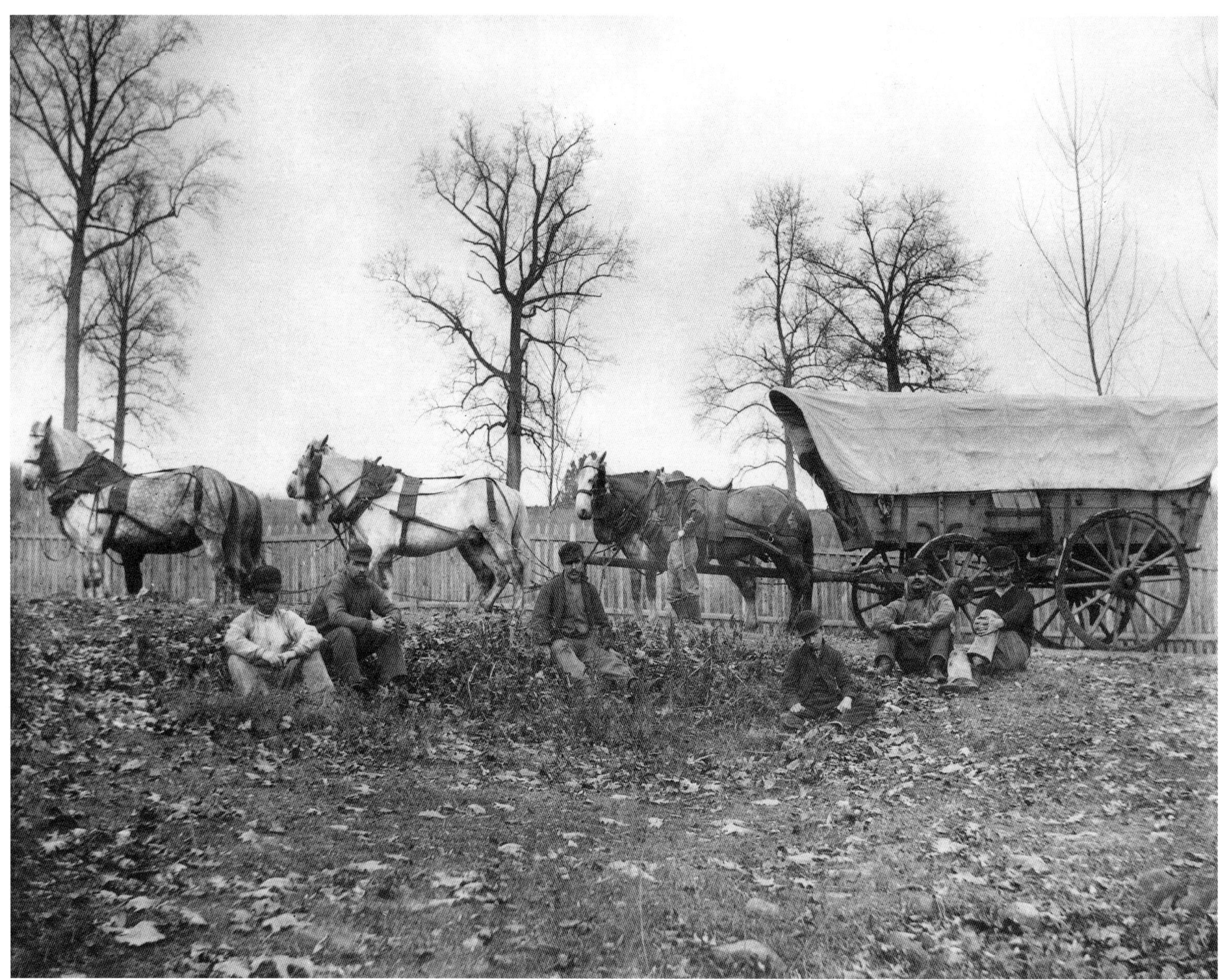

In the late 1800s, four fine gentlemen pose outside Harrison's Town and Country Store, identified as a ship chandler's store, in New Castle. Though it is no longer a store, New Castle residents still recall it as Boulden's Store. This image is evidence of New Castle's ties to the Delaware River and how many earlier residents made their living from it.

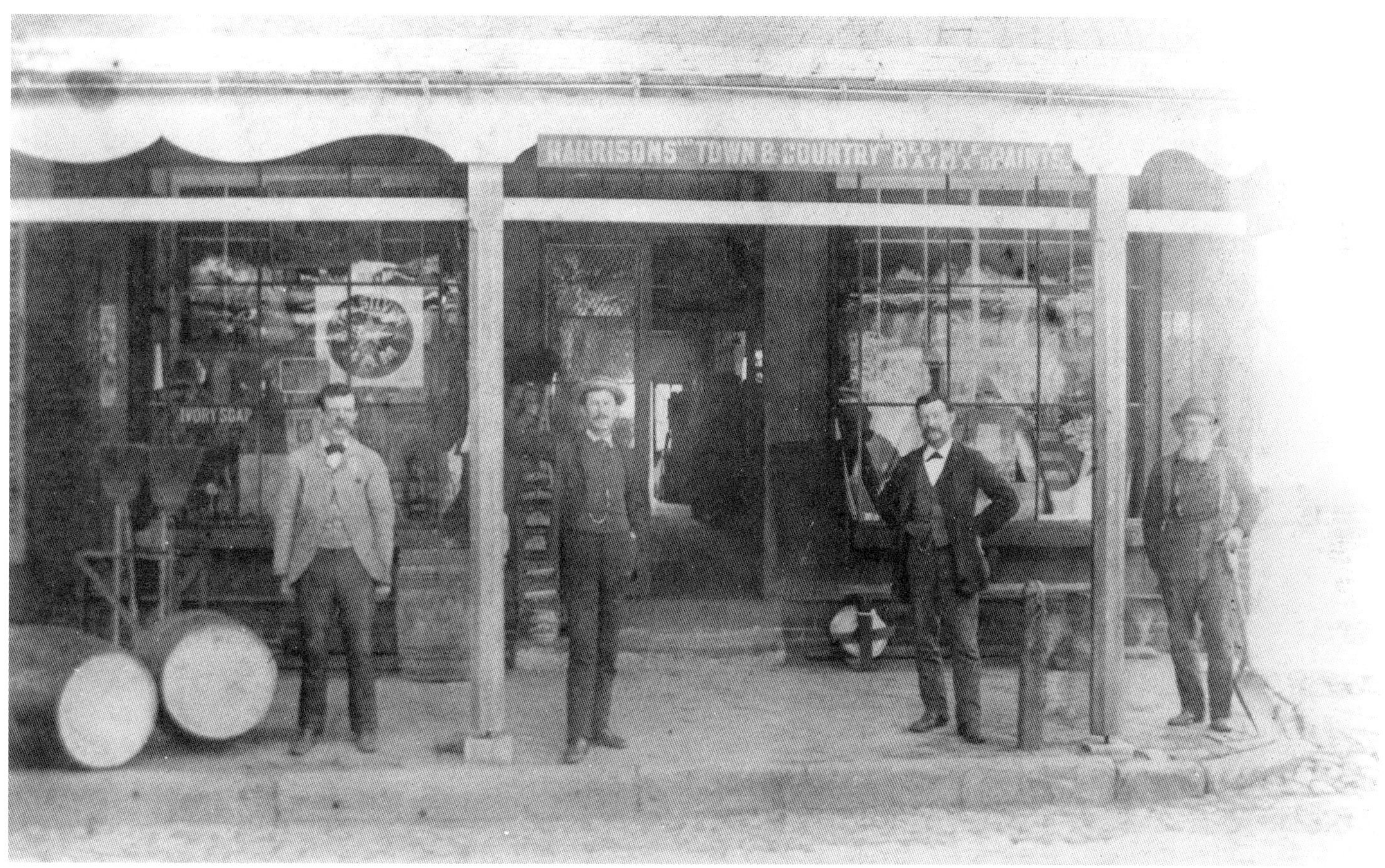

The need for the Harbor of Refuge is clearly shown in this picturesque view of destruction. Five distant figures seen at the far end of the Breakwater overlook the wreckage of the ship. In its early years the town of Lewes was a working town of pilots, ship chandlers, and salvage shops. Today it is known largely as a vacation spot and home to the University of Delaware's College of Marine Studies.

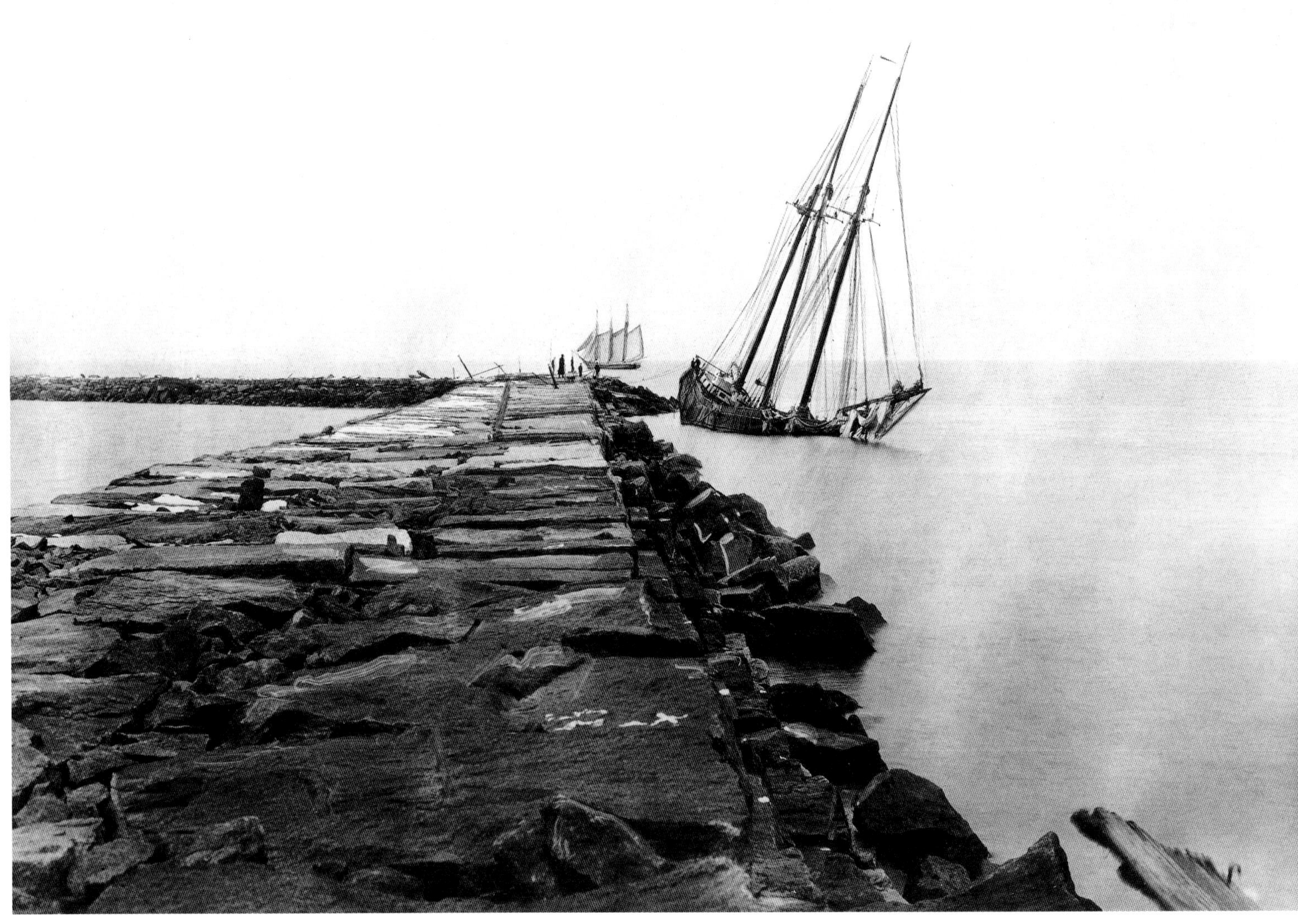

Located on the grounds of Hagley Museum and Library, the Henry Clay Village and Henry Clay Mill are shown from atop the Rockford Water Tower. The mill, seen at center, is known today as the Visitors Center. Henry Clay, the American statesman, was a friend to the du Pont family and visited the powder yards. The family paid gratitude to their friend by naming a portion of the mill after him.

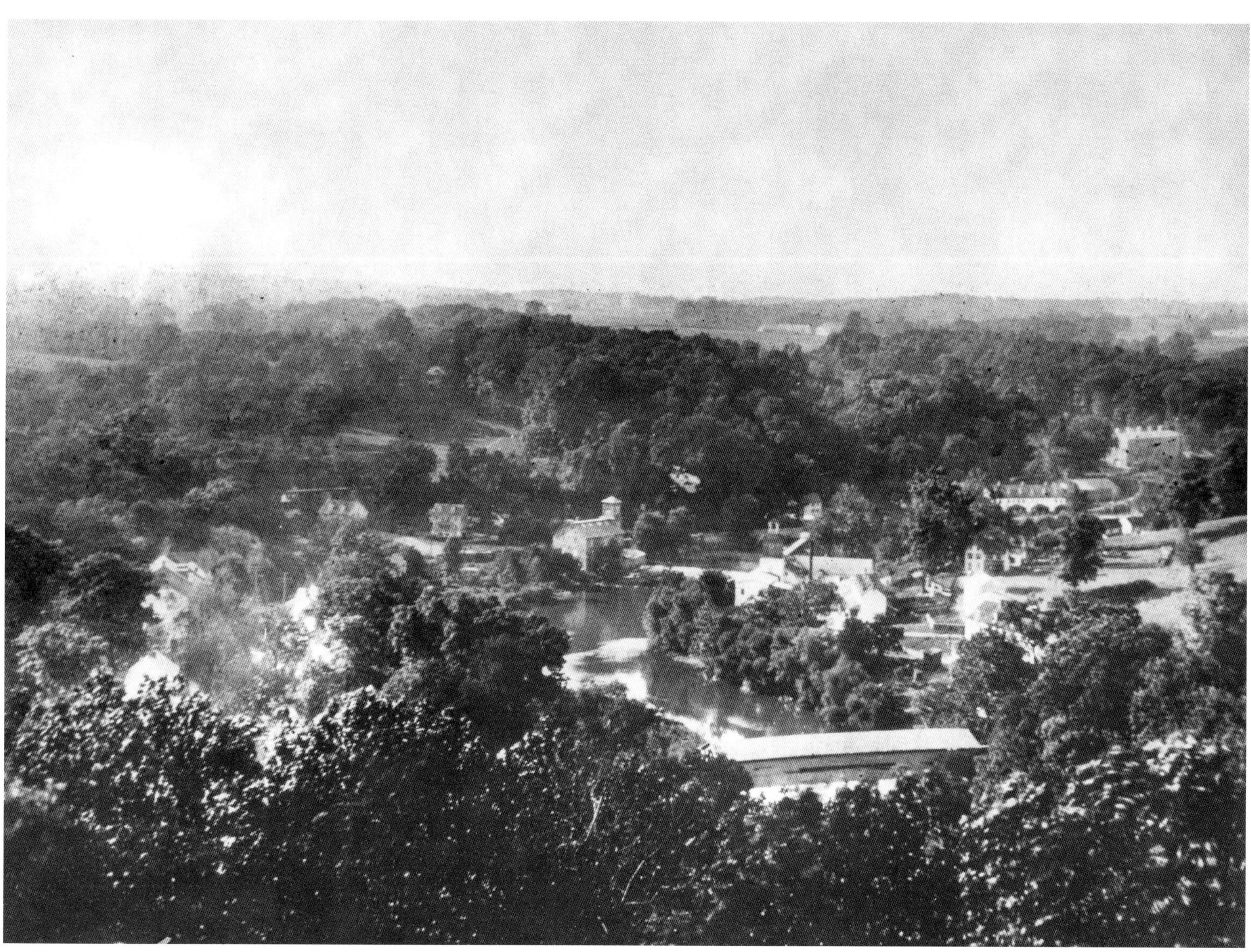

Wilmington's late-nineteenth-century skilled labor force crafted some of the very finest railroad passenger cars. This view shows the interior of a Central Pacific "Silver Palace" car. Two Wilmington car builders—Jackson and Sharp, and Harlan and Hollingsworth—produced these stunning cars.

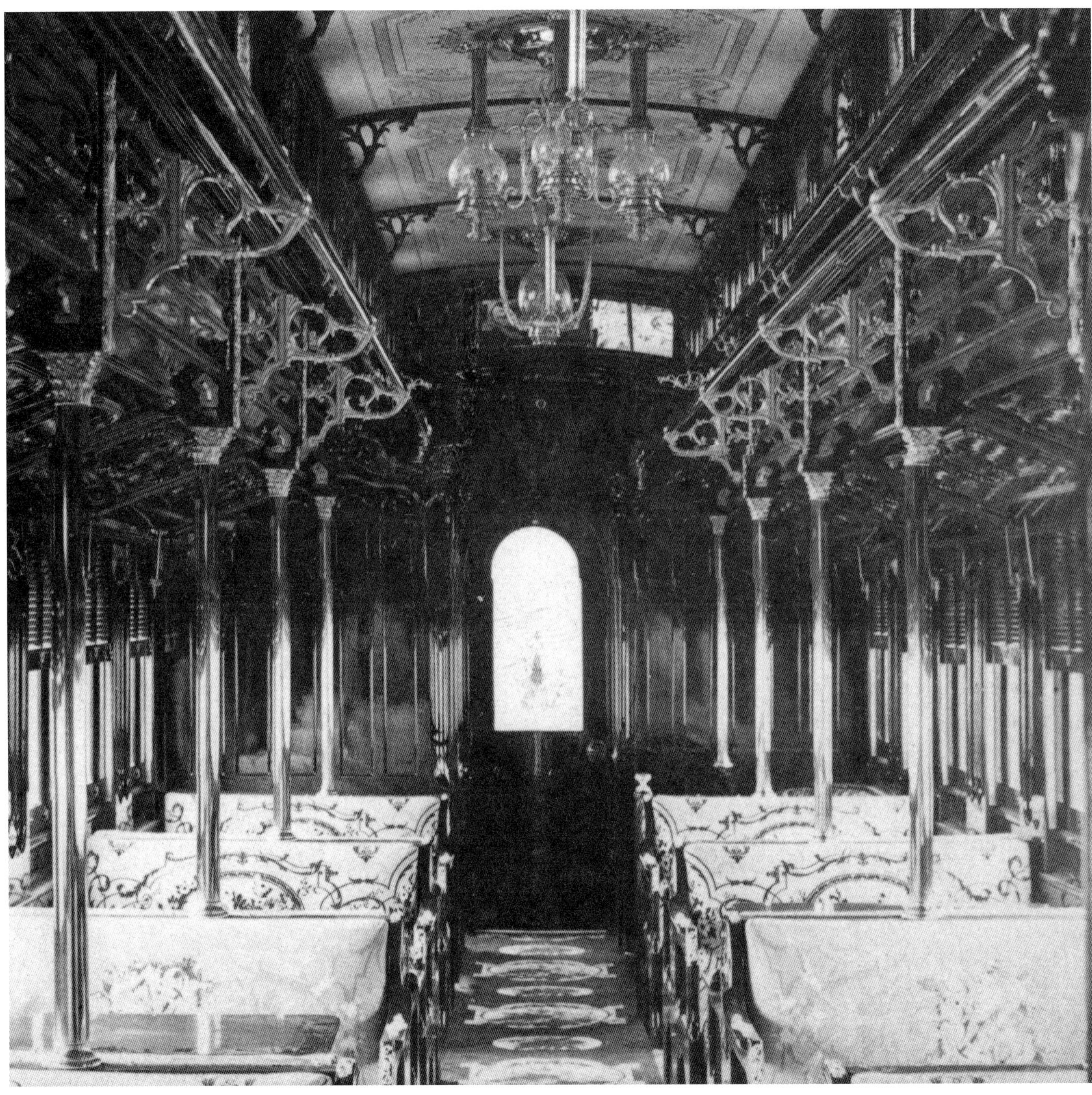

Shown here in 1895 is the Harmon McDonald house and mill located in Greenbank. Built in 1760 as a merchant mill to export flour, and gutted by fire in 1969, it stands refurbished today as Greenbank Mill, with an active educational and recreational calendar each year.

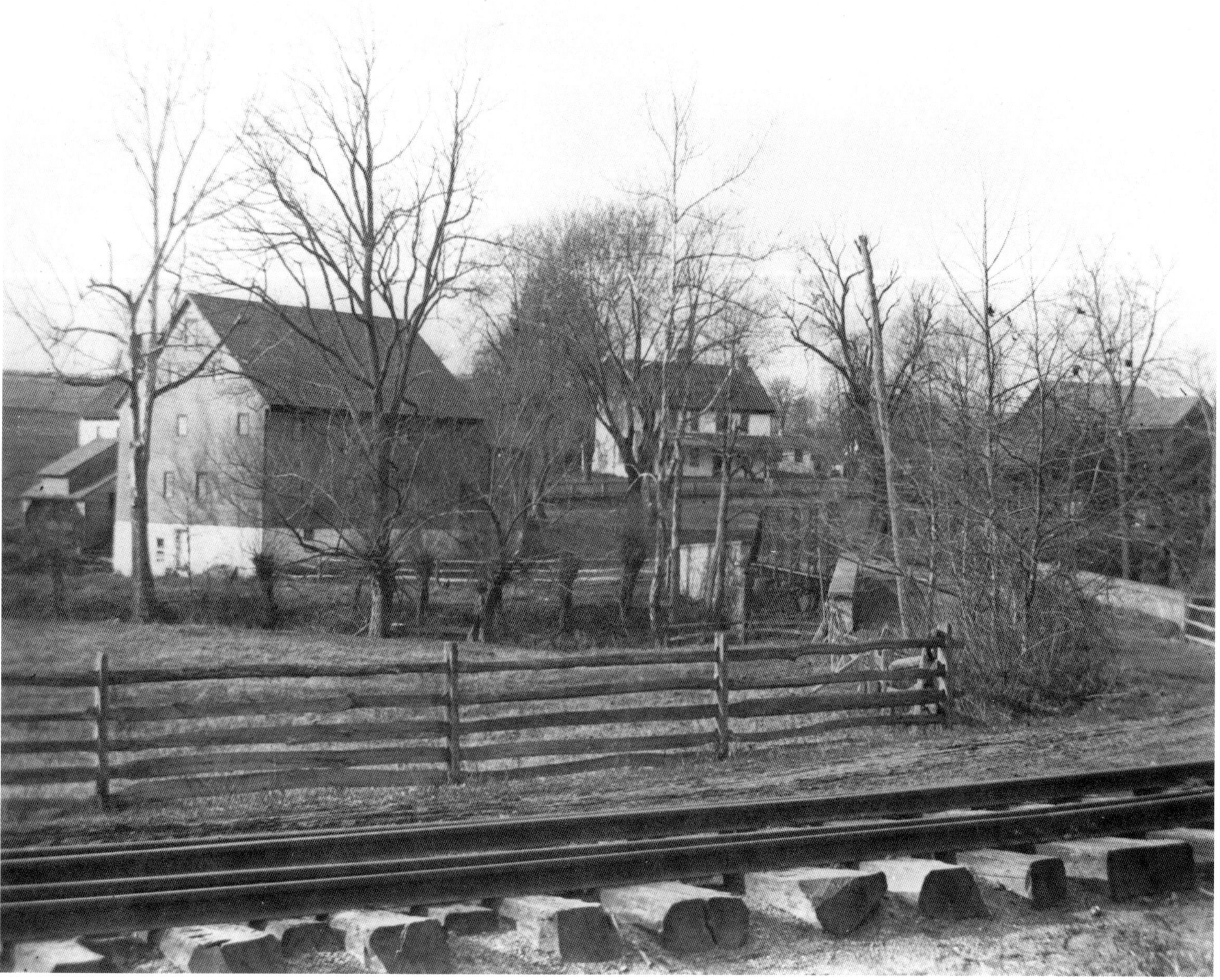

Annie Jump Cannon (1863–1941) is one of Delaware's most overlooked achievers. Born and raised in Dover, she graduated from Wellesley College in 1884. At the Harvard Observatory she became an expert in spectral photography. Cataloging more than a quarter-million stars, she devised the Harvard Classification System still used today. In 1931, she was the first woman to win astronomy's highest award, the Draper Award from the National Academy of Sciences.

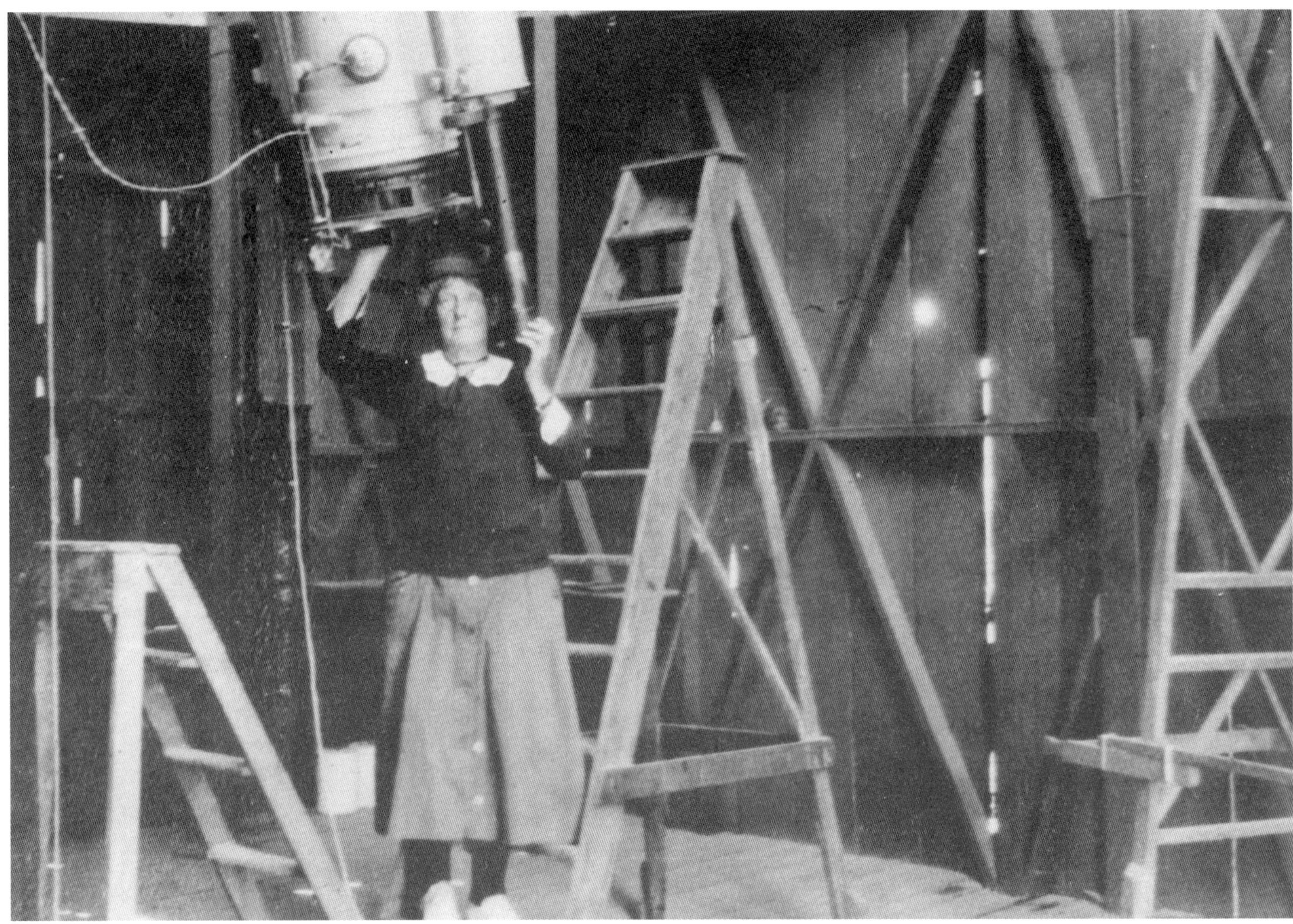

Ship christenings were elaborate affairs where both dignitaries and shipbuilders stood in attendance. Here a bottle of champagne is broken on the bow of an unidentified ship in the early 1890s. During this period the company celebrated anywhere from five to ten christenings a year. Workmen worked 60 hours a week.

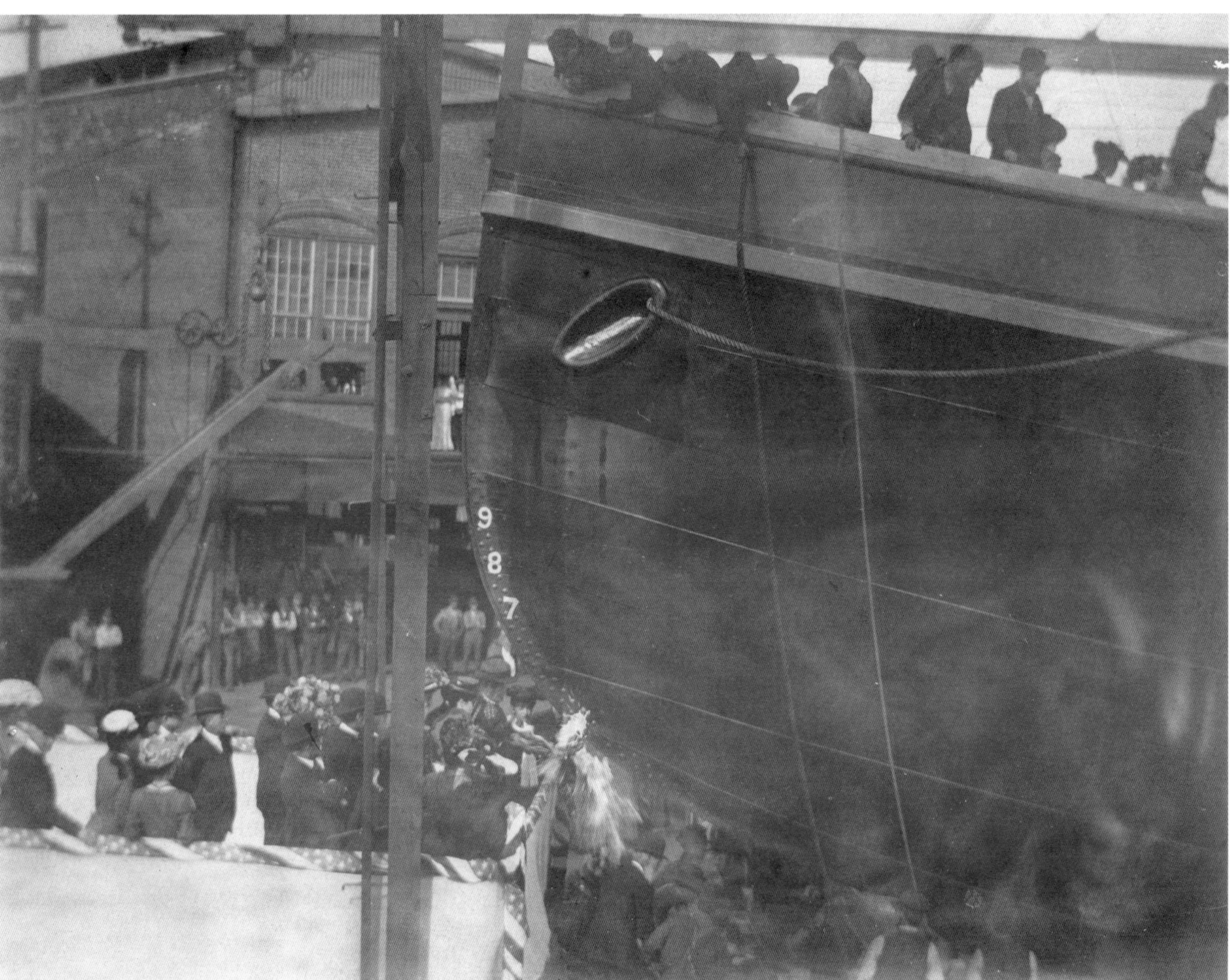

Four young cyclists and a pair of newsies pose for the photographer. The cobbled streets must have given them a jarring ride. Some enthusiasts were decried by the local papers of the time as "scorchers," for terrorizing people on the streets with their high speed and low regard for pedestrian safety.

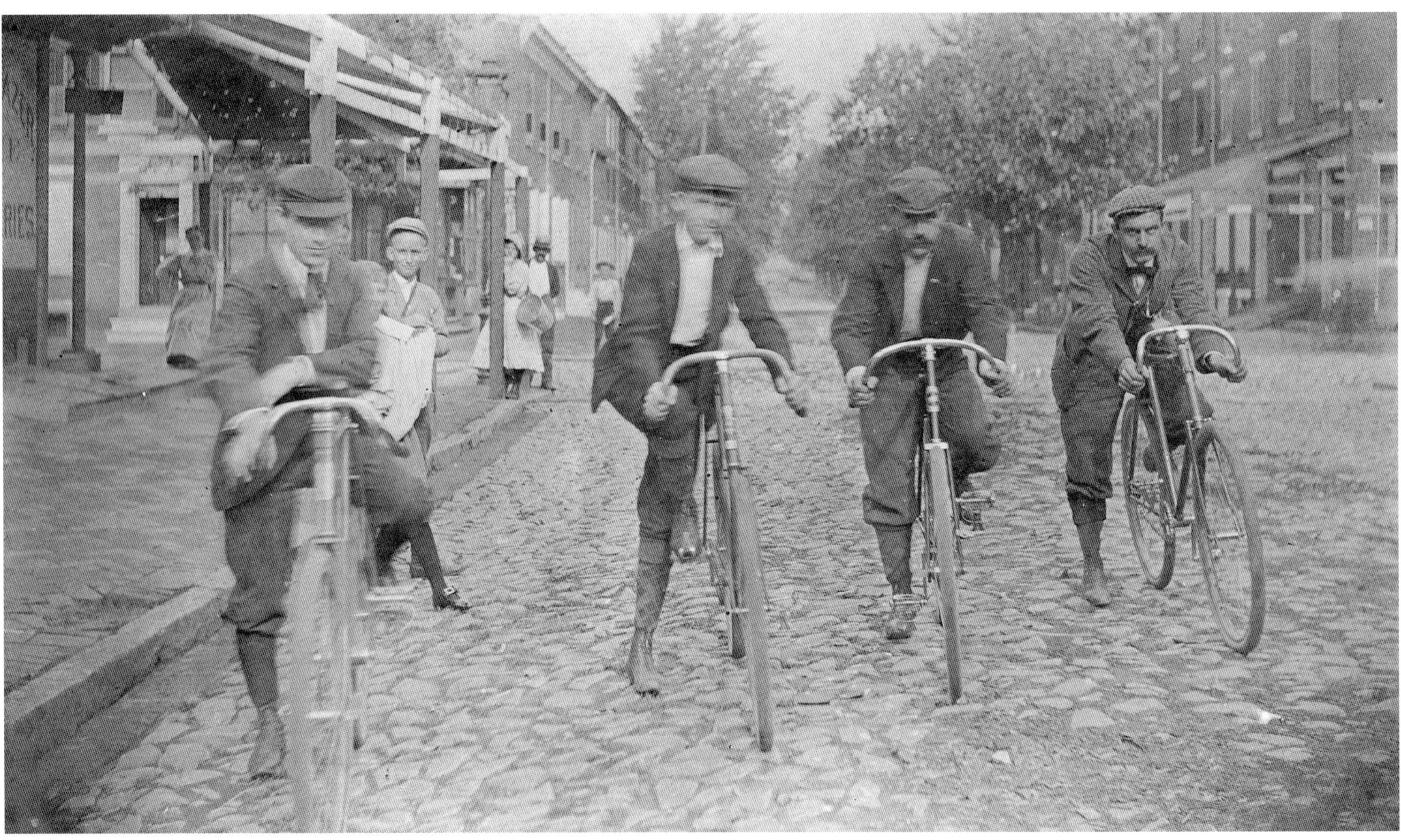

The New Castle Courthouse, seen here around 1890, is the oldest surviving government building in the state. Its earliest section was built in 1732. It served as the state's first capitol in 1776 before the capital moved to Dover in 1777. A treasured part of the colonial city's past, the building was restored and opened as a state museum in 1960.

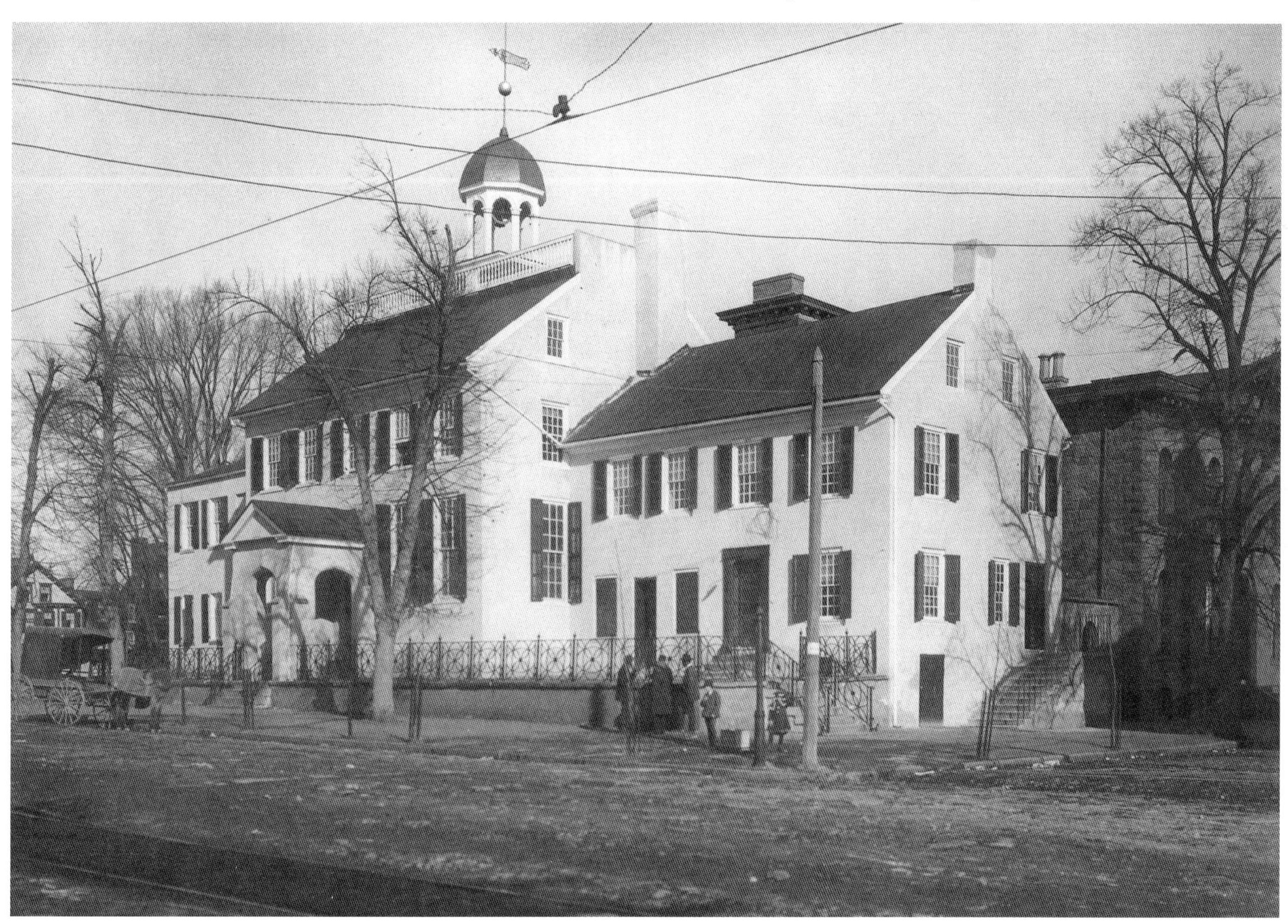

Lou Kerrigan (second from left) stands among other vendors at the Second Street Market House in Wilmington. This wonderful interior view provides a glimpse of what market day might have been like for our grandparents and great-grandparents.

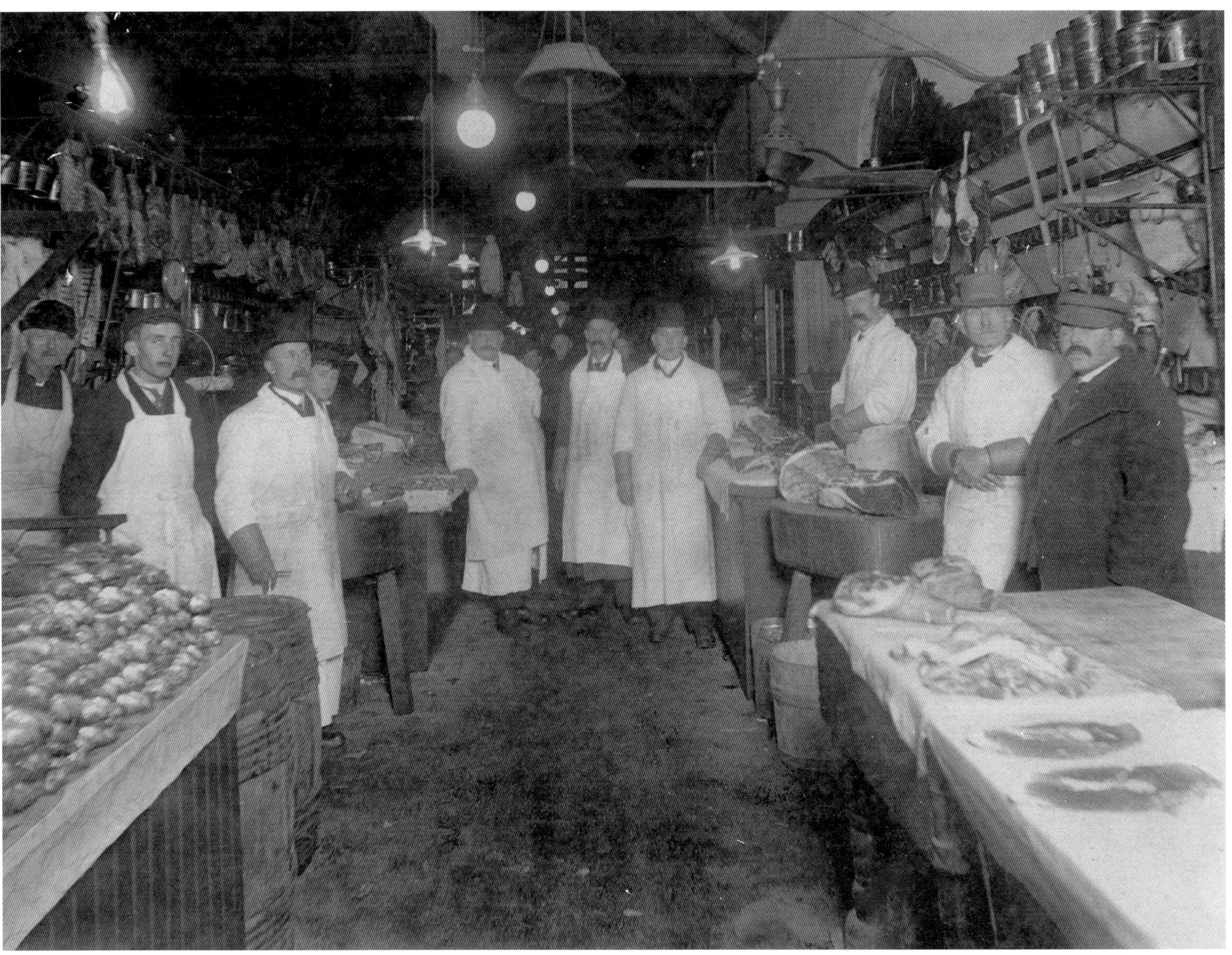

The congregation poses outside Christ Church in Laurel in the 1890s. Built in 1771 in what was considered Maryland at the time, the building is one of about a dozen churches along the Atlantic Coast that have remained unaltered since before the Revolutionary War. Its interior is unpainted heart-of-pine with a barrel-vaulted ceiling and a simple table for its altar.

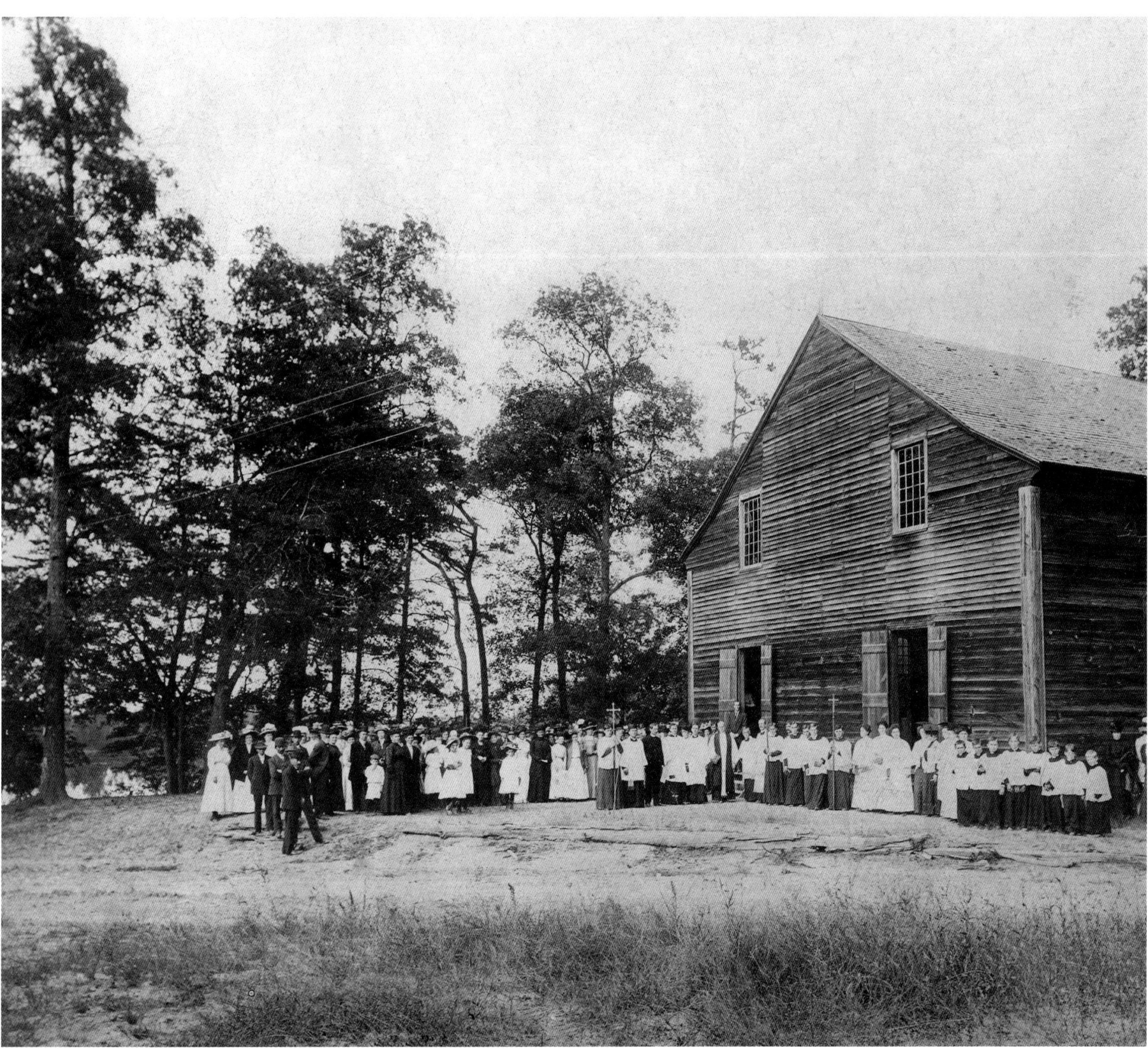

The *Lord Baltimore* at Delaware City is shown here around 1890. The Chesapeake and Delaware Canal opened in 1829 at a cost of $2.2 million and remains one of two commercially vital sea-level canals in the country today. Fourteen miles long between the Delaware River and Chesapeake Bay, the canal is 35 feet deep and 350 feet wide, shortening the trip between Baltimore and Philadelphia by 316 miles.

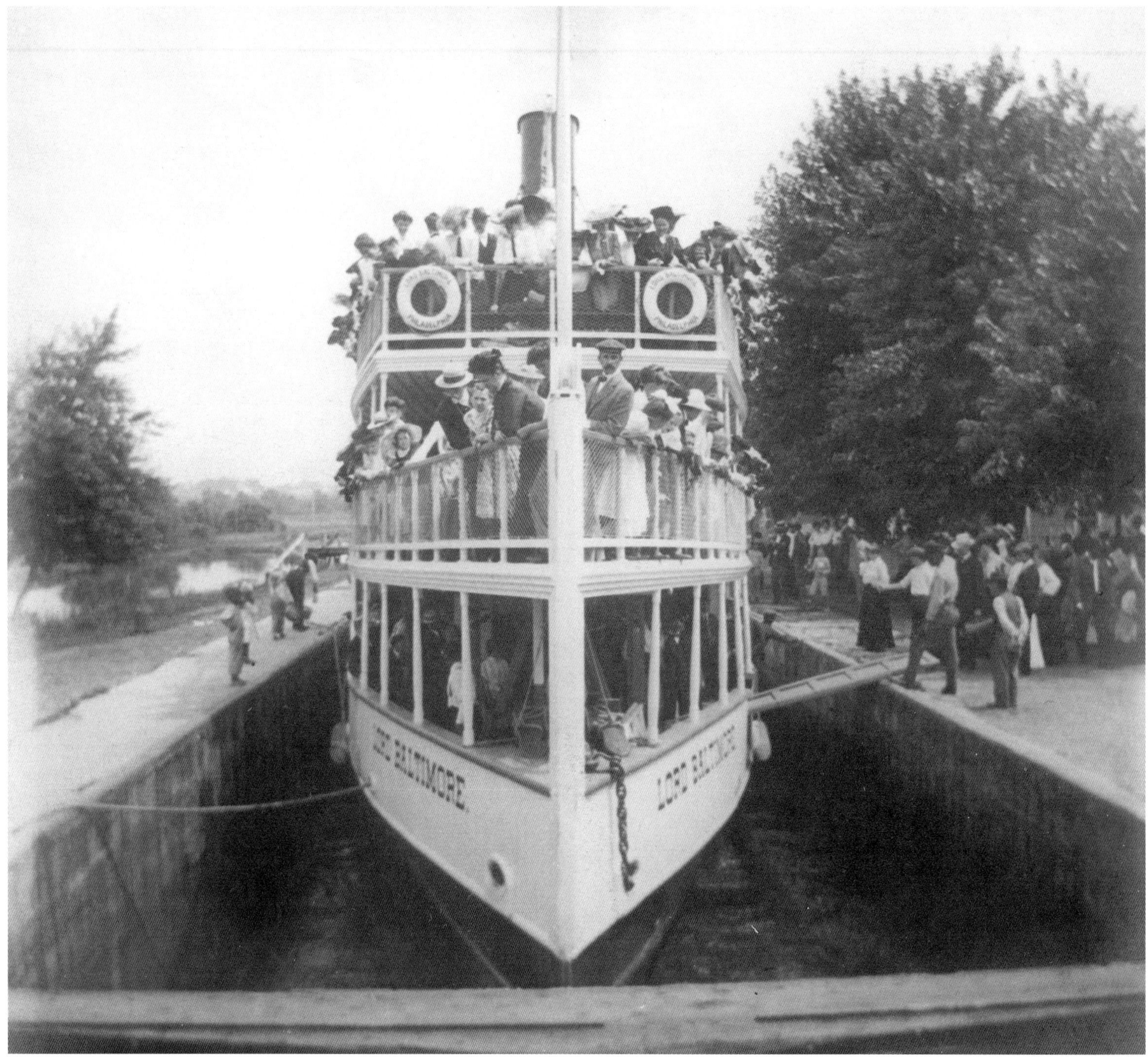

Artist and educator Clawson S. Hammitt (1857–1927) was a leading figure in Wilmington's art community for more than 40 years. In 1882, he started what is considered Delaware's first art school in the Institute Building at 8th and Market streets. He studied at the Pennsylvania Academy of Fine Arts and throughout Europe before settling in Wilmington. This photograph was taken in his studio at 502 Shipley Street.

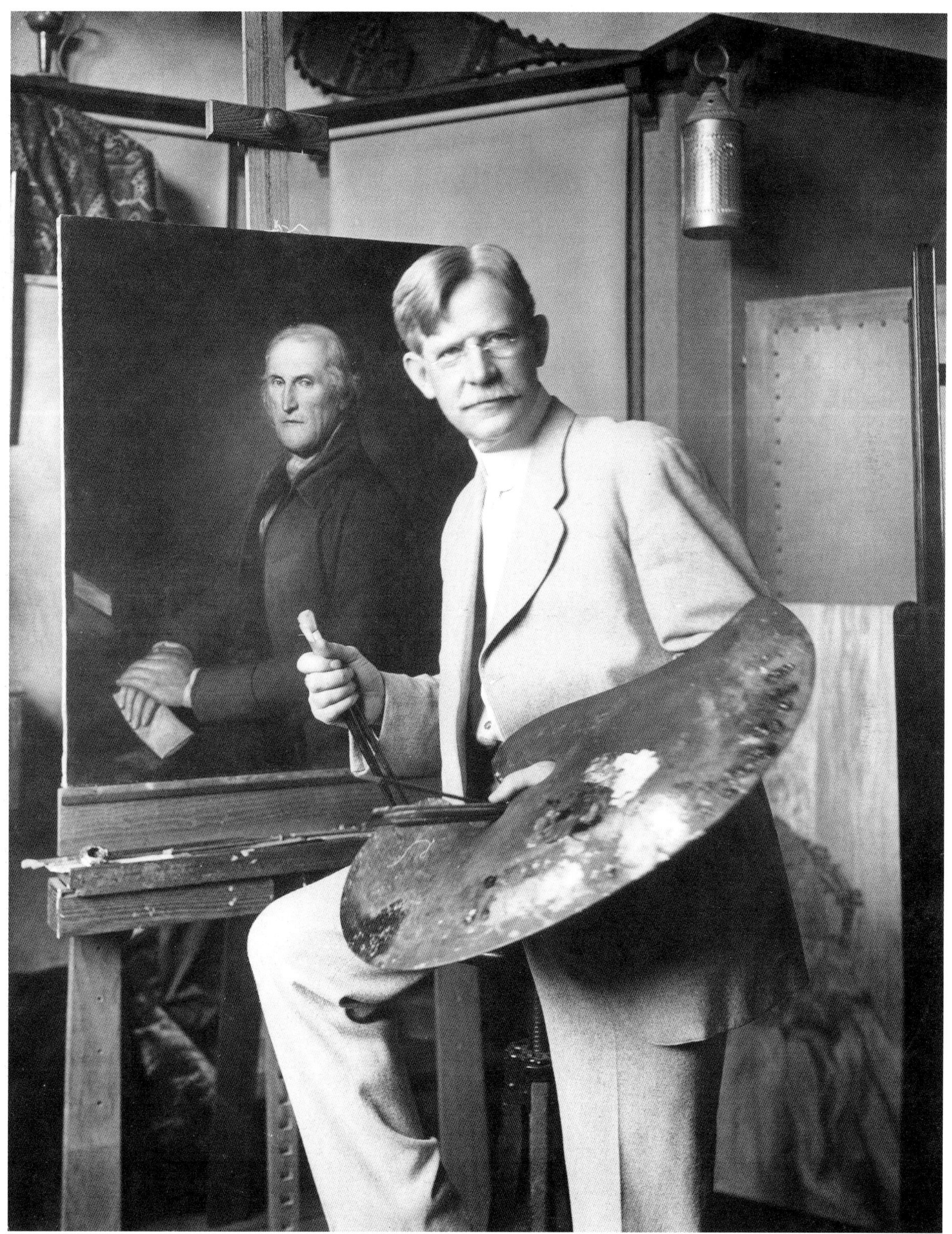

The “Republican Invincibles” are gathered at a small shack near Smalley’s Dam. They include Henry McComb Lang, E. Kettlewood, Joseph Wiggelsworth, Al Neutze, Sam Chadwick, Harvey Wigglesworth, George Neutze, and two others.

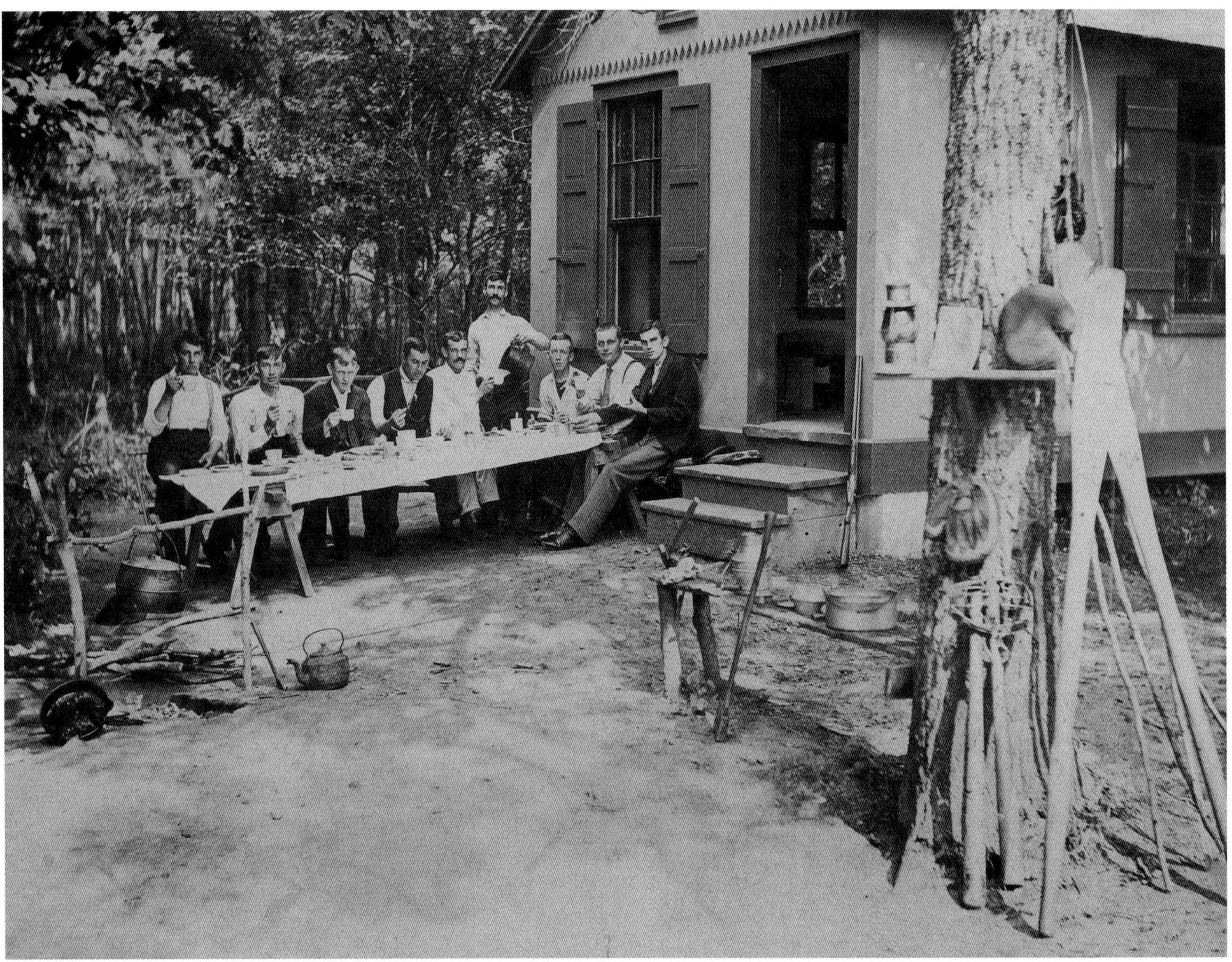

The Yacht *Volunteer* is under full sail here in 1891. Built by the Pusey and Jones Company of Wilmington, this racing yacht was launched in 1887. It was 106 feet long and carried more than 9,000 square feet of sail. After winning trial races in New York, the *Volunteer* successfully defended against the British challenger *Thistle* to win the America's Cup in 1887.

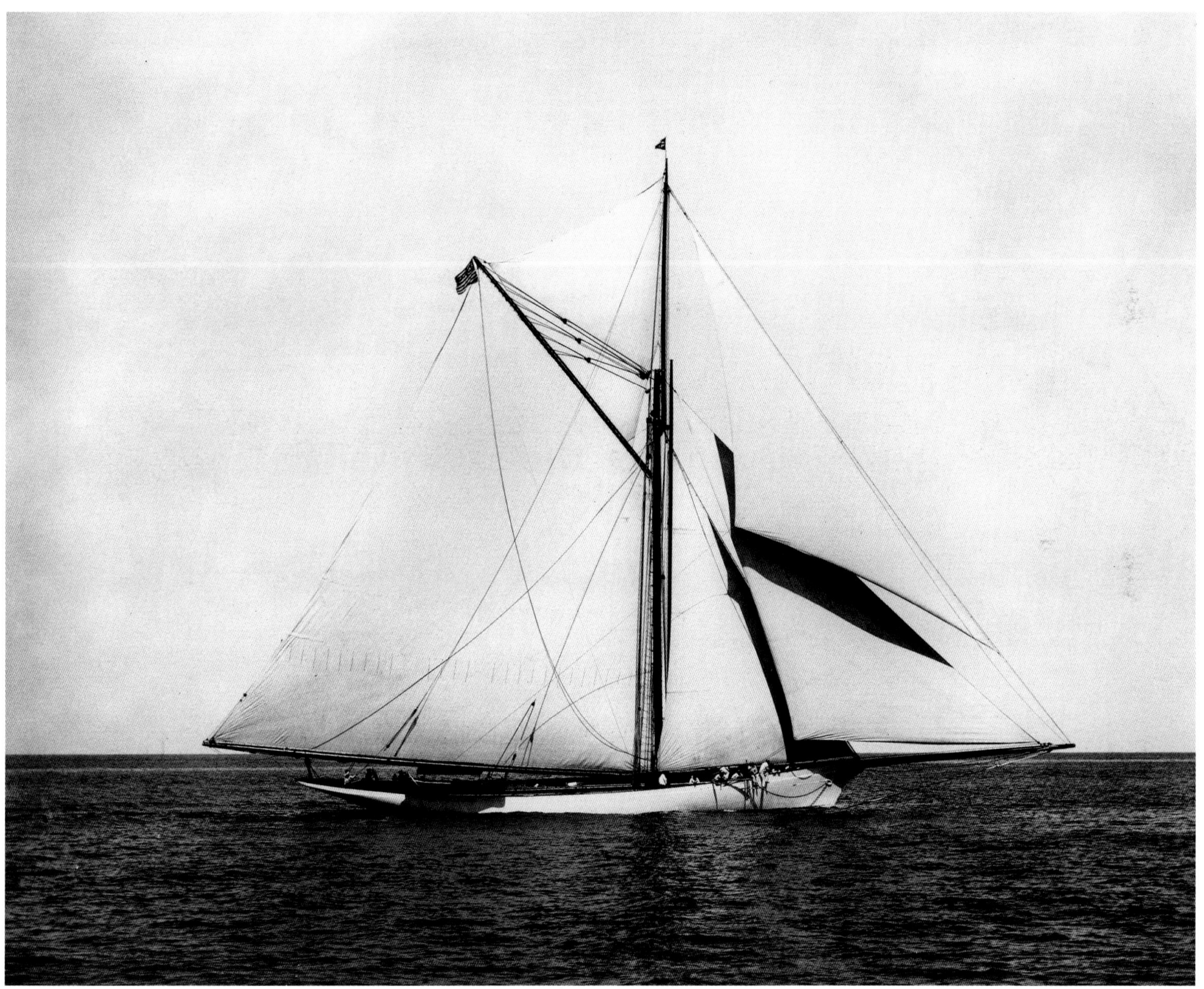

Located at the southwest corner of Delaware Avenue and DuPont streets in Wilmington, this station once proudly served the Baltimore and Ohio Railroad but has since been torn down. Today the station and trolley depot lend their name to the shopping center located there. The station was replaced by an Acme Market and parking lot.

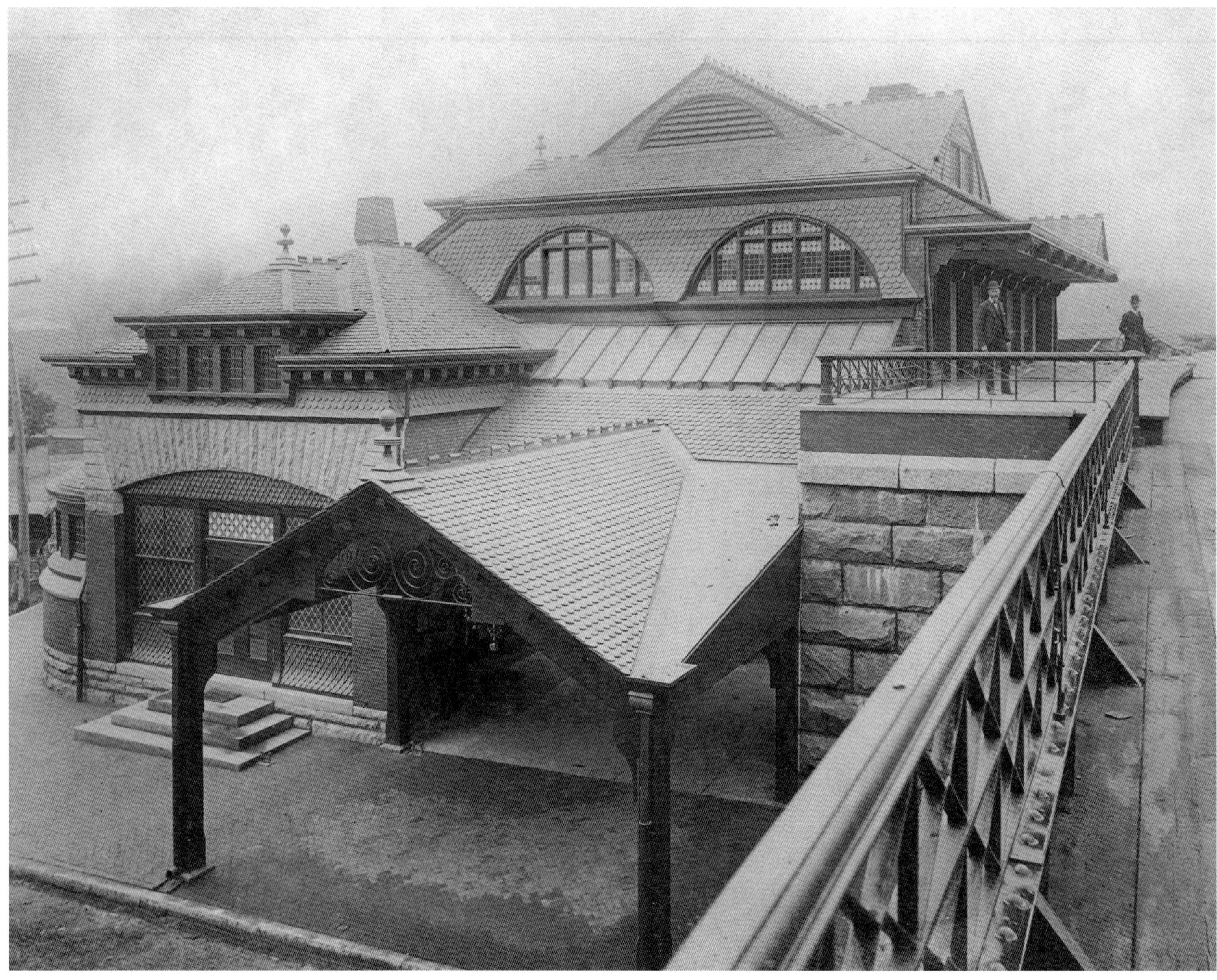

Crowds gather on the street and in the windows above to watch a parade of National Guard or Regular Army soldiers. For years, Wilmington's Market Street was the parade route for many soldiers as they headed toward the train station on the Christina River. Dressed in shirt-waist blouses, spectators in the foreground strike the classical silhouette of the Gibson Girl, a version of the feminine ideal made popular by artist Charles Dana Gibson.

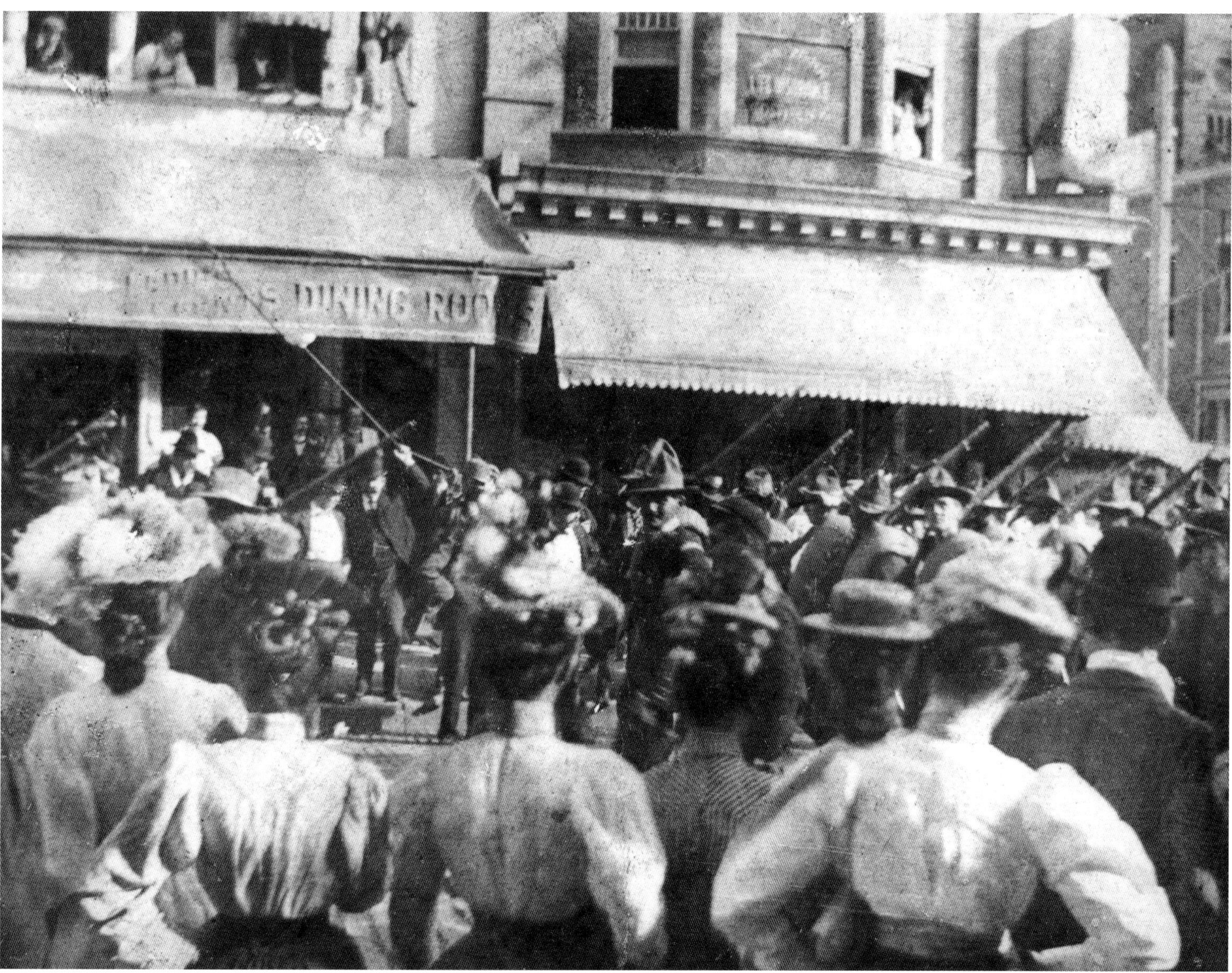

The Claymont Brick Works is shown around the turn of the century. It is likely that the man next to the wagon is Mr. Comstock, proprietor of the brickworks.

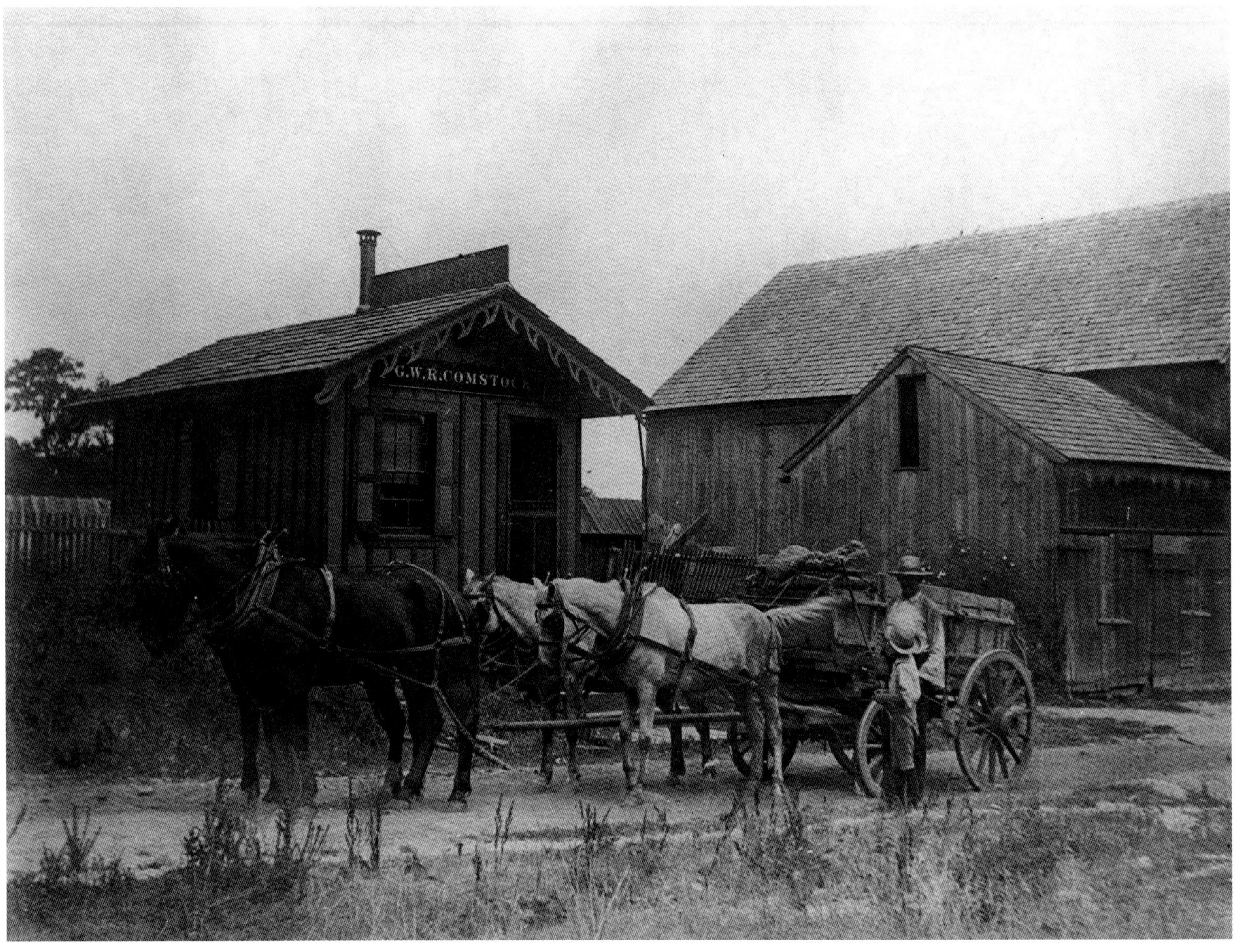

A New Century

(1900–1919)

On the heels of the Industrial Revolution an era of progress and reform infused the country. Telephones, electricity, water and sewer systems, and trolley cars changed the look and workings of cities and towns across the nation and in Delaware. By 1920, the state's 1890s appearance had been completely transformed.

In education, the Women's College was established in 1914 at the University of Delaware, and P. S. du Pont founded Service Citizens to oversee a statewide program for the construction of new schools. A new tax and administrative structure upgraded the state's public education system to provide better education for students of all races. Mr. du Pont personally invested $6 million in the project.

T. Coleman du Pont loved automobiles. He foresaw Delaware's need to pave roads for better commerce, safety, and comfort. In 1908, he proposed to the state assembly to build a highway for Delaware. The result was Route 13 from Claymont to Dover and Route 113 from Dover to Selbyville. The first section was completed in 1917, and though the State Highway Department was established before the road was completed in 1924, du Pont oversaw the work, personally spending $4 million on the project.

Between 1900 and 1905, Wilmington lost 15 manufactories and 1,000 industrial jobs. Shipbuilding and railroad manufacturing moved to the Midwest. It appeared that Wilmington, with a third of the state's population, was heading into decline.

In 1902, leadership of the DuPont Company fell to three du Pont cousins—Irenee, Pierre S., and Alfred I. du Pont—starting a new era for the company and its home city and state. The cousins discarded antiquated business practices and procedures. They diversified and bought out competitors throughout the country. In an era of big business, DuPont soon rivaled the nation's largest companies in size and power.

Large numbers of skilled immigrants found work along the Christina River. But in 1907, the DuPont Company headquarters opened at Rodney Square, precipitating a switch from blue-collar to white-collar work. By the outbreak of World War I, Wilmington was a corporate and banking center.

Delaware's beach communities were booming, too. Rehoboth was growing, and small picnic communities along the railroad became popular destinations—places like Augustine Beach, Woodland Beach, Bowers Beach, and Kitts Hummock enjoyed great popularity.

This view from the early 1900s shows the Delaware City Hotel and businesses along Clinton Street. The hotel was originally built on the waterfront in 1829, shortly after the Chesapeake and Delaware Canal opened, to entice travelers along the canal to stay a night in Delaware City. Though the main canal entrance for commercial shipping has since been relocated, this neighborhood is remarkably well preserved.

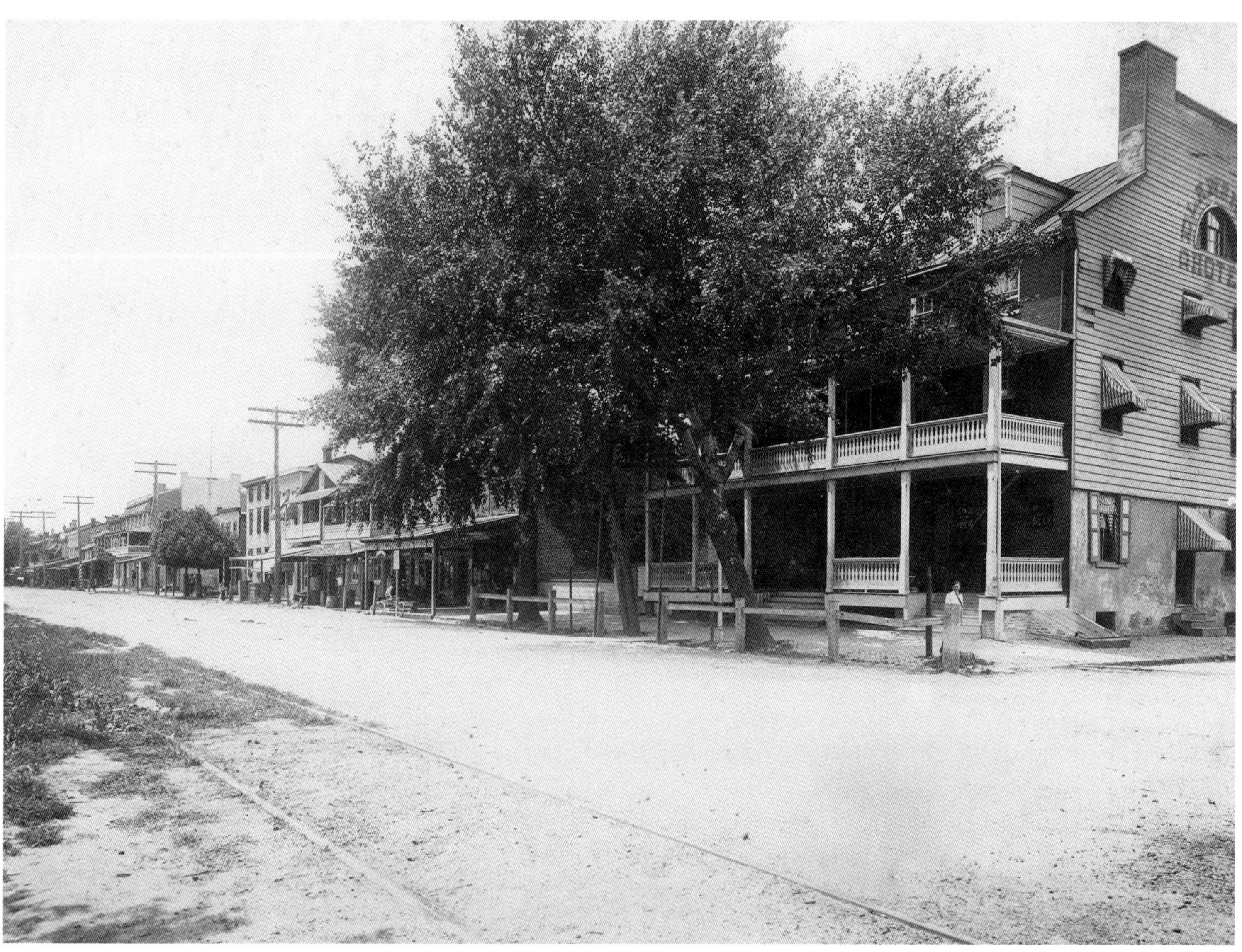

These jaunty men pose on a small recreational boat just offshore on the Christina River in Wilmington. In the background are the shipyards and businesses of the Old Swedes neighborhood.

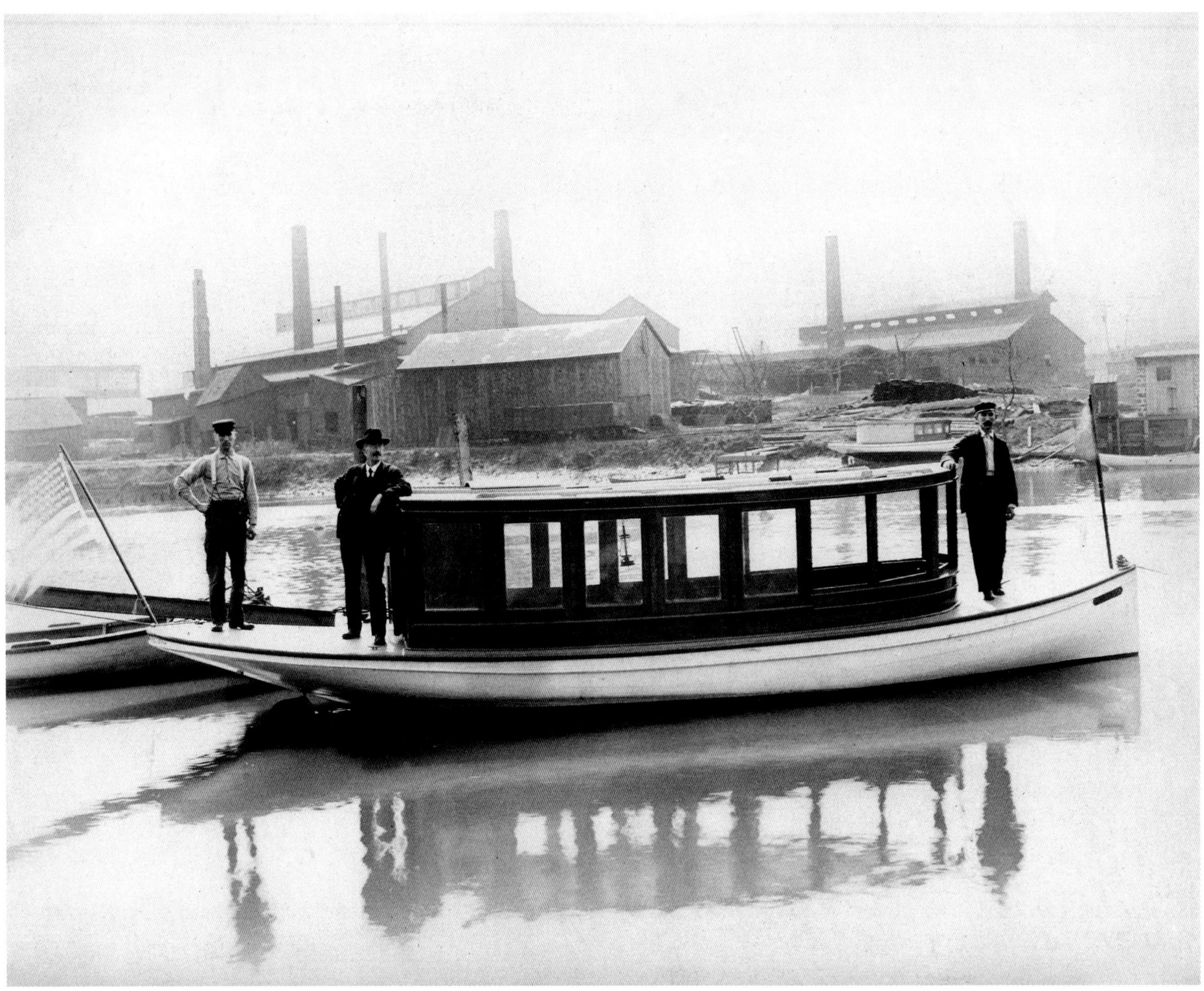

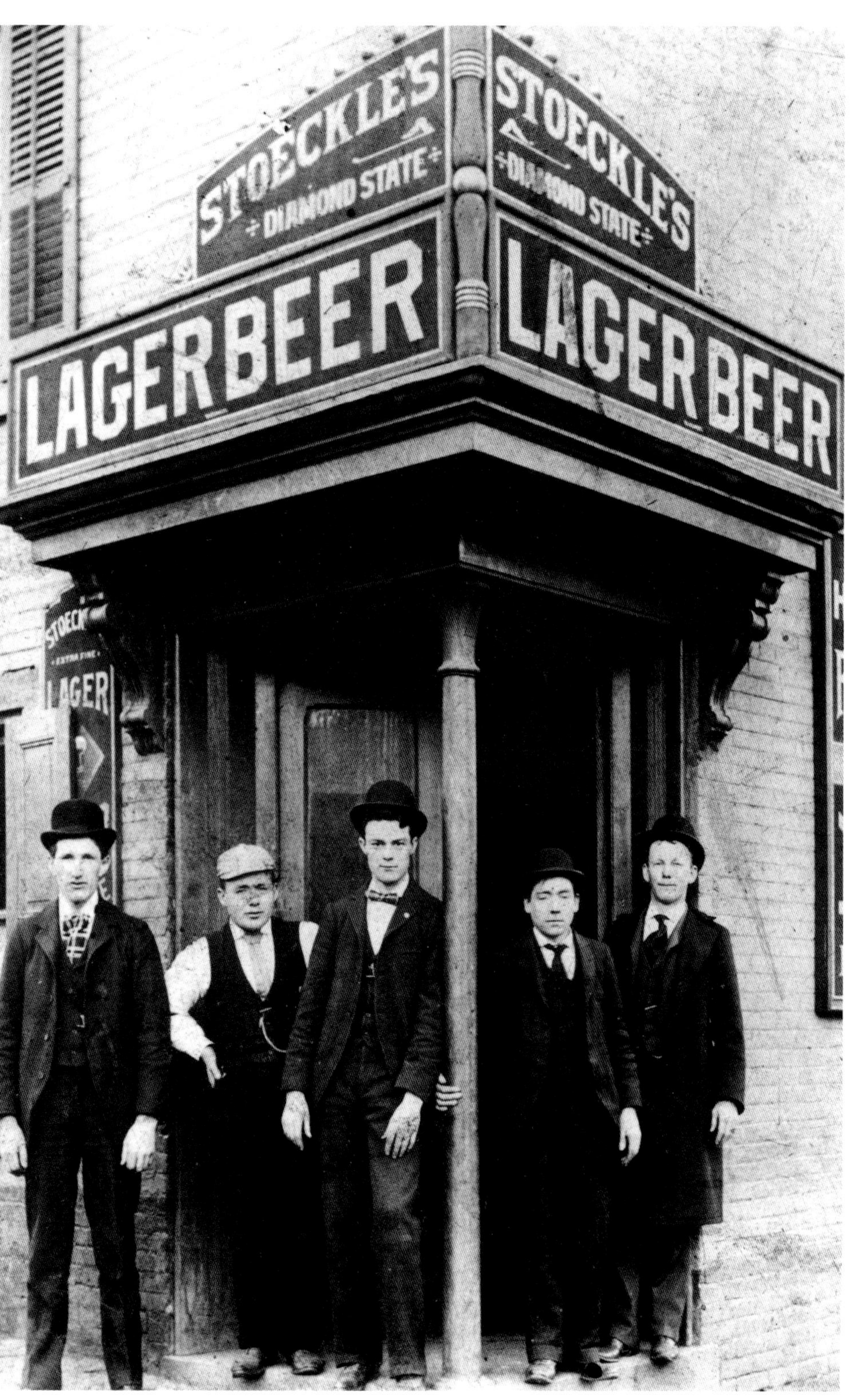

Joseph E. McCullin ran a small tavern at the corner of 5th and Tatnall streets in Wilmington between 1900 and 1902, where he proudly displayed Stoeckle's Brewery beer signs. Stoeckle's was located just a few blocks to the west at 5th and Adams streets.

Onlookers gather to see their townsman in the stocks. Corporal punishment included the whipping post, the stocks, and public hangings, and was used on both blacks and whites. Though the last flogging took place in 1952, corporal punishment was not revoked in Delaware until 1972.

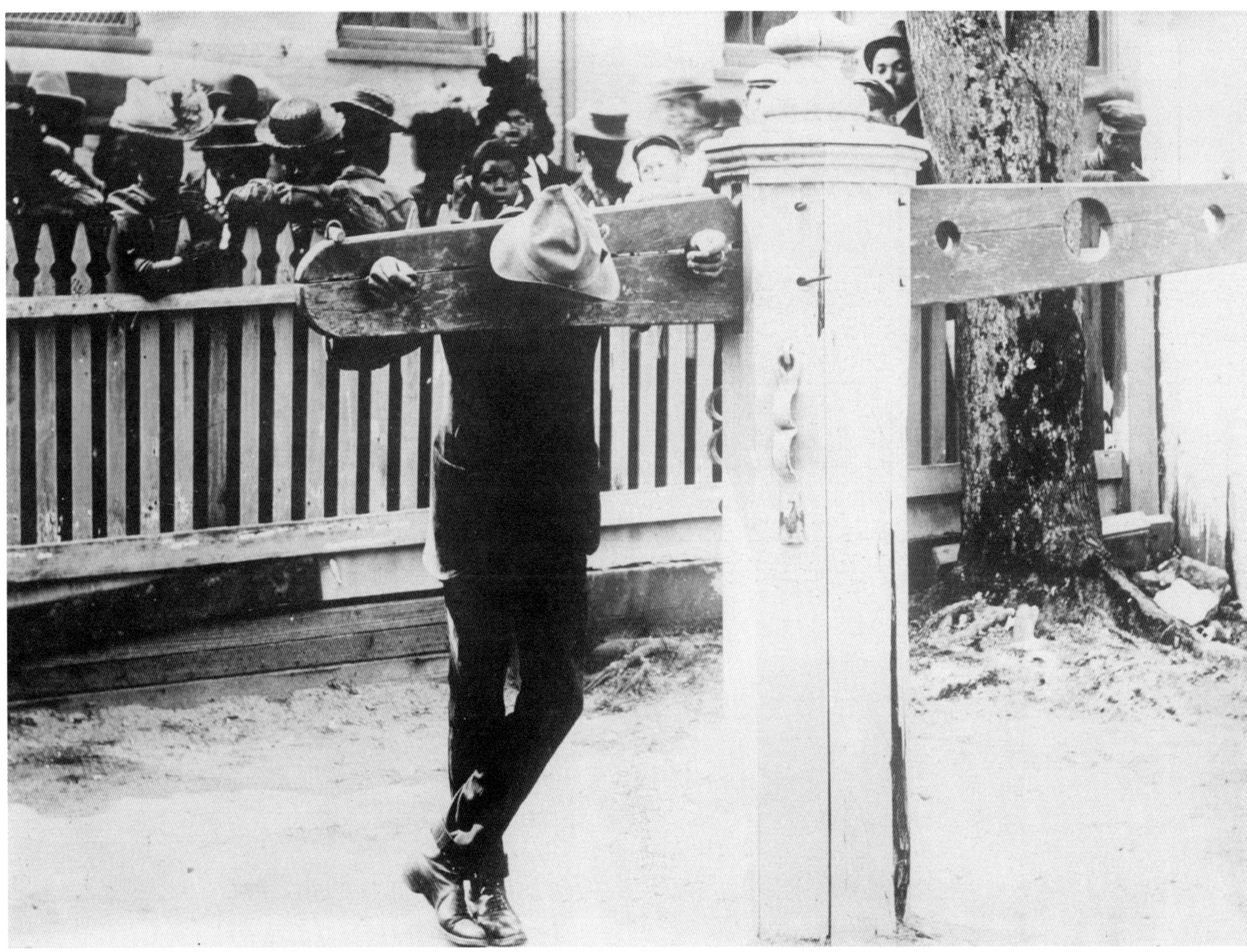

Hundreds of people turned out to watch the launching of a torpedo boat destroyer at the Harlan and Hollingsworth yards in 1901. Harlan and Hollingsworth had been national leaders in building ironclad ships, ferries, and yachts throughout the second half of the nineteenth century, but by 1901 the glory days had passed. Changes in company leadership and within the industry were causing shipbuilding in Wilmington to decline.

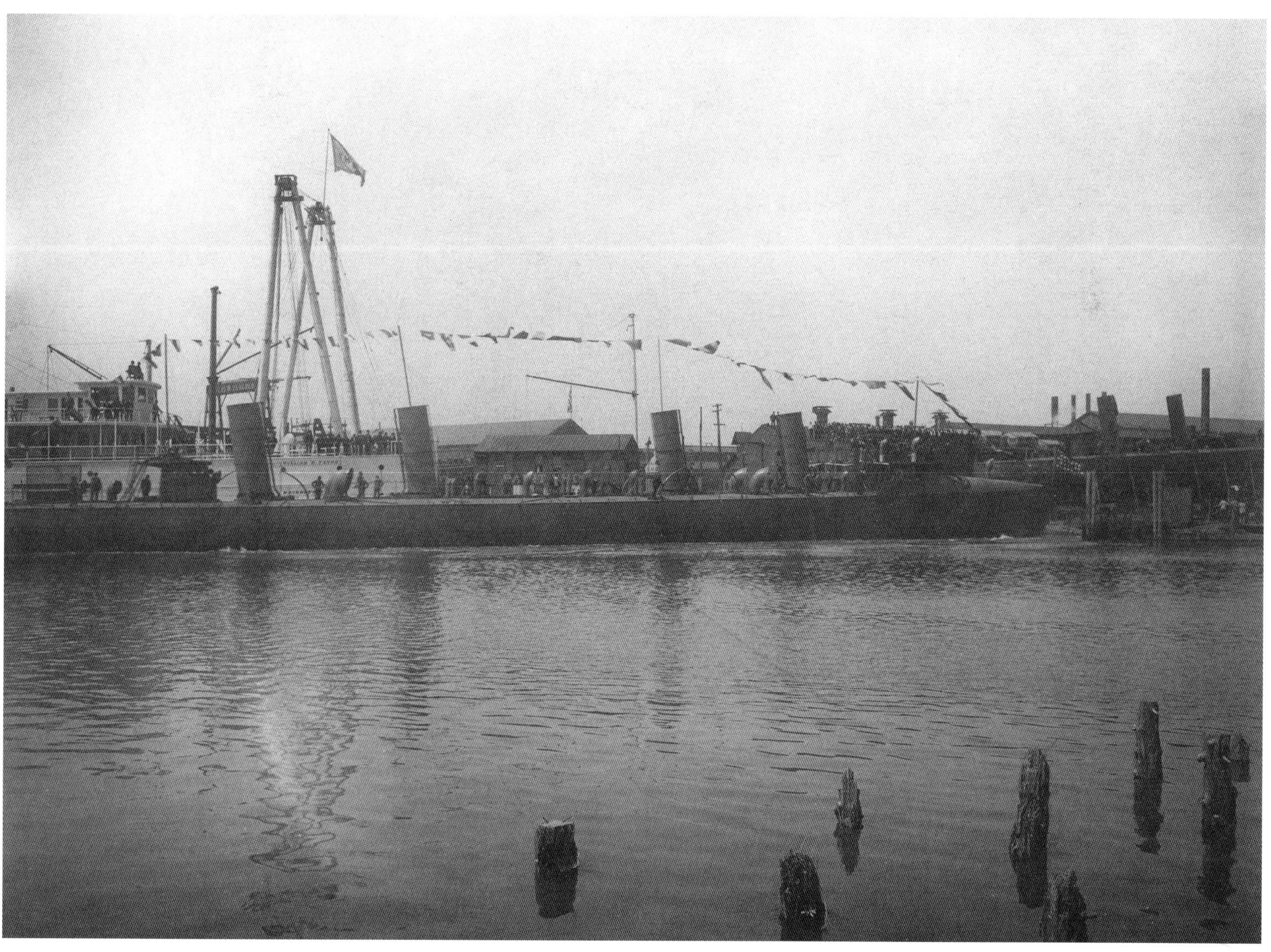

Snowbound and treetop, these children pose for posterity in front of E. Arnold Greenabaum's home on High Street in Seaford after a February 1901 snowstorm. The children are identified as Earl Donoho, William Ross, Ridgely Hargrove, Sam Scott, Ashby Shipley, Page Shipley, and Samuel Robinson. The Greenabaums operated one of the largest canneries on the Eastern Shore.

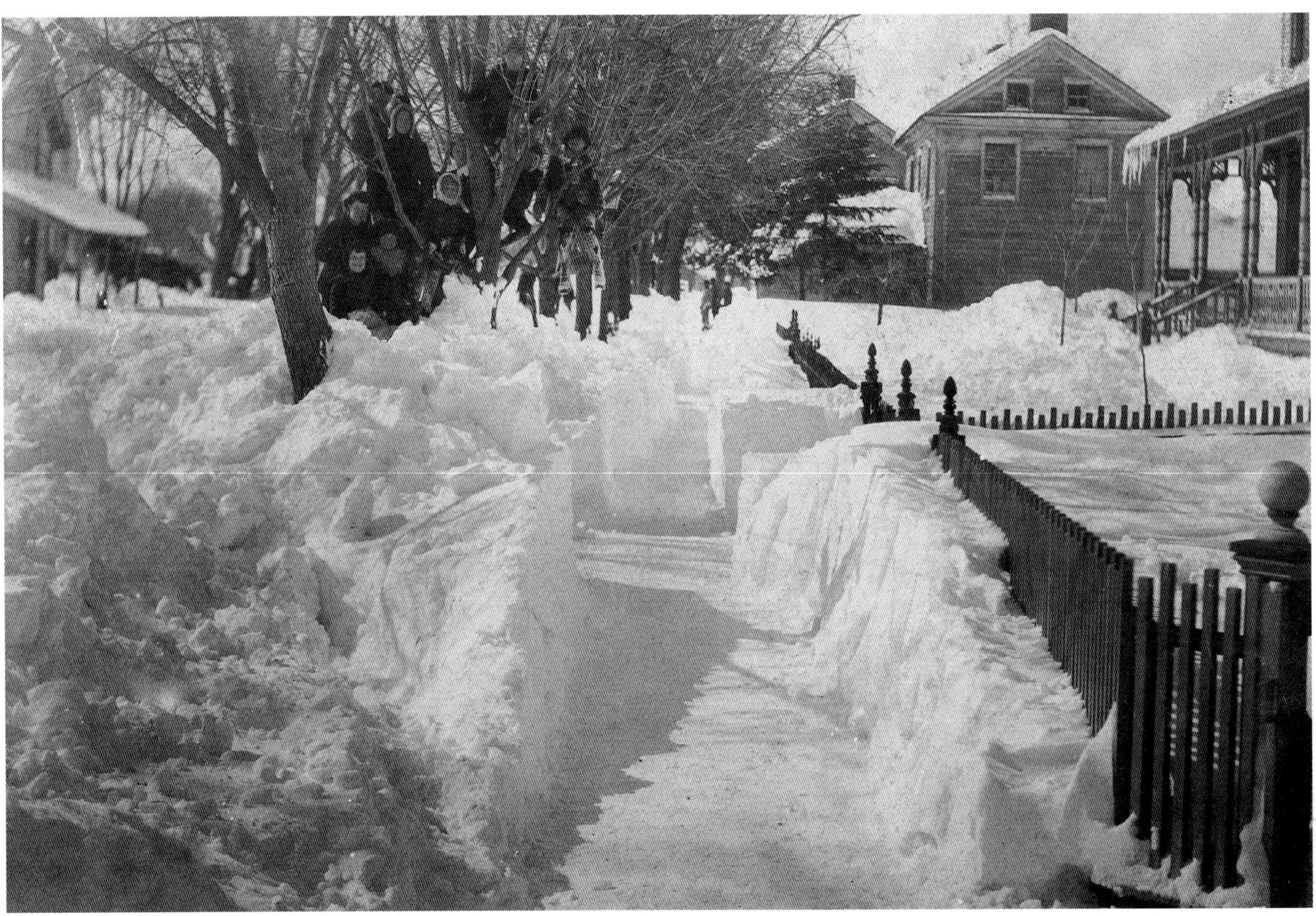

Celebrating Delaware's Revolutionary War heritage, this band is identified only as "Colonial Band." Although the band met for social reasons, they look quite stern in this photograph.

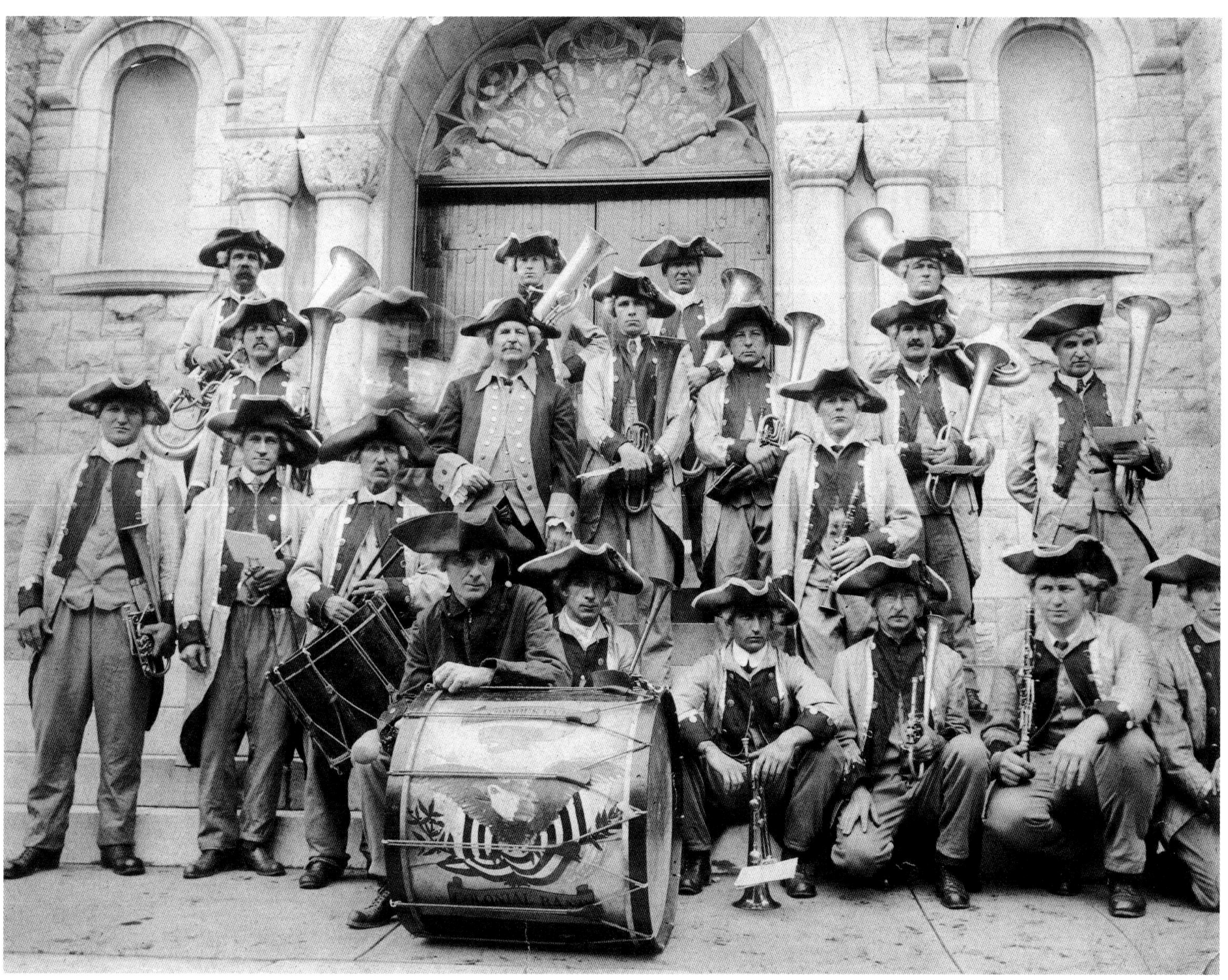

Following Spread: Photographed by F. A. Shipley, this view shows a pretty, tree-lined residential street in Seaford just after 1900.

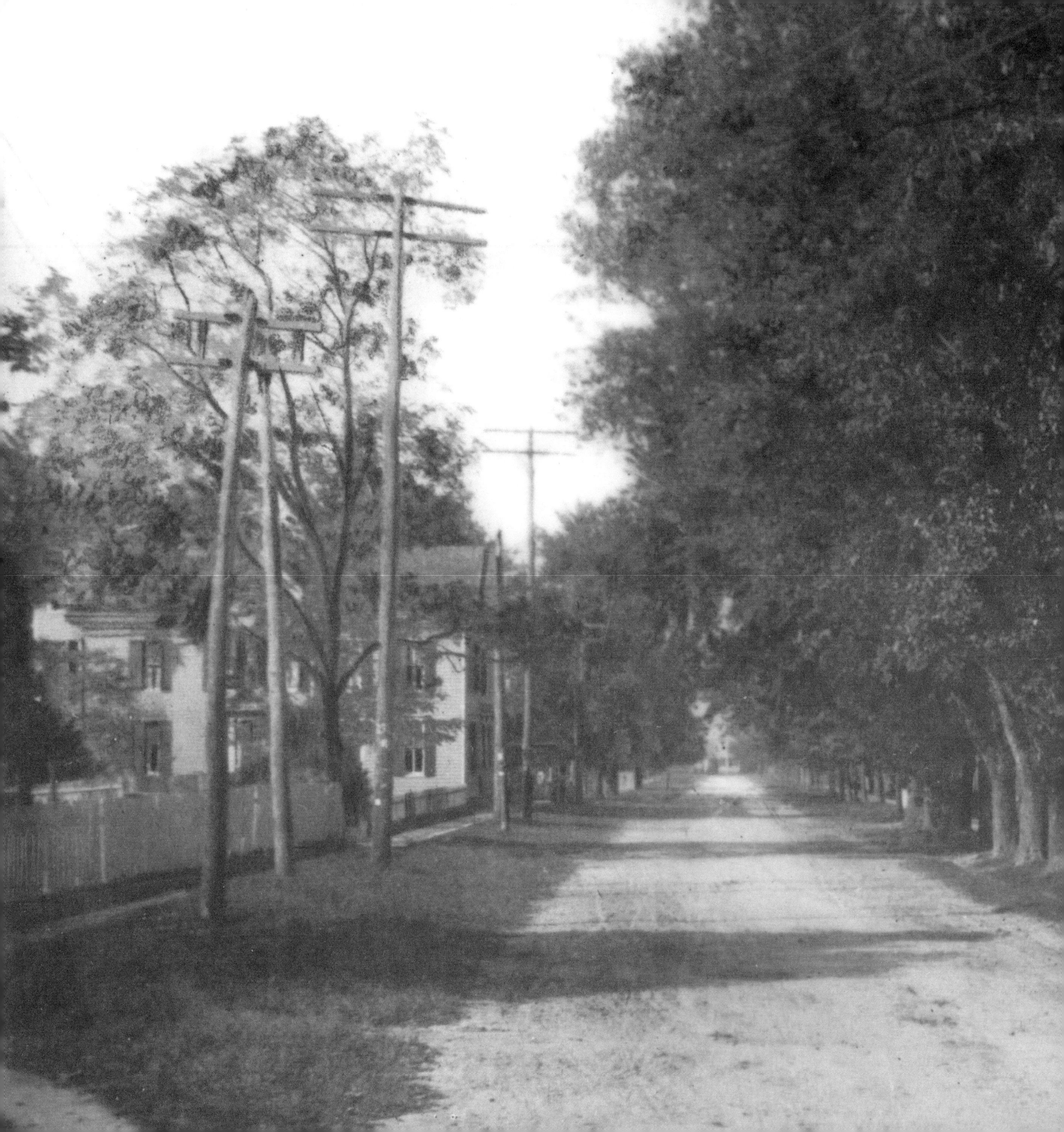

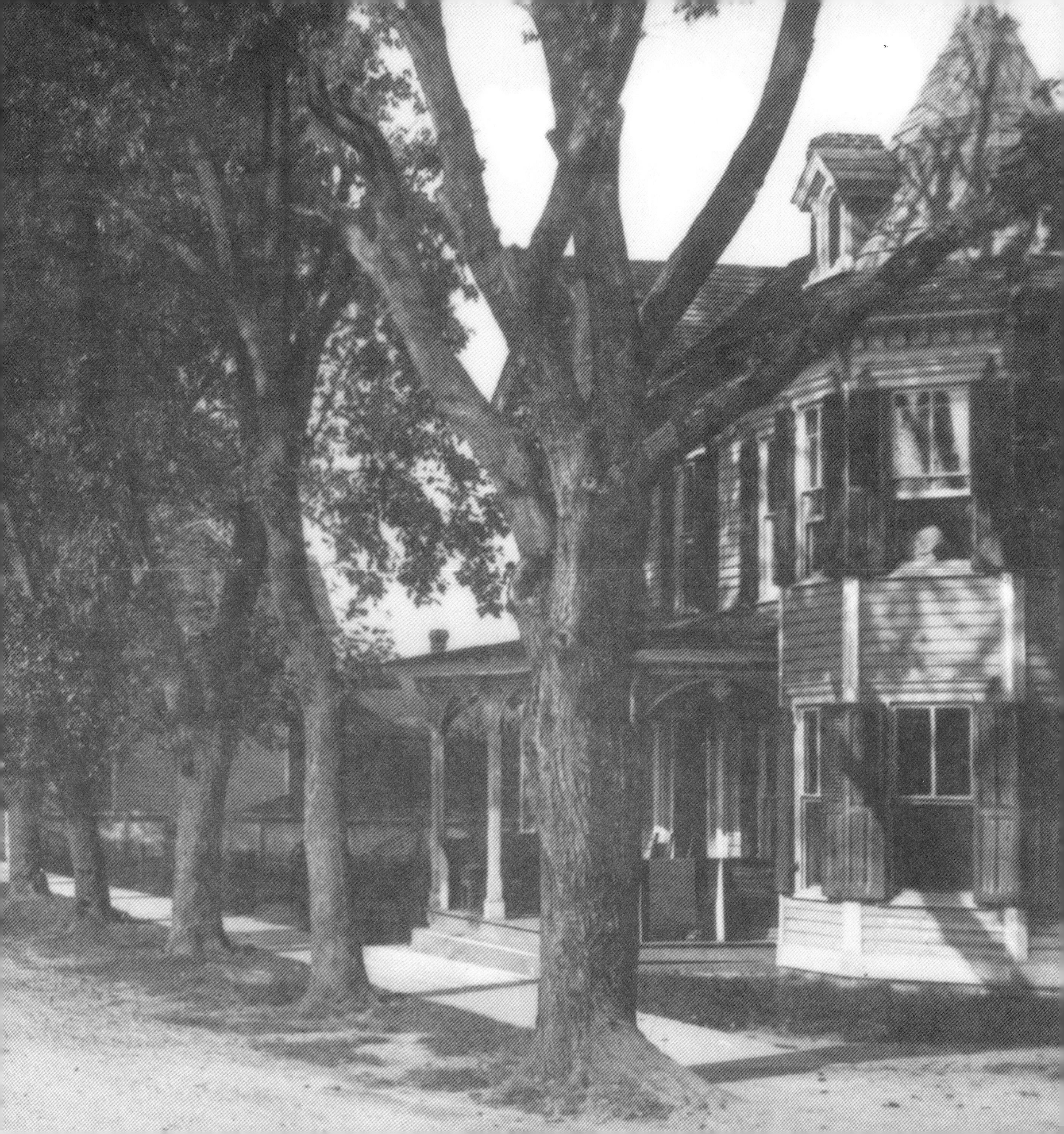

Local governments made many civic and sanitary improvements during the progressive years of the early 1900s. Here workers lay the first water and sewer lines for the town of Laurel around 1904.

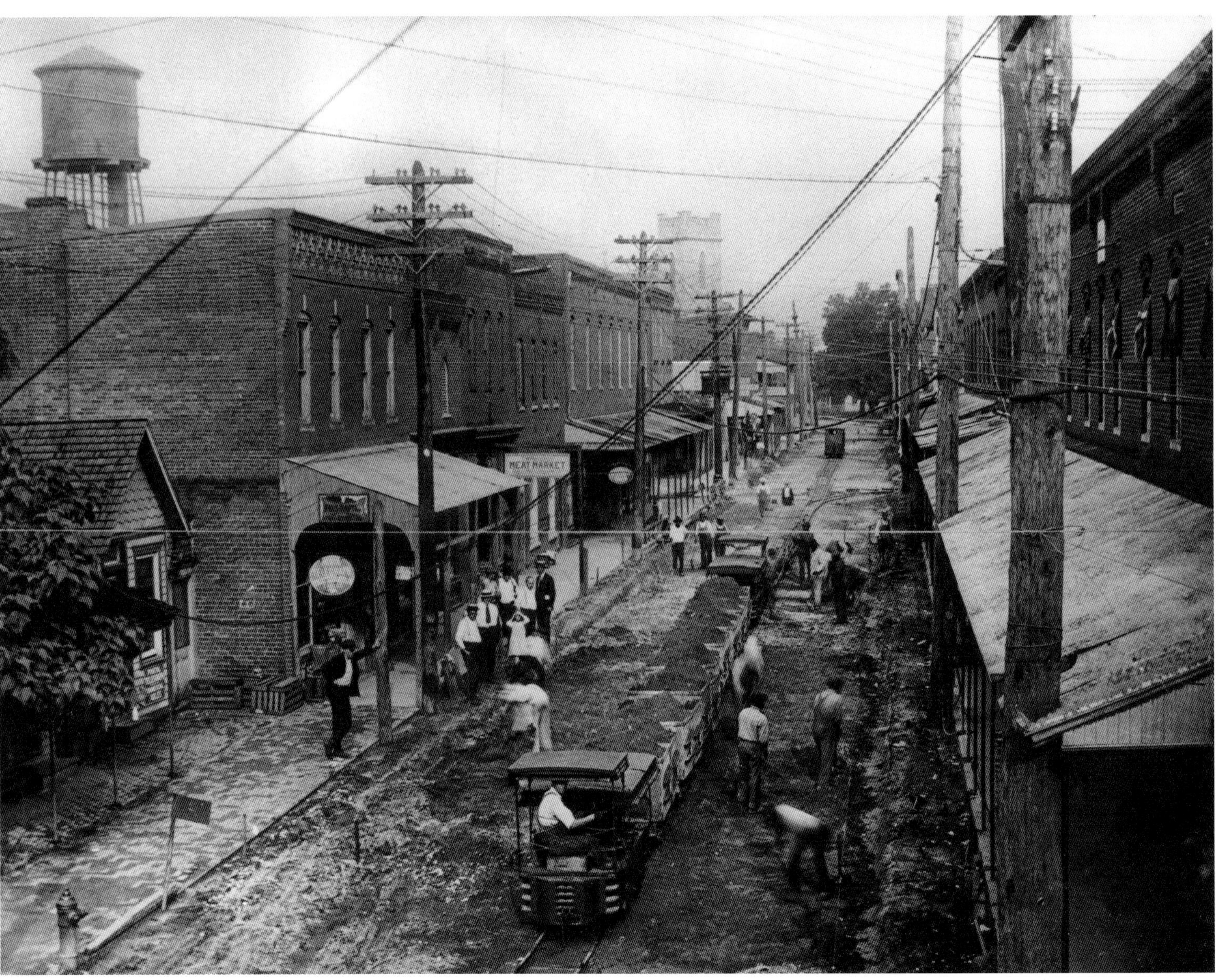

Three men pose beside the fancy delivery wagon outside B. and T. J. Dalton's dry goods, grocery, and general merchandise store in Centerville around 1905. Sherwin-Williams Paints and Syracuse Plows are advertised under the window at left.

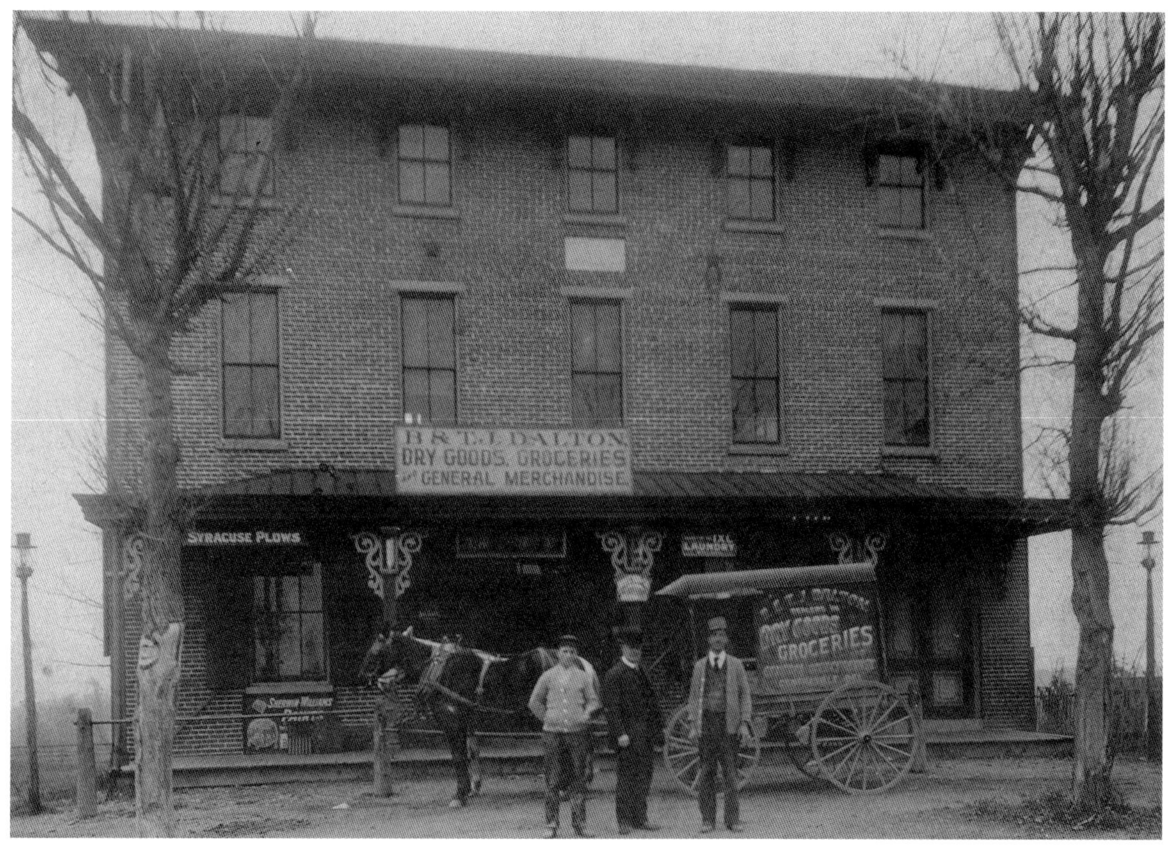

In this view of Wilmington, facing north from the railroad tracks between 1909 and 1918, White Brothers is visible at 100–104 Orange Street, and the Delaware Hardware Company fronts Shipley Street. The building above the water tower is the DuPont Building at Rodney Square. In this era, the neighborhoods near the railroad tracks included a mixture of family-run businesses with the family living above the storefront, a few larger businesses, stables, and warehouses.

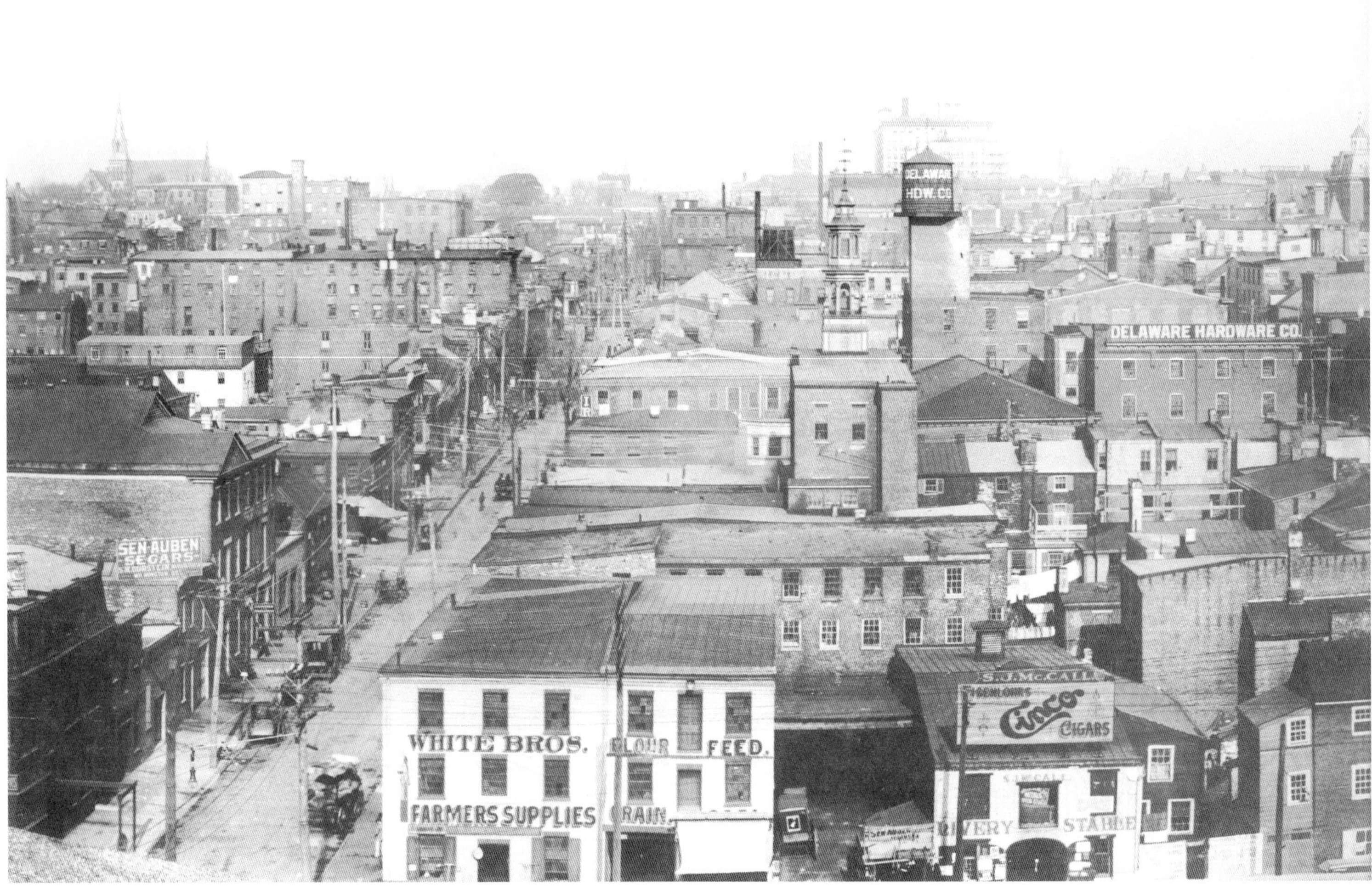

This is an interior view of a silk mill in New Castle around 1904. The family of Emma V. Zepp, who is pictured at far-right, donated this rare image of the interior of this mill long-since closed. This view raises more questions about the working of a silk mill than it answers.

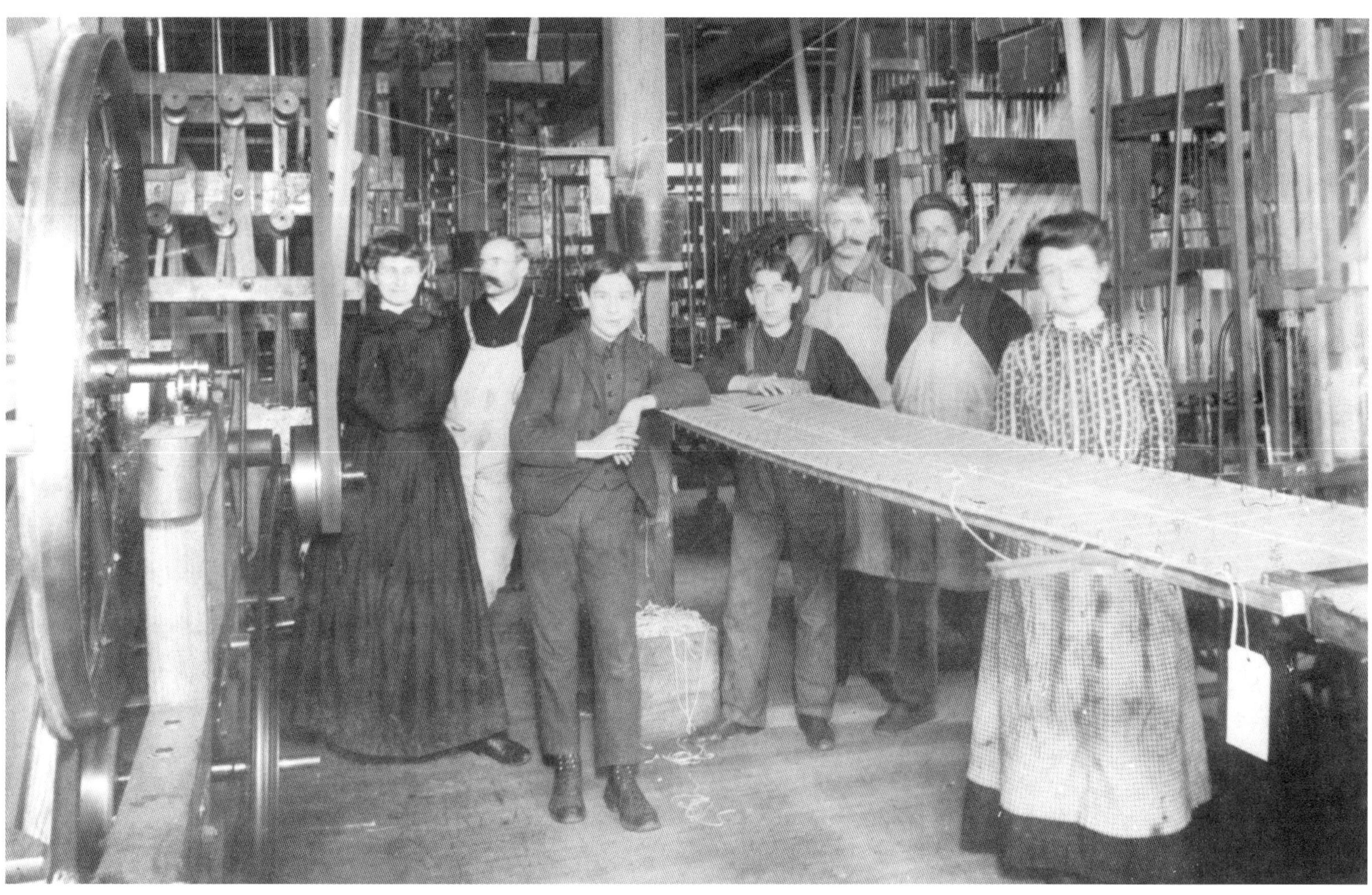

This operating room was a part of the Delaware Homeopathic Hospital. Located at 1501-09 Van Buren Street in Wilmington, the hospital had a staff of eleven men and women. A sign posted near the door announces that visitors are welcome only on Wednesdays and Sundays from 2:00 until 5:00 P.M.

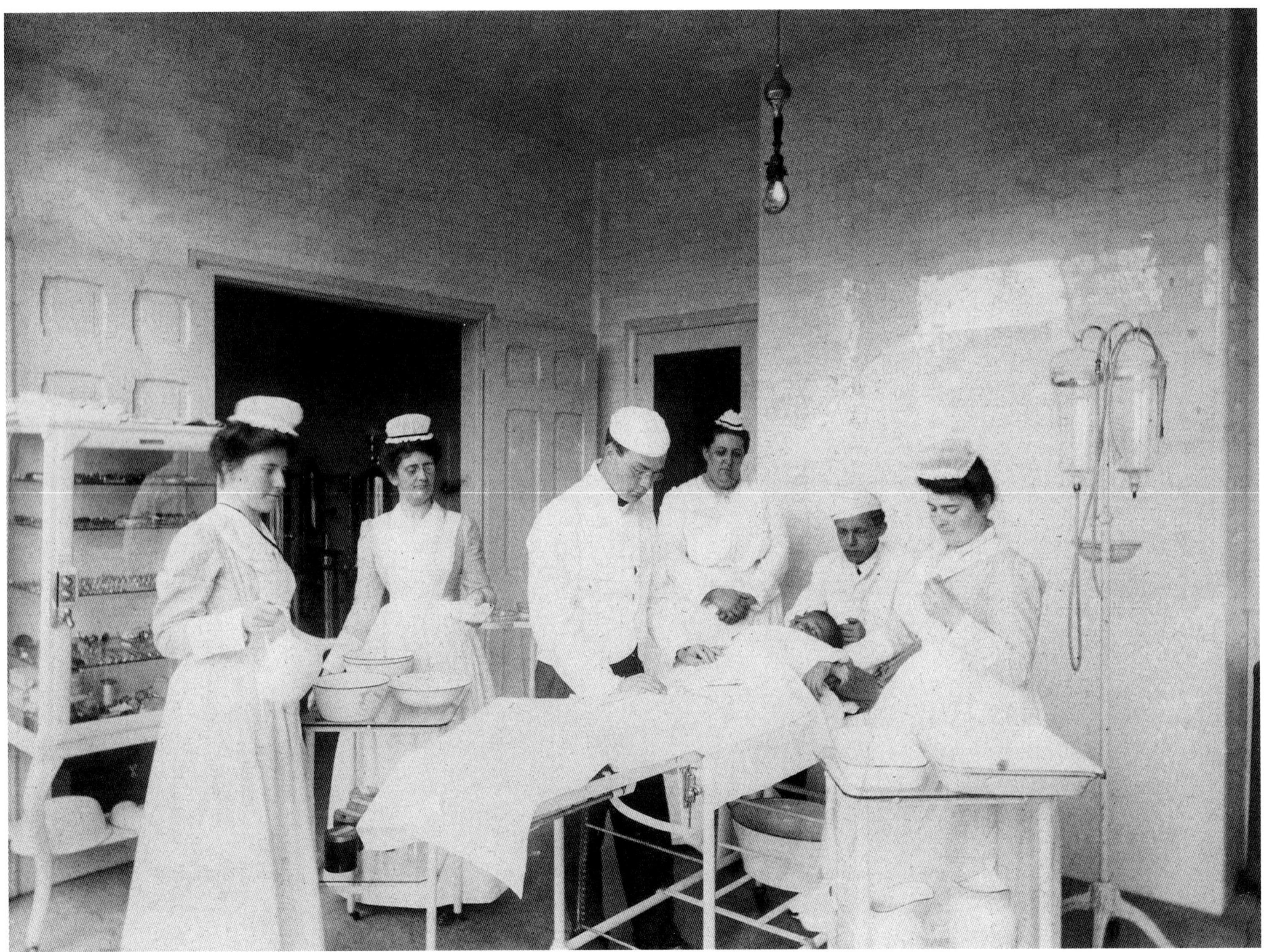

Young apprentices are hard at work learning to use a metal lathe in this Delaware machine shop.

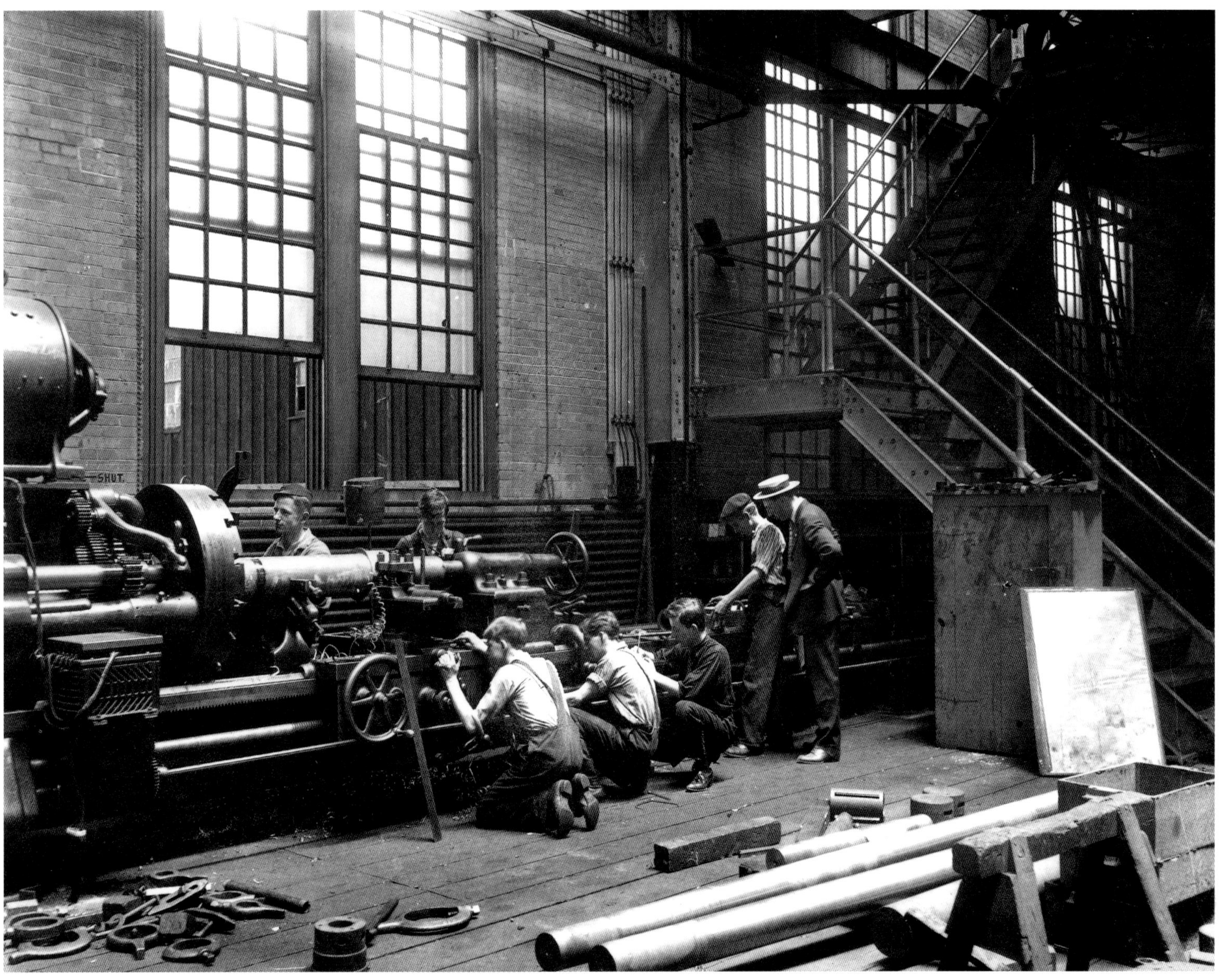

Emile Bucher photographed the proud staff of Freihofer's Vienna Bakery in 1906. Even the horses wore traditional Viennese headdress. In business for many years, the bakery was located here at the northeast corner of 5th and Orange streets in Wilmington from 1903 to 1907.

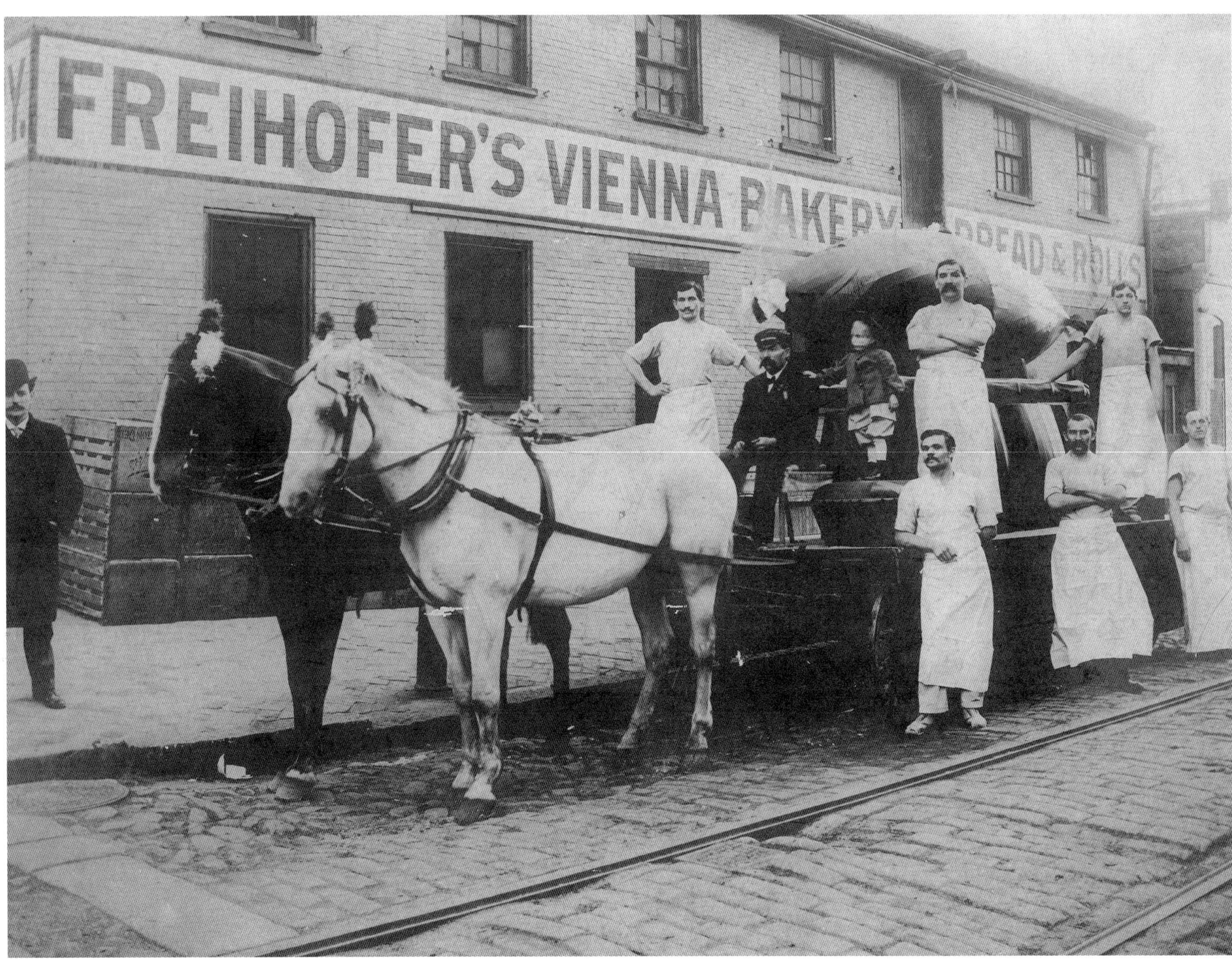

In 1902, Alfred I. T. Coleman and Pierre S. du Pont took over management of the DuPont Company. They directed its emergence into a modern corporation. After debate they agreed to remain in Wilmington and to build a company headquarters downtown, a multi-year and multi-stage construction project. Shown here in 1905 is the excavation site for the first section of the building at 10th and Market streets. The headquarters opened in 1907.

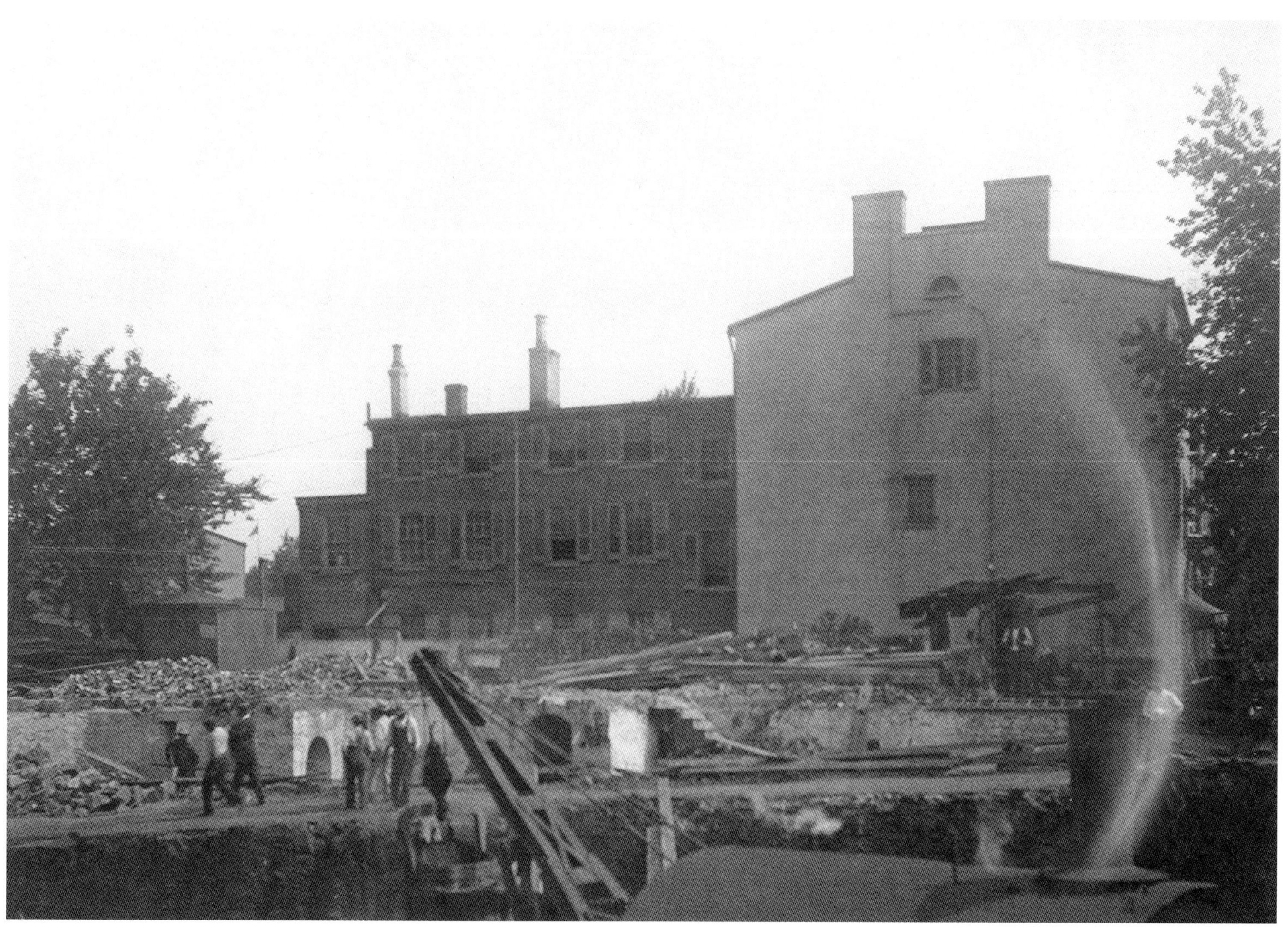

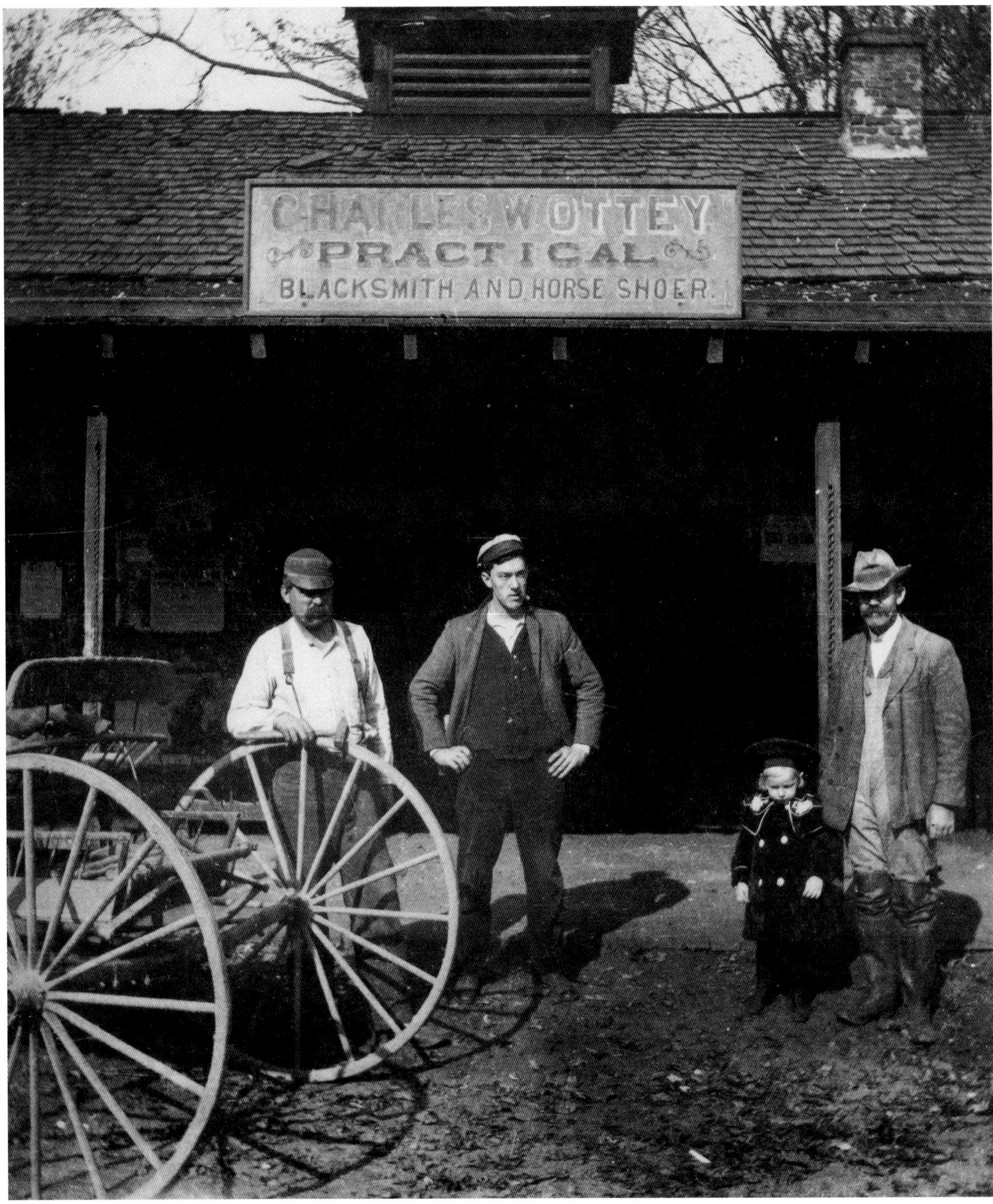

Charles Ottey ran his blacksmith shop at the intersection of Naaman's Road and Philadelphia Pike. Standing left to right are Ottey, Herbert Hemphill, Paulie Baldwin, and William Hoopes. Blacksmiths were skilled at any number of jobs, from shoeing horses to building and repairing farm machinery to making household tools, hinges, and hardware.

Three young boys pose on the corner of 7th and Market streets in Wilmington in mid September 1905. The town was decorated for the Union Veterans' 20th National Encampment, which took place for four days throughout the city. Govatos Candies, a longtime favorite of Wilmingtonians, had already been on Market Street for a decade when this photograph was taken.

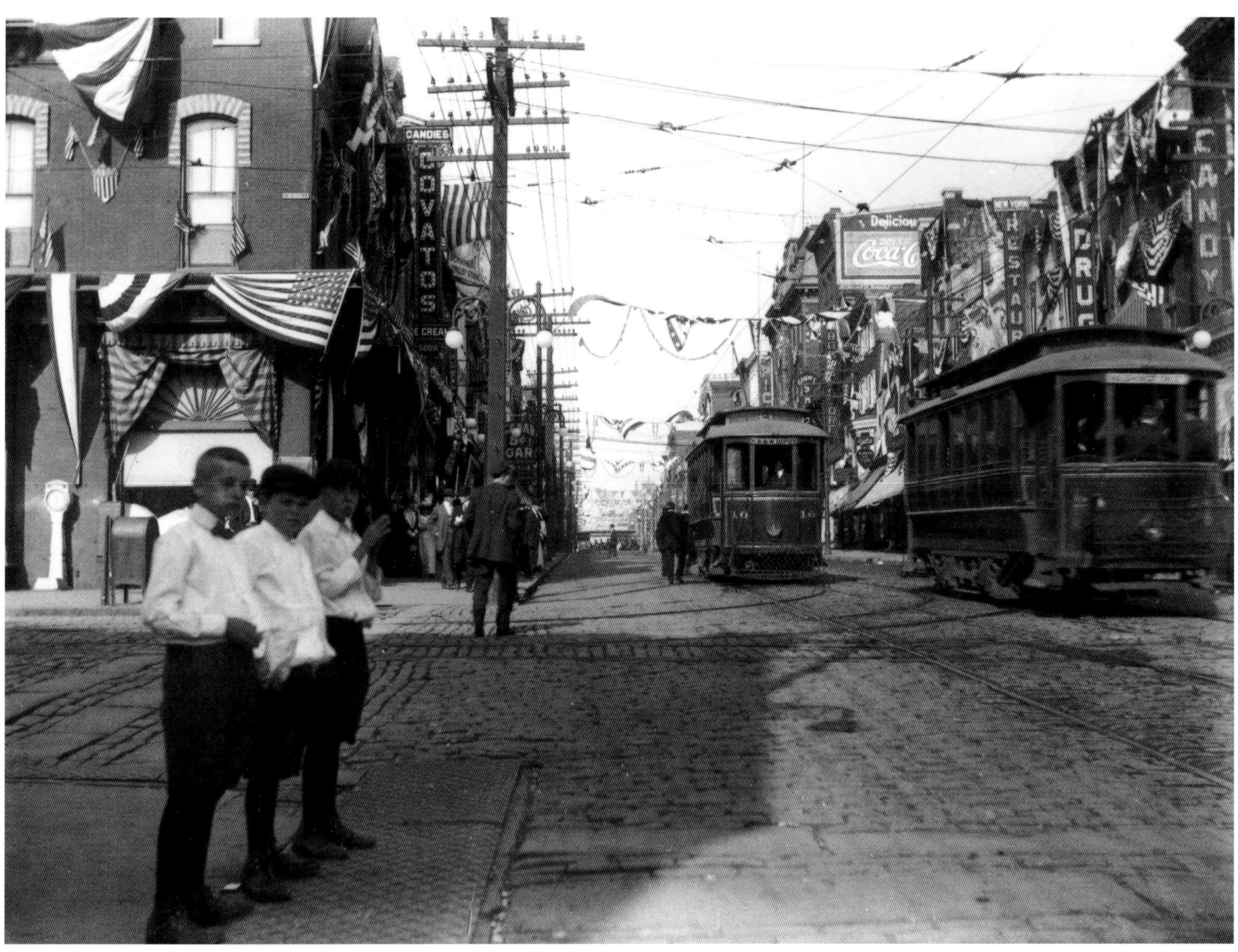

Each October, Delaware's cities and towns once held "Old Home Week," giving people a chance to celebrate their communities. A large, enthusiastic crowd in Wilmington has gathered here at the 300 block of Market Street outside Lippincott's Department Store to wait for the coming parade.

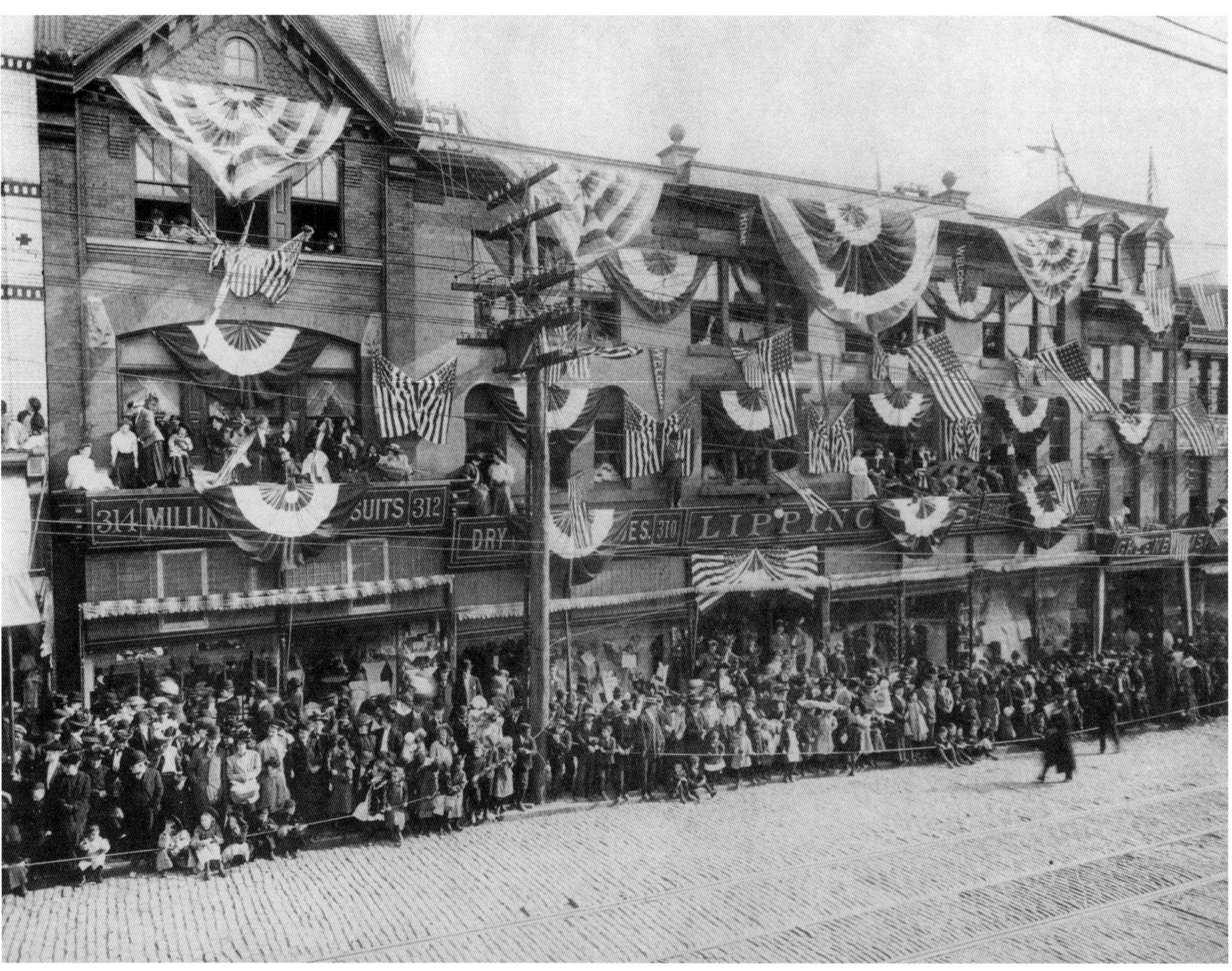

The intersection of Walnut and S.E. Front streets in Milford is shown here in 1906.

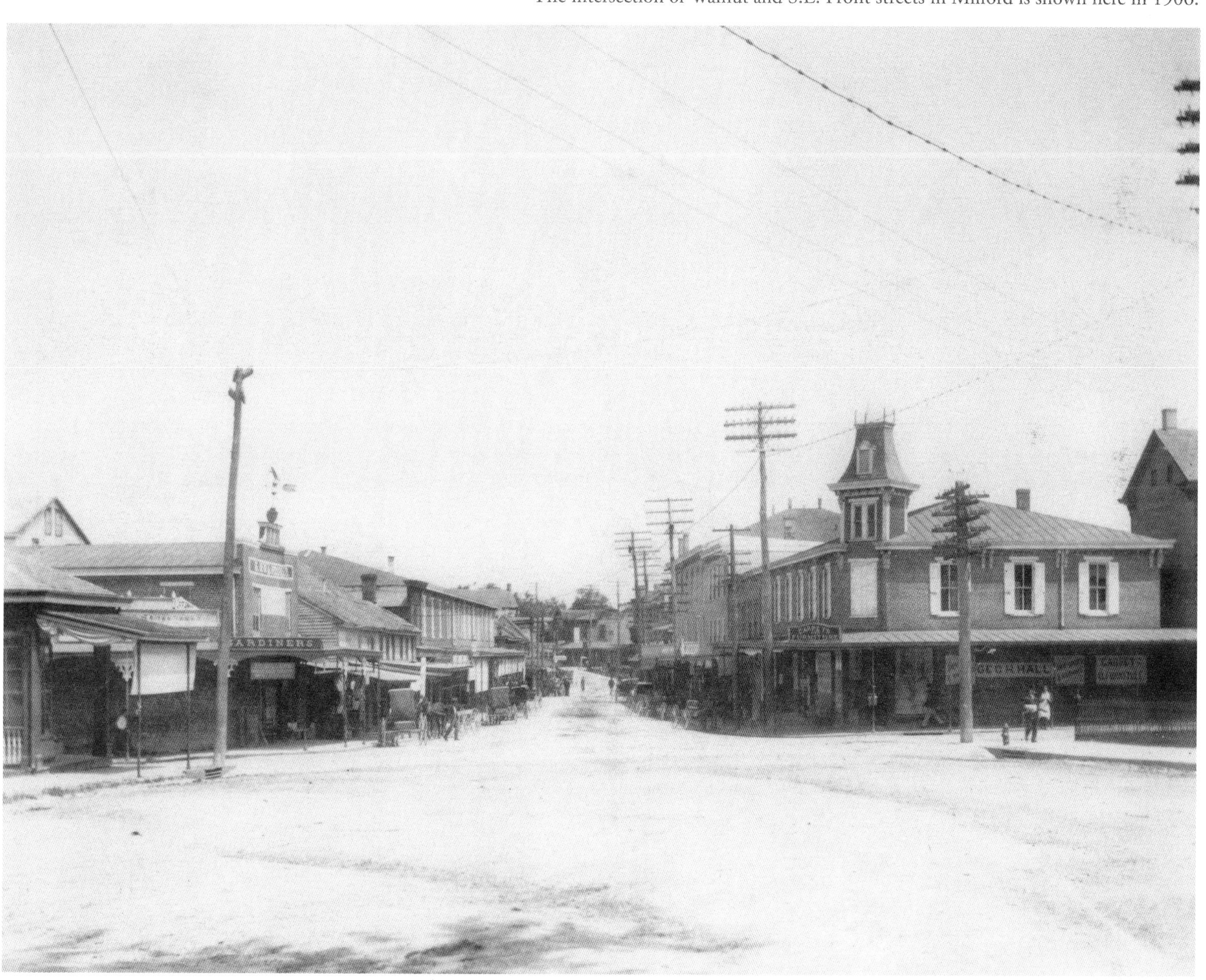

H. Eaton is probably one of the men pictured here at his store in Felton. The large and ornate stove seems as much a part of the group as any person. On the wall behind the men, posters and calendars advertise the products of Schlitz beer and Gulf oil, as well as the handmade tires of Marion, Pecan Valley's peanut butter, and others.

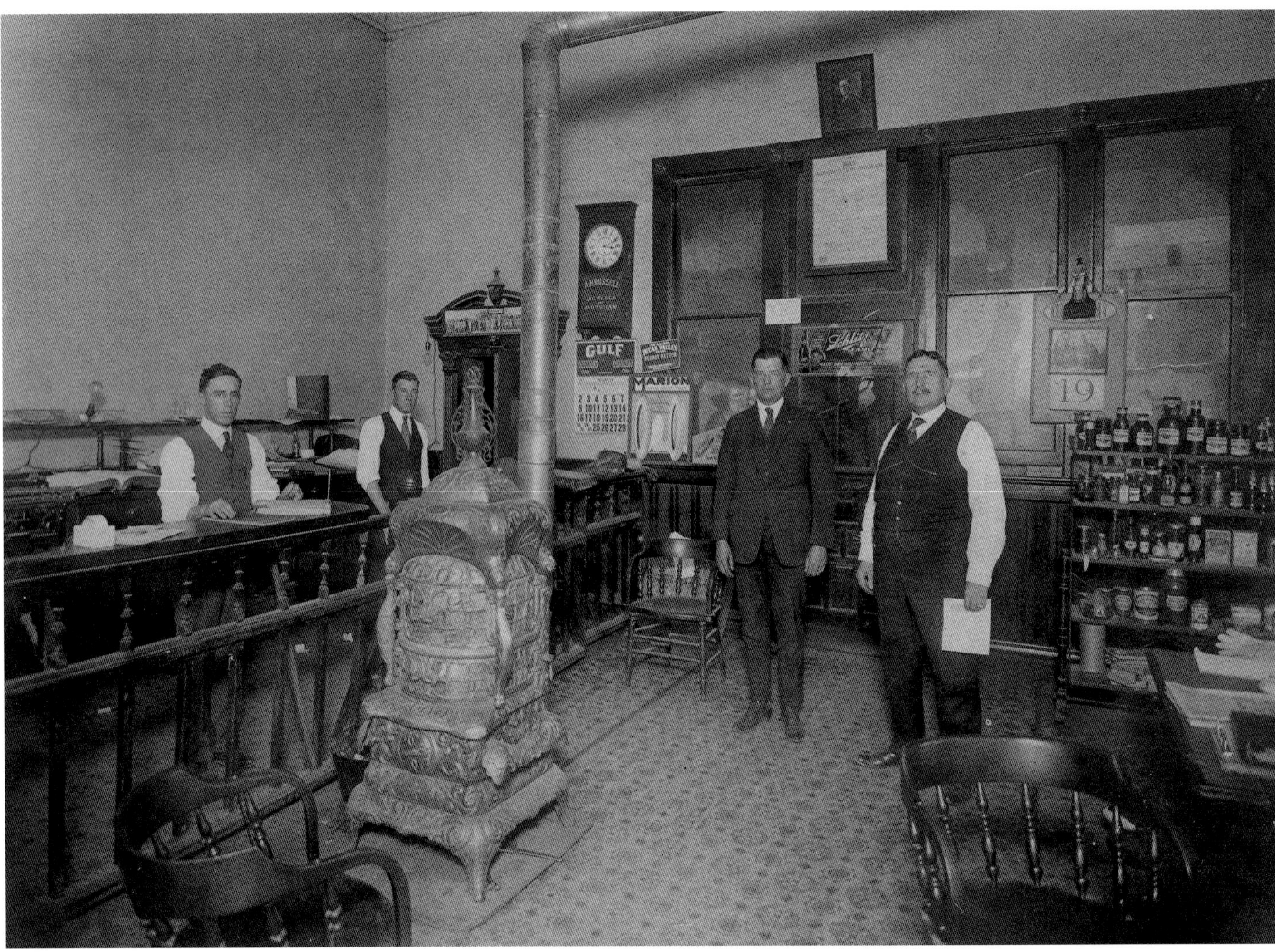

Harvey Buchanan of 608 N. Van Buren Street began working for the Postal Telegraph Company as a messenger at age 13. He began at 7:00 A.M. and regularly worked until 6:00 P.M. He earned $4 a week and admitted to smoking and visiting houses of prostitution. This was the biography Harvey gave to photographer Lewis Hine and an investigator in May 1910.

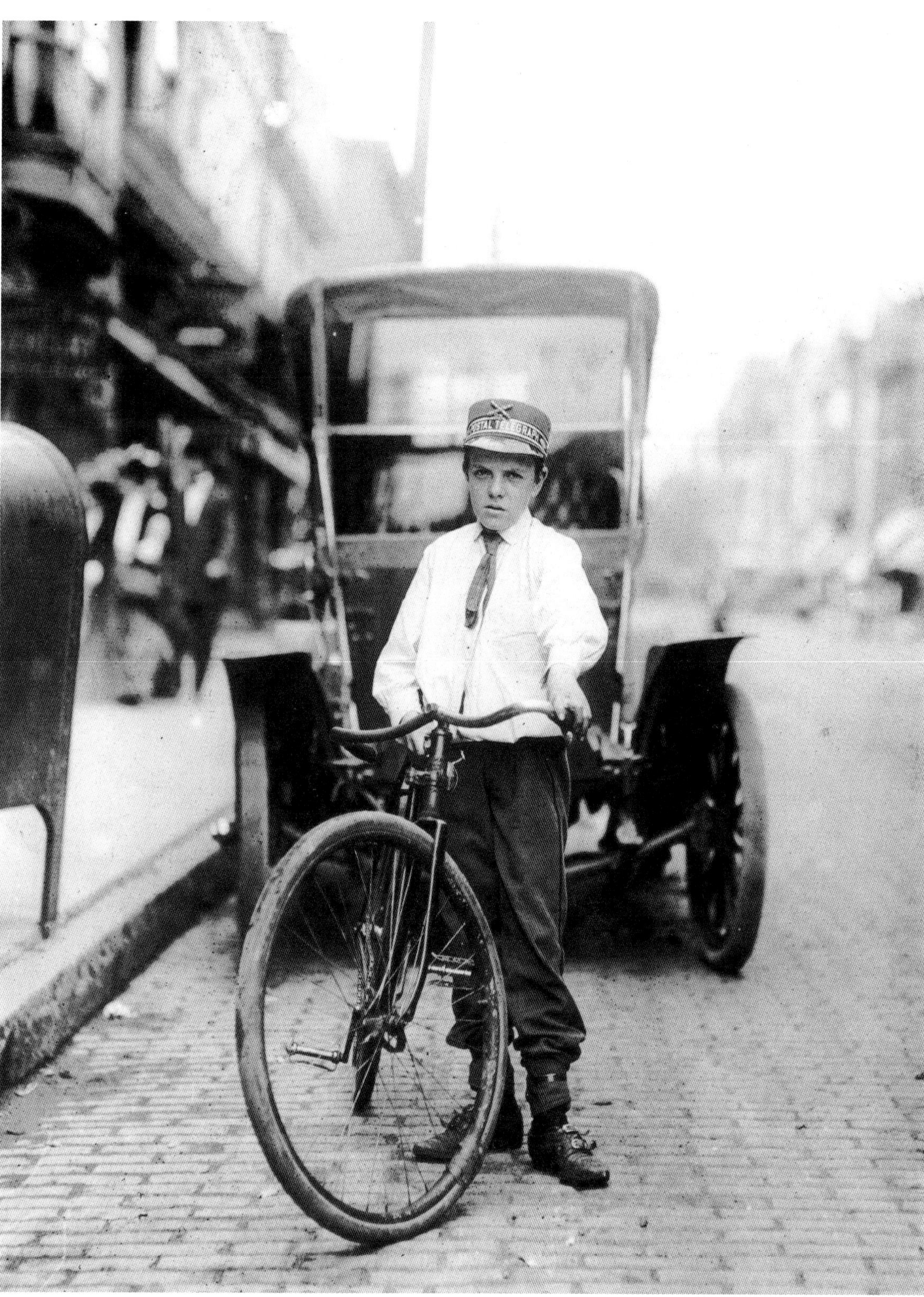

Daisy Langford, at front, is 8 years old and is working in her first season at Ross's Canneries in Seaford. She told Lewis Hine that although she worked full-time placing caps on cans at the rate of 40 a minute, she could not manage to "keep up." Hine photographed children like Daisy to document unsafe working conditions.

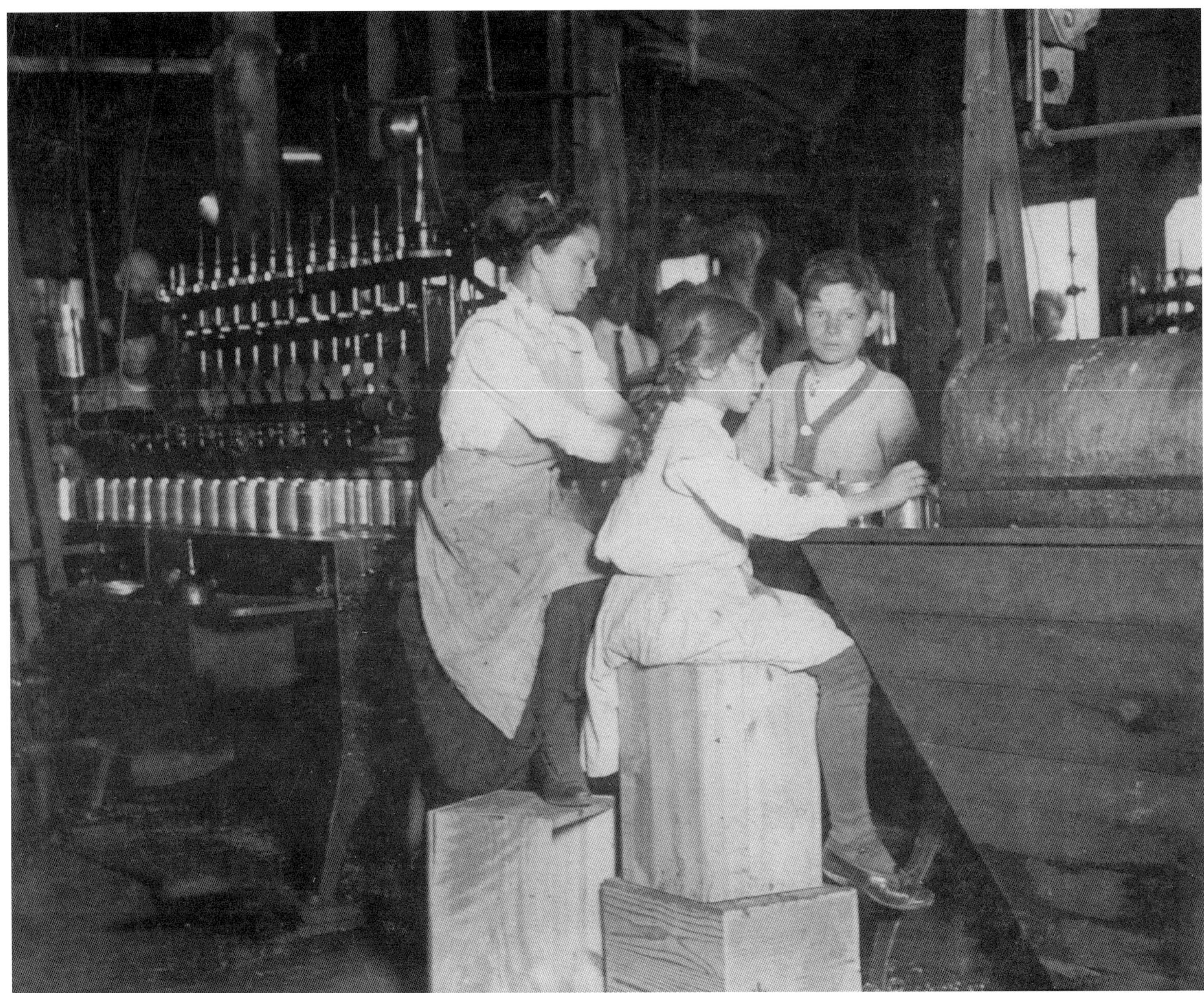

The *City of Wilmington,* purchased in 1910 by the Wilson Line, plied the waters of the Delaware River many times each day. The Wilson Line's passenger ferries traveled between Philadelphia, Chester, Penns Grove (and the popular Riverview Beach Park), and Wilmington. Founded in 1882, the Wilson Line was a favorite mode of transportation for generations and was in business for 80 years.

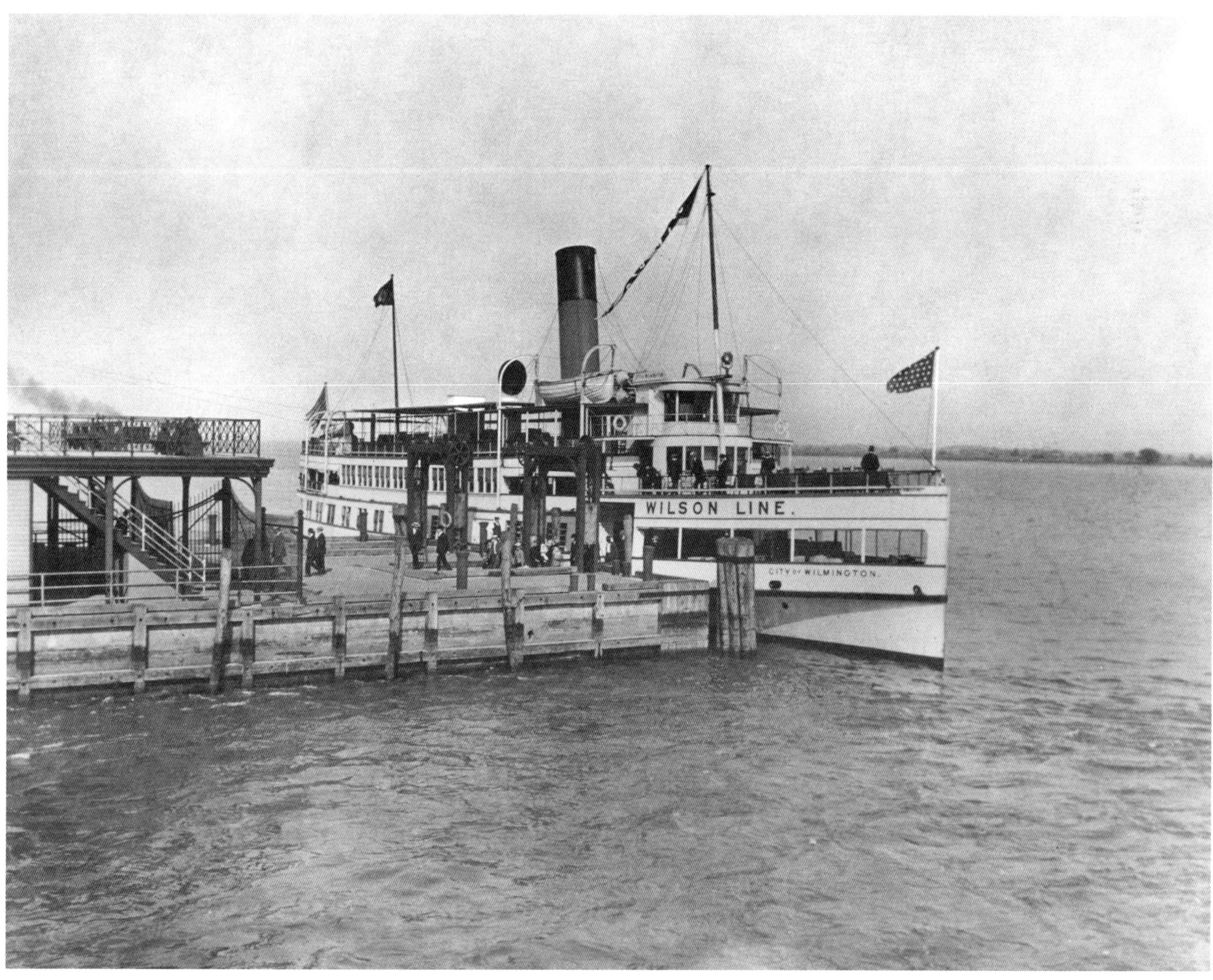

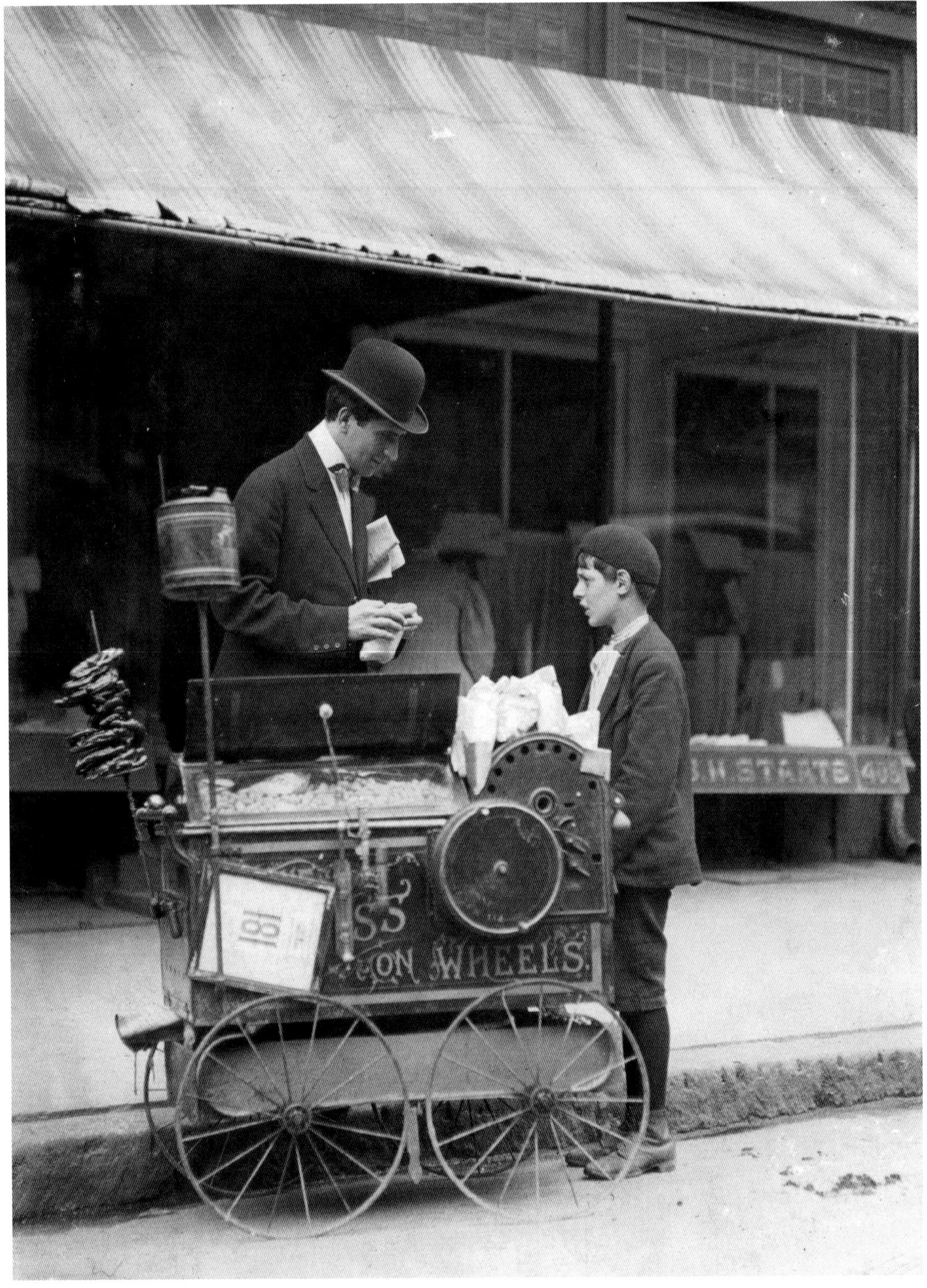

Photographer Lewis Hine reported that at age 11, Joseph Severio had been selling peanuts in Wilmington for two years. He worked 6 hours a day and gave his earnings to his father. He was working until midnight this day in May 1910.

Little Michael Mero is photographed at work on May 21, 1910. Photographer Lewis Hine learned from Michael that he was 12 years old and lived at 2 West 4th Street. He said he had been working as a bootblack for one year at his own choosing. He claimed that he usually worked 6 hours a day. According to Hine, that night Mero was out after 11:00 P.M.

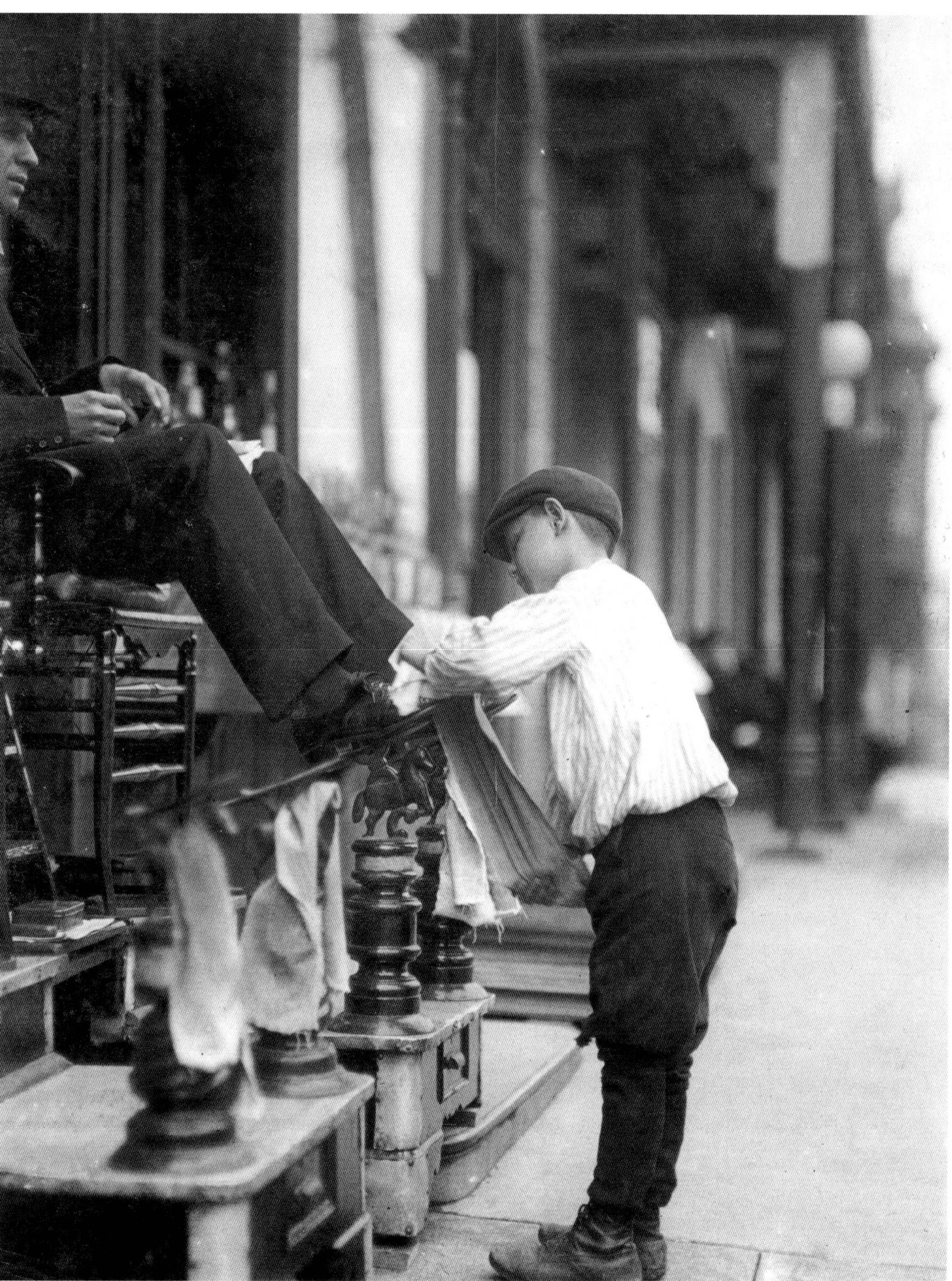

F. R. Vernon poses with his beautiful new truck in Claymont. Newfangled automobiles and trucks and ice cream were popular when this photograph was taken in April 1910, and Vernon was the latest with the greatest. At that time, Wilmington boasted nine ice cream manufacturers.

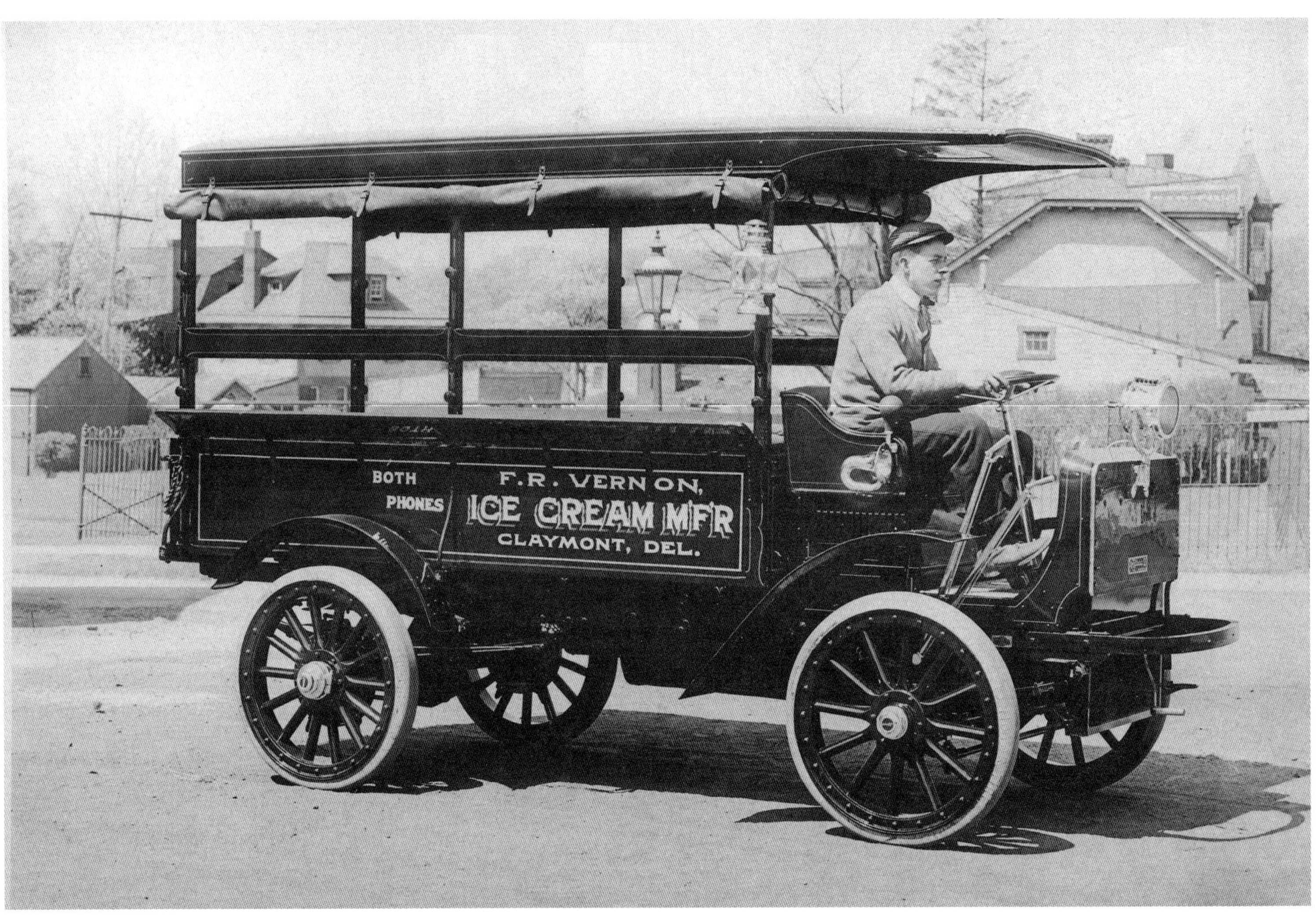

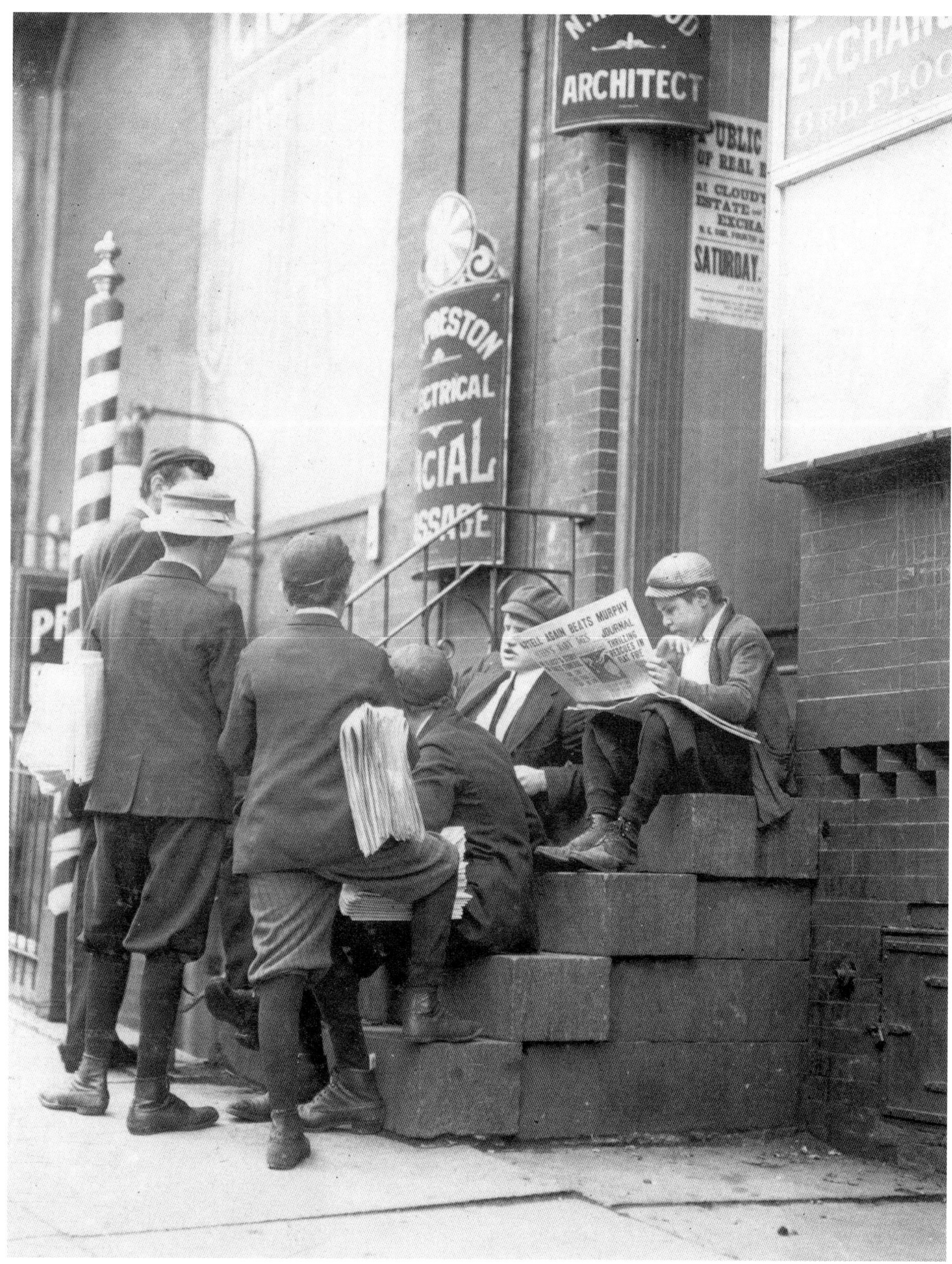

These young newsies sit together on a stoop at 4th and Market streets in Wilmington. They said to the photographer, "Take our mugs, mister," probably unaware that the photograph would be used by the National Child Labor Committee to argue that they should be in school. In the newspaper headlines on this day, boxer Attell had beaten Murphy—again.

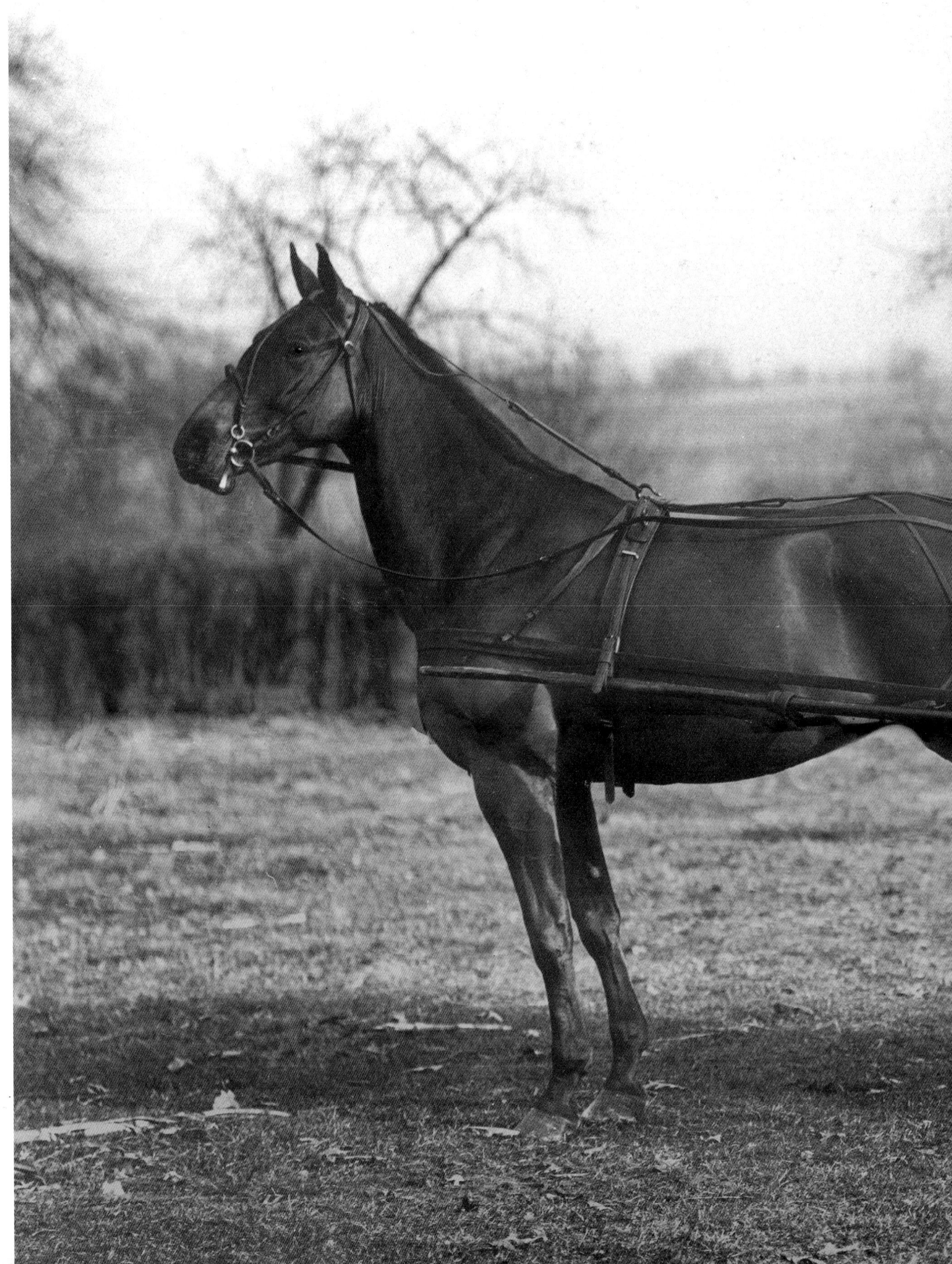

Lillie Donohoe, who lived in Edgemoor, was a mail carrier in Claymont. Here she poses in her "Light Runner" delivery cart. Lillie must have been proud of her work and her horse as several images of her on duty have survived the years. She used a similar image, taken after a snowfall, to send as a Christmas greeting to the people on her route. This photograph was taken by Schreiber in December 1910.

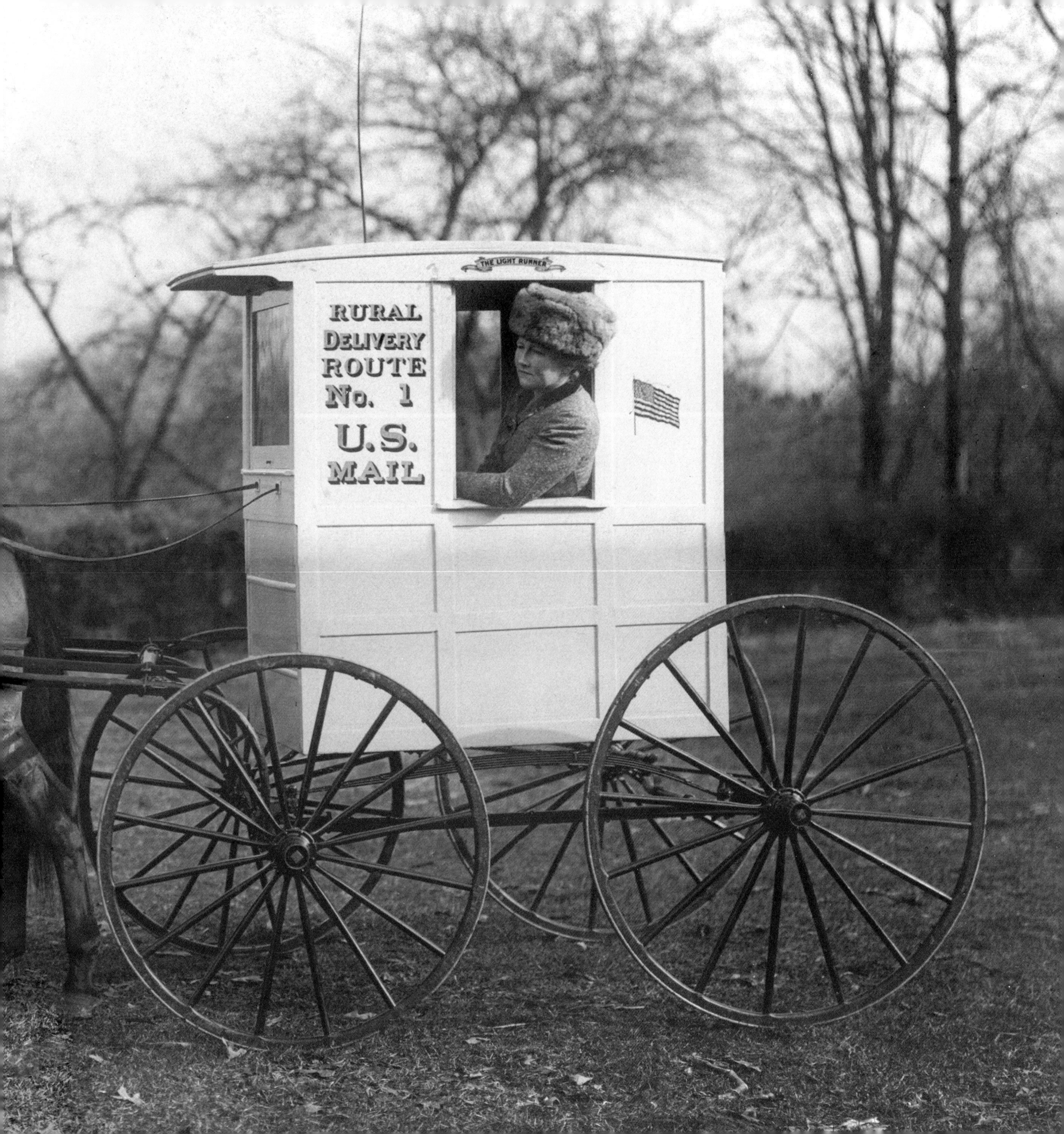
THE LIGHT RUNNER
RURAL
DELIVERY
ROUTE
No. 1
U.S.
MAIL

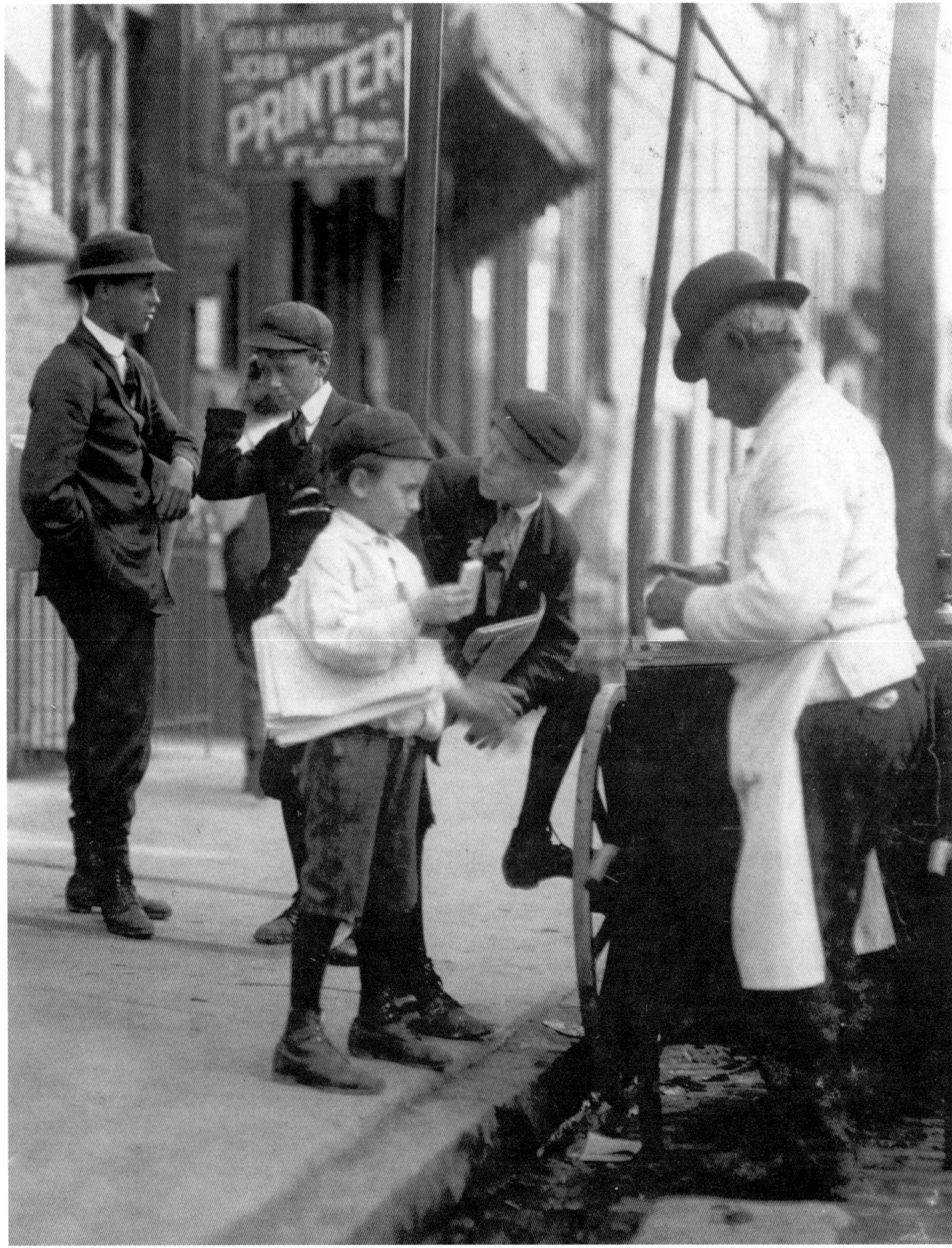

This Wilmington newsie spends his earnings for lunch at the cart of a street vendor. Lewis Hine recorded this view in May 1910.

A view along Delaware Street toward the Delaware River in New Castle around 1910. There is plenty of activity along the street and much interest in the photographer.

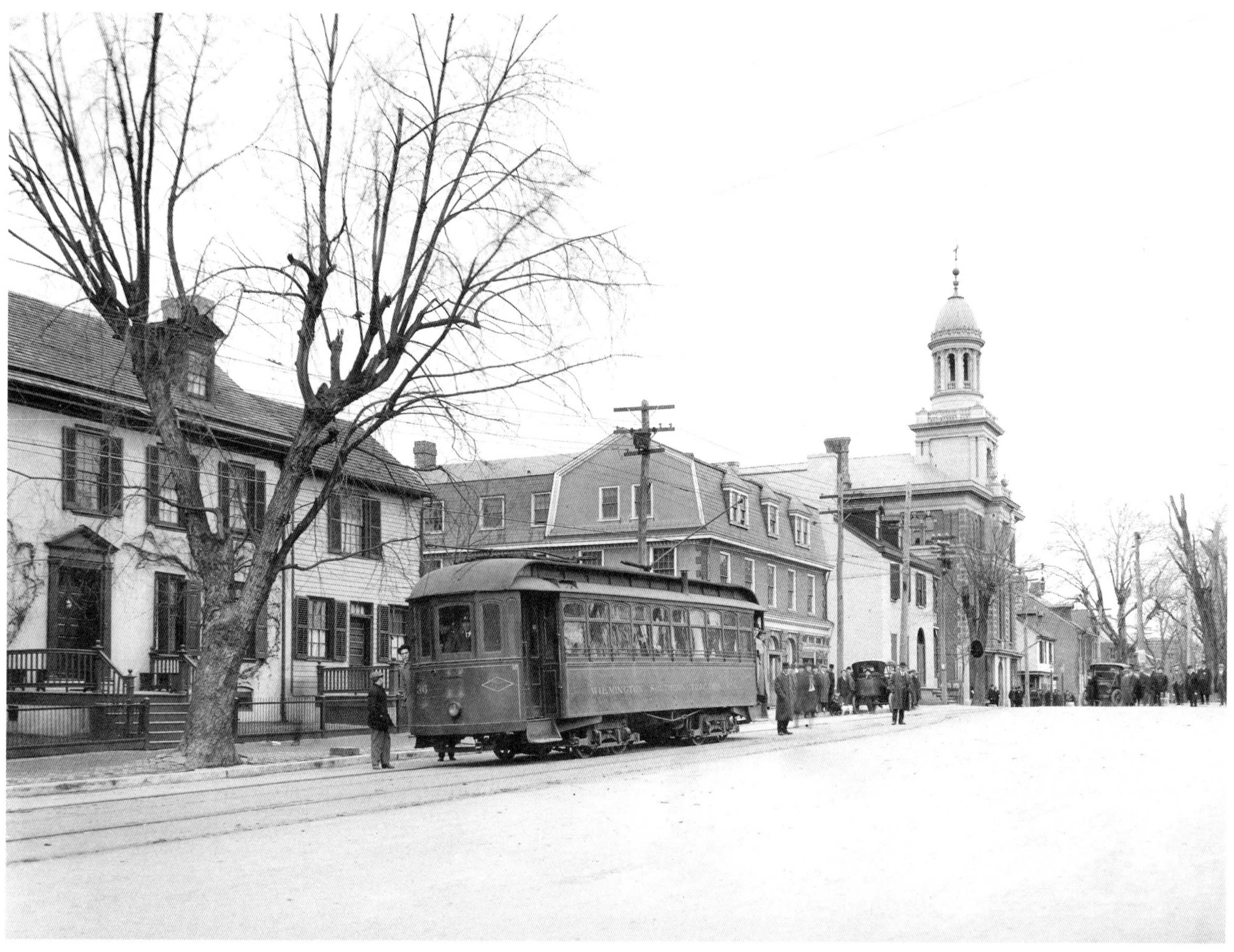

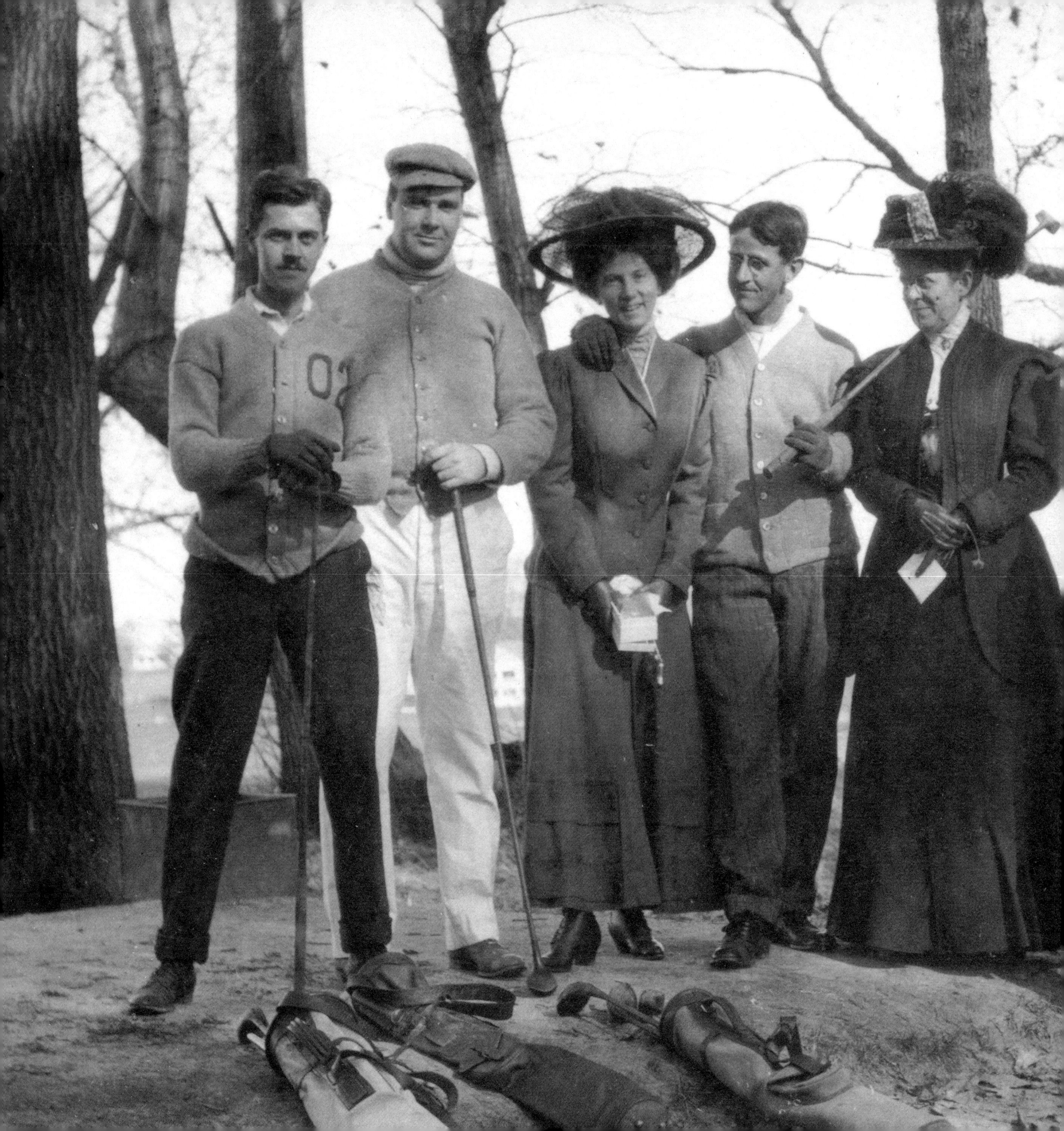
02

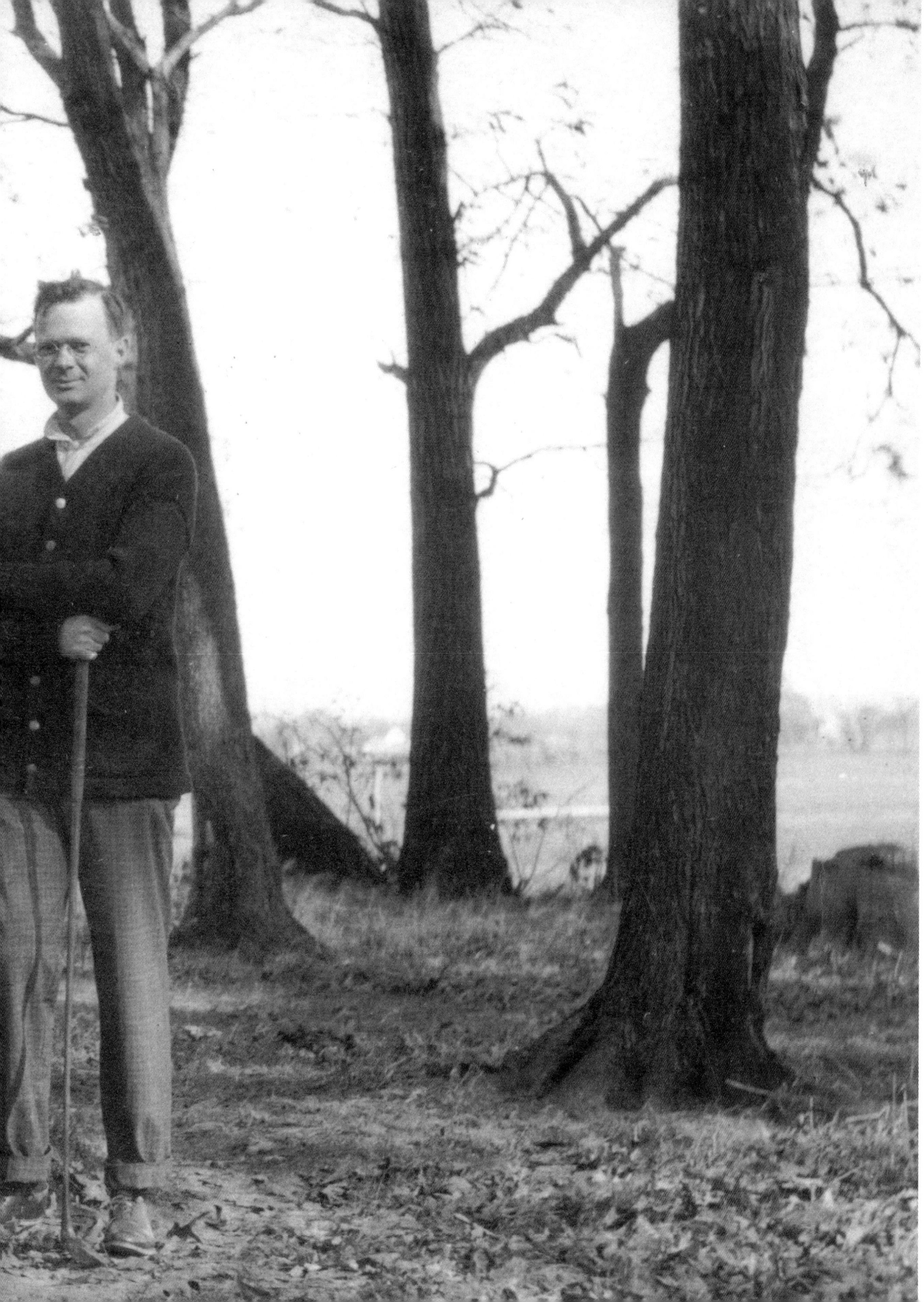

Charles Rumford took this photograph of his friends on the golf course at the Wilmington Country Club around 1910.

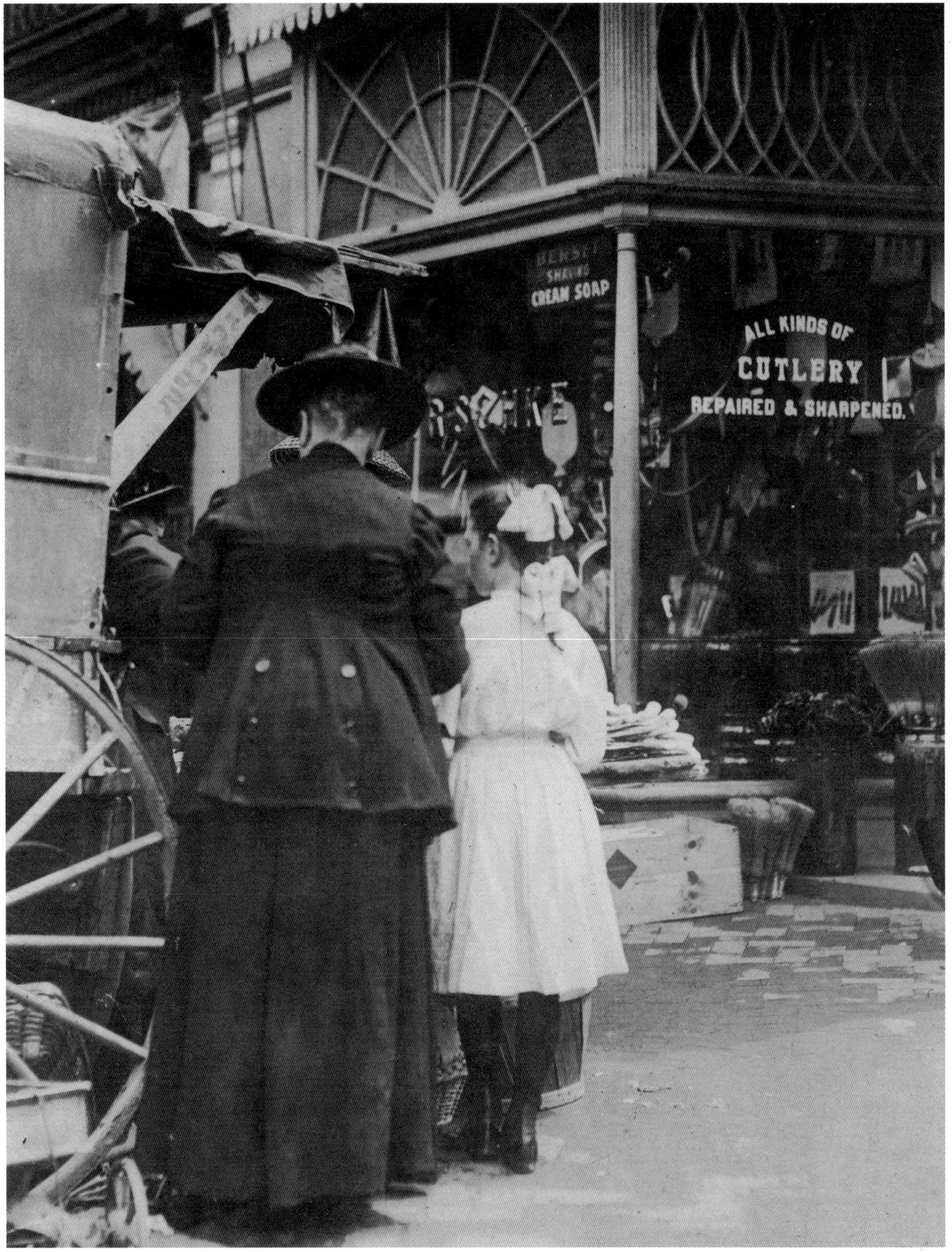

This is a Lewis Hine photograph of a young street vendor in Wilmington selling goods from the back of a wagon. Hine and the National Child Labor Committee pushed for compulsory education and laws against child labor. These laws were eventually enacted. The Committee continues operating today.

The engine of a Pennsylvania, Wilmington, and Baltimore train is hoisted up after the railroad bridge over Broad Creek collapsed just west of the town of Laurel. A handful of spectators watch what must have been an incredible sight.

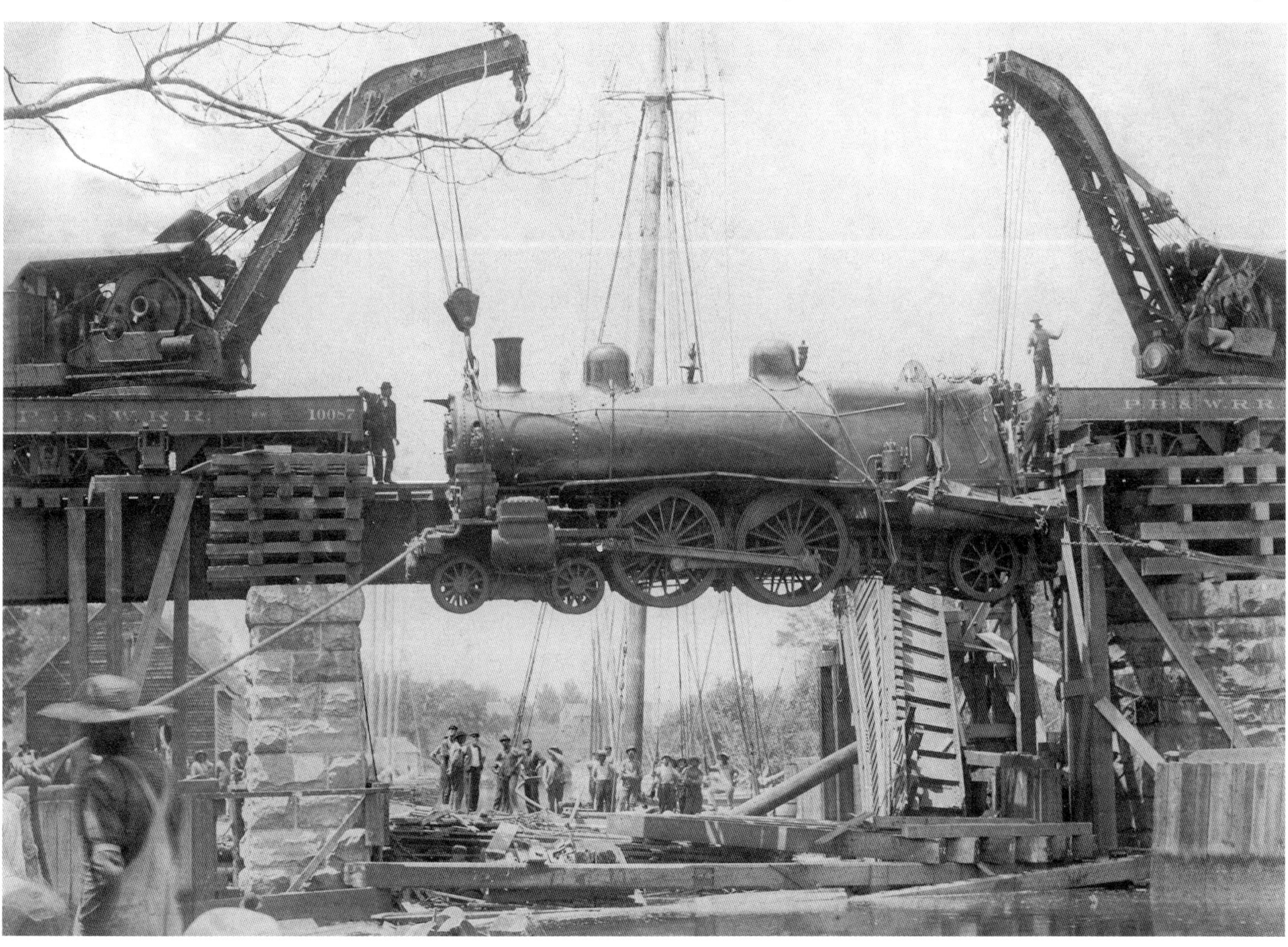

Photographer Lewis Hine traveled the United States in 1910 documenting child labor and advocating its abolition. He photographed five-year-old Helen with her stepsisters hulling strawberries at Johnson's Hulling Station in Seaford. He learned that Helen, once an orphan, had been adopted by the Hope family in Seaford. This was her second summer of work. On this day she began work at 6:00 A.M. and was still working at 6:00 P.M.

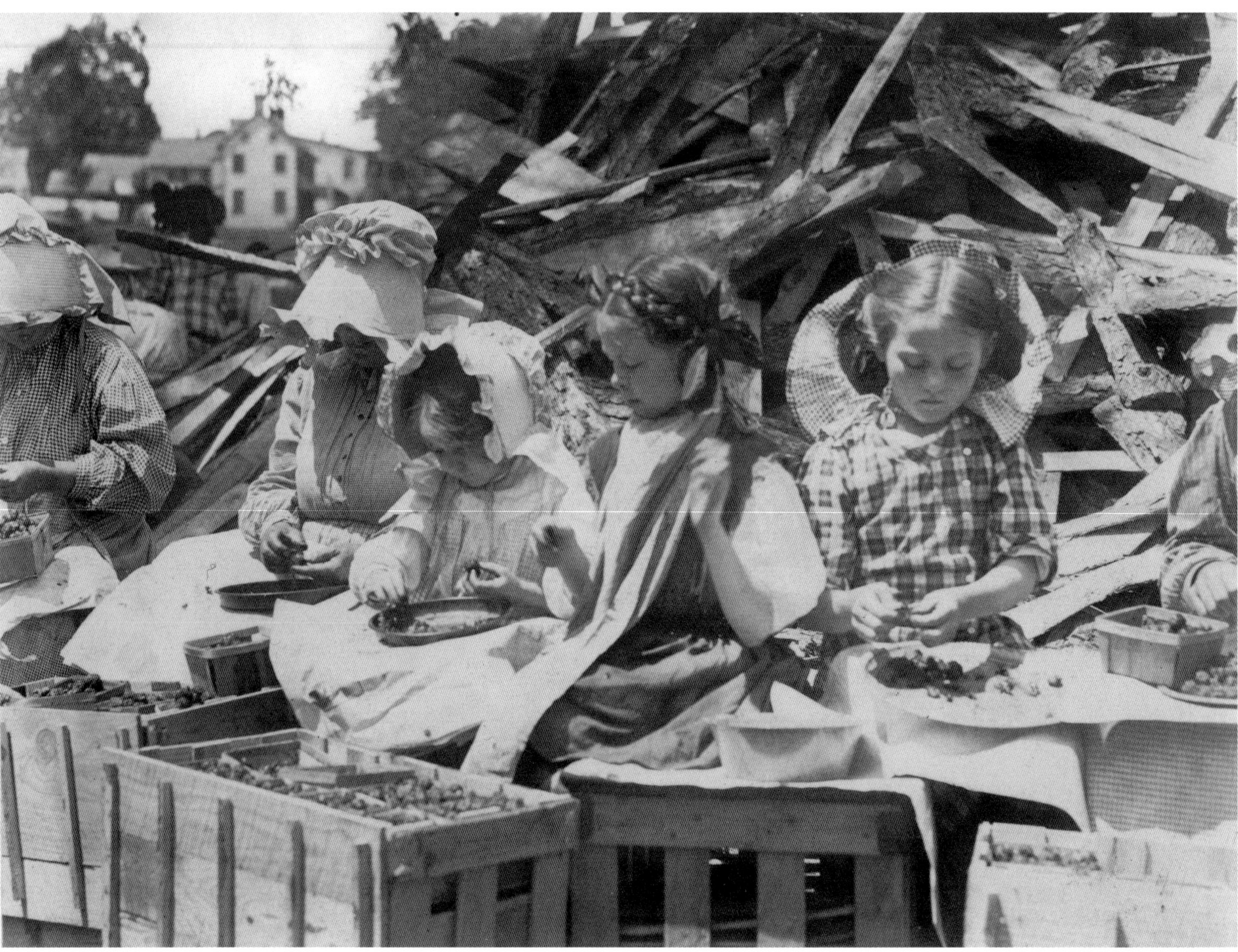

This electric trolley, with open sides for the summer, traveled the Delaware Avenue line. Trolleys made possible the expansion of the city limits by offering inexpensive and convenient transport for workers. As soon as the first horse-drawn trolleys began operating in Wilmington in the 1860s, many who could afford it began to move out to new "trolley car suburbs."

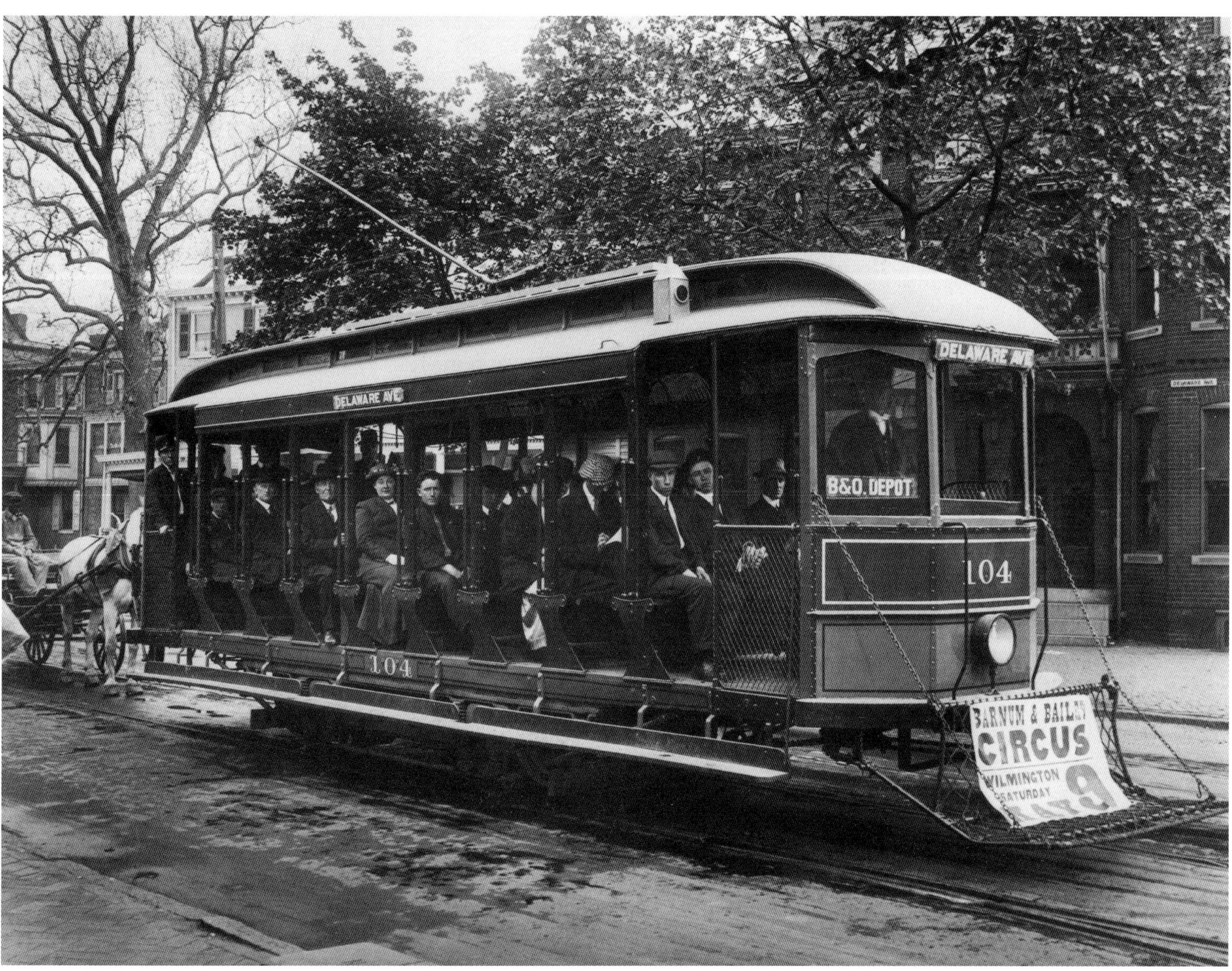

Lewis Hine photographed this newsie on the streets of Wilmington in May 1910. His name was James Lequlla. He was 12 and had been selling papers for three years, averaging about fifty cents a week and working about 7 hours a day. He told investigators that his family did not need his earnings. He said he did not smoke but did visit saloons.

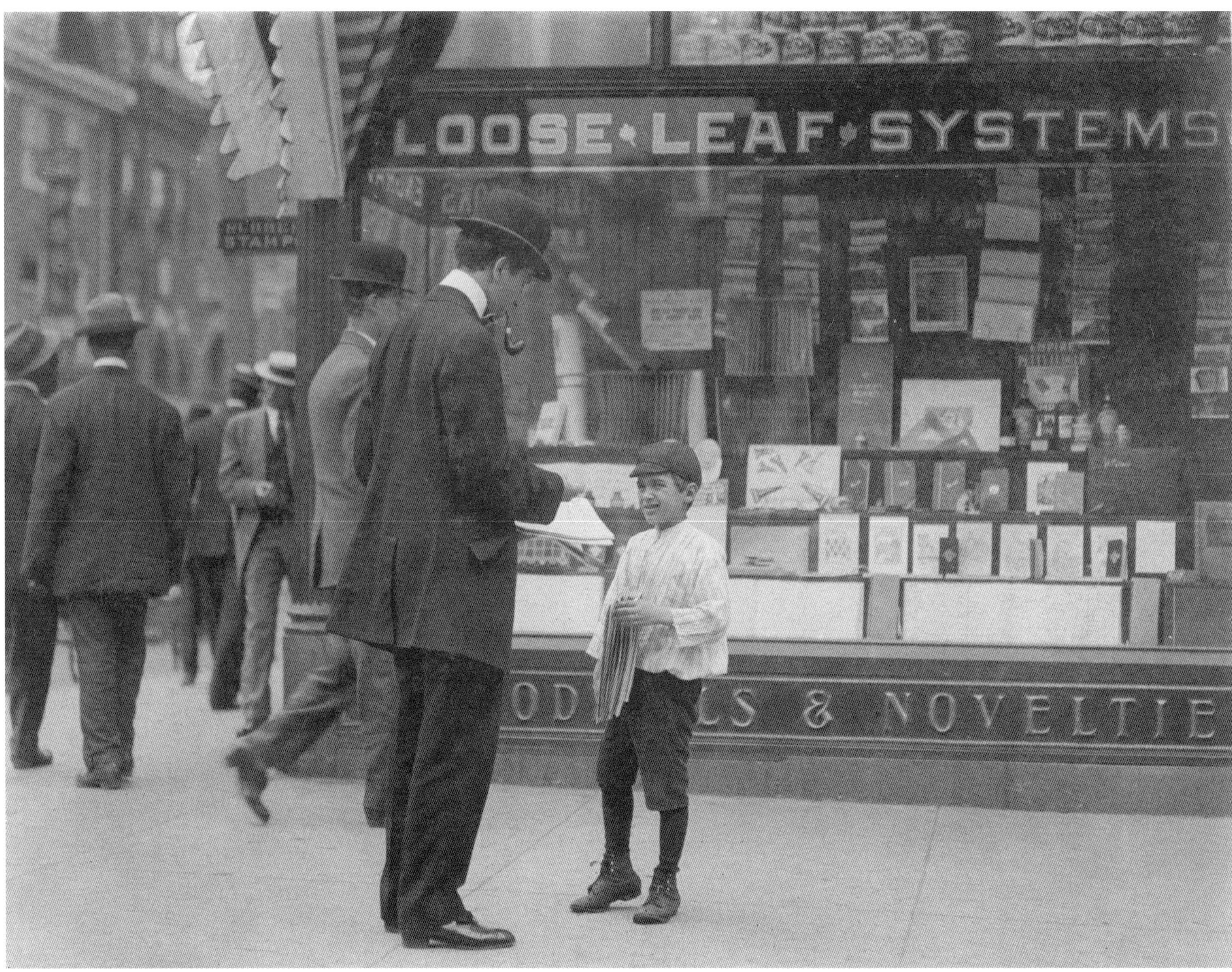

Wilmington mayor James Price attends the laying of the cornerstone for the City-County Building in 1914. Two buildings are joined behind one facade. Spanning the entire block from King to French streets and from 10th to 11th streets, the city offices were housed in the 10th Street half and the county courts were housed in the 11th Street half of the building. Since its completion, Rodney Square has served as the focal and economic heart of the city.

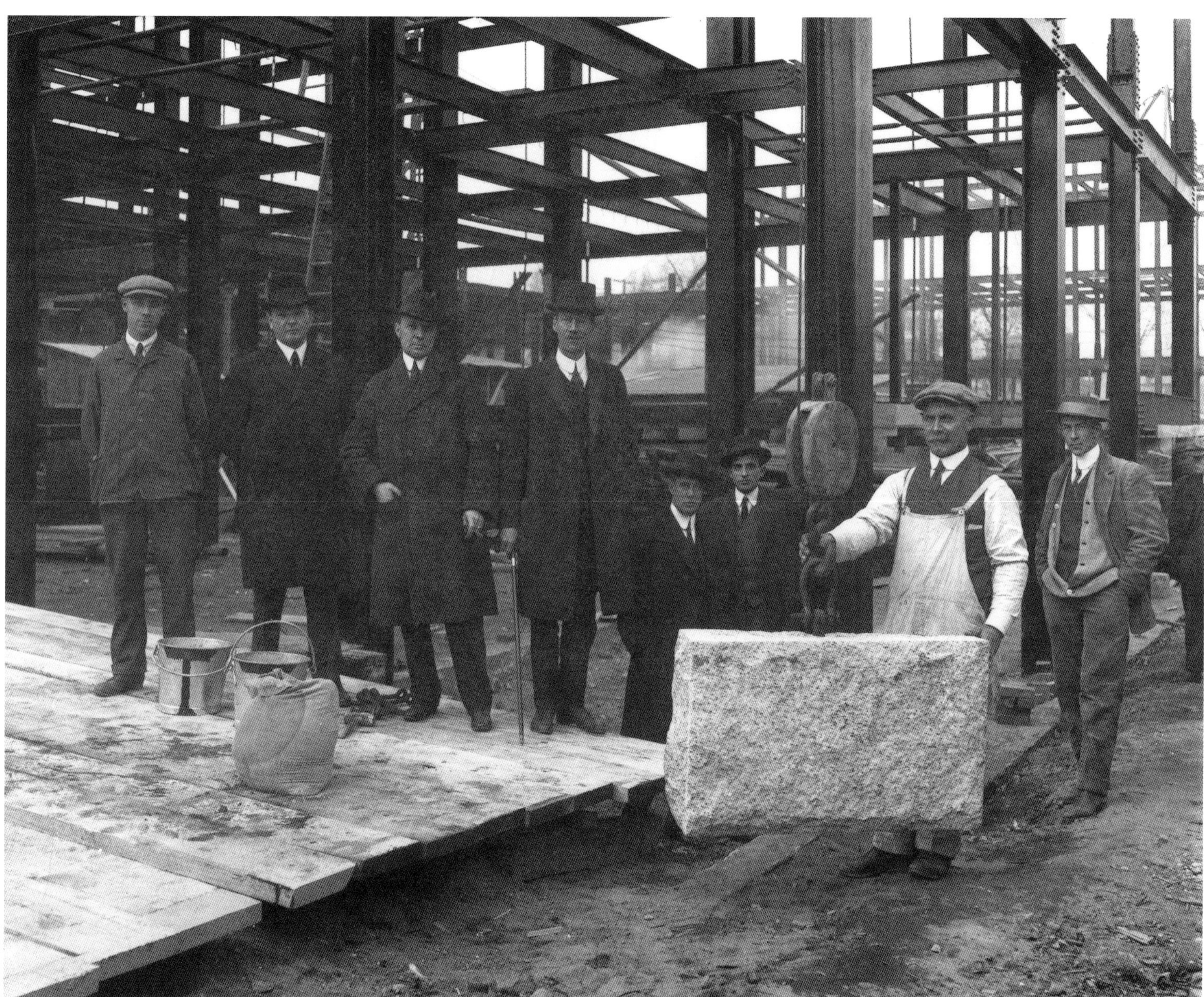

The churchyard of First Presbyterian Church is seen here at 10th and Market streets in Wilmington. When the Wilmington Institute Free Library site was purchased in 1916, the main church building (not shown), the education building (at far-left), the cemetery, and first church (center), now located on Park Drive on the Brandywine River, were moved. Market Street runs along the bottom of the photograph.

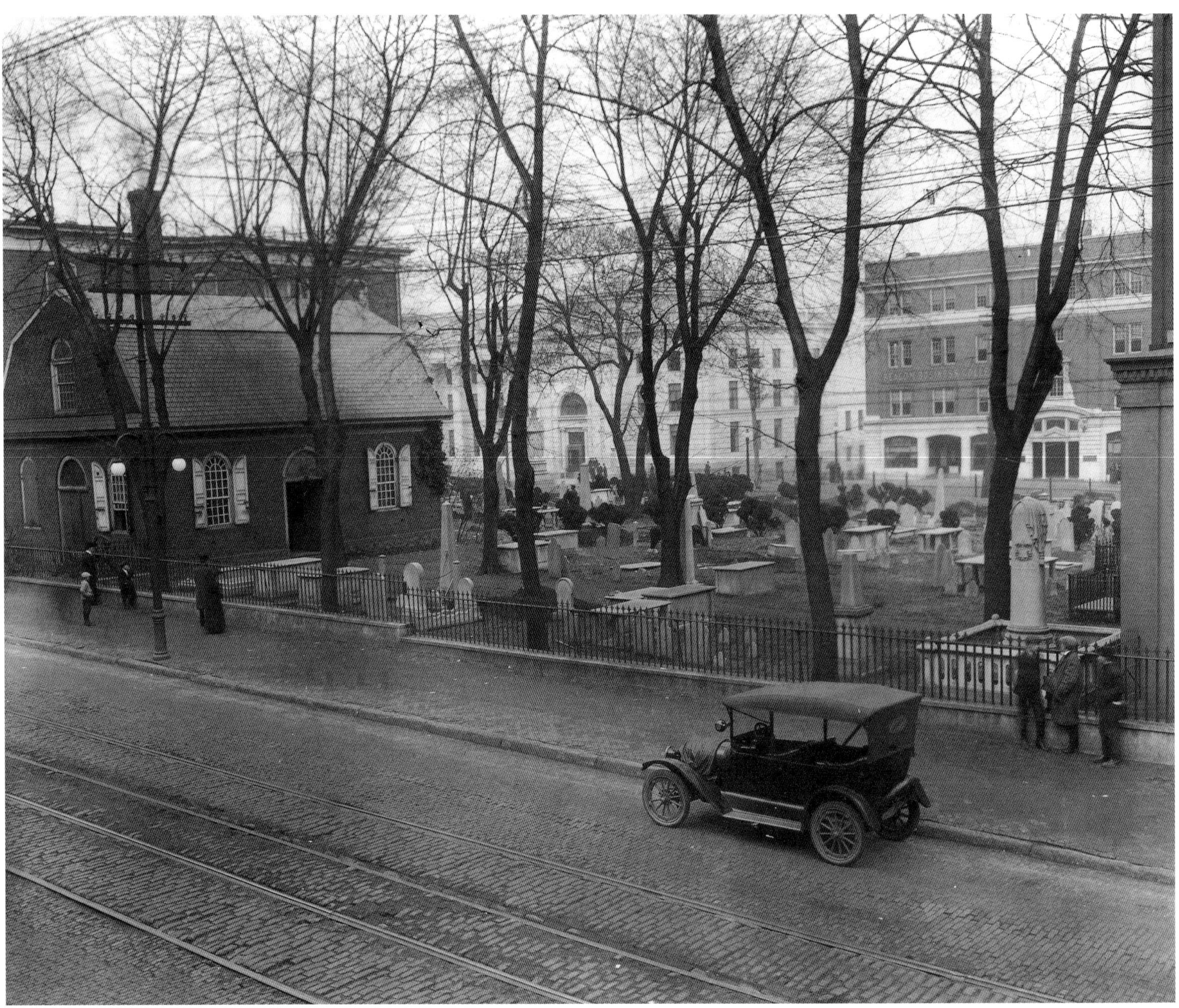

This dapper crowd includes, from left to right, Fred Fuller, Ruly Carpenter, Elsie Fuller, Irene S. du Pont, "Peggy" Margaretta Carpenter, and "Bus" Irenee du Pont.

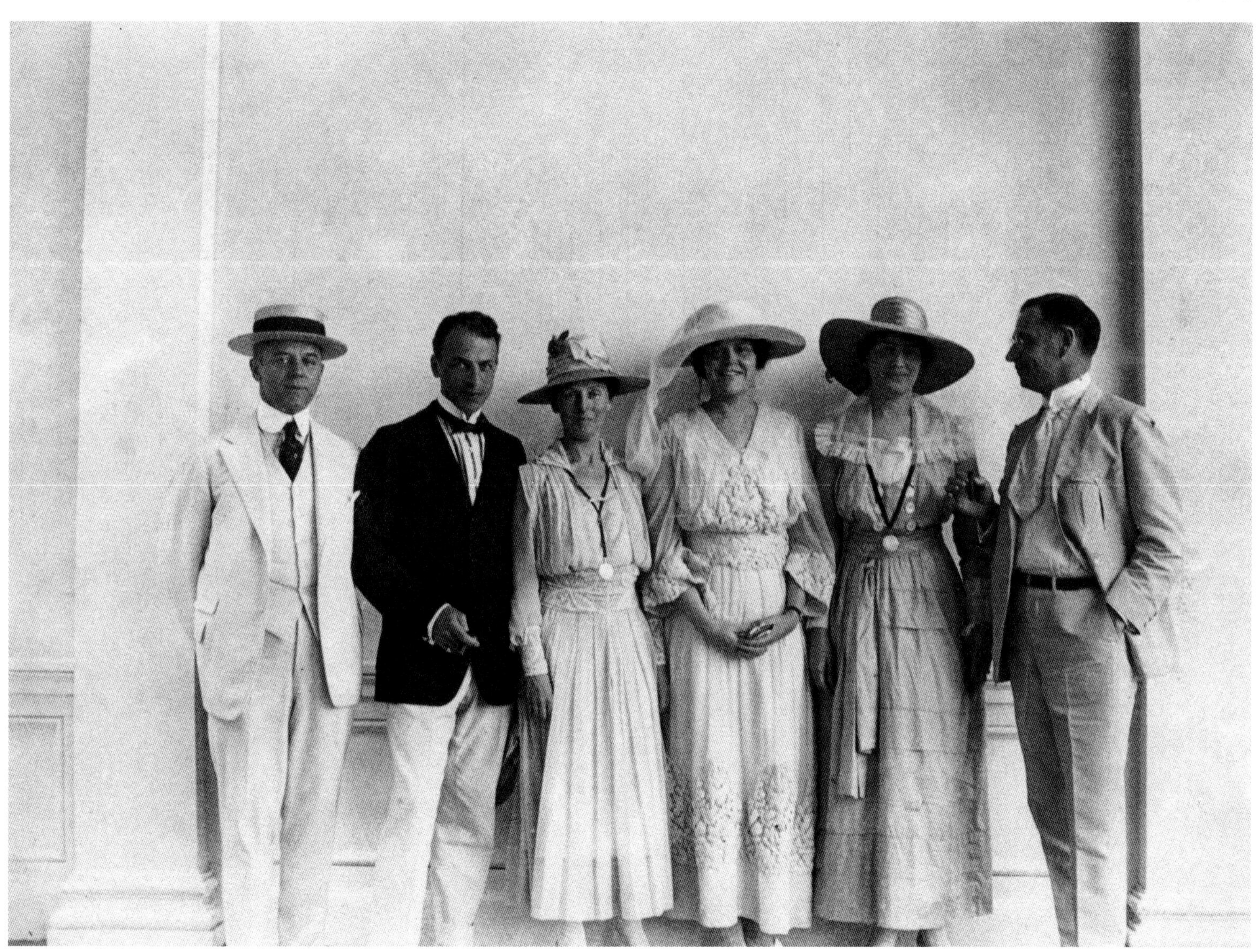

Emile Bucher took this photograph of the New Castle Rear Range Lighthouse in 1912. Built in 1876 as a home and tower, the structure had a light that was 50 feet above the base and 90 feet above the water. The light was 2 feet in diameter and the glass window was 44 inches square. The Coast Guard sold the lighthouse as excess property in the early 1950s. At the request of the owner it was burned in 1982.

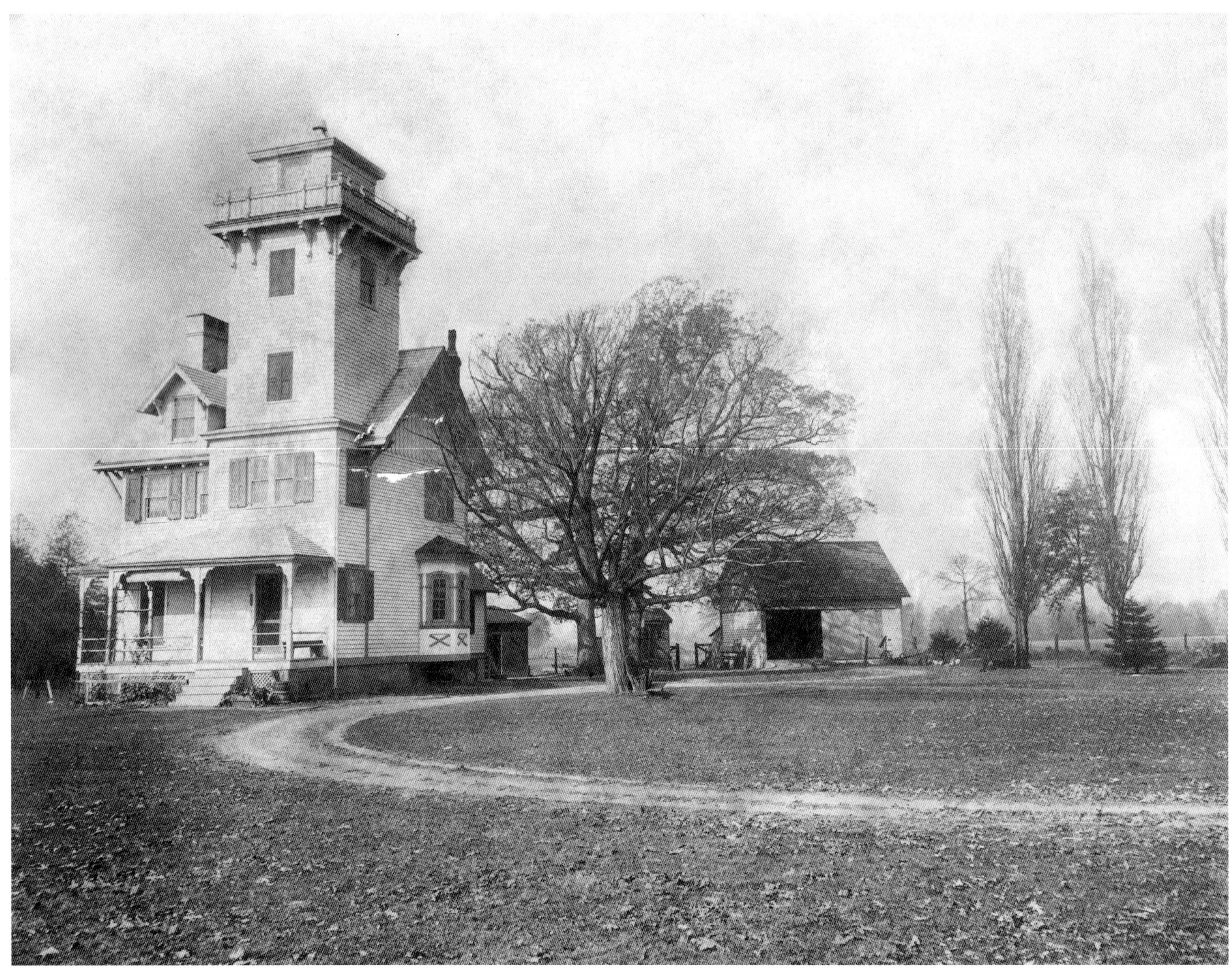

This whimsical view was recorded on the grounds of Francis G. du Pont's home during his annual Brandywine Picnic. Here he is with two young family members, Eleuthere "Paul" and Archibald "Archie" M. L. du Pont around 1912.

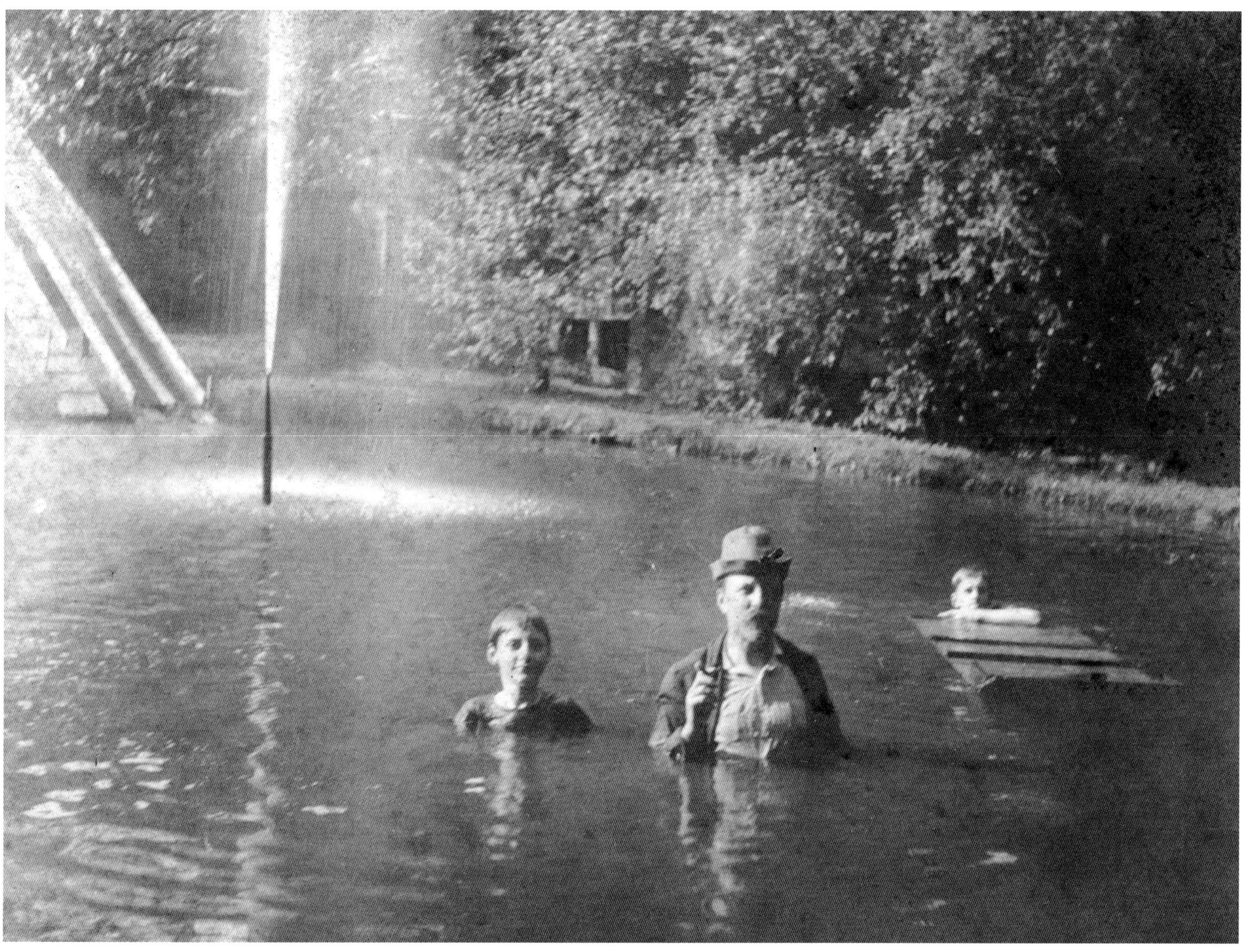

Members of the Delaware National Guard pose at Camp MacDonough in July 1913. The photograph was taken during a weeklong encampment at the Delaware State Rifle Range in New Castle. Camp MacDonough was named for Delaware's naval hero Thomas MacDonough, a commander of the decisive Battle of Lake Champlain in 1814 in the War of 1812. MacDonough was lost at sea in 1825, dying at the age of 42.

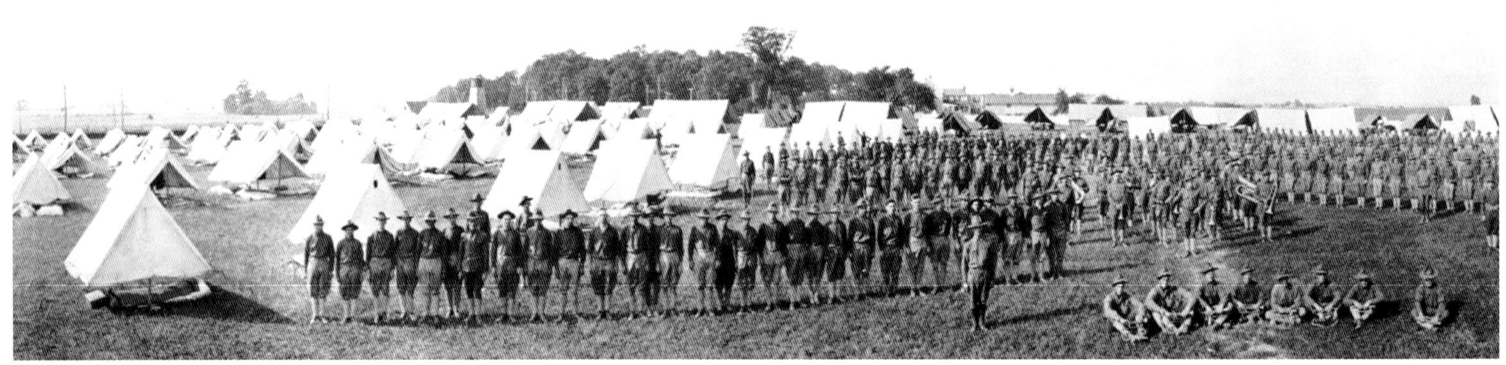

In 1915, this Wilmington police officer had a pretty nice ride. The department proudly traces its history to 1738 and the founding of the city. In 1891, the department began offering a salary to its members. In 1914, in response to the automobile and its effect on public safety and city streets, the Traffic Department was created.

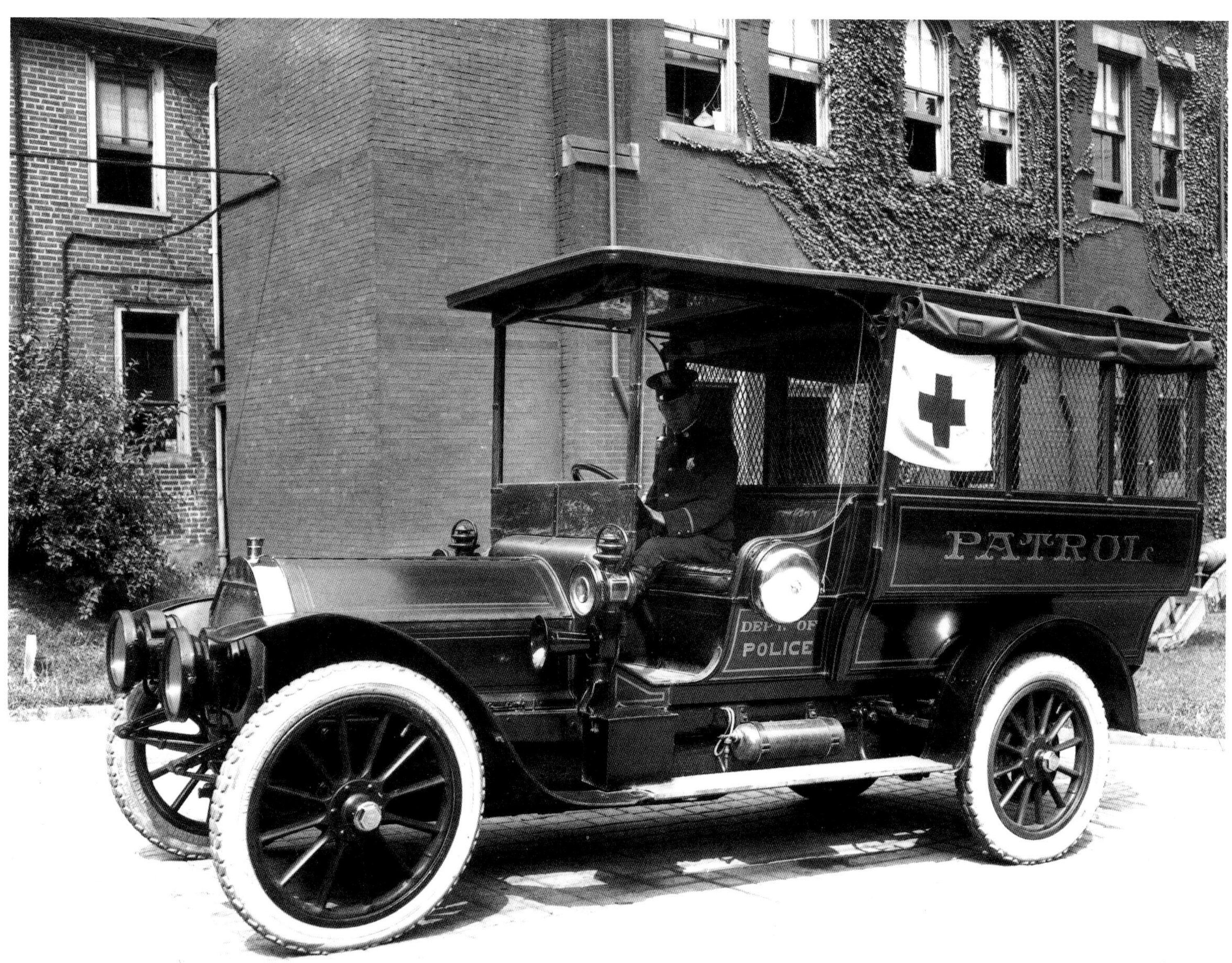

Spectators line the dusty track at Wawaset Park in Wilmington in 1916. Before the fairgrounds in Harrington were chosen to host the state fair, it was held in Wawaset Park. Today the neighborhood is a beautiful residential area, but in the early 1900s many large sporting events were held there.

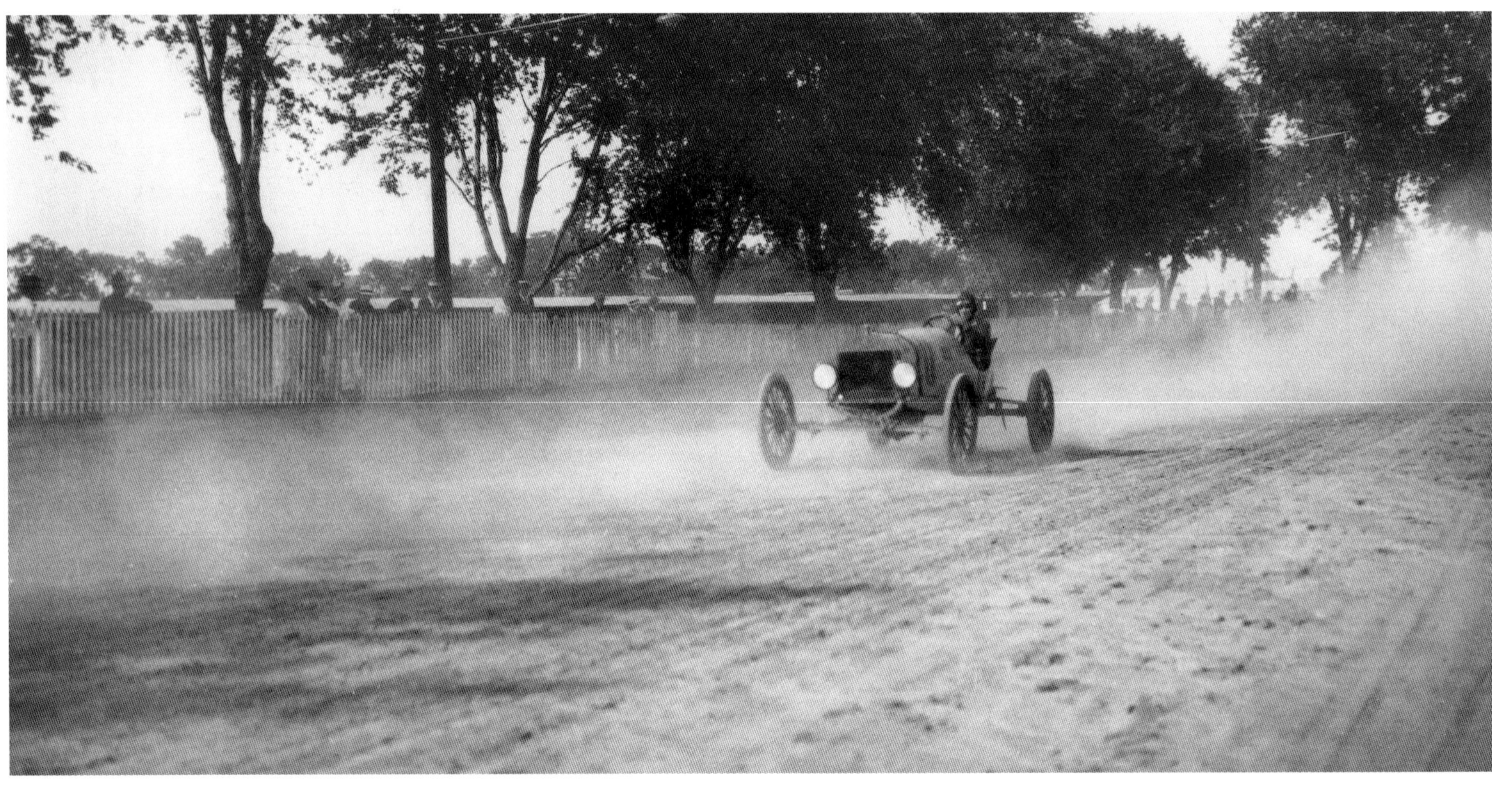

Nan Brown, Helen Wardell, and Nellie Webb Casperson stand outside Nellie's shop at 402 King Street in Wilmington. Webb's Millinery provided a good living for Casperson. She ran her business from this location between 1911 and 1933.

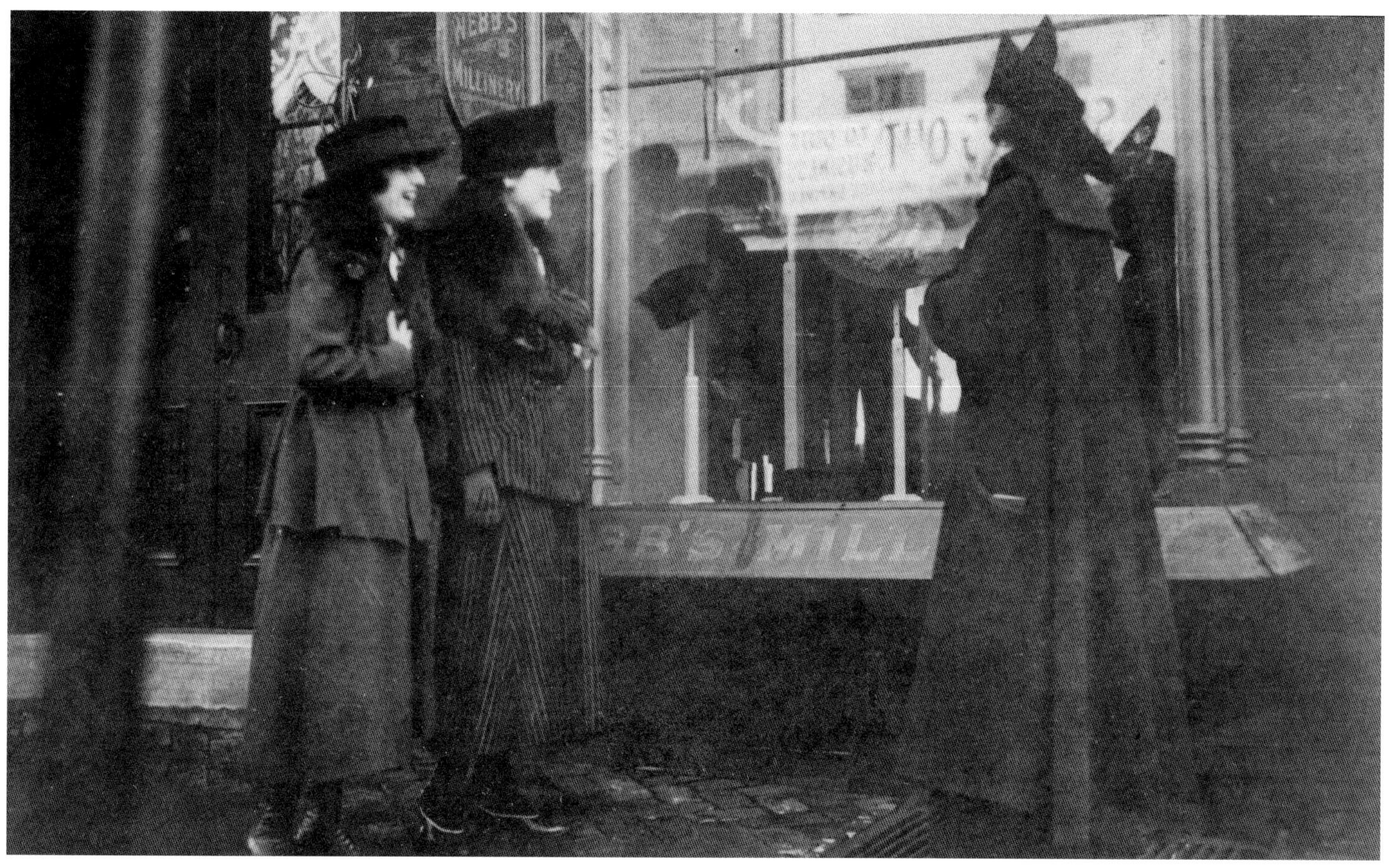

This picturesque scene was recorded at Little Creek along Broad Creek just west of Laurel.

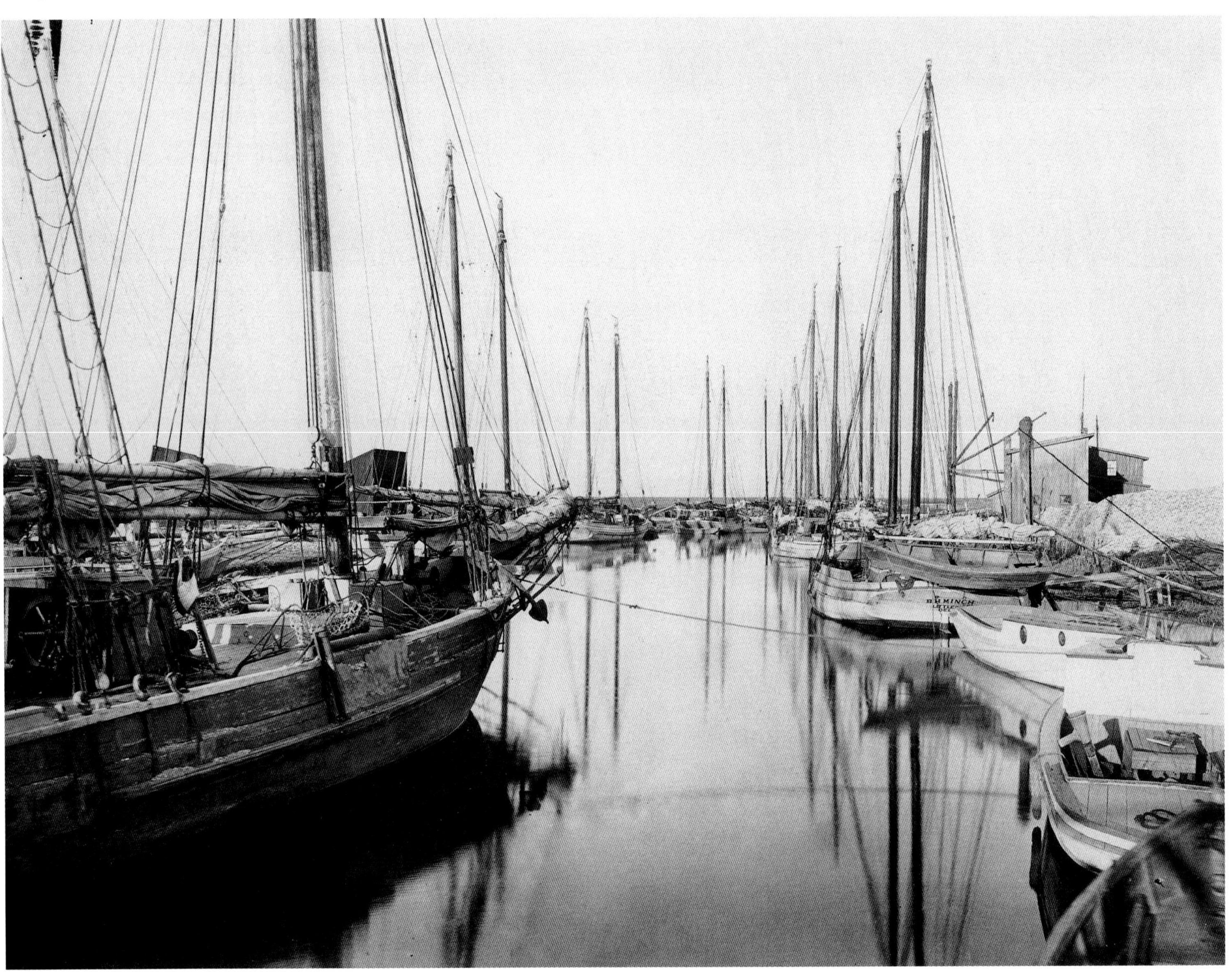

Wilmingtonians listen from King Street and from windows during the opening ceremony for the Public Building on May 28, 1916. For years Town Hall and the Court House had been declared outdated and overcrowded. Wilmington could at last celebrate a public building in keeping with the modern look of downtown, which had begun its transformation when the DuPont Building opened on Rodney Square in 1907.

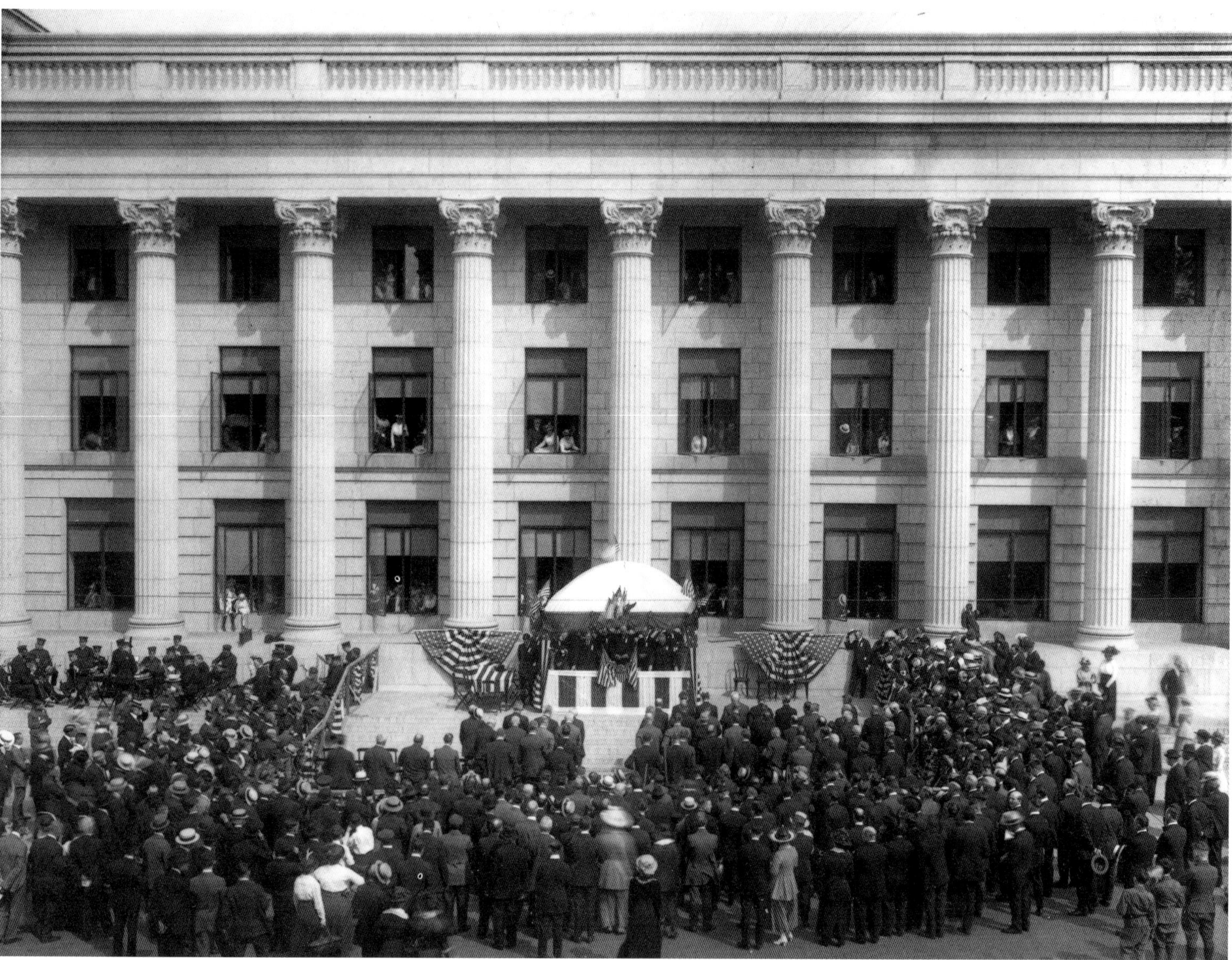

Even the dogs participated in this World War I–era parade down Clinton Street in Delaware City.

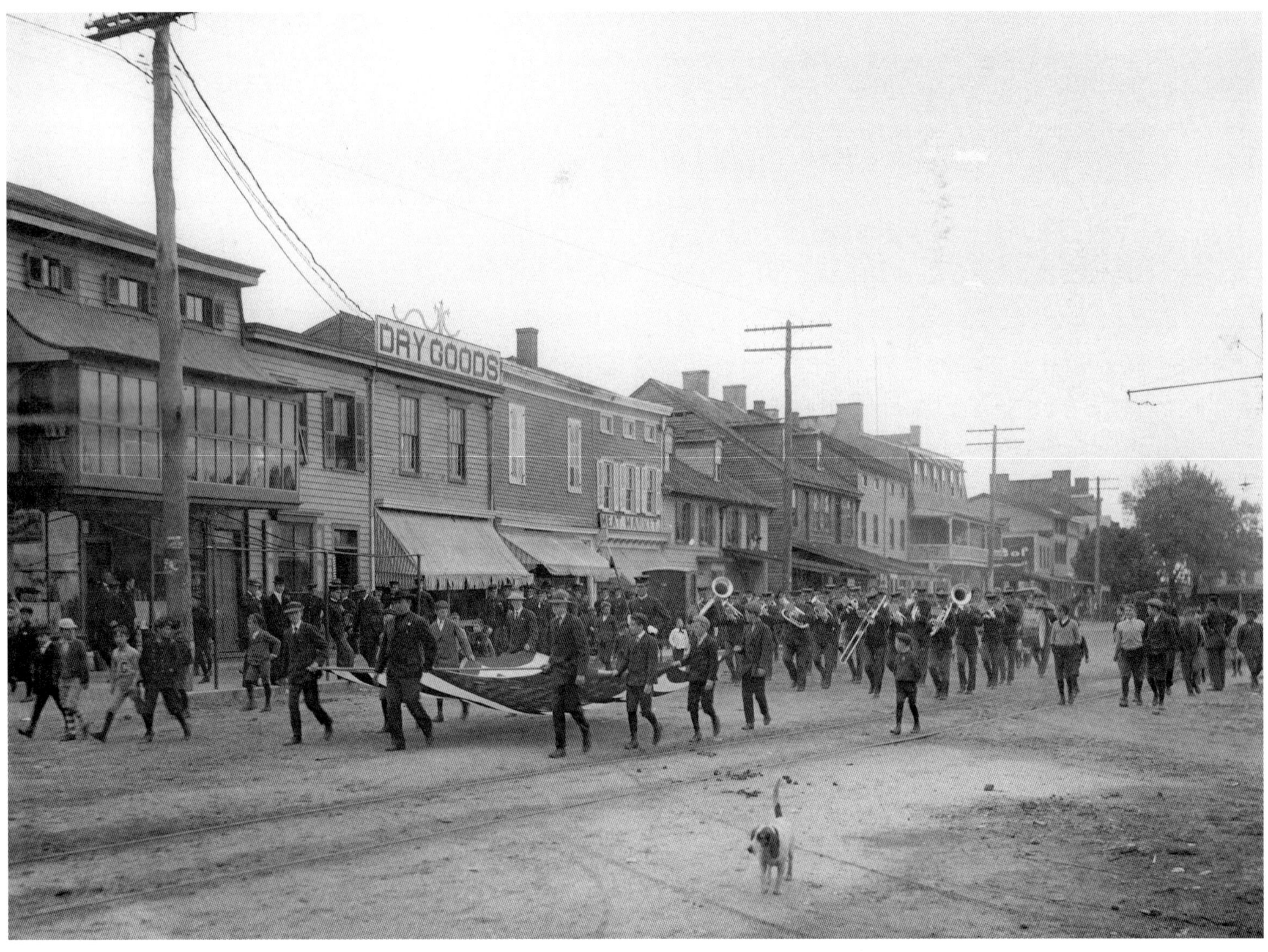

On Armistice Day, November 11, 1918, a parade passed along Wilmington's Market Street celebrating the downfall of the German kaiser and cheering President Woodrow Wilson and the troops.

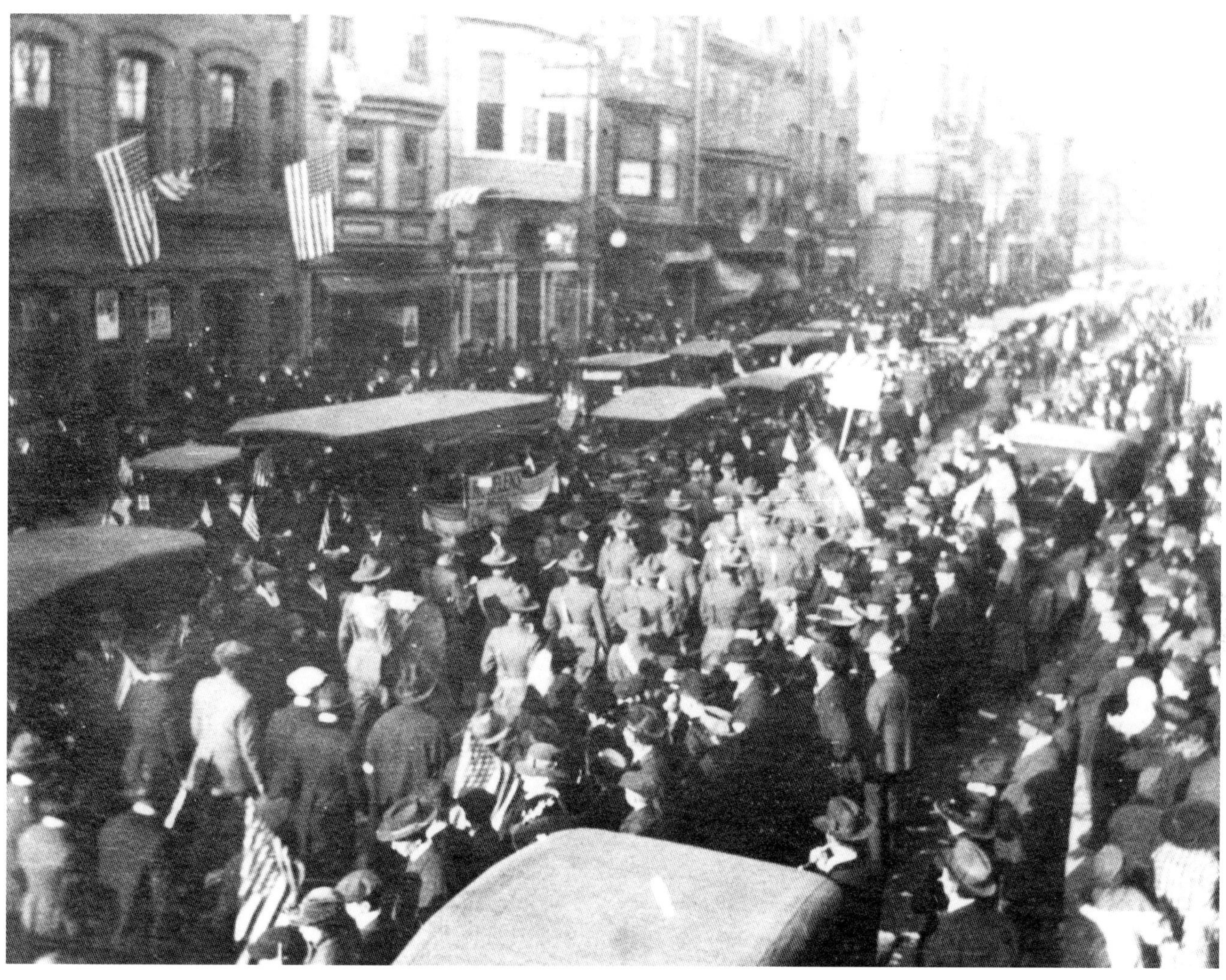

At Fort Delaware, the outer wall and moat dwarf the people standing on the bridge at left. Located on Pea Patch Island in the middle of the Delaware River, it was originally intended to fortify the river and served as a prisoner-of-war camp during the Civil War. Prisoners began arriving in July 1861, and at one point 12,500 people inhabited the island. In all, 30,000 prisoners passed through the camp.

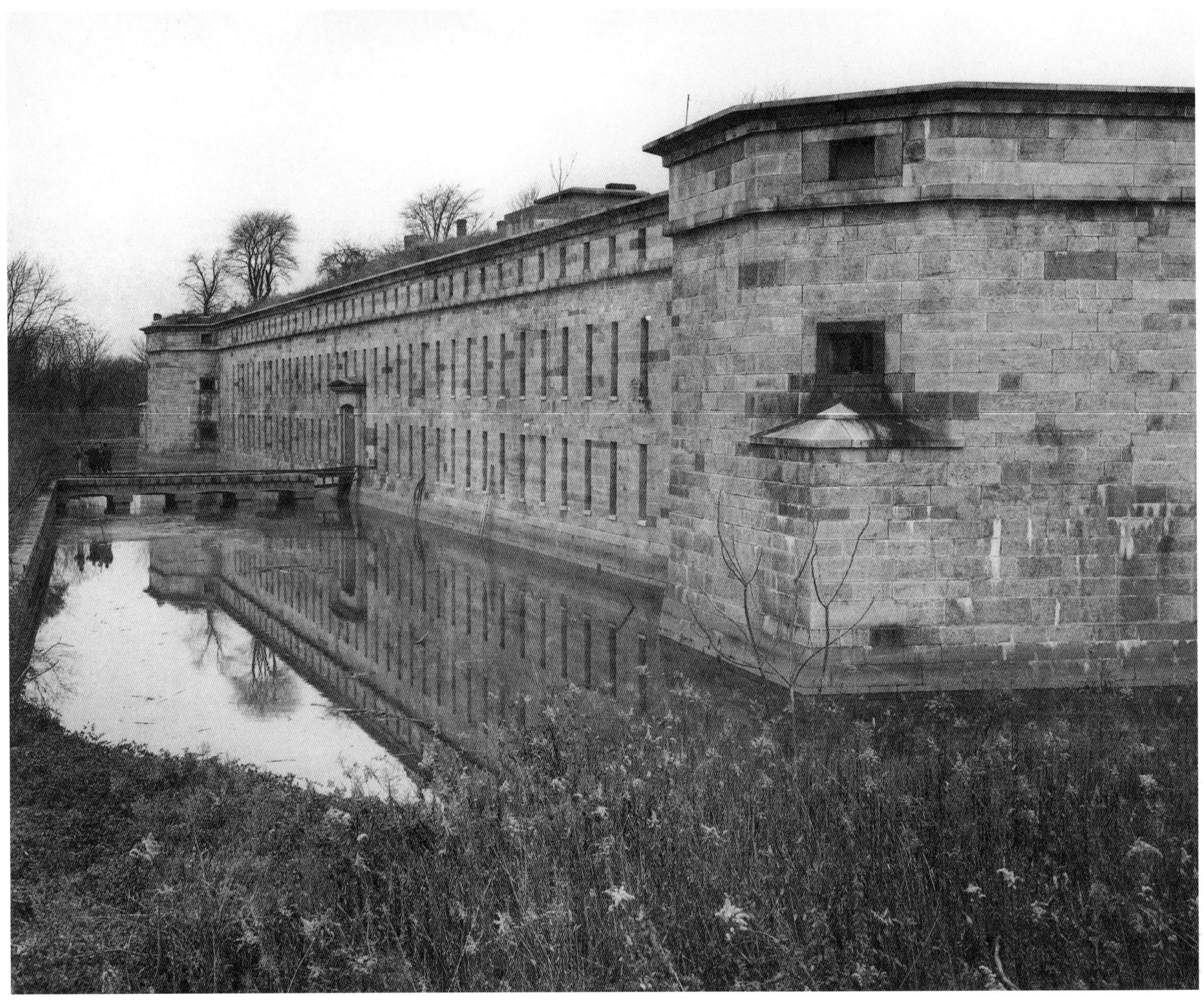

Mrs. Ether Ball Staniar, Red Cross Motor Corps captain (at the wheel), and Miss Mary Moran, director of the Red Cross Training Center, Bureau of Hygiene, are seen helping a young patient at the Edgewood Sanatorium in Marshallton in 1919. This sanatorium served the state's African American tuberculosis patients.

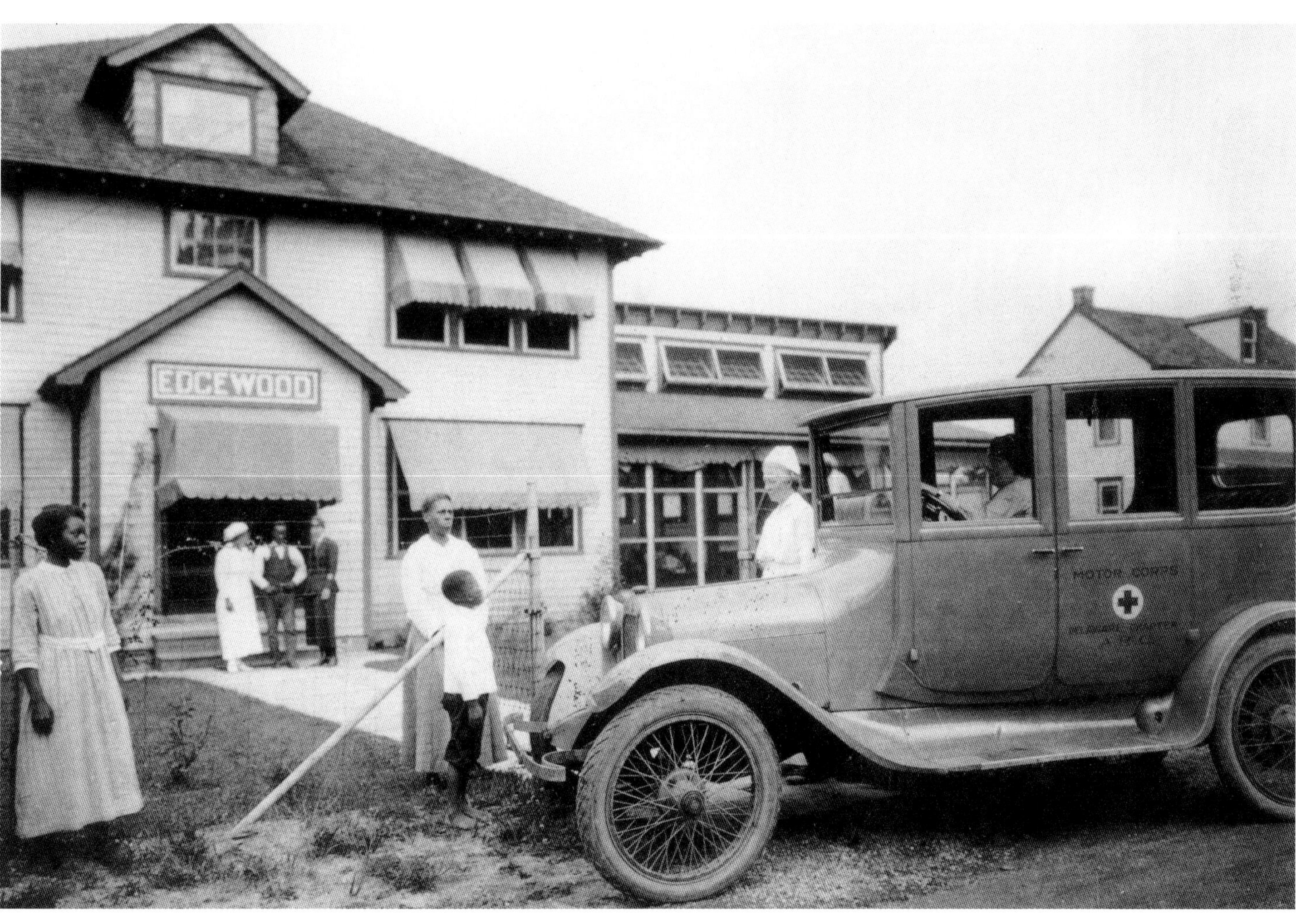

Helen Jones, at far-right, poses with friends and her father in Dover just before leaving home on a nationwide adventure on July 4, 1920. Traveling alone, she stayed with friends and relatives along the way. She documented her remarkable journey with photographs, postcards, and notes in a scrapbook found in the library of the Delaware Historical Society.

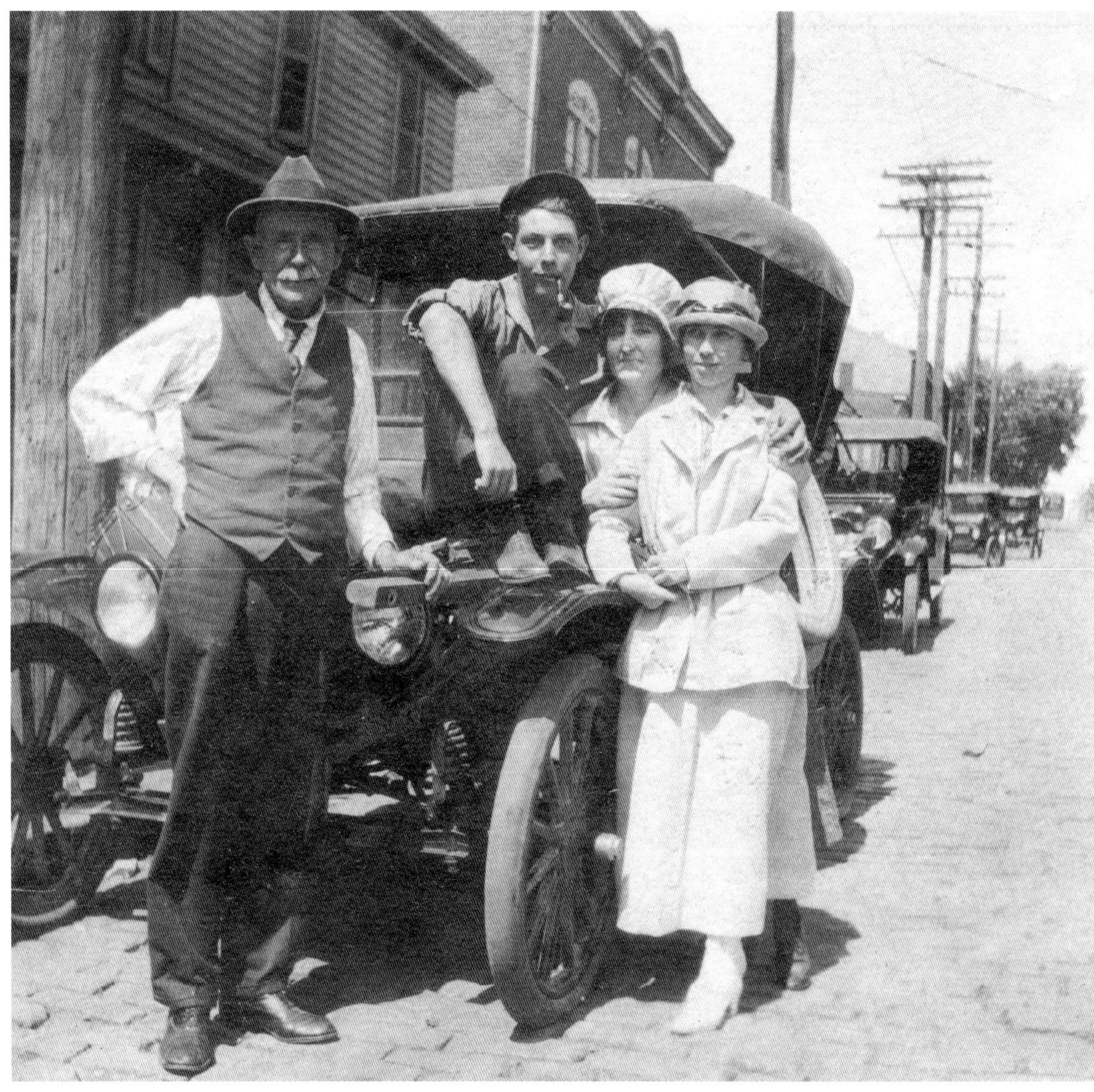

Influences from Beyond the Border

(1920–1945)

Outside influences shaped Delaware during the World Wars and the Great Depression. Delaware lost 262 soldiers during World War I, and sadly, the "War to End All Wars" didn't. Aiding the war industry, shipbuilding experienced a brief boom in Milford, Seaford, and Wilmington.

An important economic boost came through luck and Delaware's proximity to large markets. In 1923, Cecile Steele of Ocean View ordered too many chicks, unwittingly starting the fantastically successful broiler industry. Between 1925 and 1942, broiler production increased 670 percent. Sussex County became one of the nation's richest agricultural counties, producing one-fourth of the nation's broilers.

Kent and Sussex counties weathered the Great Depression better than New Castle County. No major banks failed, and the DuPont Company's construction of two plants, a pigment plant at Edgemoor in 1935 and a nylon plant in Seaford in 1939, provided jobs. In 1934, over 90 percent of the state's families without a breadwinner lived in New Castle County. In November 1932, Governor Buck called for a $2 million relief allocation to supplement the work of private charities. Federal relief projects employed thousands of workers throughout the state. Relief workers cleared poorly drained areas of Sussex, clearing the way for further development of beach communities and farmland. Workers cleaned up industrial sites, widened roads, recorded the state's history, and they painted murals.

On December 7, 1941, the United States was attacked at Pearl Harbor. Two Delaware men were killed, but another, George Welch, got off the ground and shot down four Japanese planes. The war consumed the next four years and Delaware sent 30,000 soldiers to the fight. The federal government built Fort Miles at Bethany Beach to protect the Delaware River and Bay, and the New Castle Airport became an army–air force base and was used to ferry planes and supplies to Europe. The Dover Airfield was a training field for pilots and a secret testing site for America's first rockets. Delaware shipyards secured government contracts, and Dravo's work force in Wilmington rose from 400 to 11,000. DuPont, Hercules, and Atlas supplied most of the ammunition used by the army and navy. The DuPont Company produced atomic bombs in Washington State and had contracts for nylon that was produced in Seaford.

The freighter *Absecon* takes a trial trip in the Delaware Bay around 1921. The camouflaging of ships is not a familiar practice today. It was first experimented with in the United States during World War I and used in World War II.

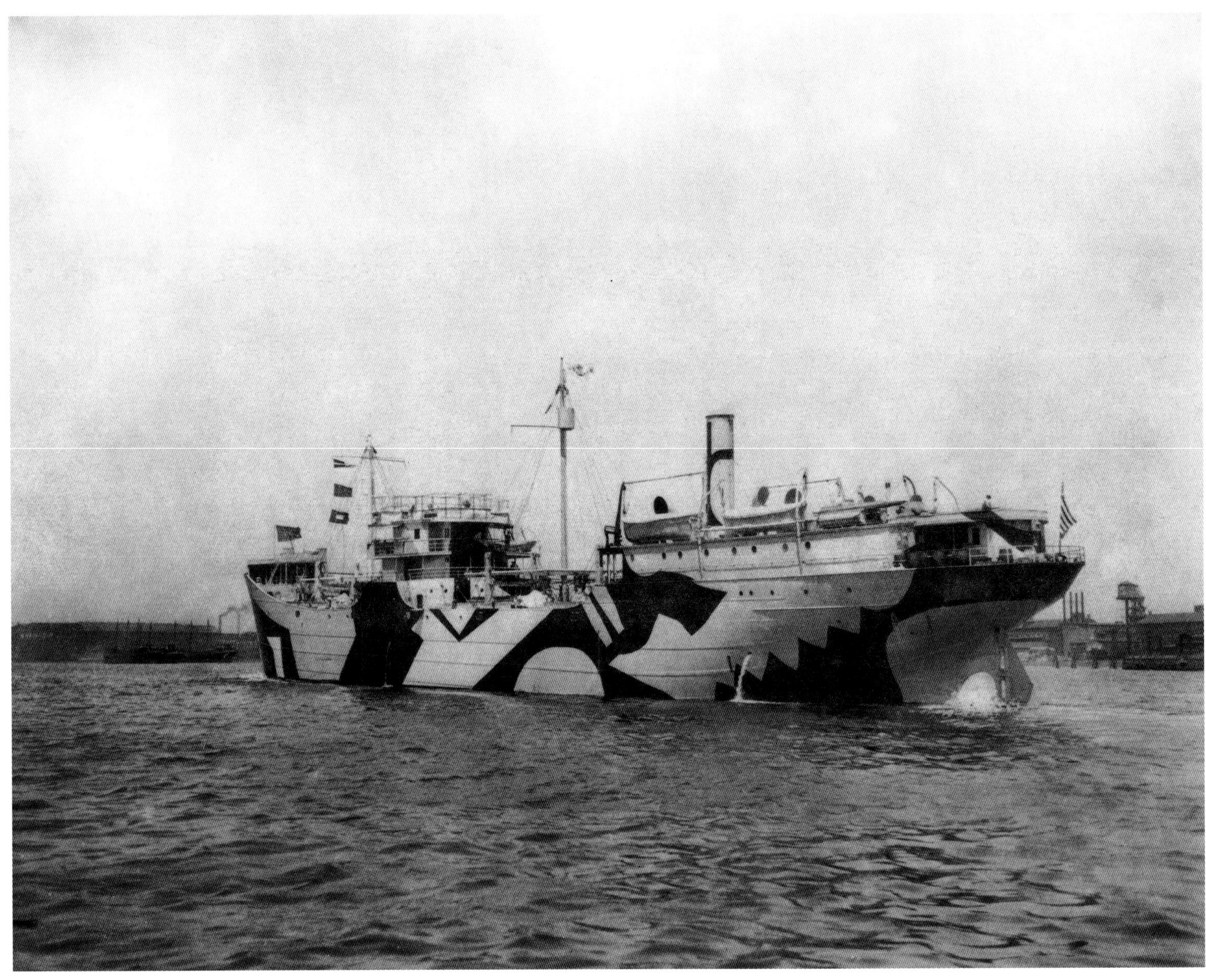

Seen here is an interior view of Tobin's Market at 414 Delaware Street in New Castle. Mr. Tobin stands proudly behind the counter on the right.

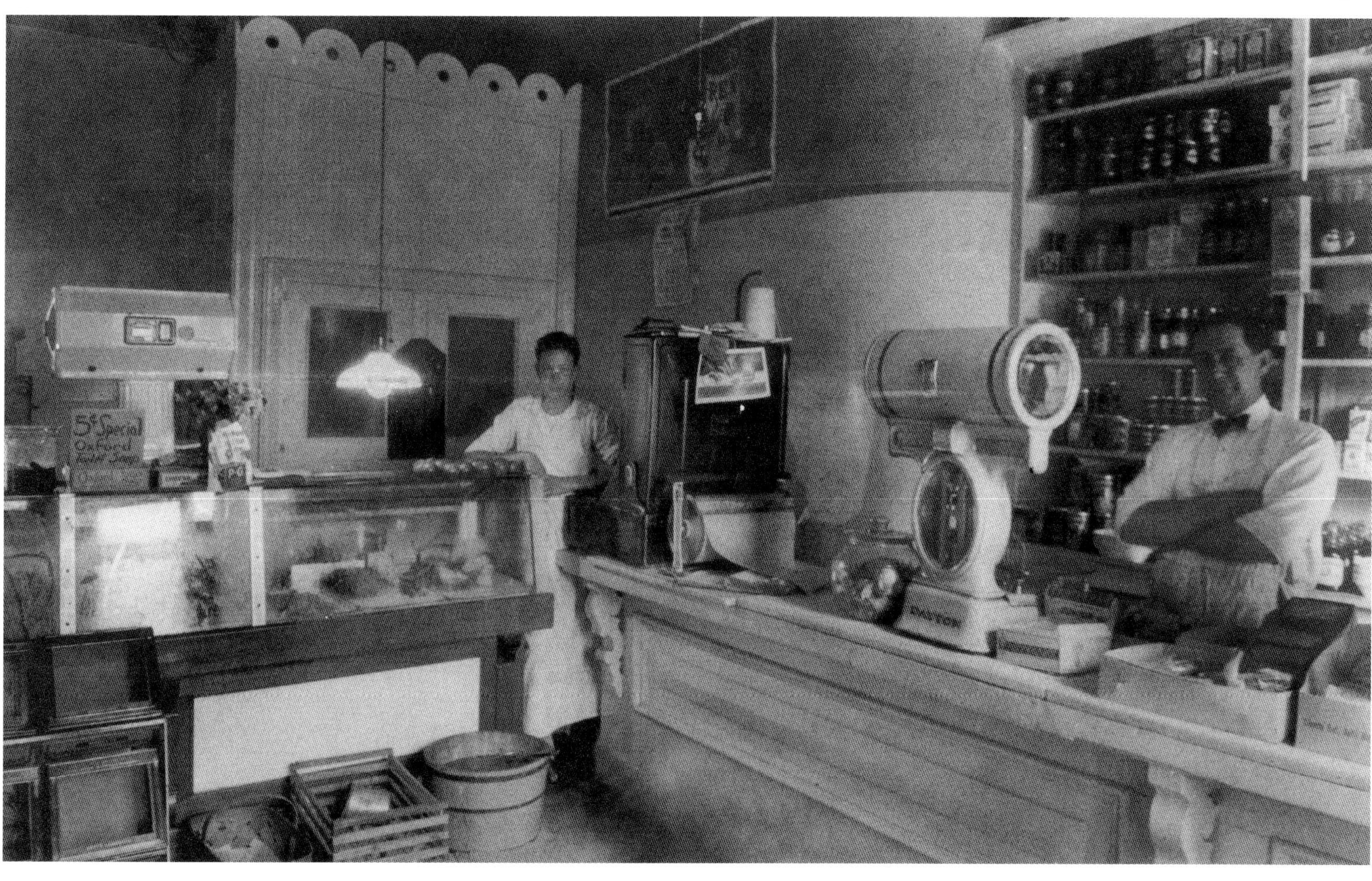

An aerial view of the town of New Castle shows the privately owned New Castle–Pennsville ferry, which plied the waters of the Delaware River. With increasing automobile traffic, a more efficient mode of transportation and relief from traffic congestion in New Castle was sorely needed. In 1945 the governments of Delaware and New Jersey agreed to build a bridge across the river.

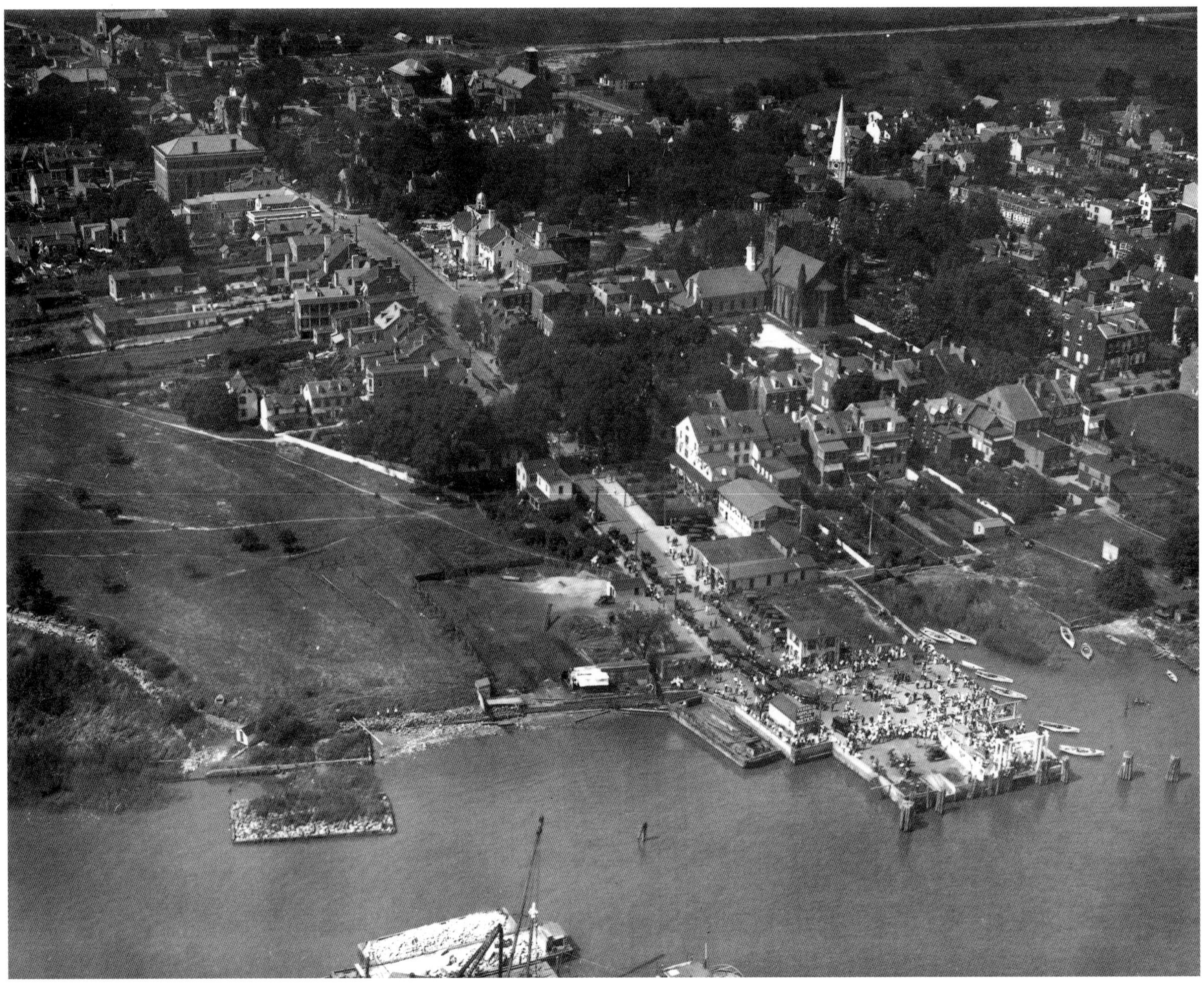

This view of a plate mill table was recorded inside the Worth Steel Company in Claymont in 1920. In 1918, Worth Steel bought 600 acres to build a mill. The company built an attractive headquarters atop a hill near the entrance to "Worthland," a housing development for steel workers and their families. The company also built 24 houses for African American employees. Still in business, the mill has had many owners over the years.

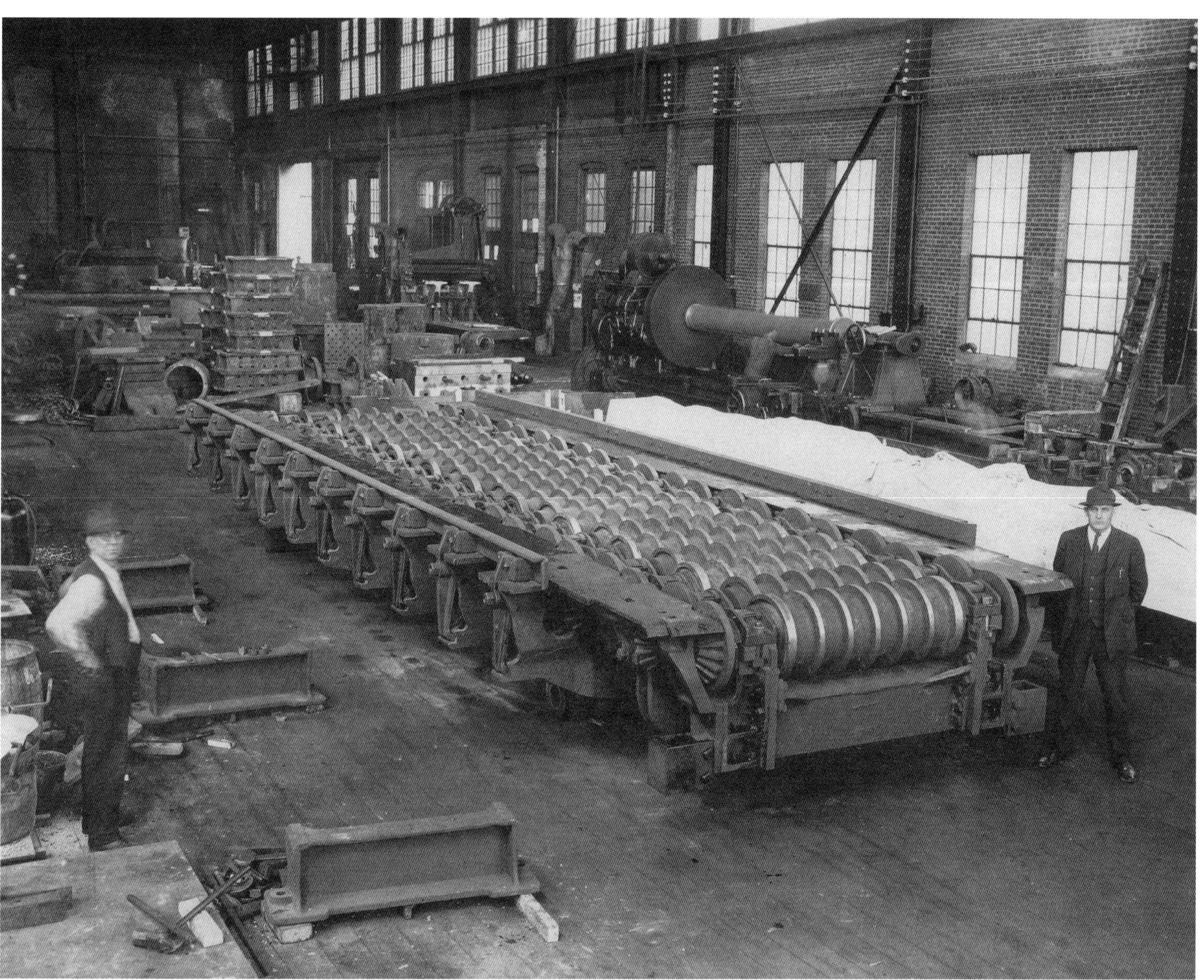

Farmers stand at their stalls along the King Street Farmers Market. Wilmington's tradition of markets is as old as the city. The market was moved from Market Street to King Street in 1872 and operated there for more than 100 years. It continues today but in a smaller capacity at various locations.

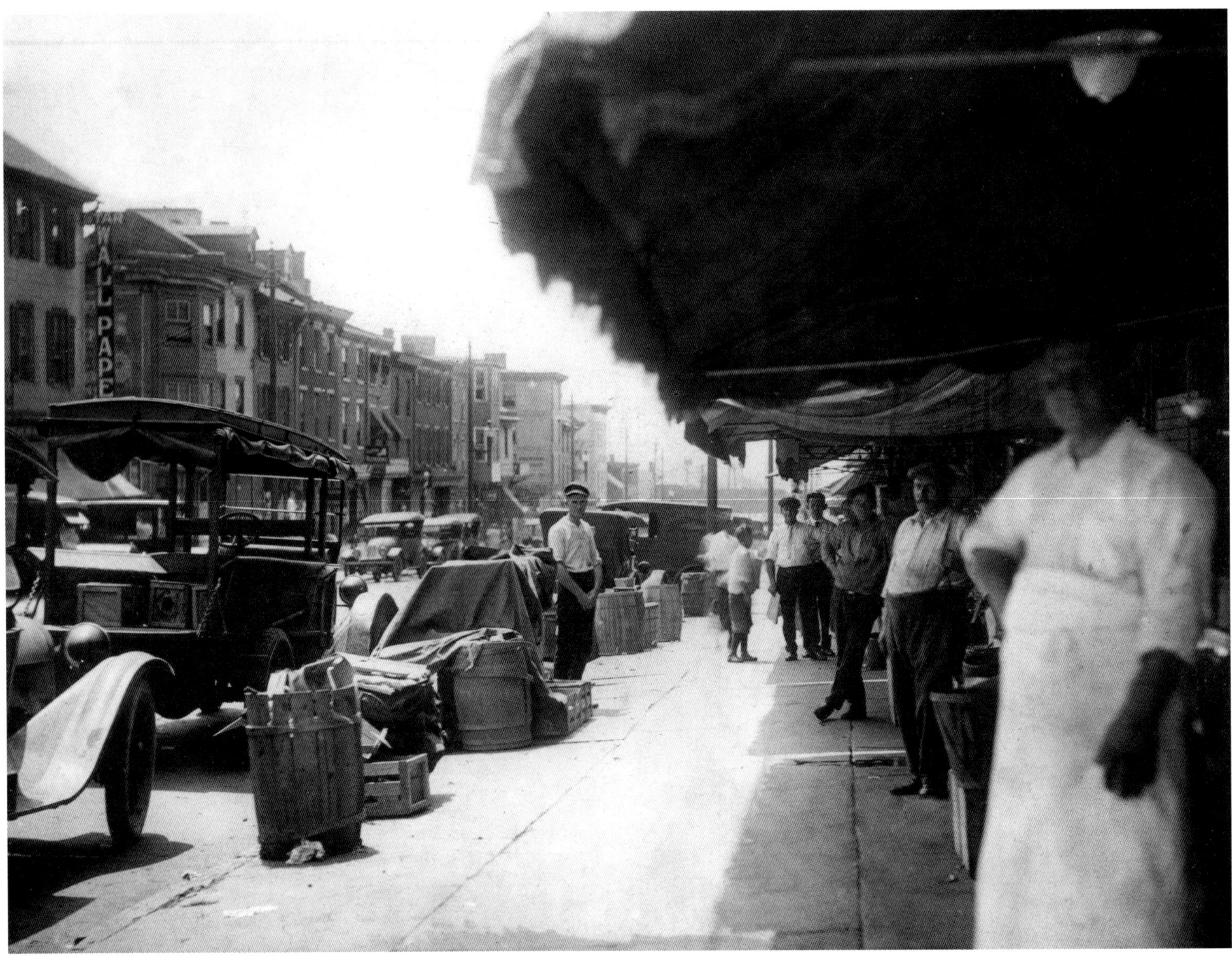

This photograph was taken in 1920 during a visit by Wilmington's Engine Company No. 6 to the Fire Station of Engine Company No. 10 at 25th and Market streets.

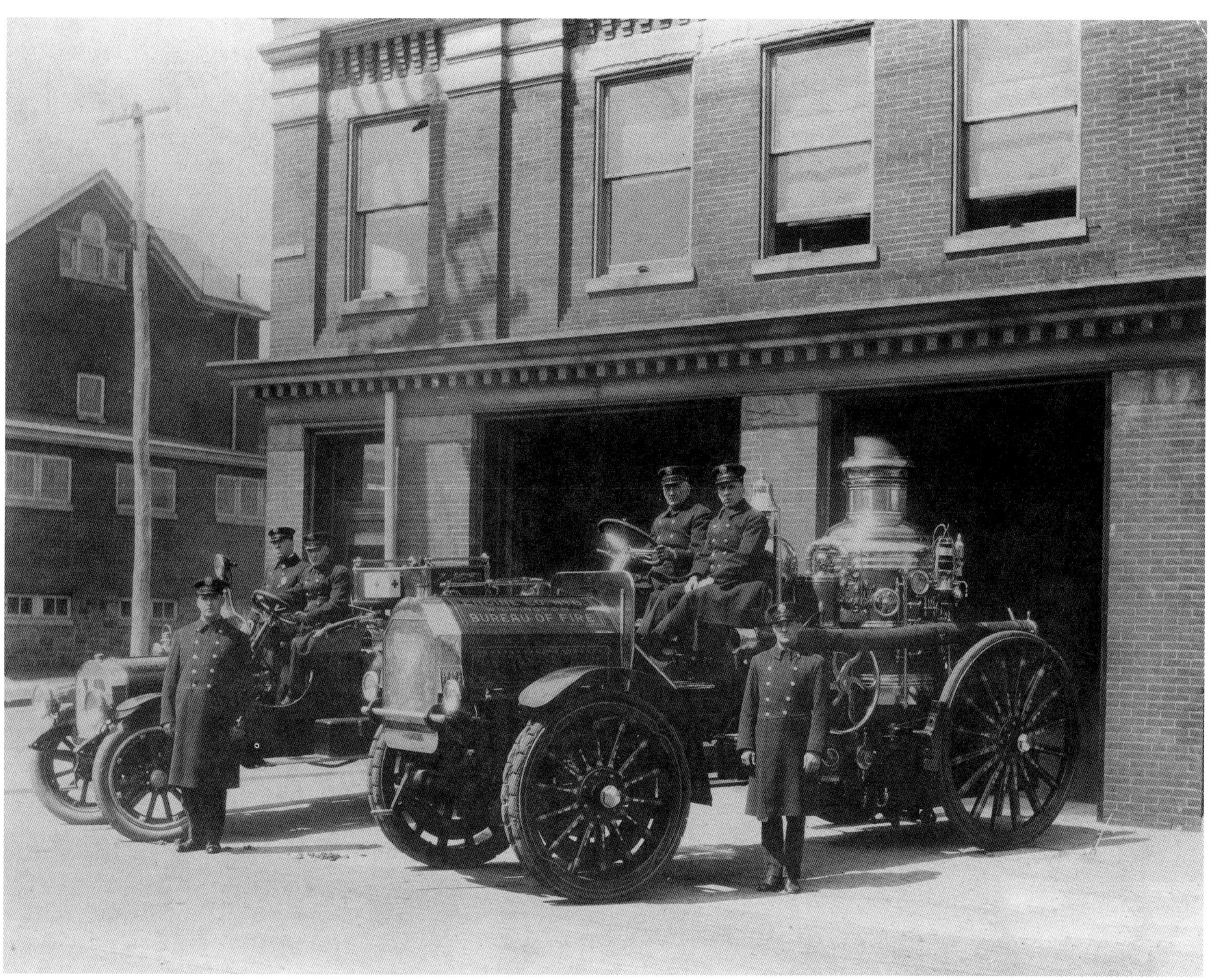

Facing east from the top of the DuPont Company building in Wilmington during the 1930s. This image shows one of the twin spires of the City-County Building, which sits across Rodney Square, and looks out over the east side of the city to the convergence of the Christina and Brandywine rivers. The low, flat housing of the working-class neighborhoods is punctuated by large factory buildings and churches.

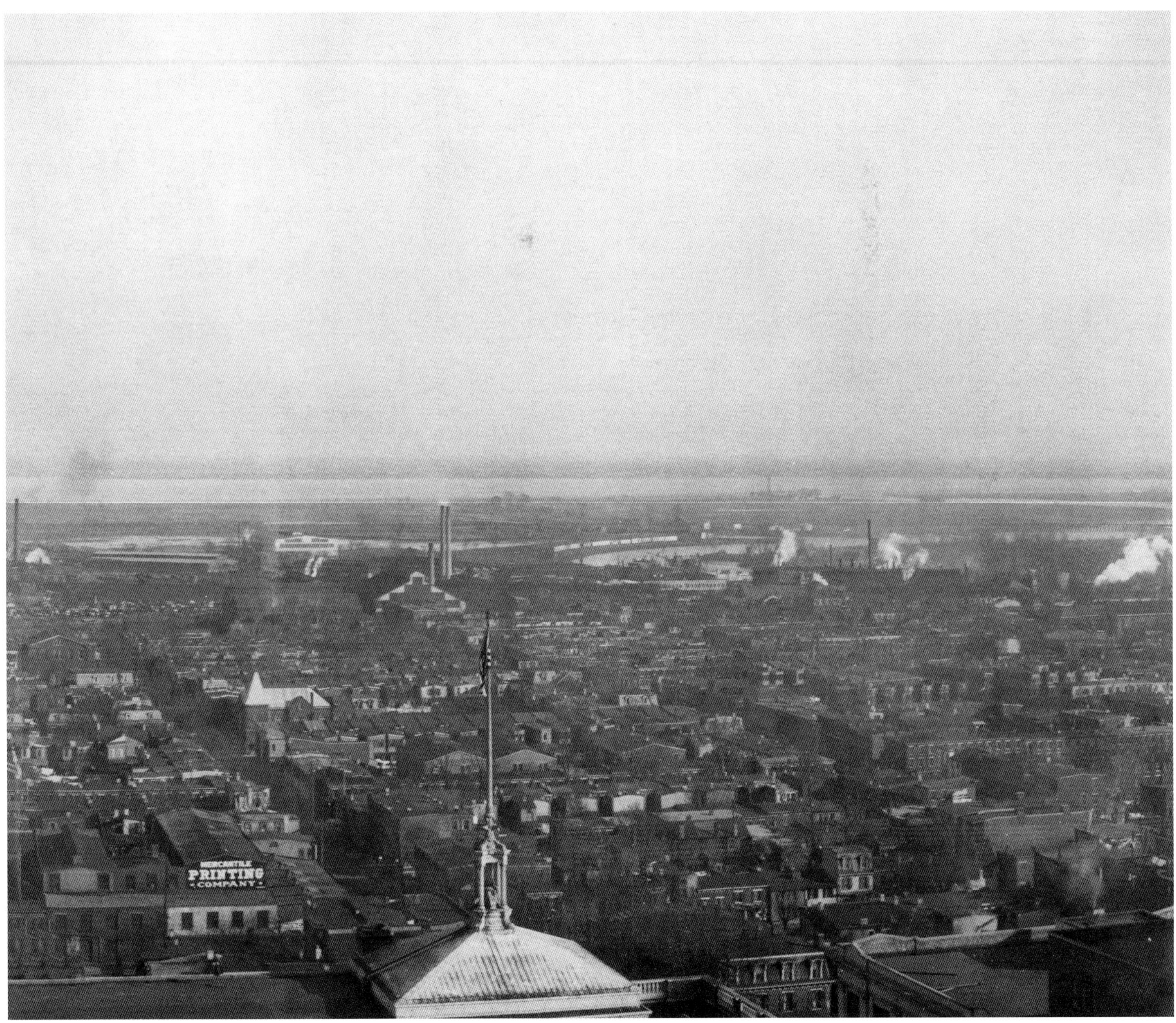

A play is performed on the open-air stage at Gild Hall in Arden. In 1900, Arden's founders, Frank Stephens and Will Price, dreamed of creating a life that was "more simple, honest, and beautiful" than the life they found in the outside world. Based on the simple-tax philosophy of Henry George, Arden remains one of only a handful of Utopian colonies in America still in existence.

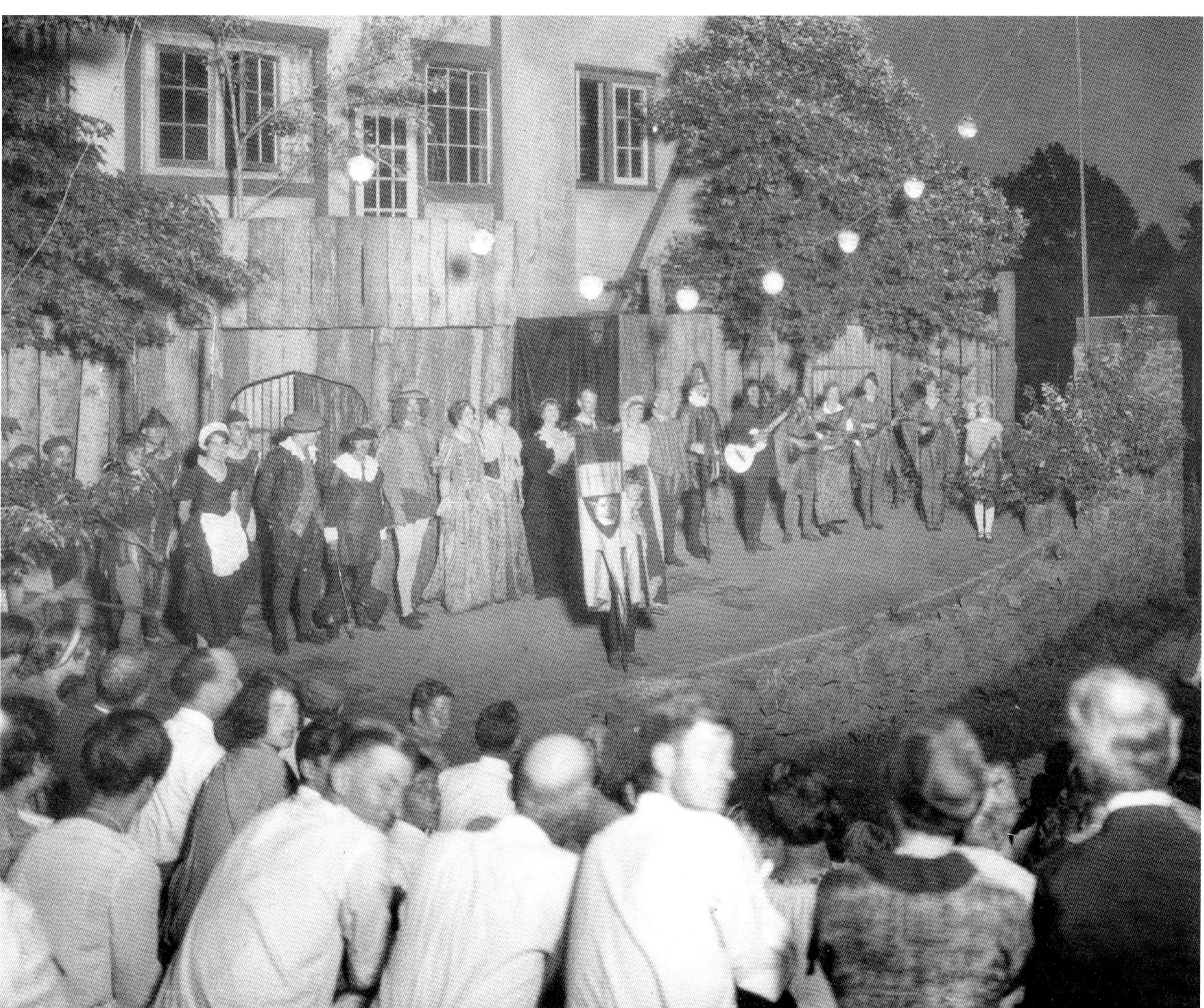

The State Road, also known as Route 13–Route 113, runs the length of Delaware from Selbyville to Claymont. The pet project of T. Coleman du Pont (1863–1930), it was originally envisioned as a dual highway with a center lane for horse-drawn vehicles. When finished, the road was a two-lane highway, considered a model for highway construction at the time. One period pamphlet called it a "concrete ribbon."

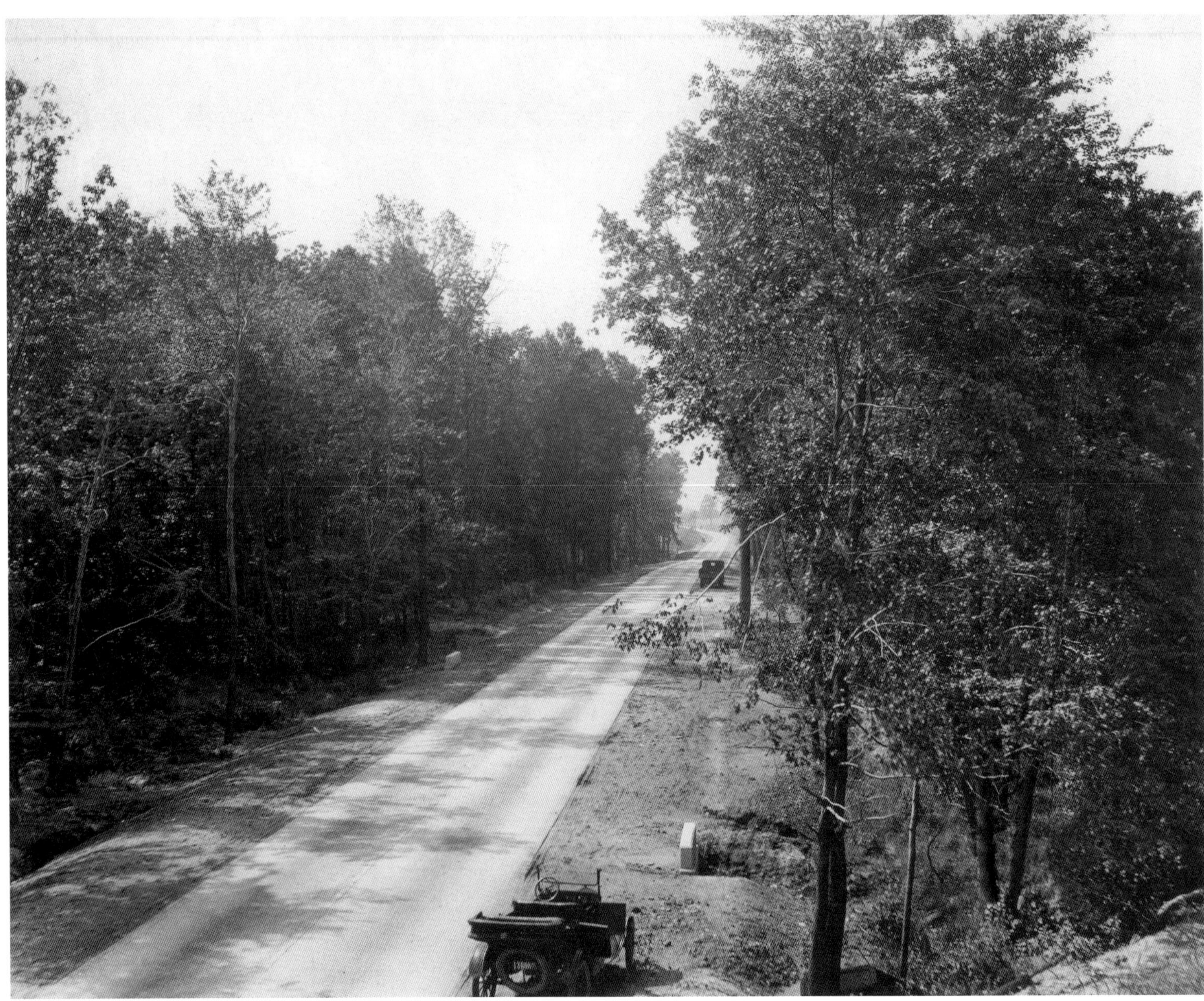

This aerial view of the Bellanca Airfield and Corporation shows the facility on the former Spring Garden farm outside New Castle about one year after it opened. A group of Delawareans headed by Henry Belin du Pont wooed Guiseppe M. Bellanca, an airplane engineer and builder, to Delaware. Bellanca, considered an aeronautical genius, ran his business from New Castle between 1928 and 1954, building more than 3,000 planes here.

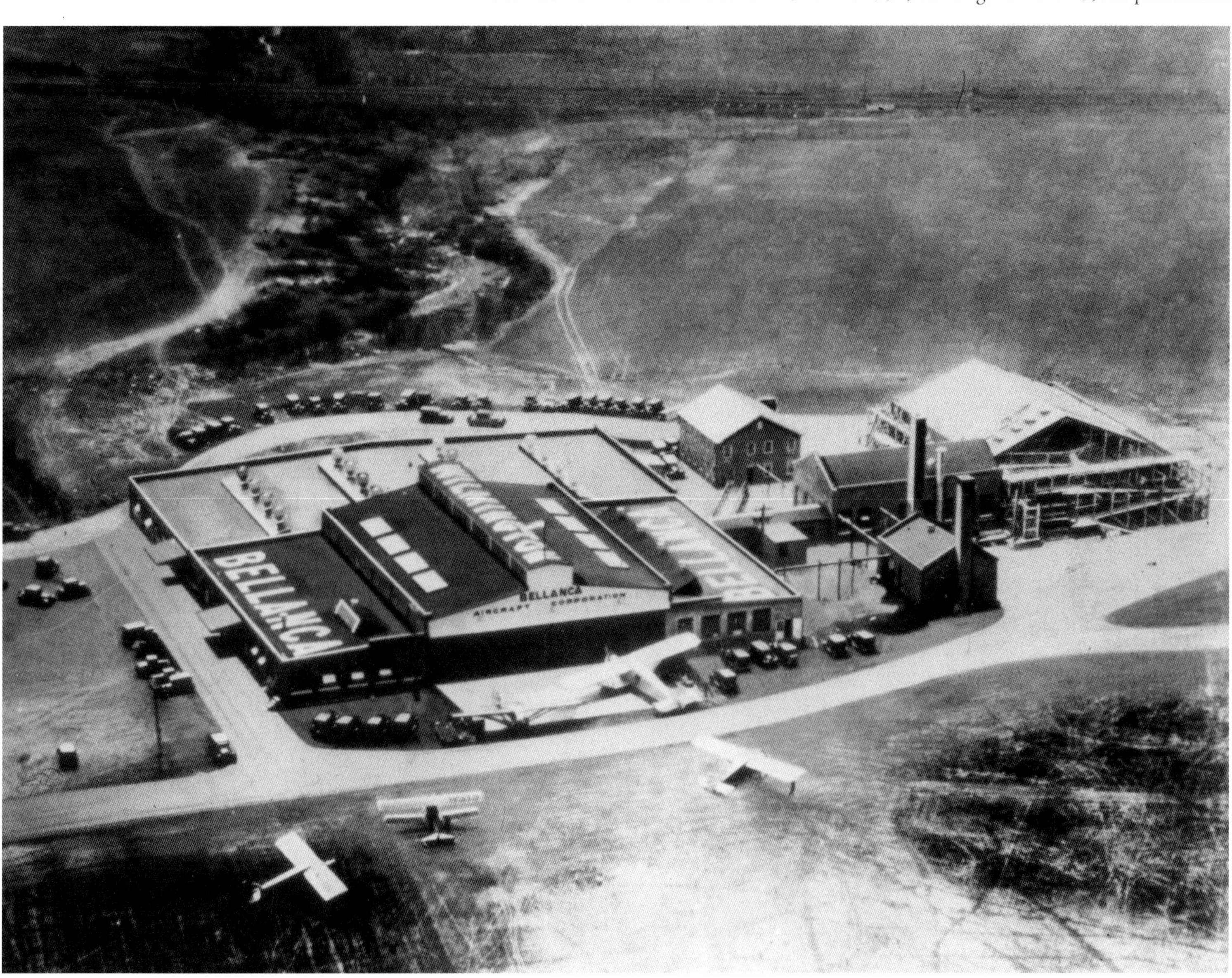

In 1927, Charles "Lucky Lindy" Lindbergh completed the first solo non-stop flight across the Atlantic Ocean. Henry Belin du Pont (at left) invited Lindbergh and the *Spirit of St. Louis* to Delaware. Lindbergh drew 50,000 people to his motorcade and festivities at Baynard Stadium, where he addressed the crowd on October 22, 1927.

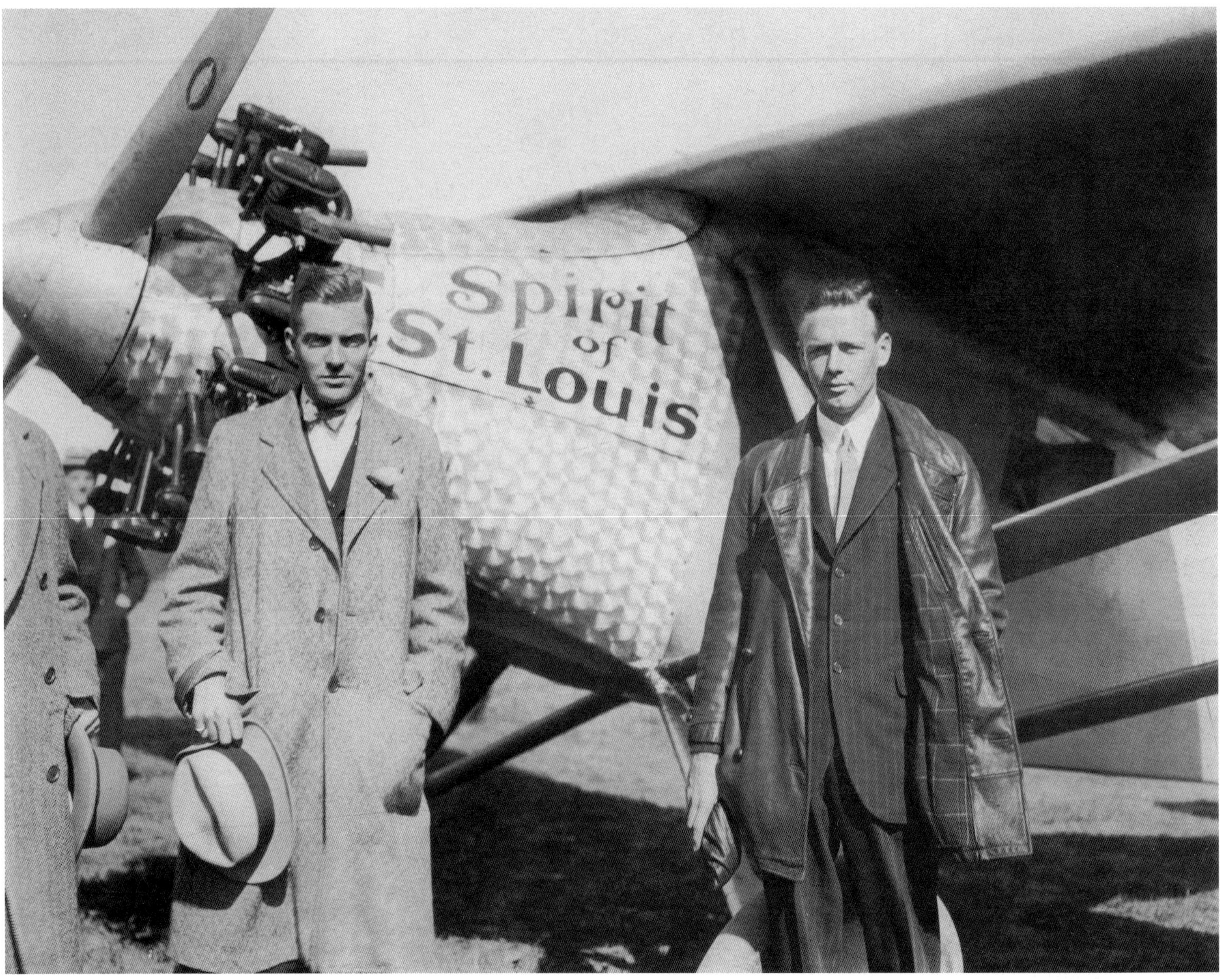

At the beach and on the boardwalk at Rehoboth Avenue in the 1920s. At far left is Dolle's, famous in Rehoboth Beach for its saltwater taffy. Next door is the bowling alley and to the right of that is the four-pillar facade of a family home. In contrast to today, the people on the boardwalk are dressed in suits with ties and dresses. It wasn't until after World War II that Americans began to dress more casually for seaside outings.

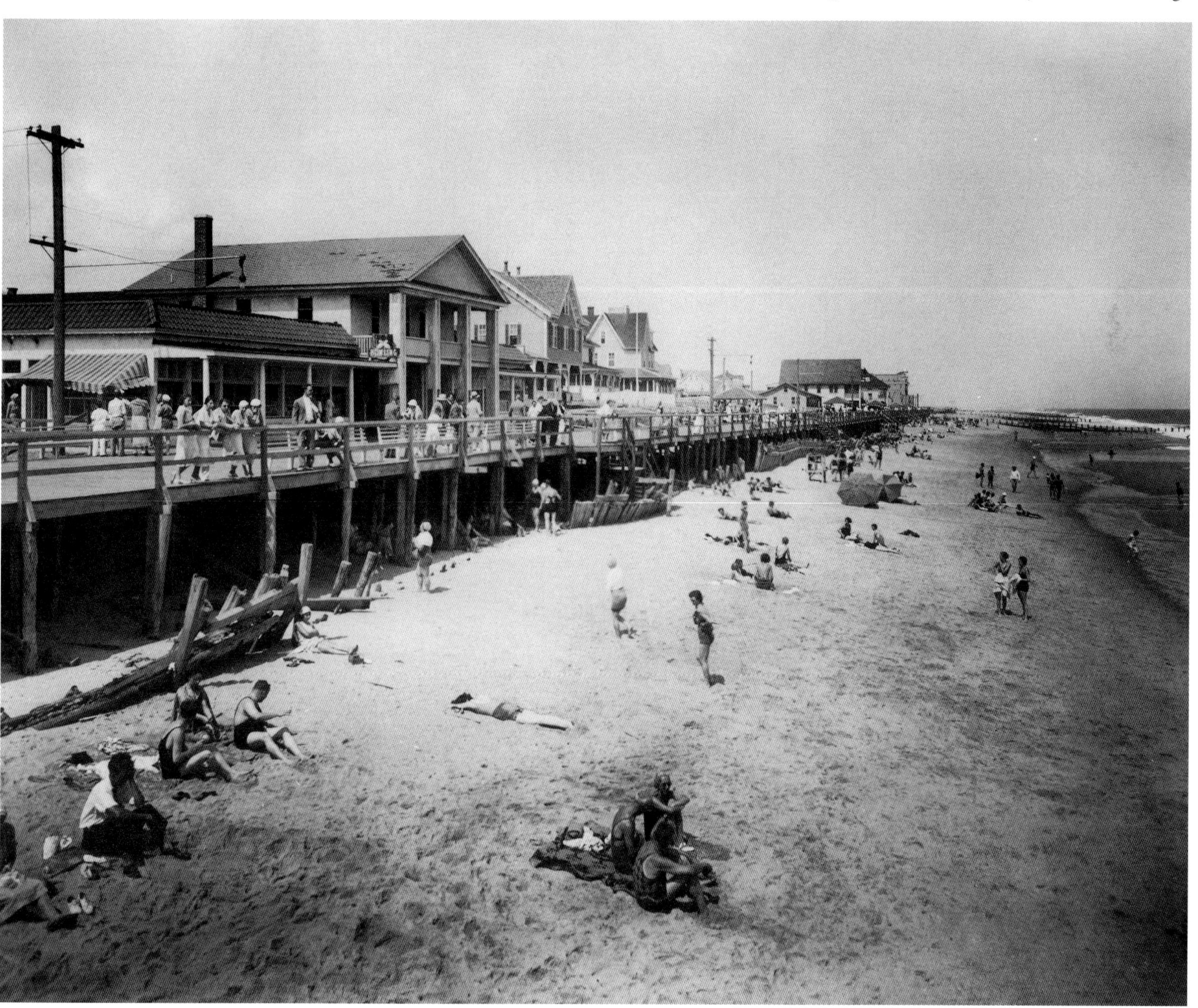

The front window of White Brothers Motor Company on the 3200 block of Market Street north of Wilmington is decorated for the holidays and year-end sales around 1927. To pique the interest of potential customers, the latest in transportation convenience is compared with the outmoded one-horse sleigh of a generation before.

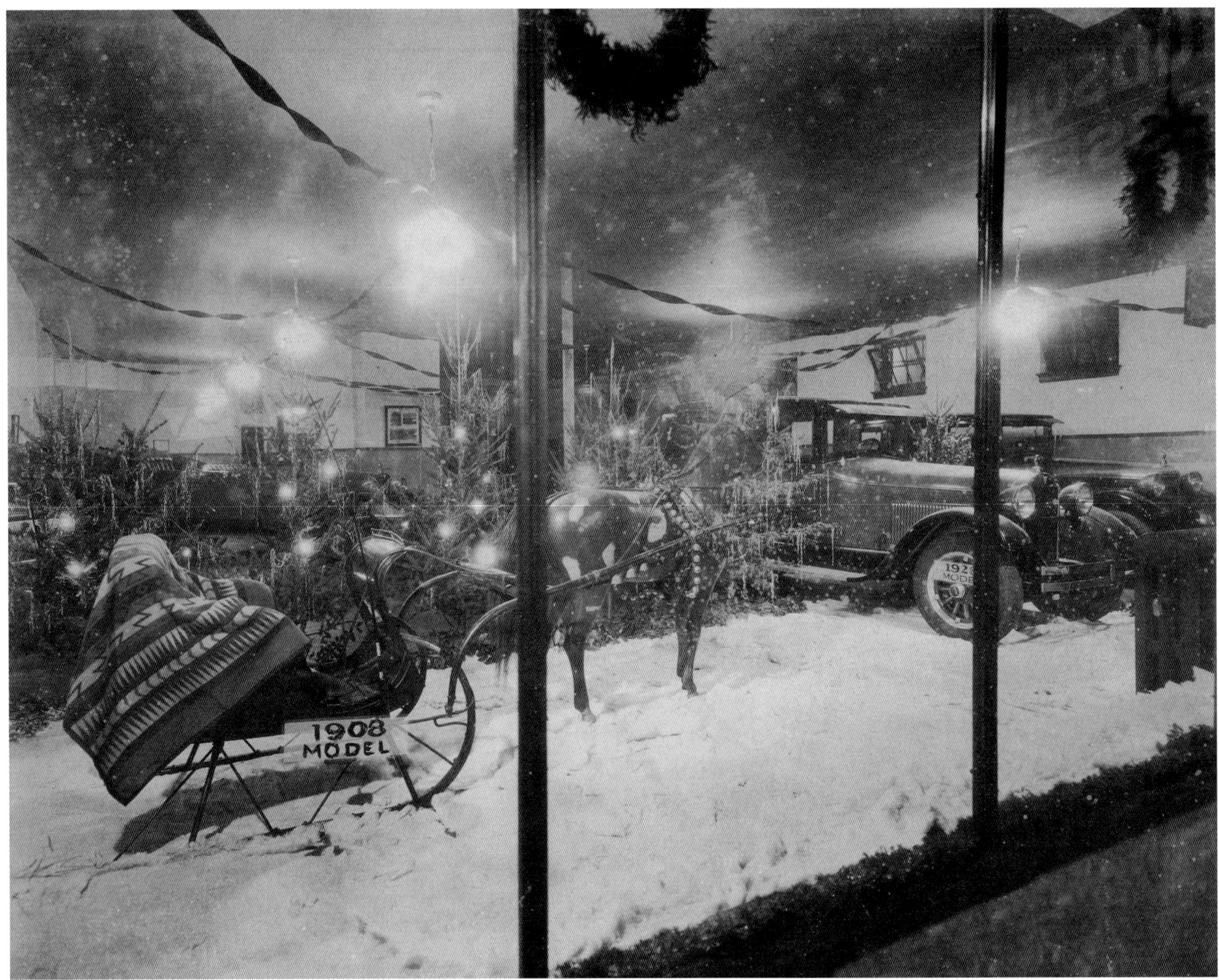

The Adas Kodesch Synagogue was organized in 1885. In 1898, the congregation bought the Zion Lutheran Church building at 5th and French streets in Wilmington. In 1907, that building was razed and in 1908 this building was dedicated. The congregation remained here for more than 50 years. In 1957, the Adas Kodesch and Chesed Shel Emeth congregations merged and moved to Washington Boulevard in the Brandywine Hills section of Wilmington.

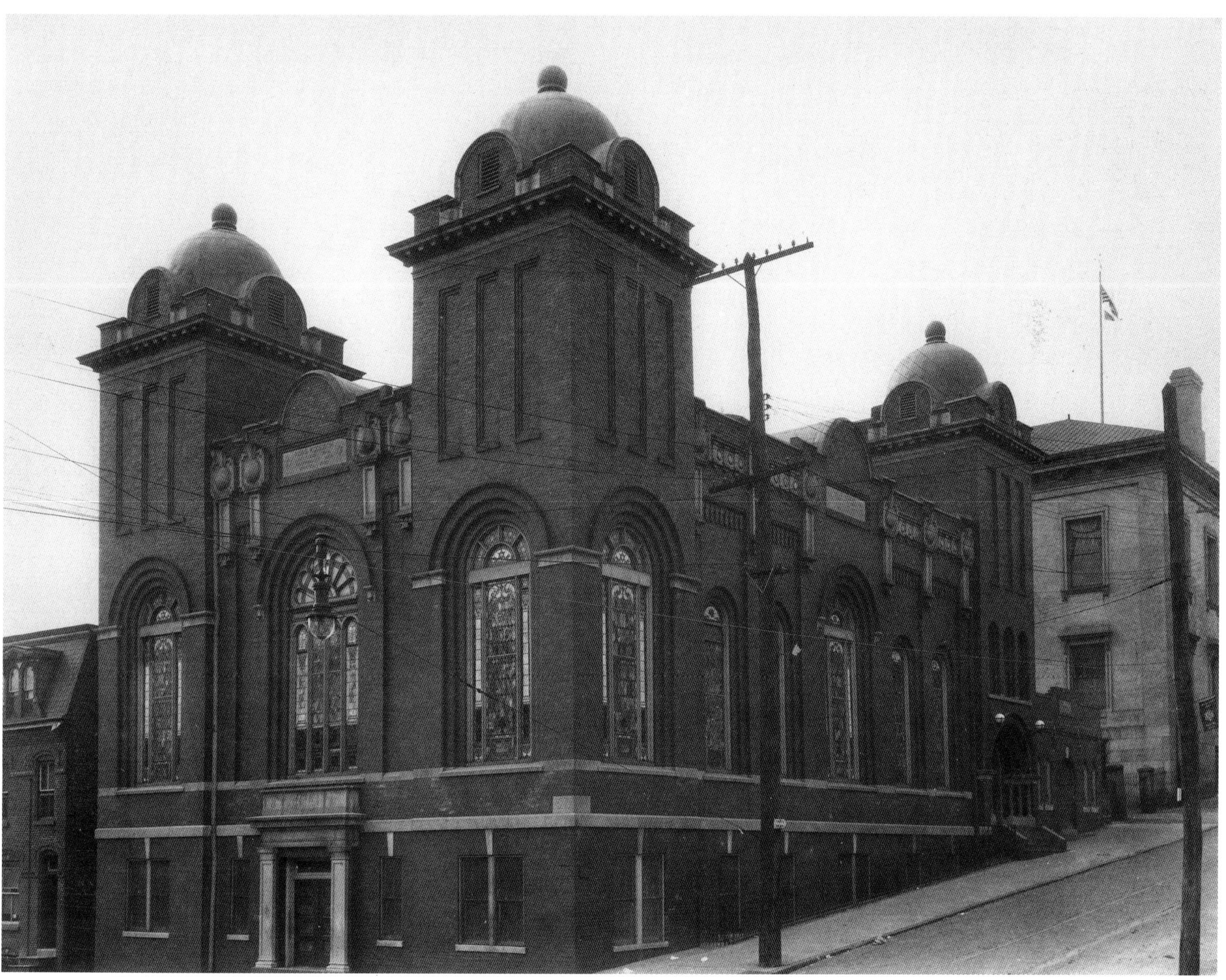

The Laurel train station grounds also held the farmers market, seen here in the 1920s. As it did in most downstate towns, the railroad cut right through Laurel and was important to the town's economy. Farmers shipped their produce to large markets by train.

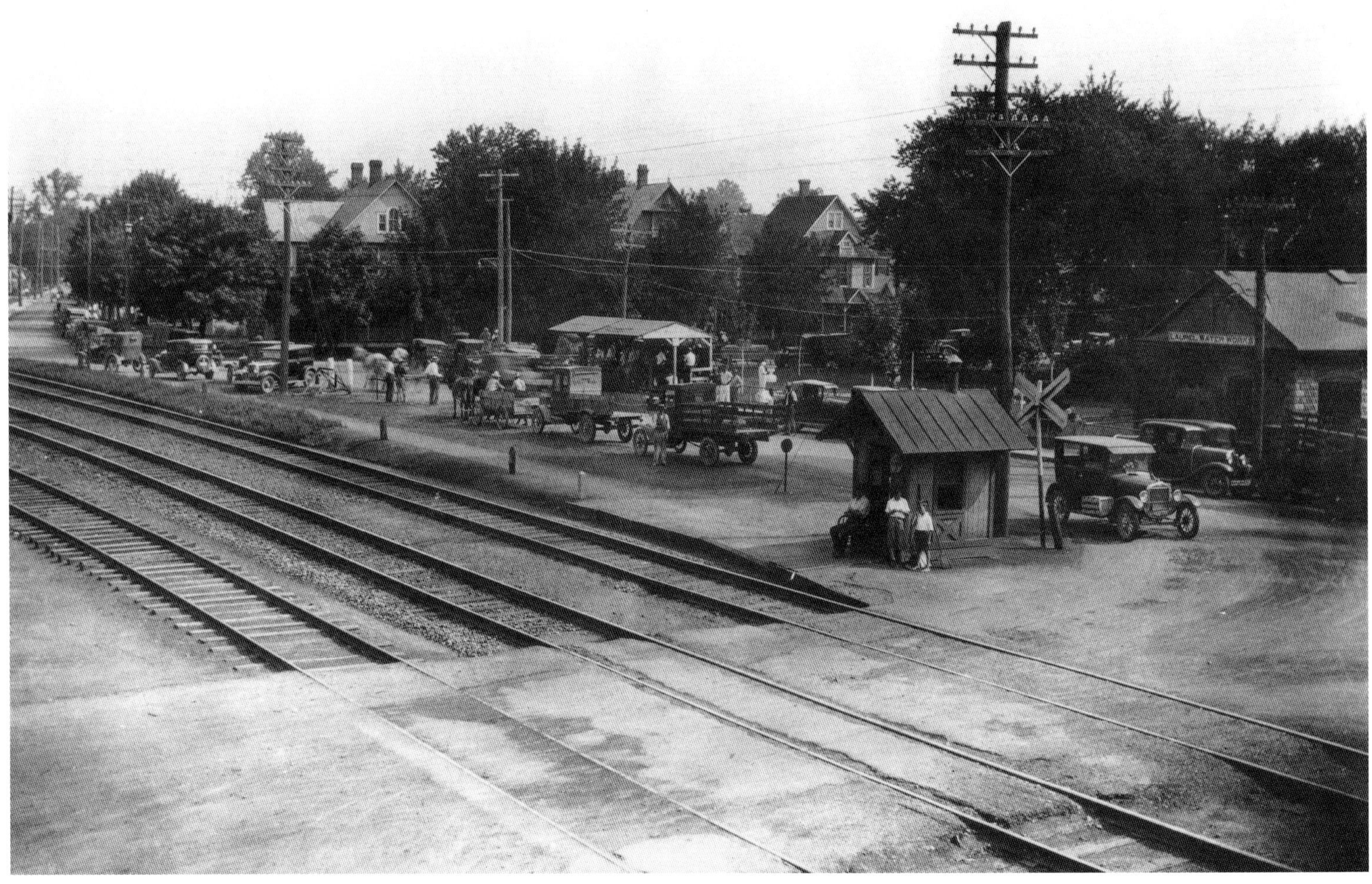

This photograph of a parade was taken in the late 1920s at the intersection of 4th and Market streets in Wilmington. Pictured here is the band of the Liberty Fire Company from New Castle Avenue and a group in Revolutionary War costume.

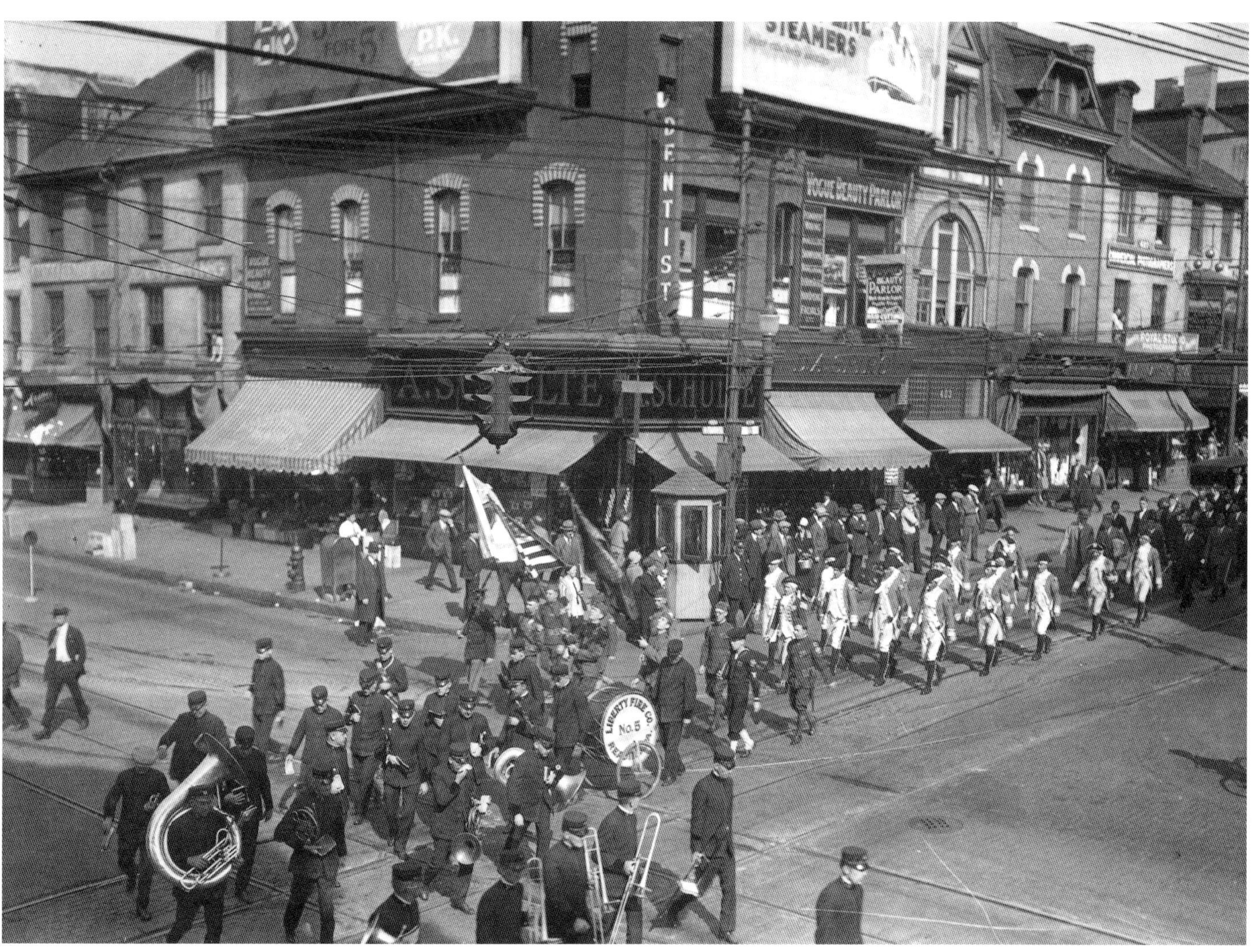

The Queen Anne Pier in Lewes, as it appeared around 1930. Built in 1898 by the Queen Anne Railroad, it was 1,202 feet long but was destroyed by storms in 1936 and again in 1940. Lewes was gaining a reputation for great saltwater fishing. Around this time the Lewes Anglers Association began running a fleet of boats for fishing hardhead, trout, bluefish, and drum. Seen here before integration, the building at center is marked "Colored."

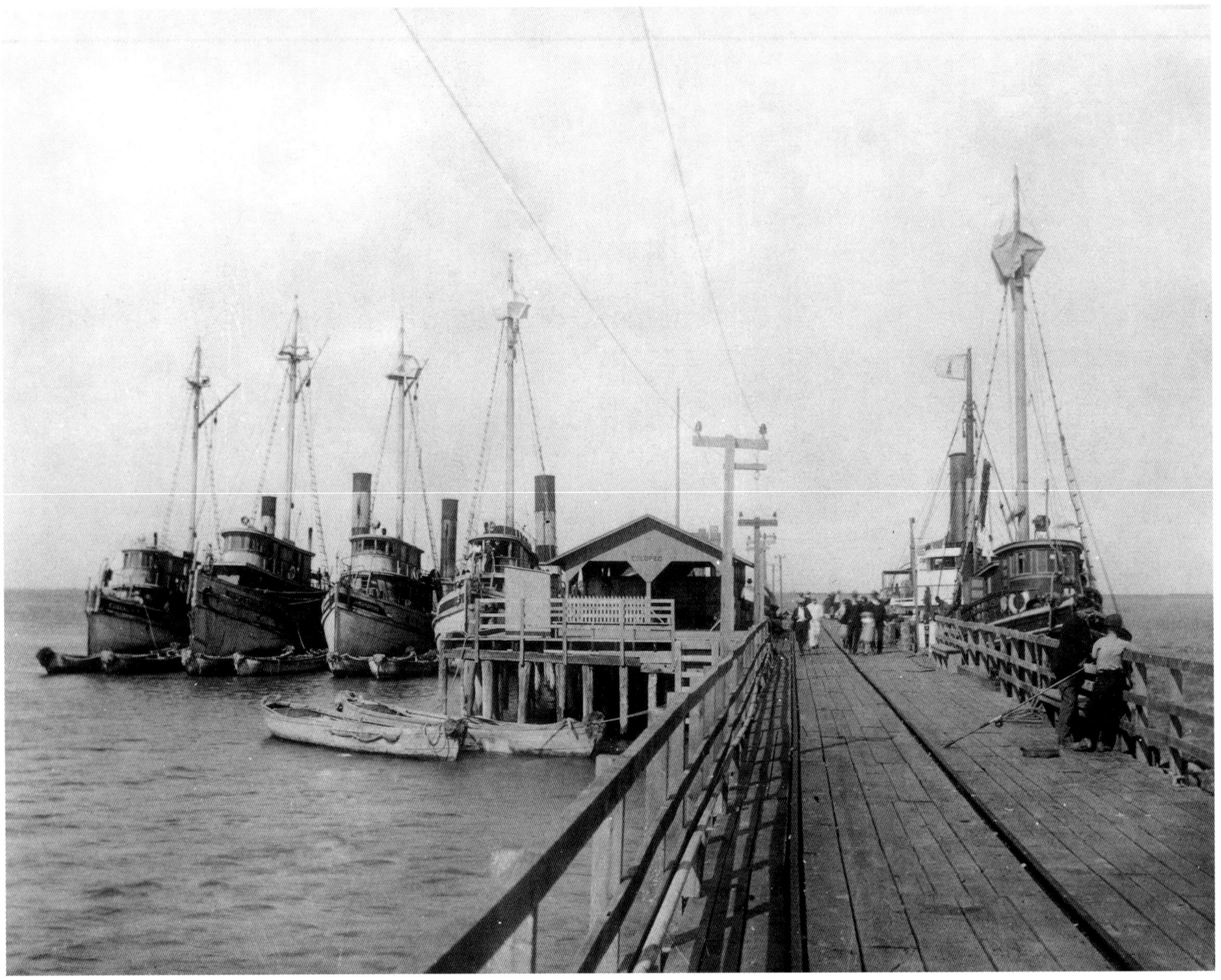

Between 1920 and 1933 the sale and use of alcohol was prohibited in the United States by the Eighteenth Amendment to the Constitution. During Prohibition the Diamond State Brewery Company changed its name to the Diamond State Bottling Company. The Twenty-first Amendment revoking Prohibition became law in 1933, and the brewing company at 5th and Adams streets in Wilmington resumed beer production.

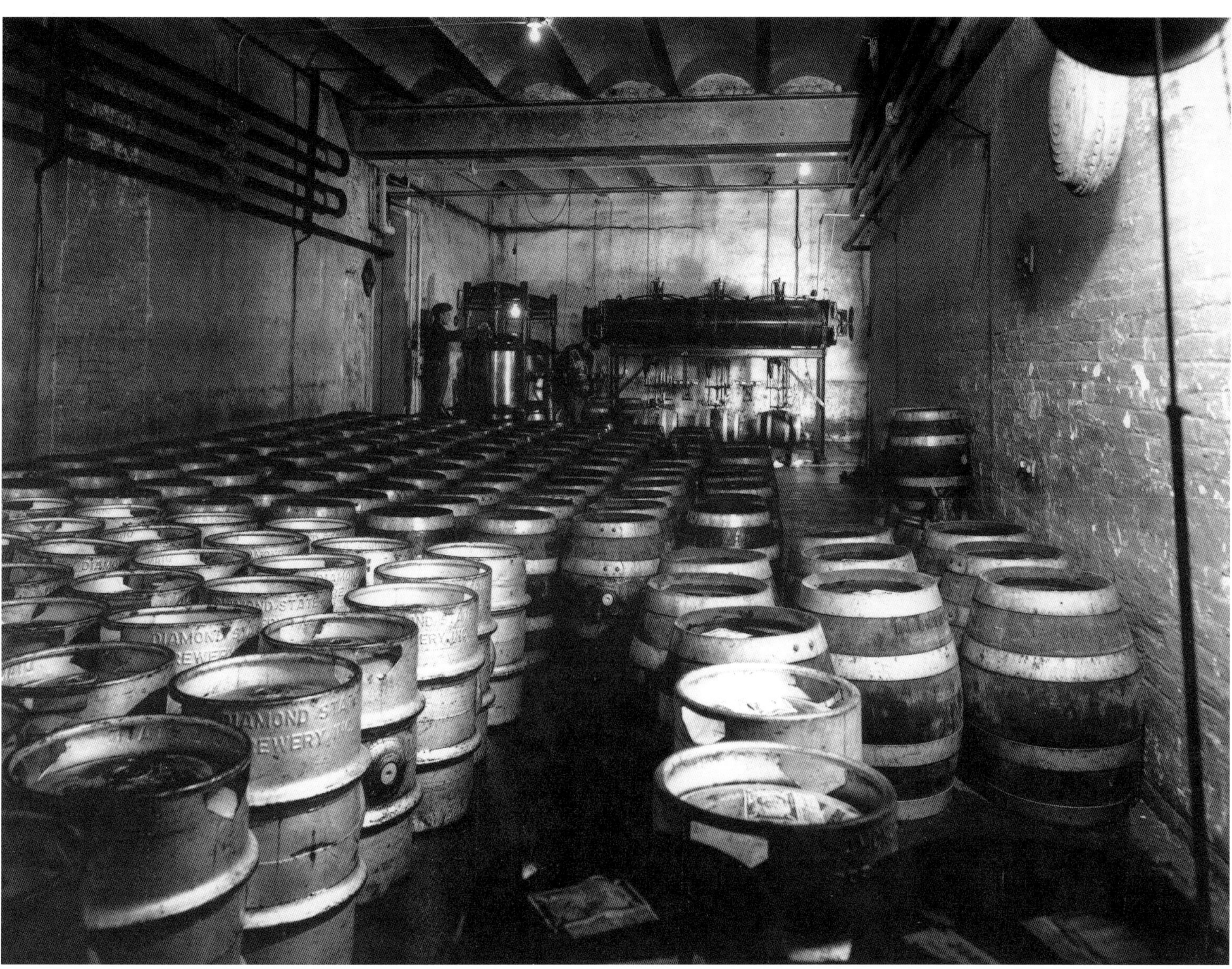

Edman Devenney (in the light suit), manager of the Savoy Theater, stands with a bunch of eager young moviegoers outside the Savoy at 517 Market Street in Wilmington in 1931. In the movie *Young Donovan's Kid,* a young crime lord adopts the son of a slain accomplice, reforms his life, and gets the girl. No wonder a clergyman supports the story and stands alongside Devenney and the children!

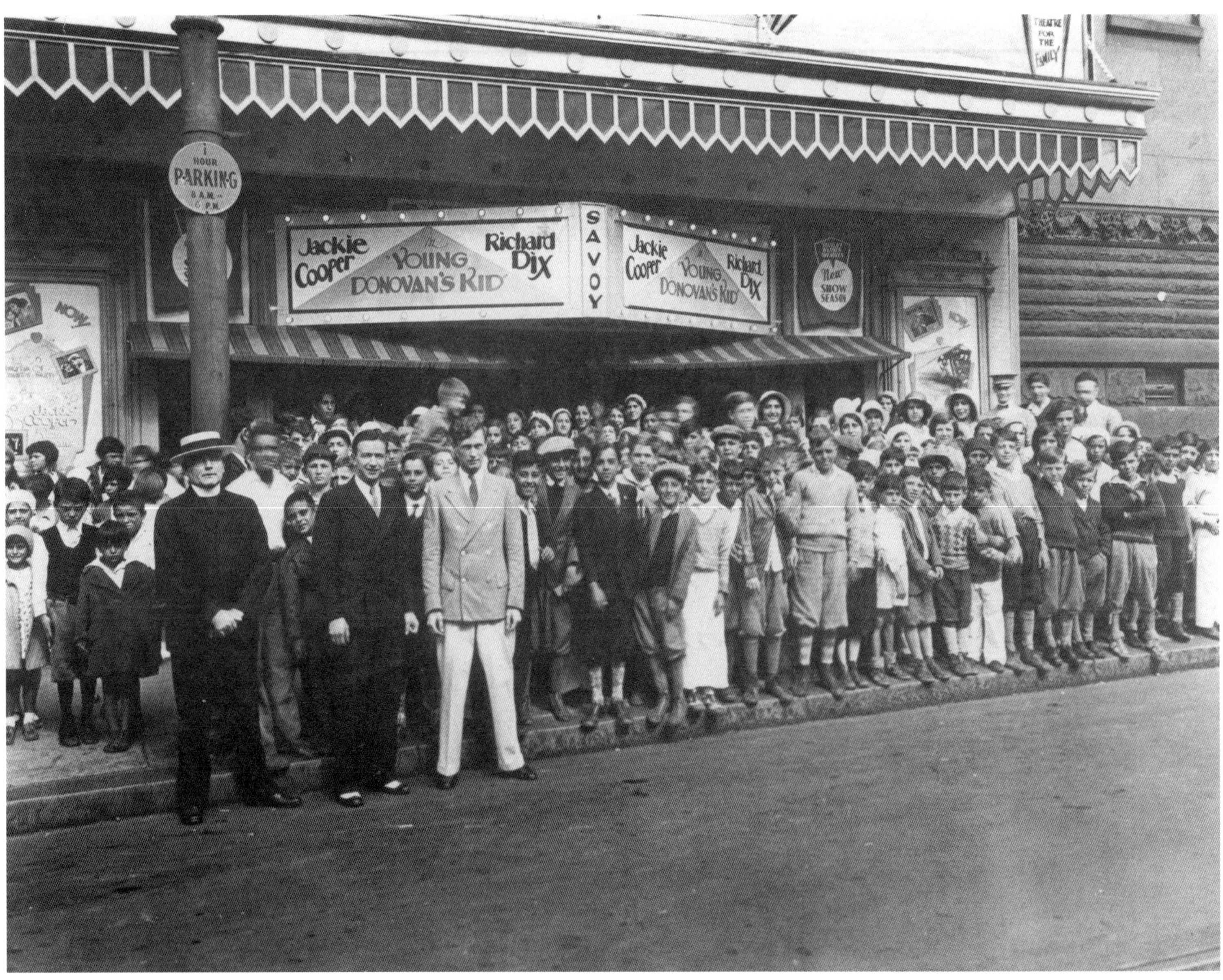

Patrons enjoy a drink at the Spot Café on French Street in Wilmington. The Spot featured distinctive murals along the walls and was well known for its good music. It was unusual at the time for black and white patrons to meet together, but music has often broken down society's barriers.

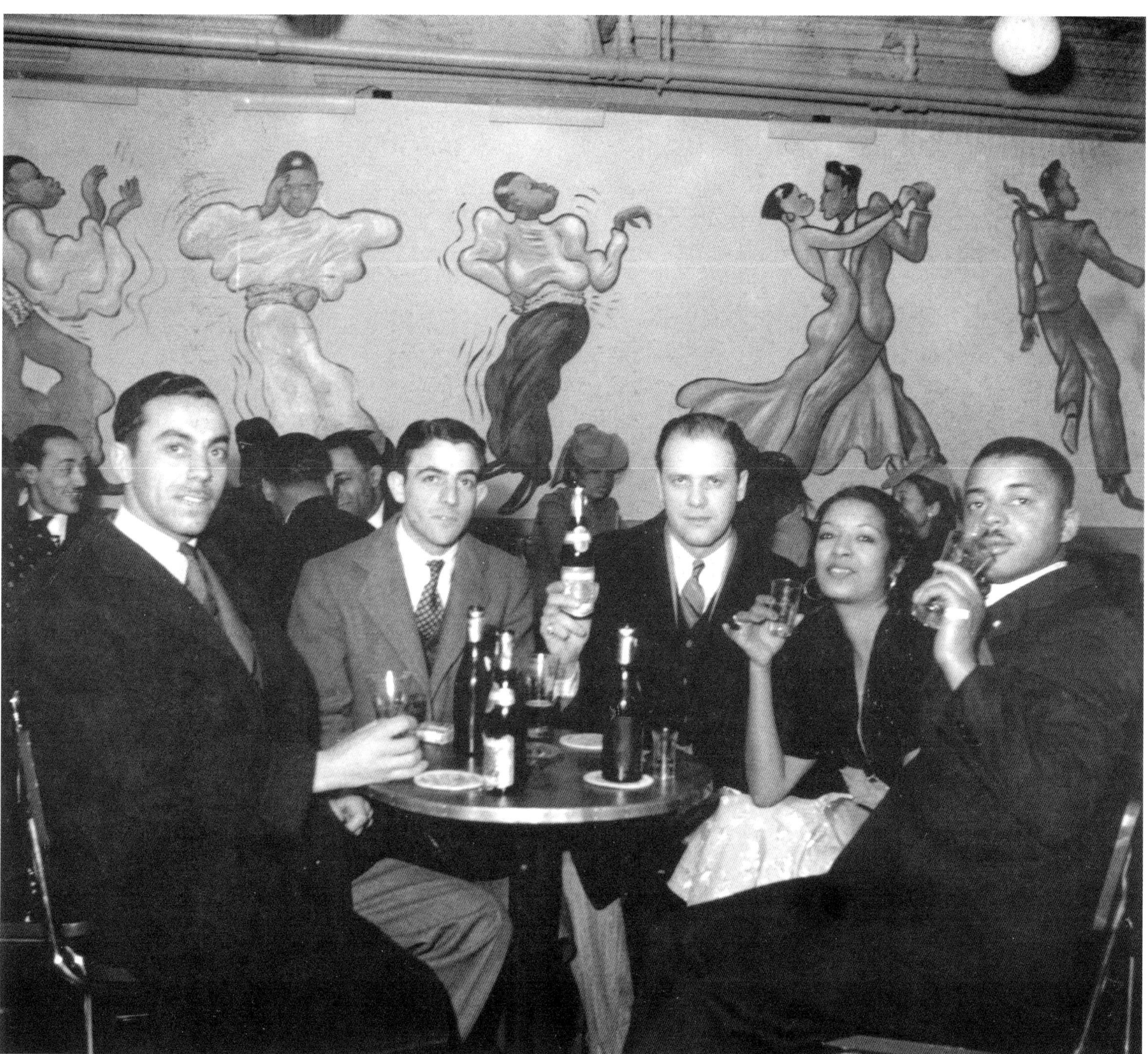

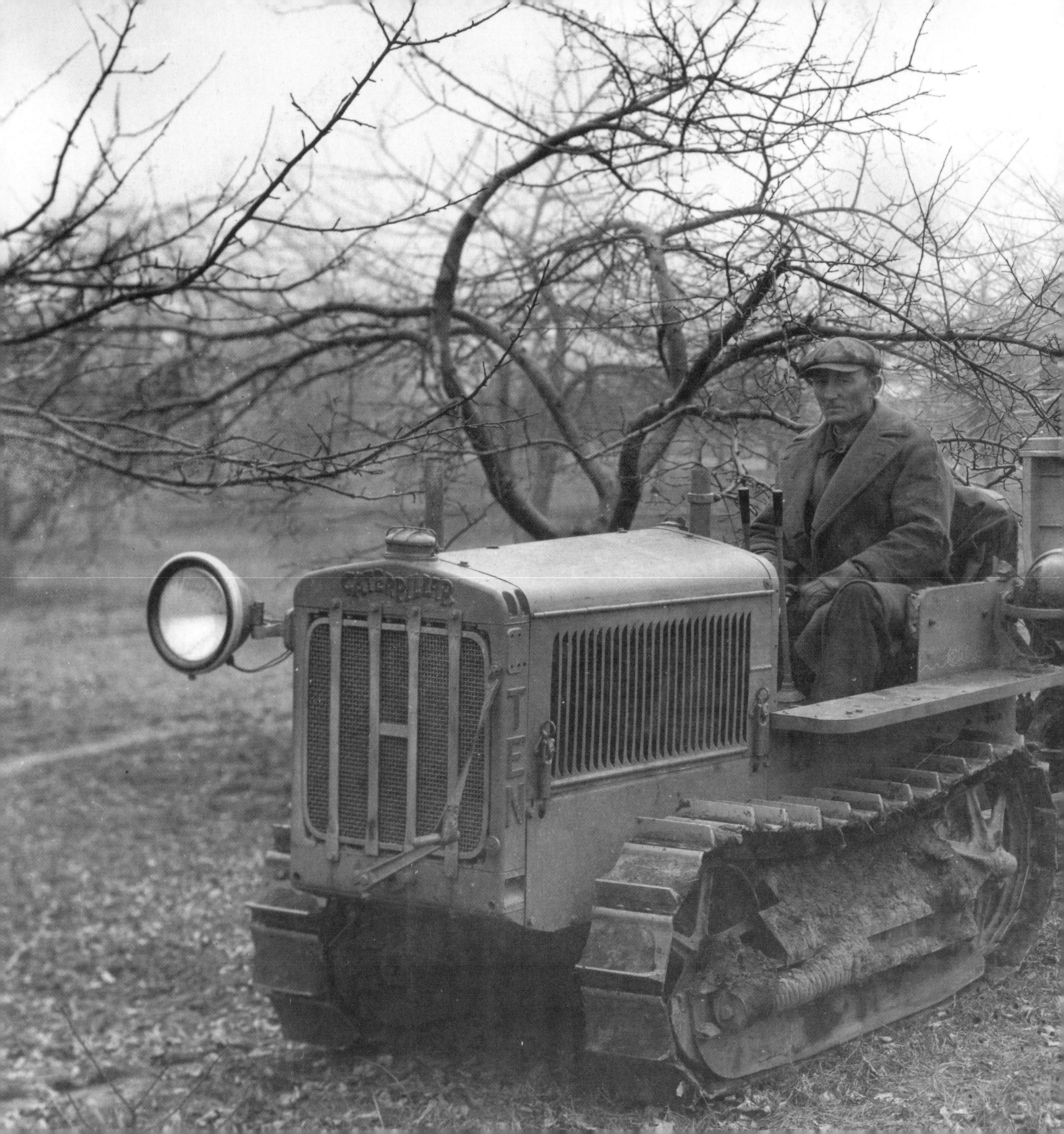
CATERPILLAR
TEN

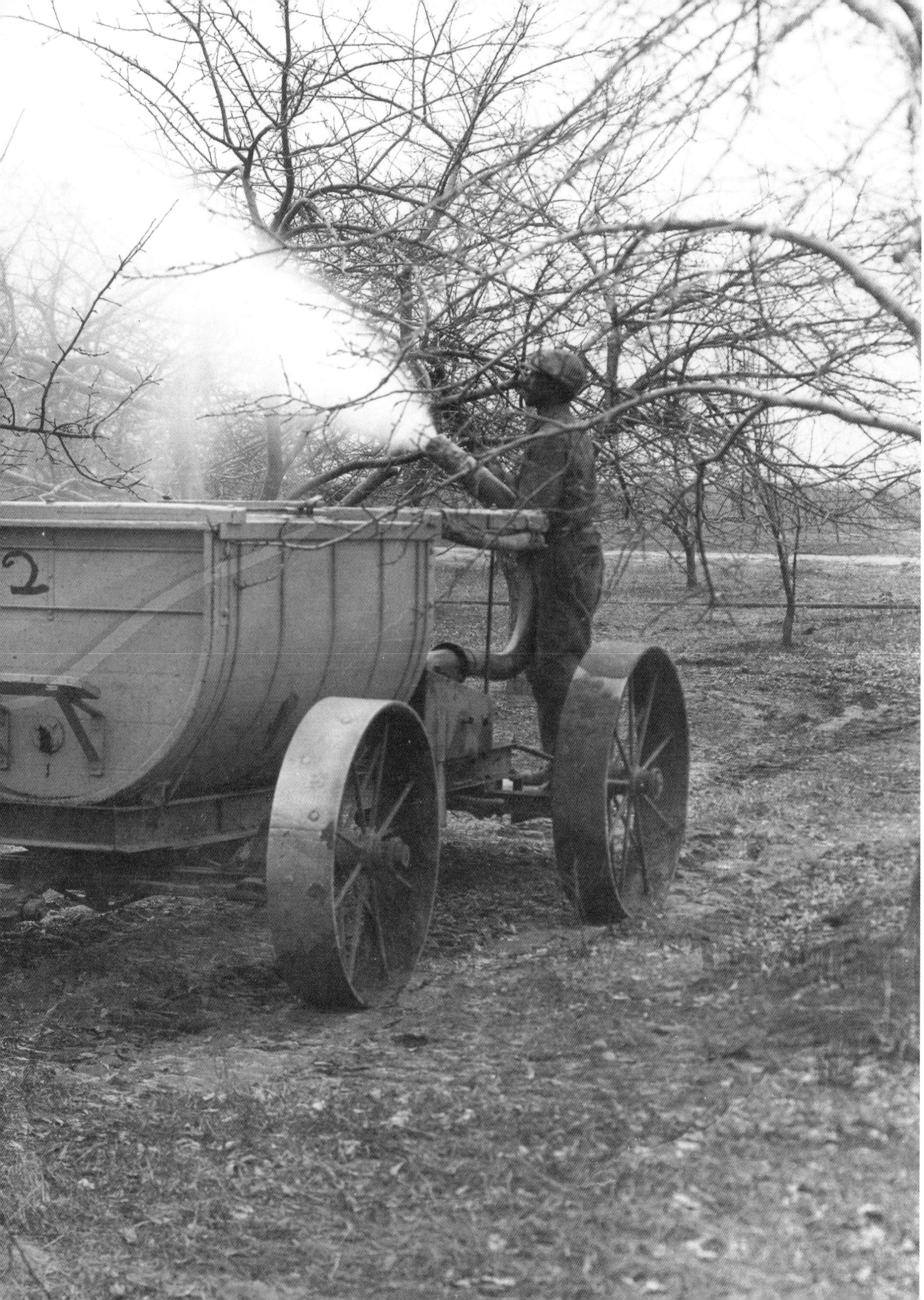

The Caterpillar Tractor Company photographed a farm worker spraying trees in the orchards of Governor John T. Townsend in Selbyville using the governor's new tractor on April 4, 1931. The governor had apple orchards scattered throughout the lower end of Sussex County, leading the *Sunday Star* to claim that Townsend's operation was one of the world's three largest.

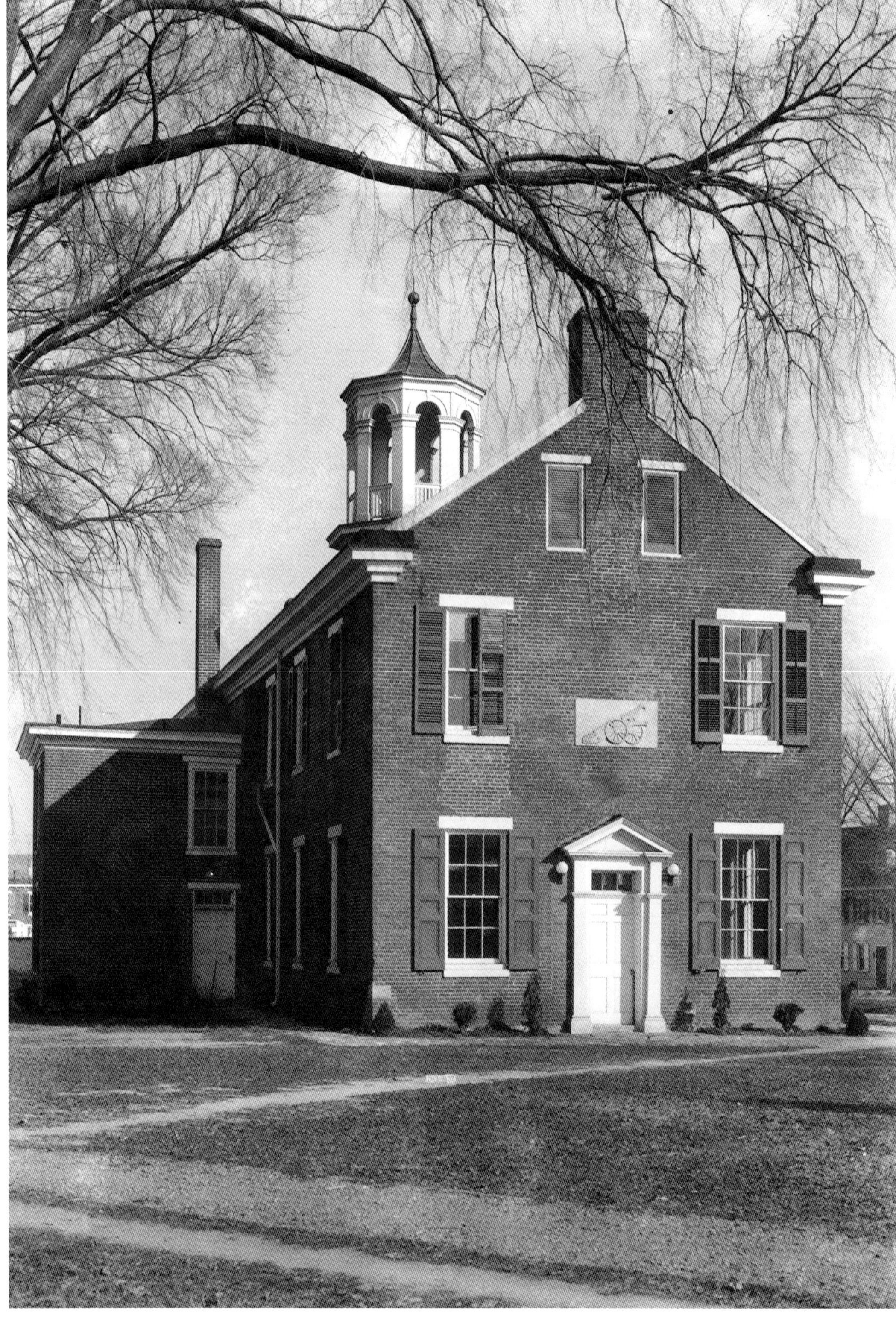

The Old Academy Building stands at Third and Harmony streets in New Castle. The academy was planned in 1772 as a "public seminary of learning." Philadelphia architect Peter Crowding designed the structure, which was built in 1798-99. It was a private school until 1852 when New Castle joined the state's public education system. It remained a public school until 1930. Today it is owned by Immanuel Episcopal Church.

The Delaware Hospital in Wilmington offered service to children in need of transportation to physical therapy sessions or doctor appointments. They could be picked up from school or home and transported in a wagon like this one. Here a nurse and driver pose with children at the hospital in 1934.

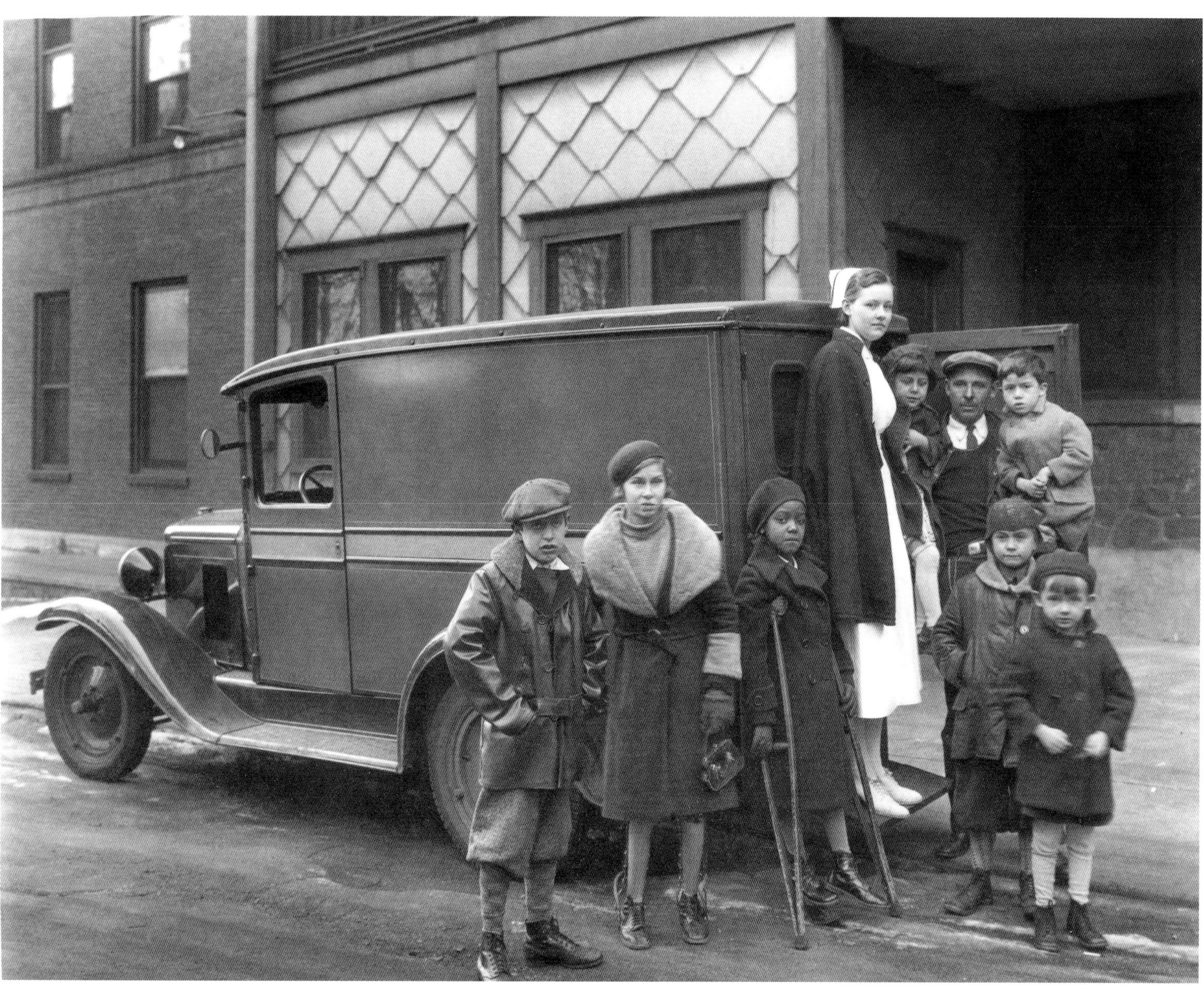

In 1933, a fierce fire destroyed the Lea Mills along the Brandywine River near Wilmington. This aerial view shows what the mills looked like before that fire. One of the early Brandywine mill companies, Lea Mills ground wheat and corn into flour. By 1922, the mill had moved to New Castle. When the fire broke out, every piece of apparatus in the city was called out to save the building, all to no avail.

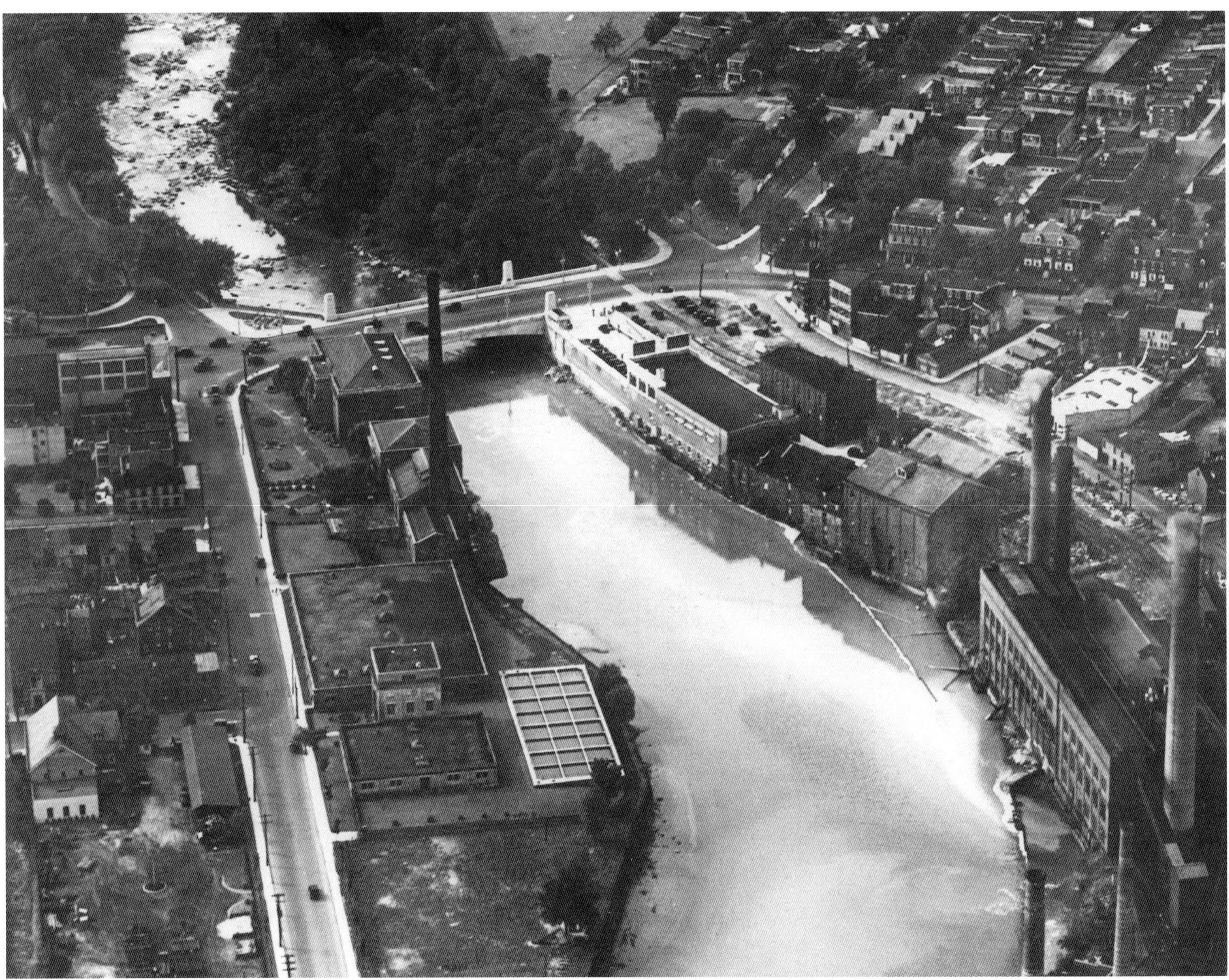

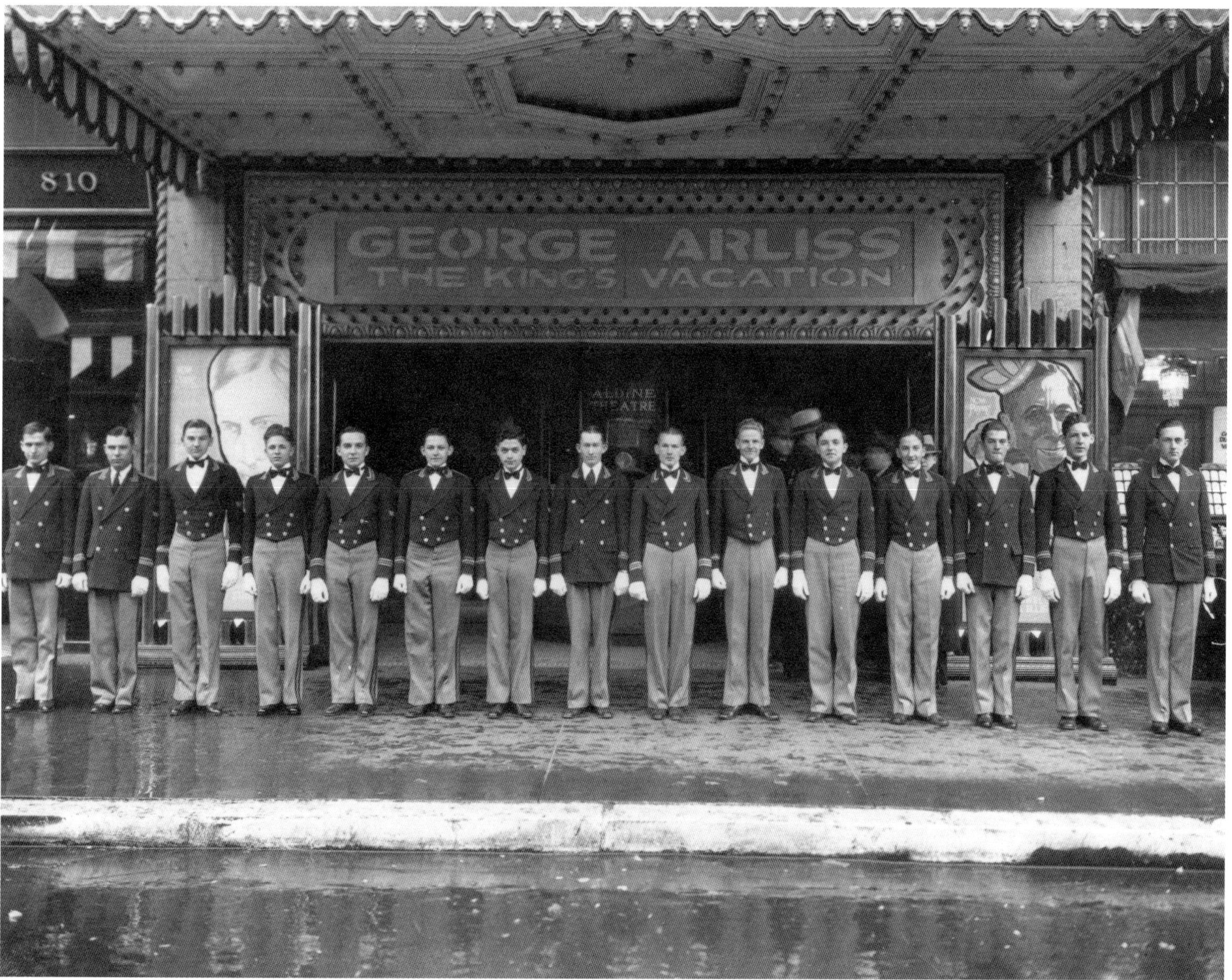

These dapper ushers stand outside the Aldine Theatre at 808 Market Street in 1933. During the heyday of the movies, Wilmington's Market Street had six theaters. This theater stood just a few doors away from the Grand Opera House.

Women sing and pray on French Street at the August Quarterly in 1939, a festival begun in 1814 by Peter Spencer, a founder of the Union Church of African Members. The Quarterly seeks to reunite family and friends, to host a religious revival, and to celebrate freedom. Before slavery was abolished, slaves and free blacks met together for the August Quarterly. The Quarterly continues today.

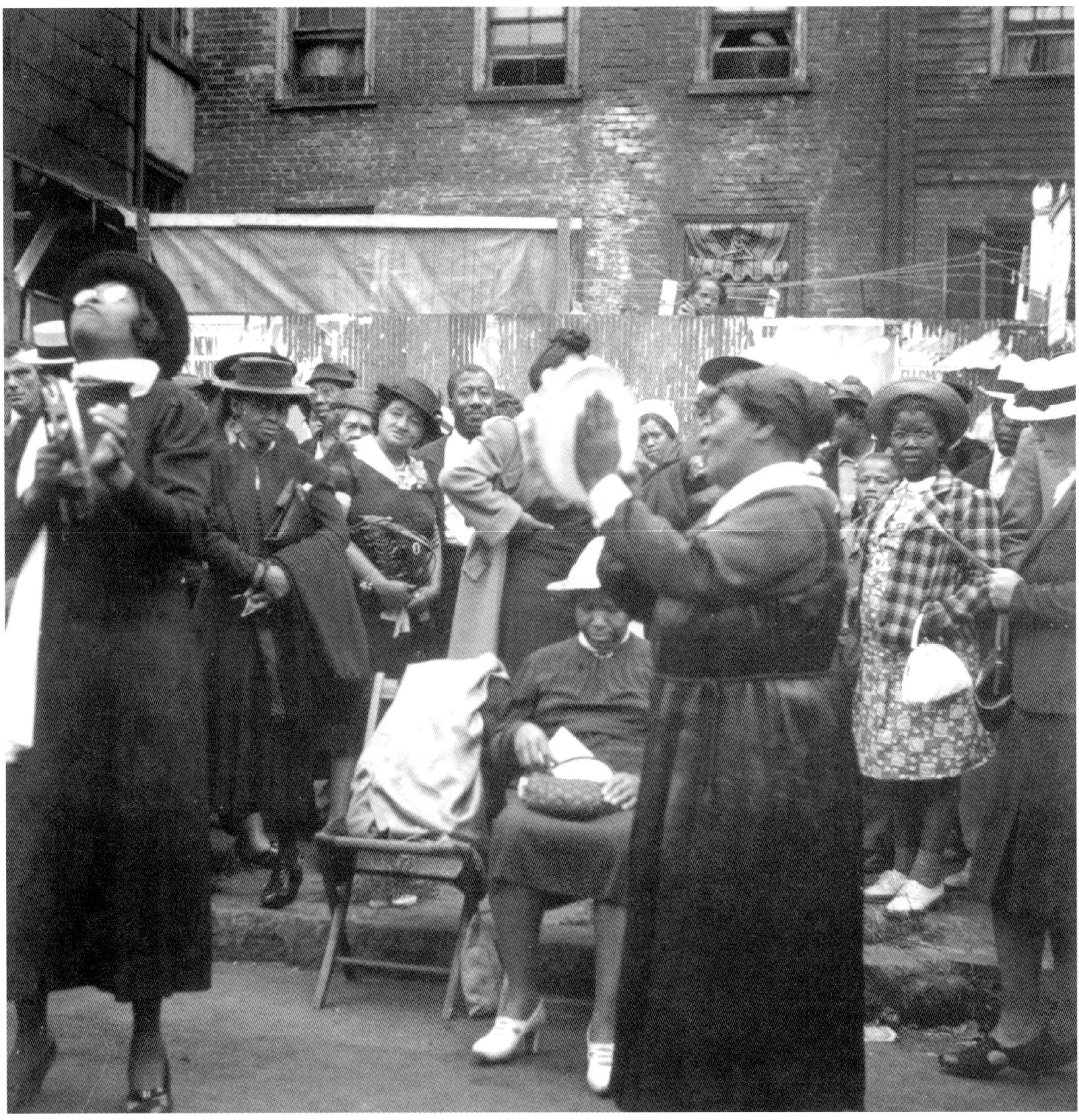

This aerial view shows how extensive H. P. Cannon and Sons in Bridgeville had grown by September 1936. In 1874, brothers Henry P. and Philip L. Cannon began farming together. In 1881, they opened a cannery in Bridgeville Station. They continued to raise crops and to can fruits and vegetables, becoming highly successful. After 100 years in business, the operation closed in 1981.

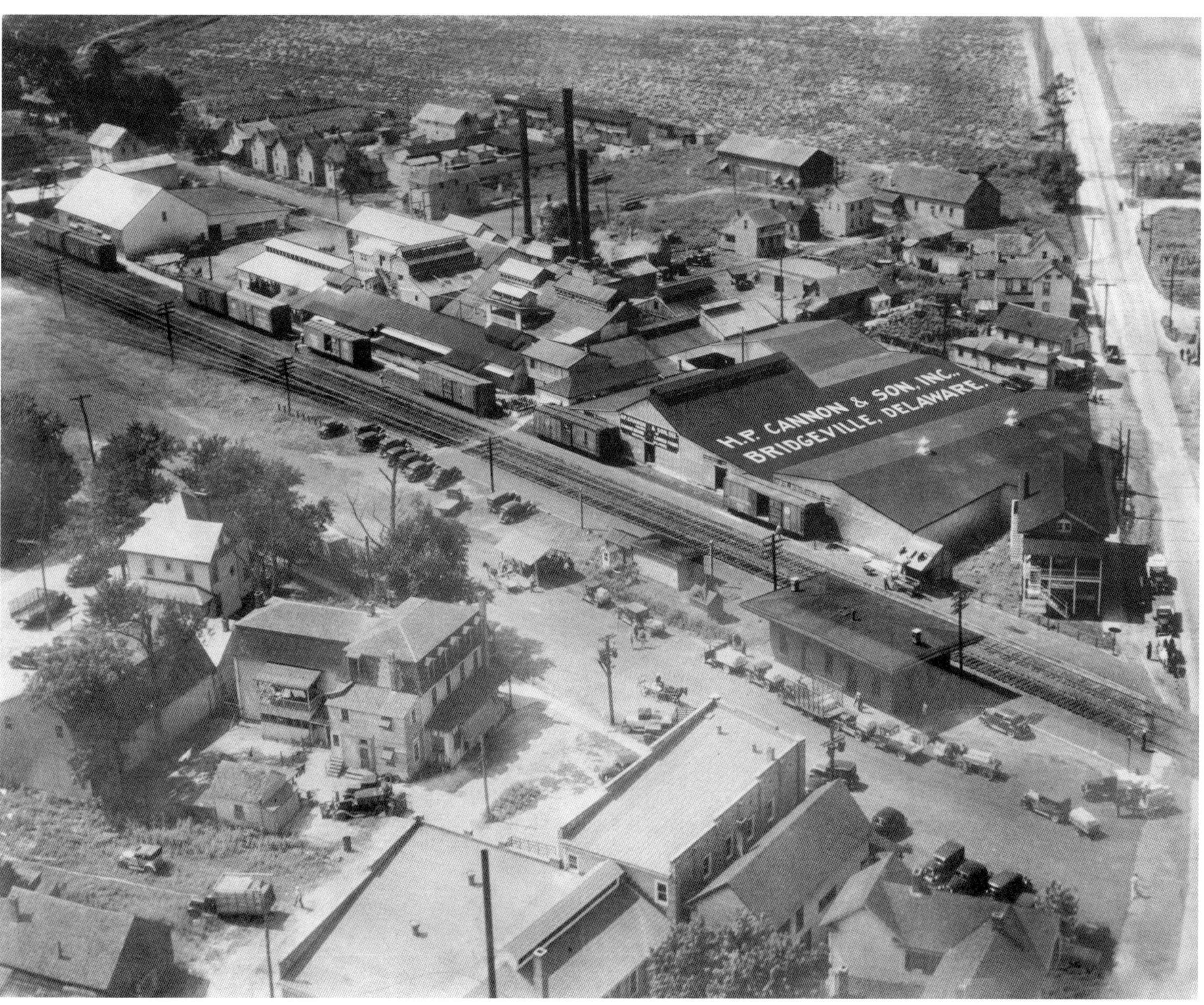

Wilmington is bustling with activity in this view south along Market Street, from the northeast corner of Market and 9th streets. At left is the Wilmington Savings Fund Society, beyond that is the sign for Rosenblum's Toy Store, and signs for the Grand and Lowes Aldine theaters are farther south. A "trackless trolley" provides transportation for locals, who would not be riding city buses until the 1950s.

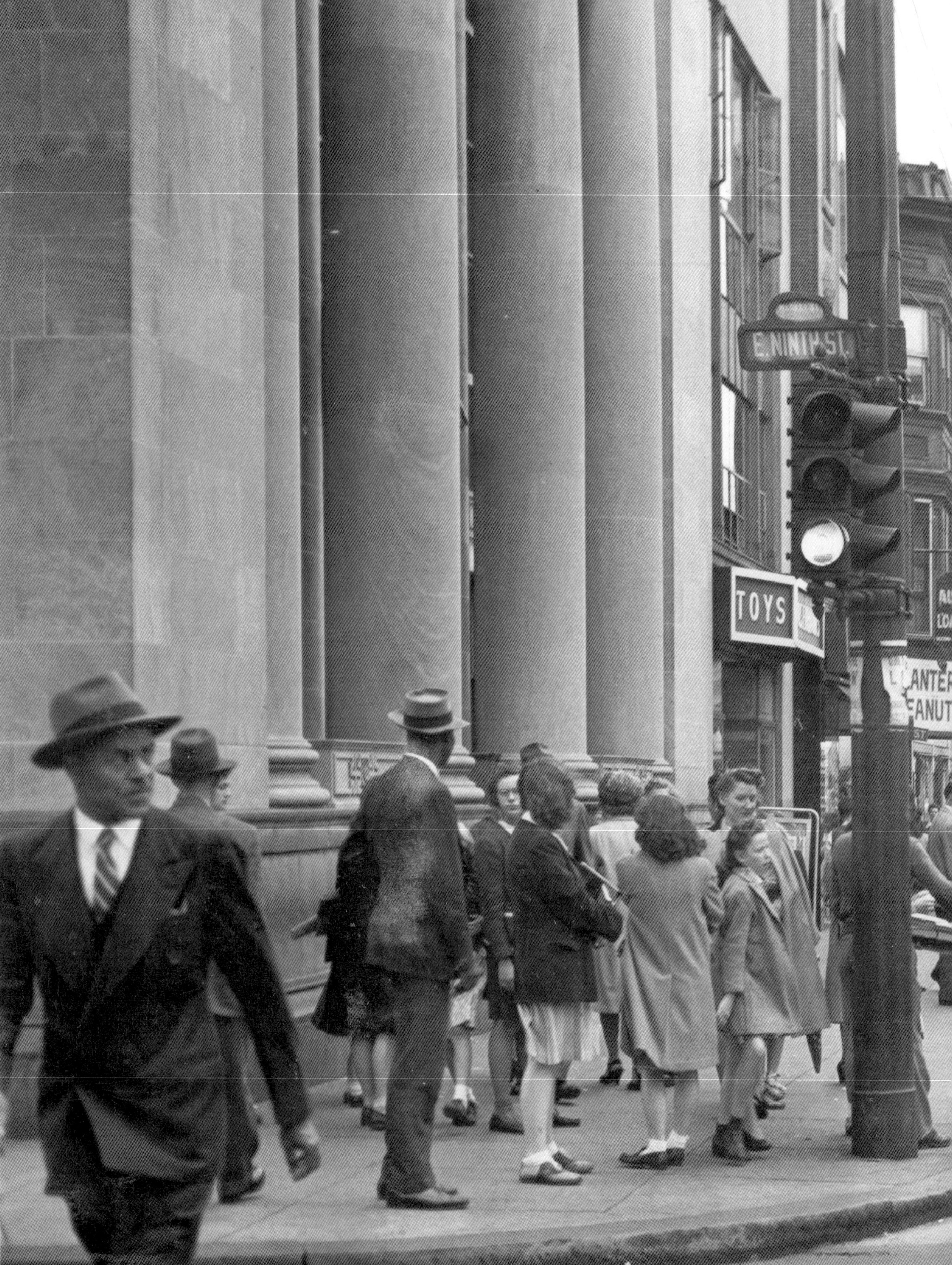

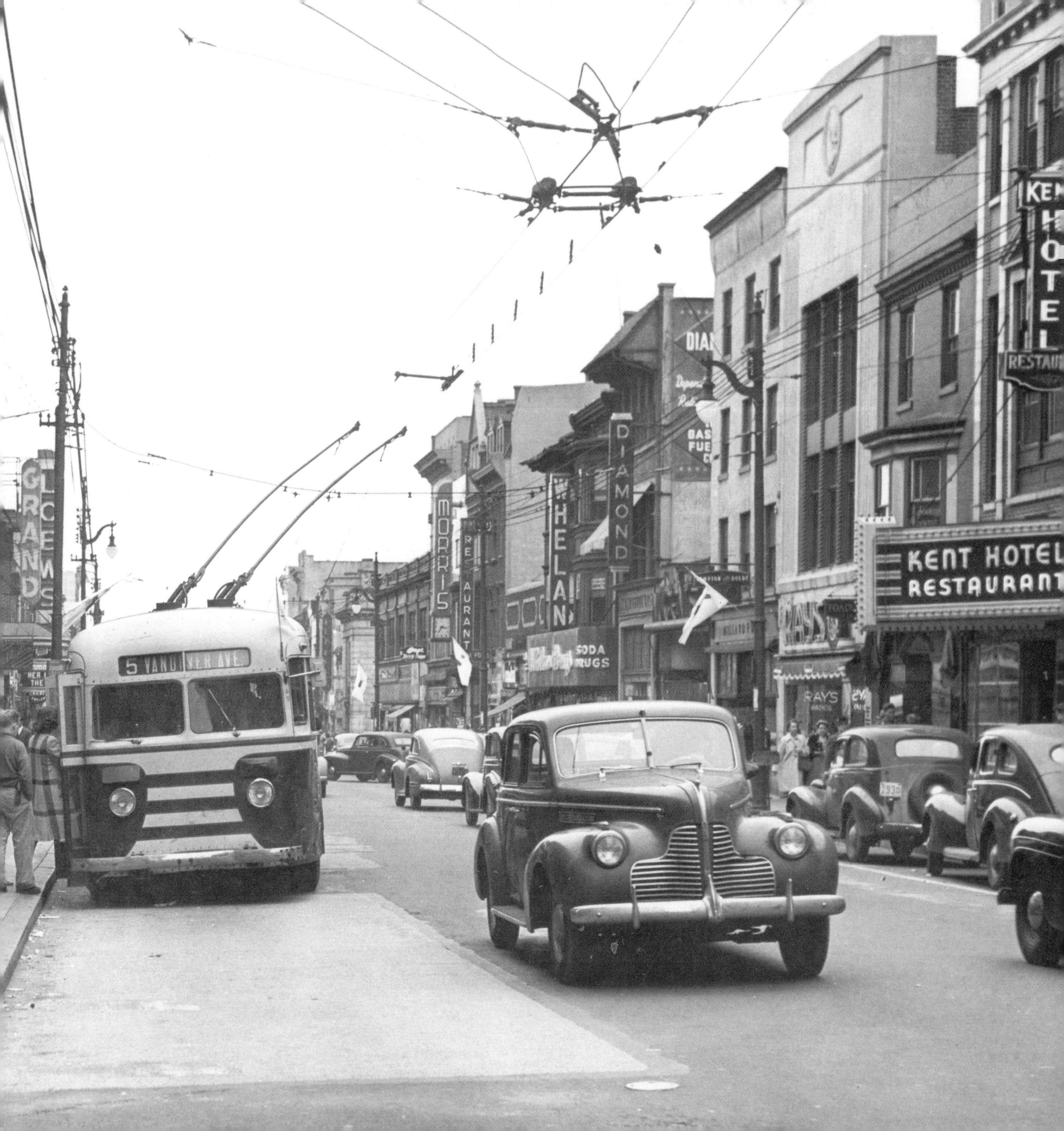
KENT HOTEL
RESTAURANT
DIAMOND
MORRIS
GRAND
LOEWS
SODA
RAYS

Race contestants assemble for the start near the Wilmington YMCA at 11th and Washington streets on May 18, 1935. This photograph was paid for by the American Legion and was taken for the *Evening Journal.*

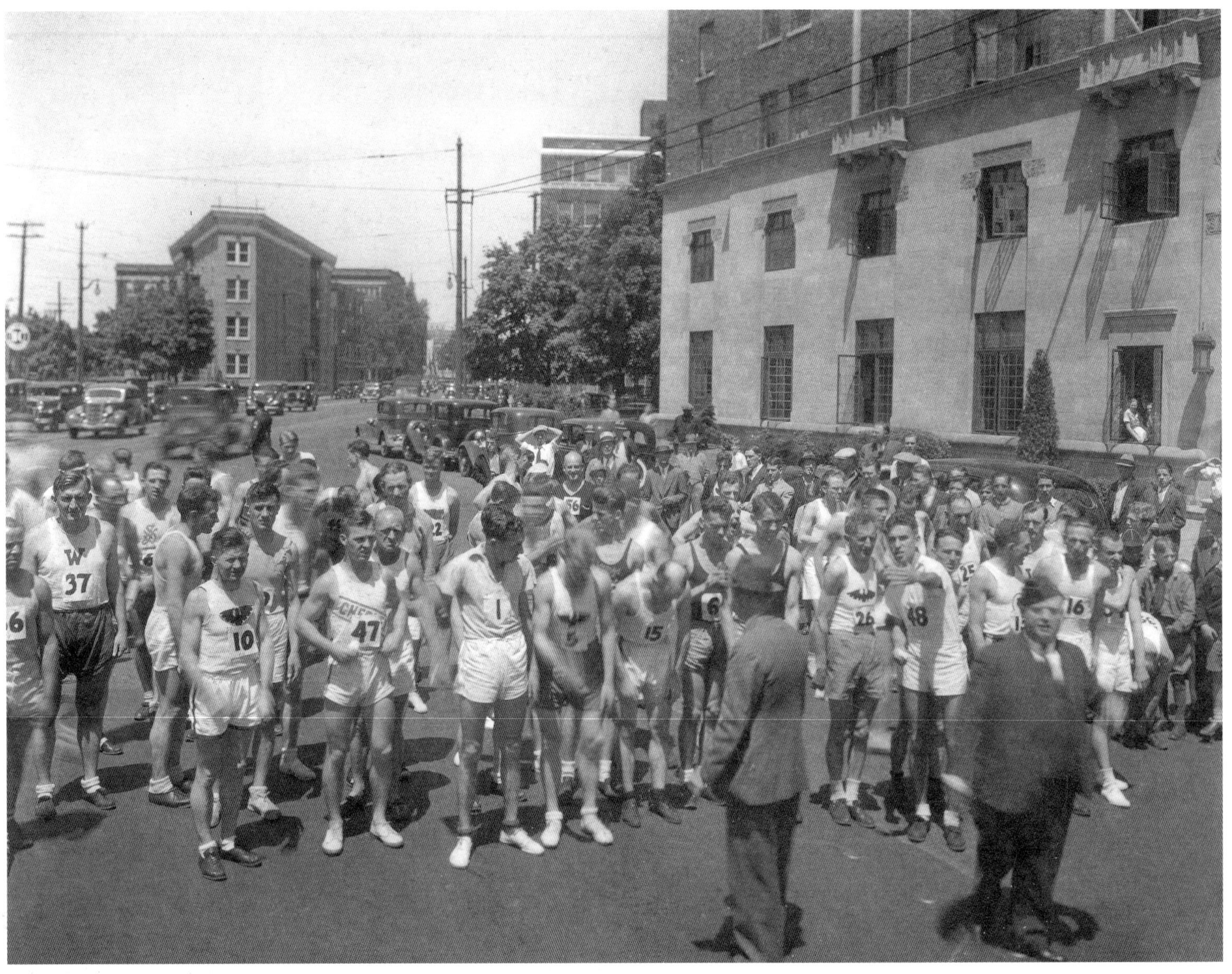

Oyster shells line the slip for this small, two-car ferry shown plying the waters of the Nanticoke River between Woodland and the road leading to Laurel. In 1930, an automobile engine was added to help power the boat, which still operates today. Before 1930, the ferryman had used long handles to pull the boat along a cable, which ran the width of the river. The ferryman, a state employee, lived in a state-owned house.

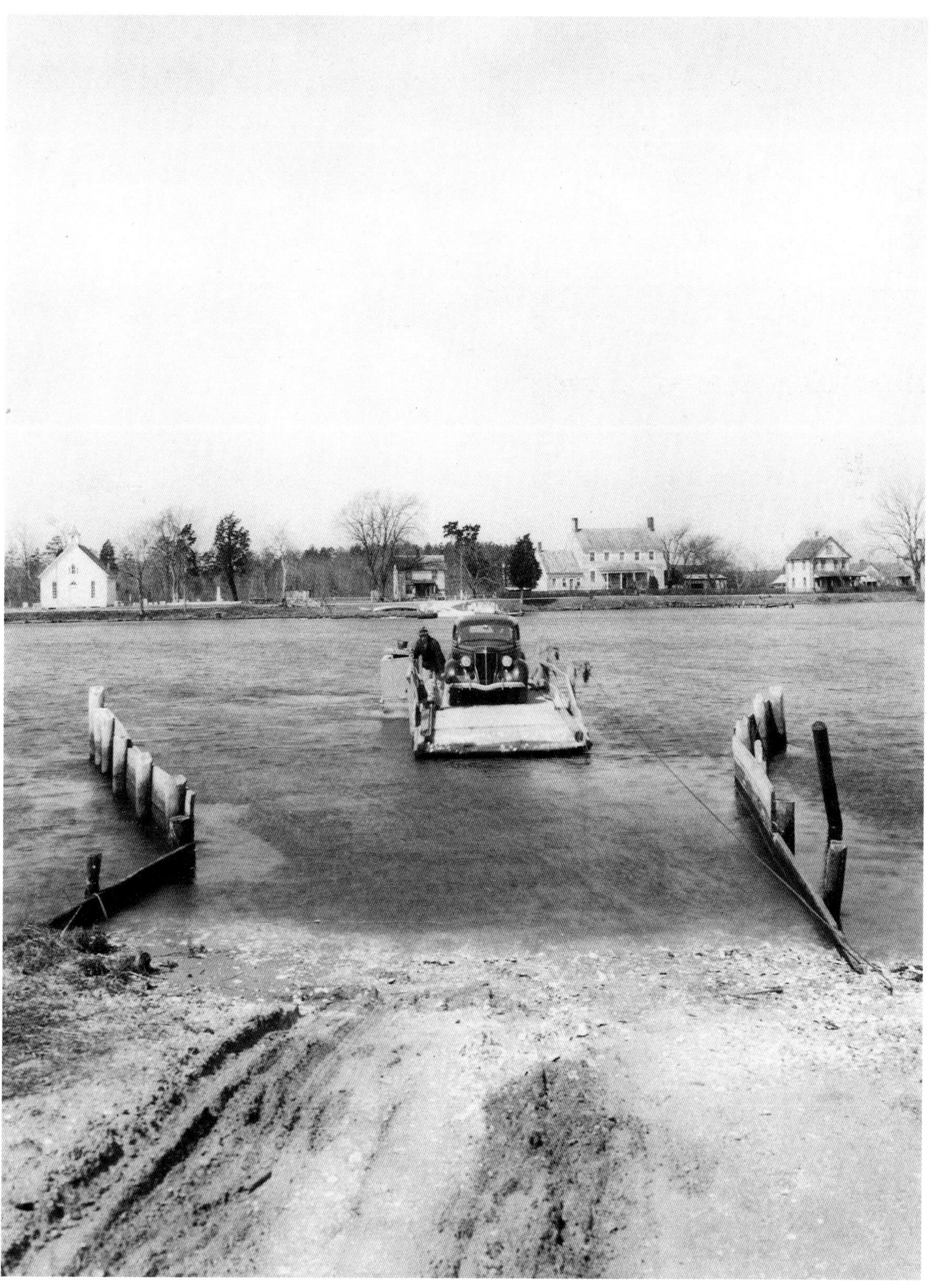

Dover celebrates its rich heritage and community each year on Dover Day. These ladies are performing around the Maypole on May 9, 1936. The celebration, which continues today, is centered on the Green near Legislative Hall.

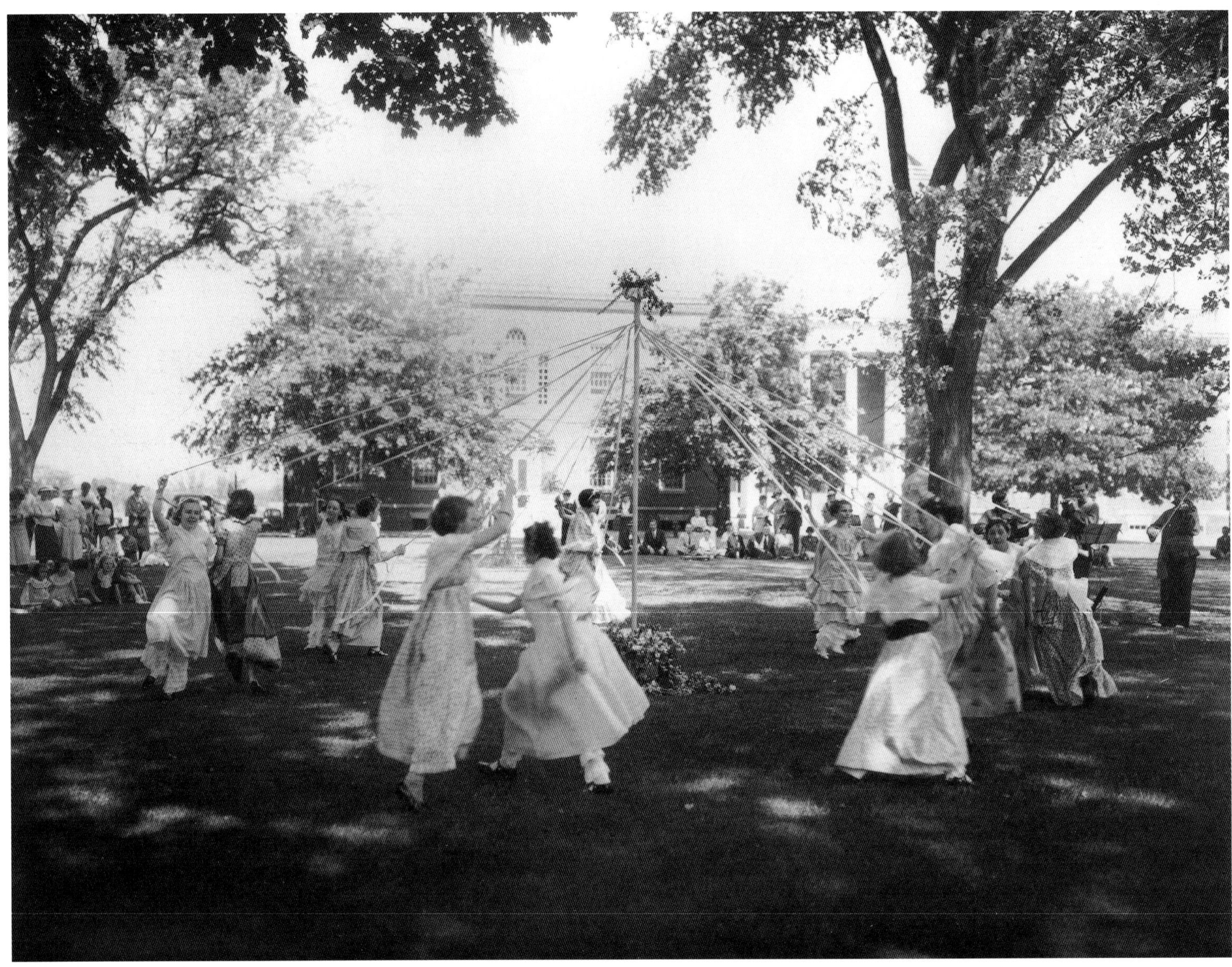

Shown here in the 1930s is the center of Middletown at the intersection of Main and Broad streets. At left, a lone gentleman poses at the corner of the five and dime store.

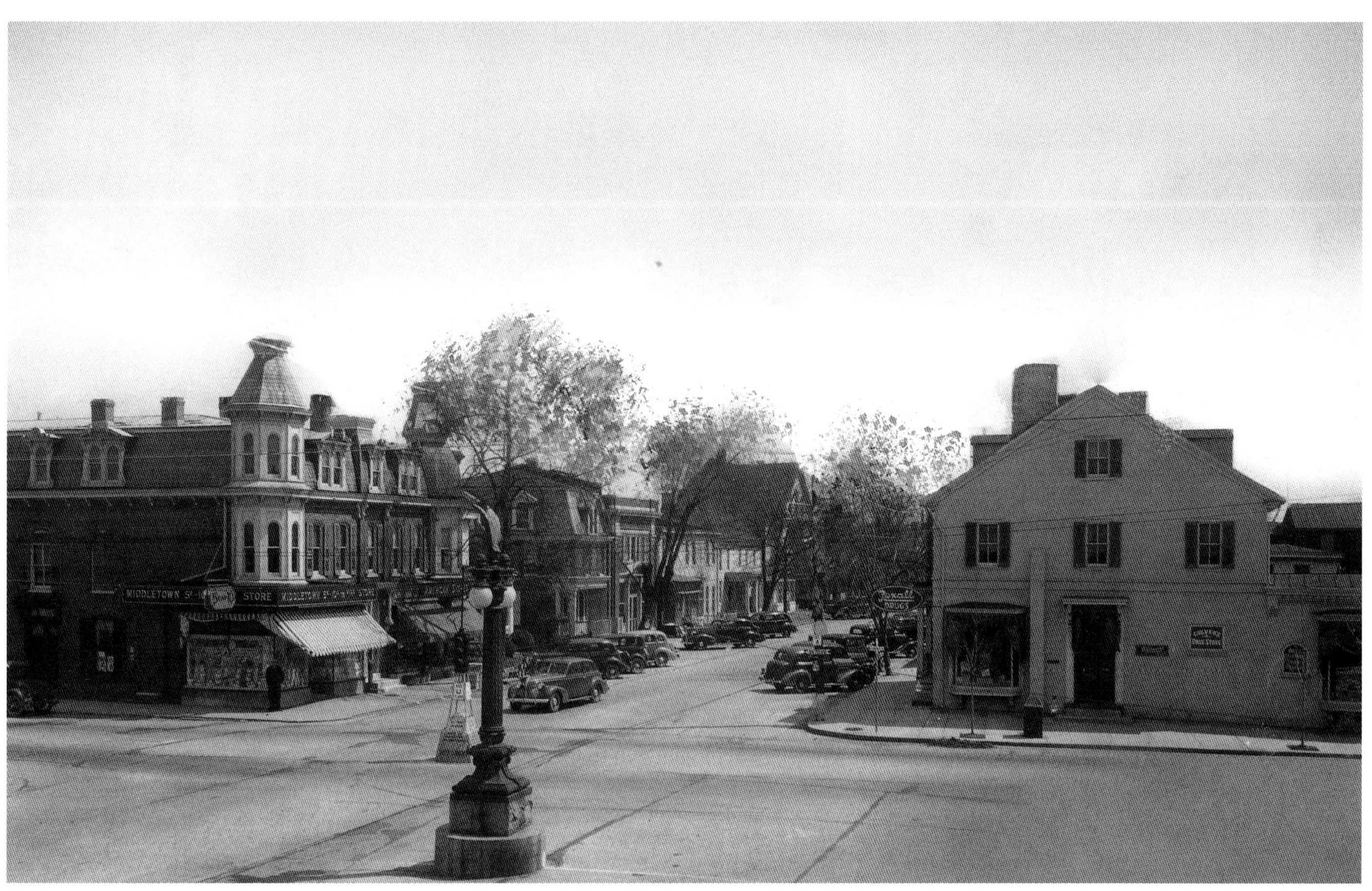

Before the United States entered World War II, Wilmington shipbuilders were fulfilling government contracts. This ship, built by Pusey and Jones, was a mine layer. It was launched in Wilmington on June 22, 1937. The plant was located at East Front and Poplar streets along the Christina River.

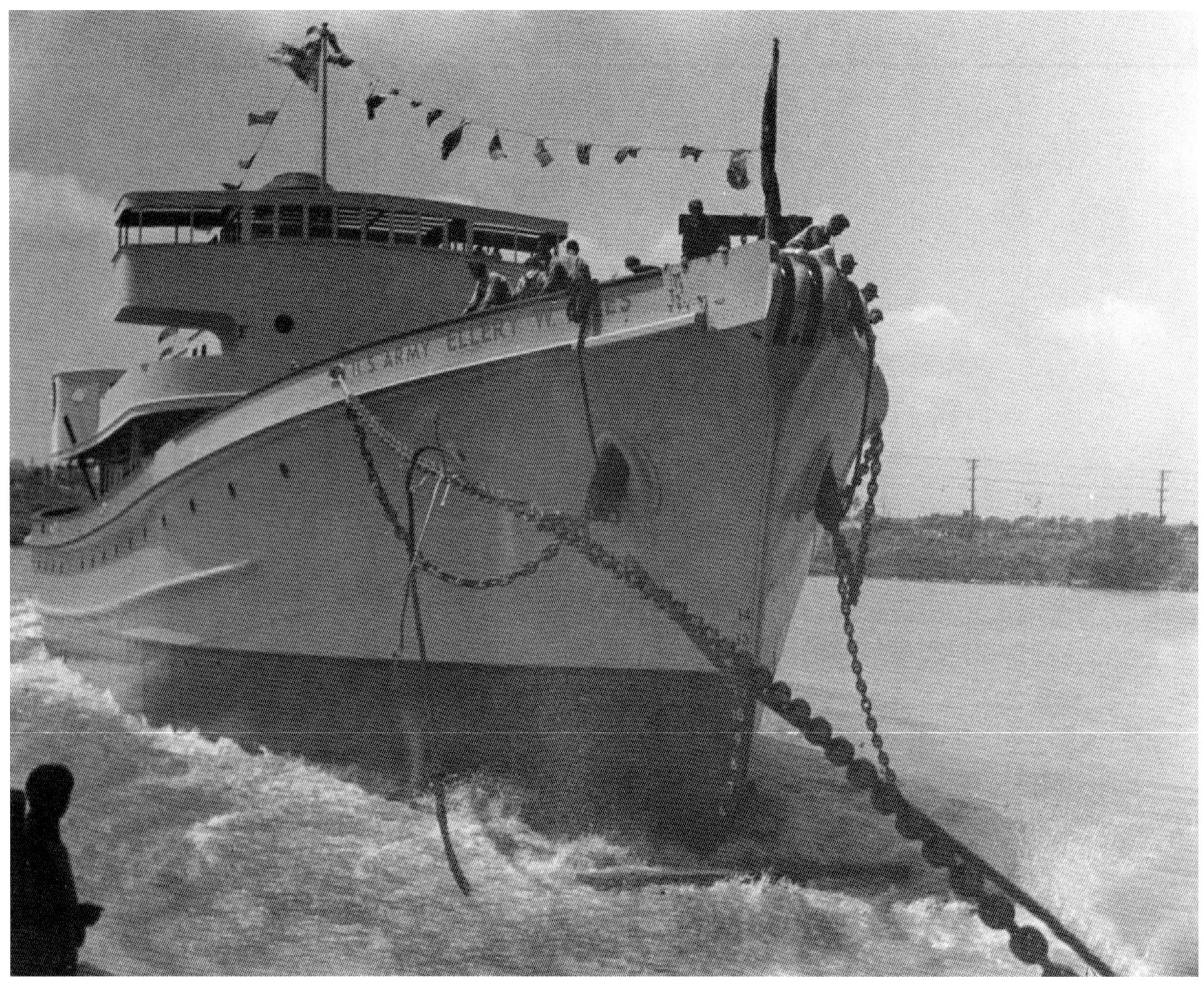

Four barbers pose at their chairs inside Burton's Tonsorial Parlor at 801 Walnut Street in Wilmington. Claude E. Burton owned this shop in 1939.

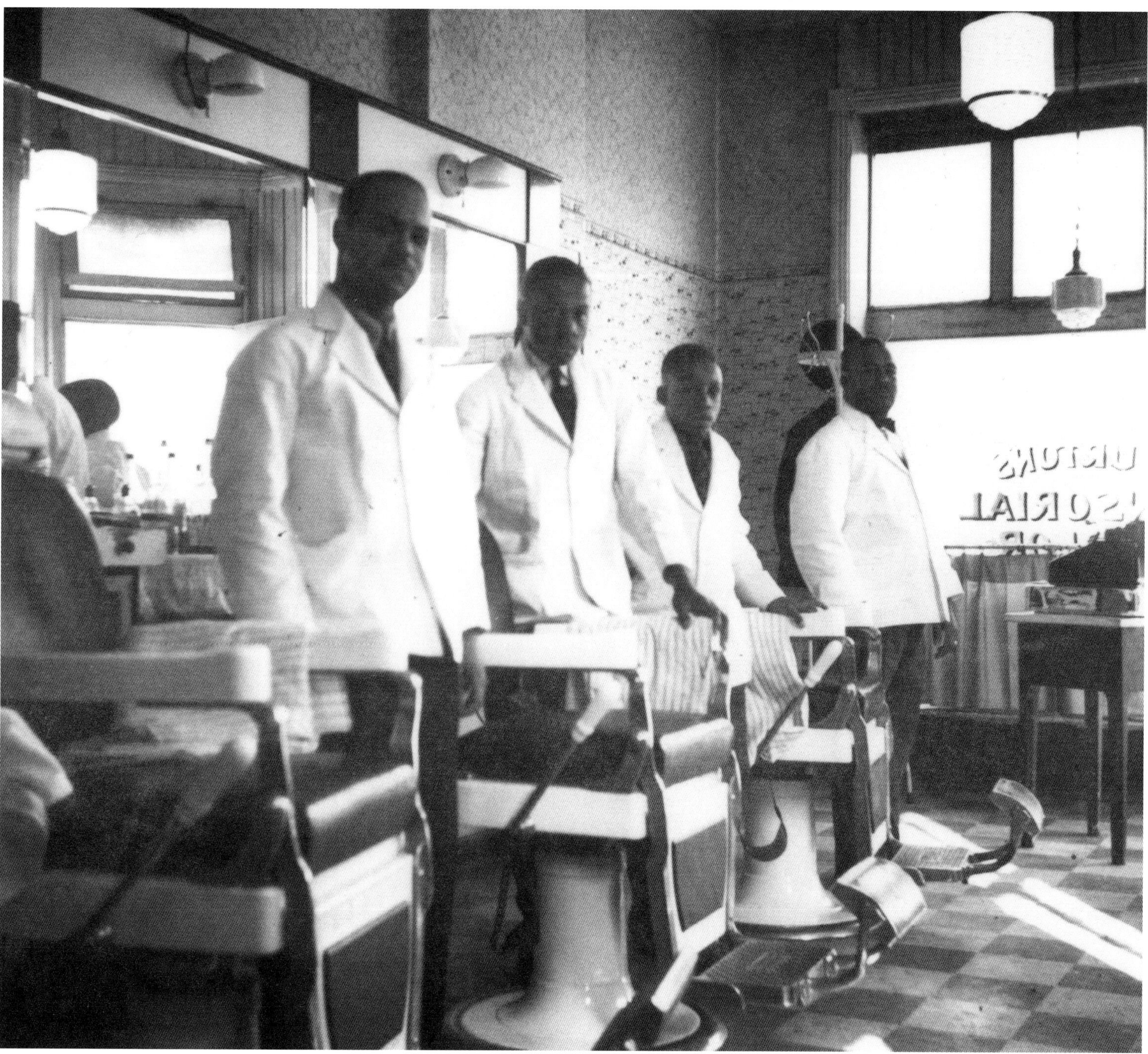

The first stop for farmers bringing peppers to H. P. Cannon's in Bridgeville for canning was the Government Inspection Shed. Every load of produce was sample-tested here for richness of color, quality, weight, and appearance.

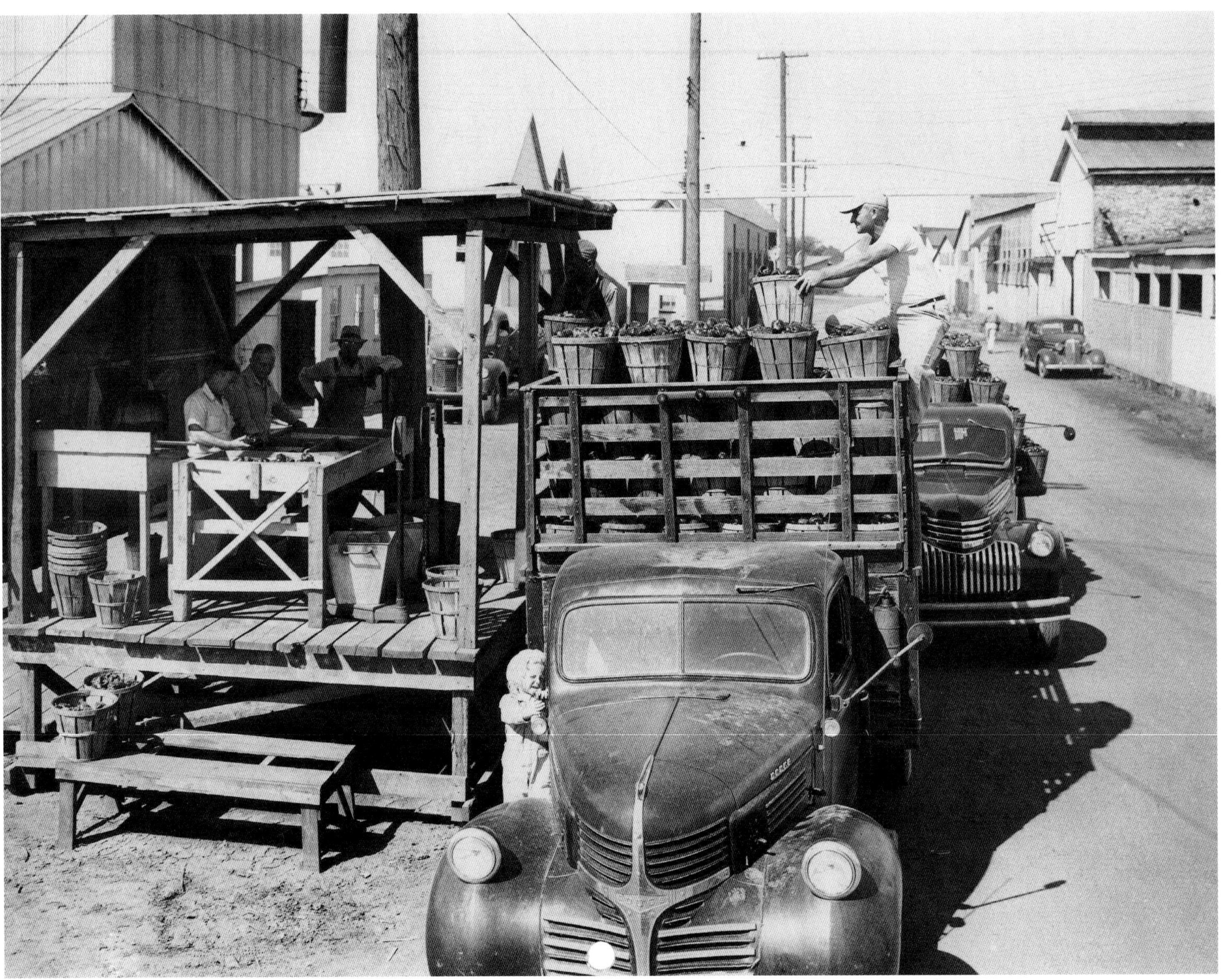

Cannon's employed a large number of women at the cannery, seen here sorting green beans. At far-right is what must have seemed to them an endless supply of beans.

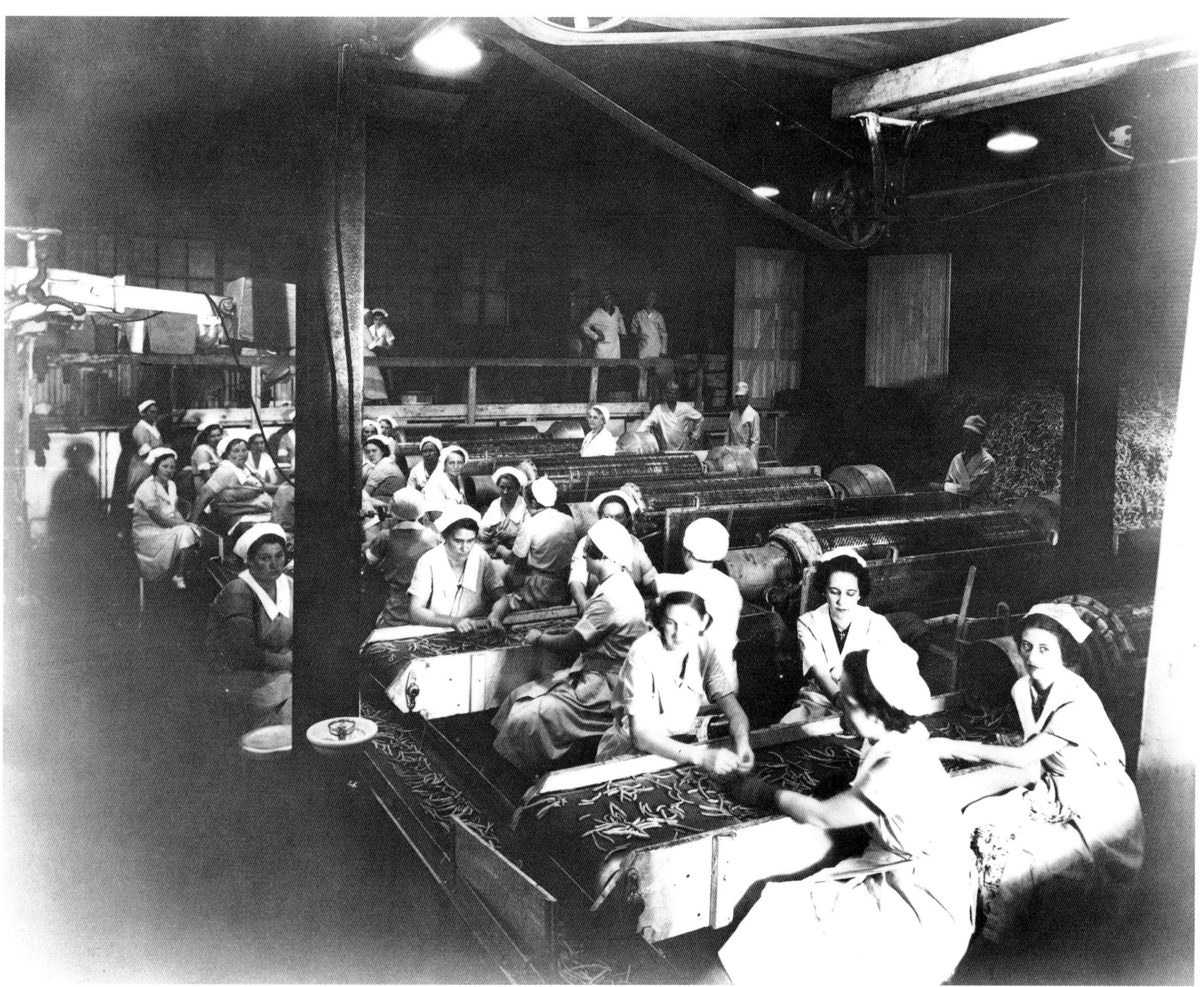

Governor C. Douglass Buck (seated at front) presides over the unveiling of the statues of Caesar Rodney and John M. Clayton in National Statuary Hall at the United States Capitol in June 1934. In 1870, it was decided that each state should be represented in the hall. State Archivist and University of Delaware Professor George Ryden is shown speaking to the 300 people assembled about Rodney, and Congressman Robert Houston of Georgetown spoke about Clayton.

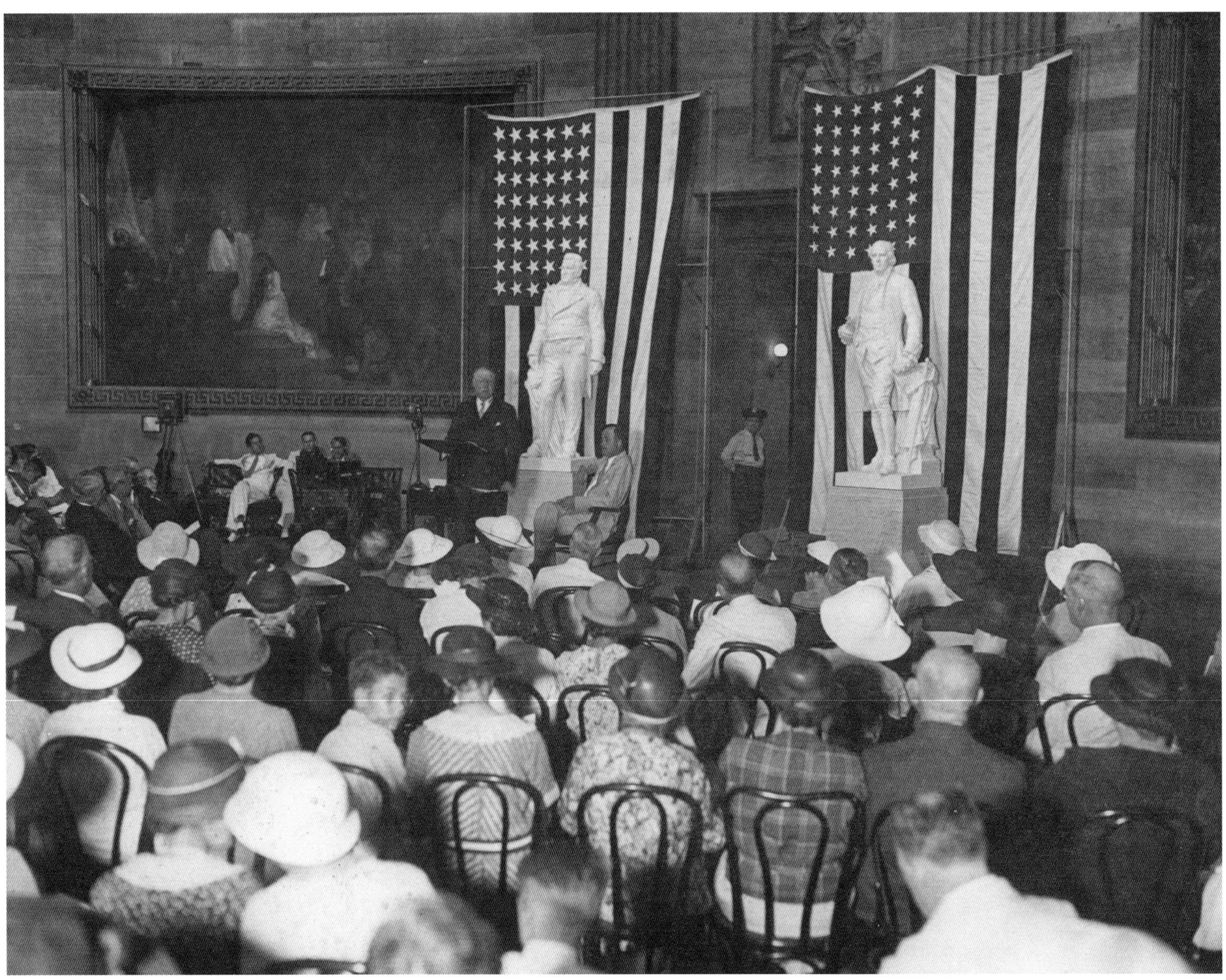

The Nursery School Committee and the children of the Works Progress Administration nursery school take a moment to pose for a photograph on June 10, 1938. During the Great Depression, the WPA offered services to America's smallest citizens, too. This nursery school met at the American Legion Log Cabin in Seaford.

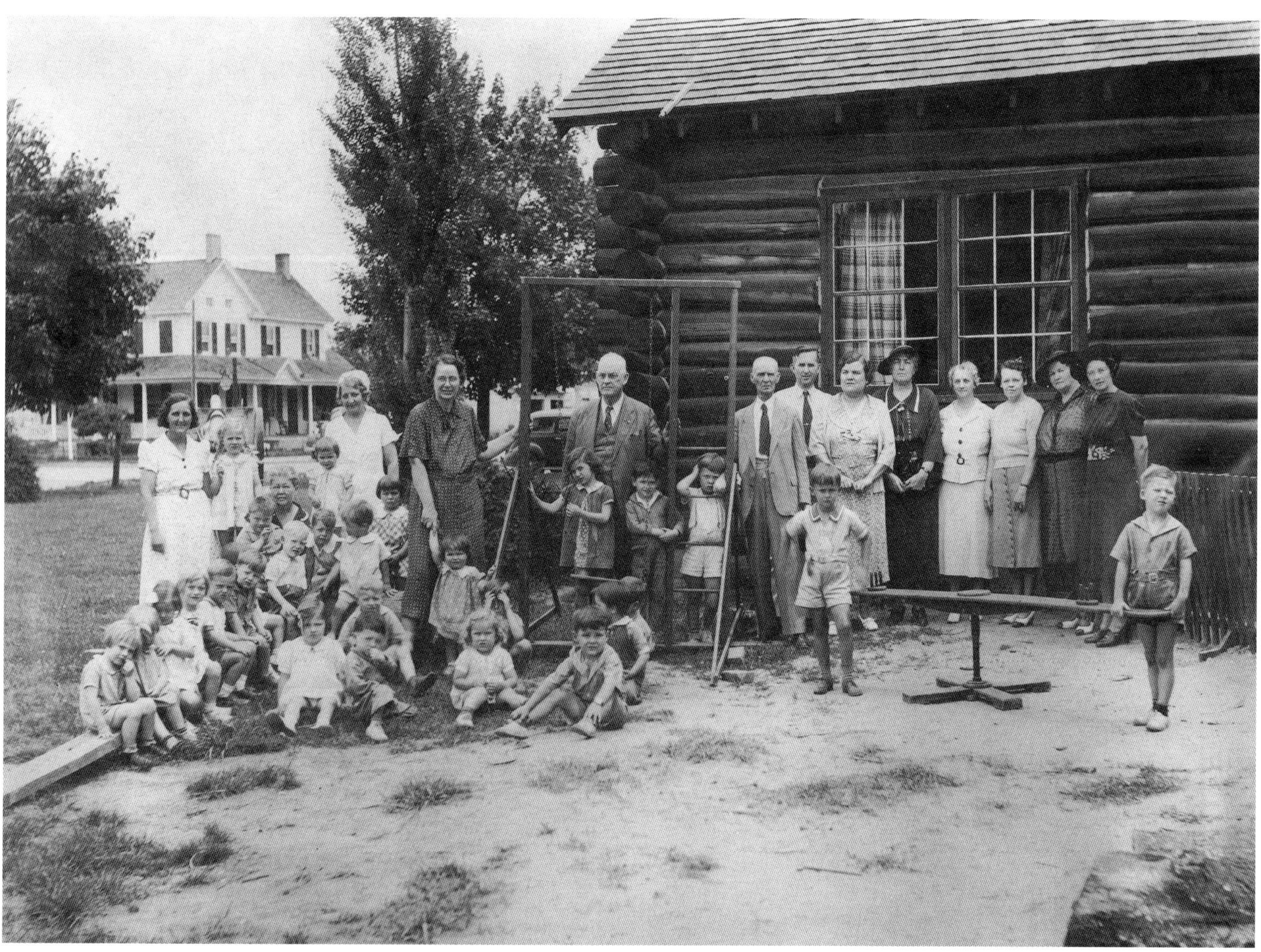

Estella Hodges, left, stands with the hairdressers in her shop, Estella's Beauty Salon, at 819 Poplar Street in Wilmington in April 1939.

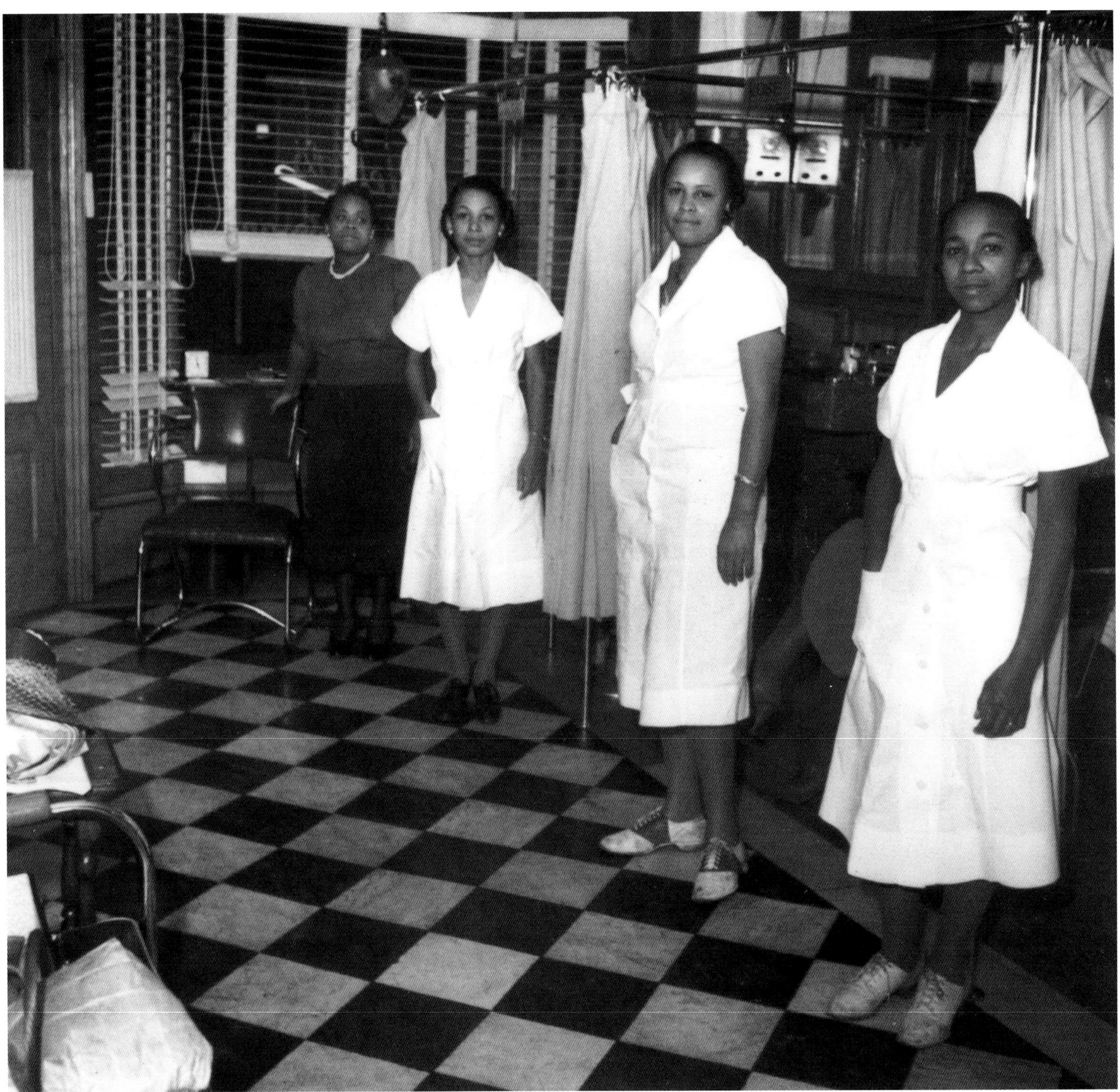

The tiny town of Christiana was overcome by floodwaters in June and July 1938. Here a number of people have gathered to watch and hope that traffic can get through.

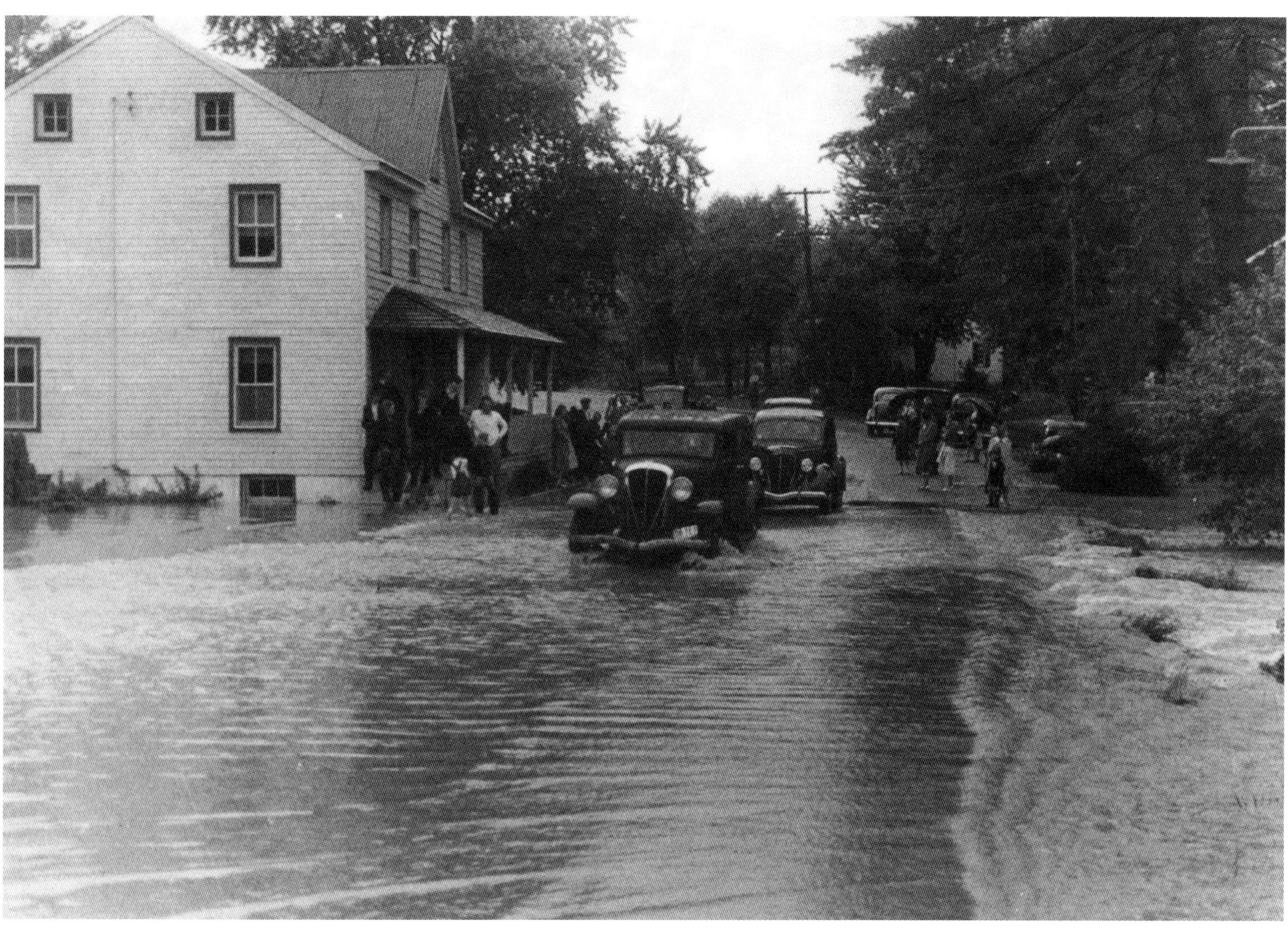

A classic roadside stop, the School Bell Colonial Court was located along the DuPont Highway. Unfortunately, it has long since disappeared from the roadway.

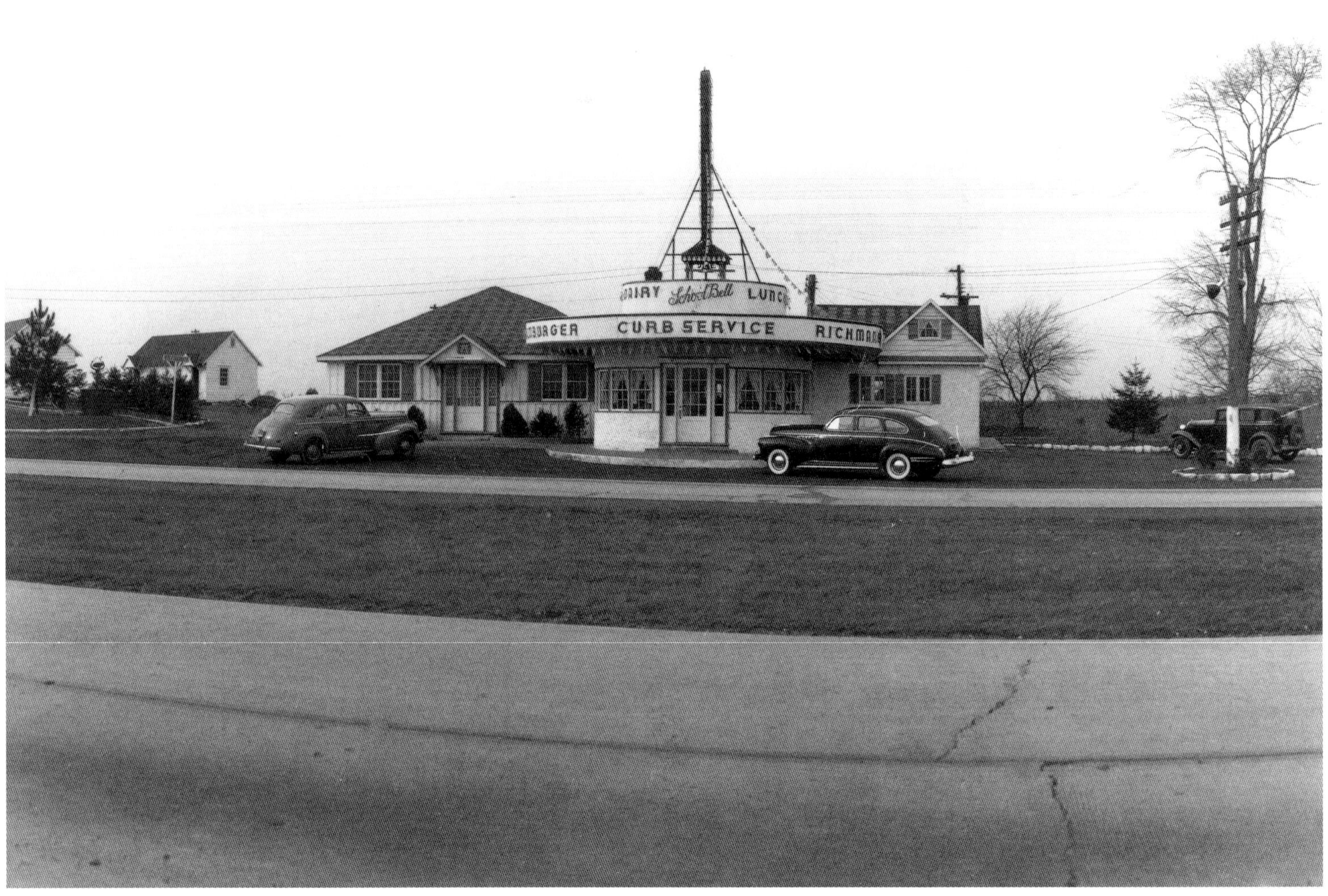

Photographer Arthur Rothstein captured this unusual situation as he traveled along Route 40 in the spring of 1939.

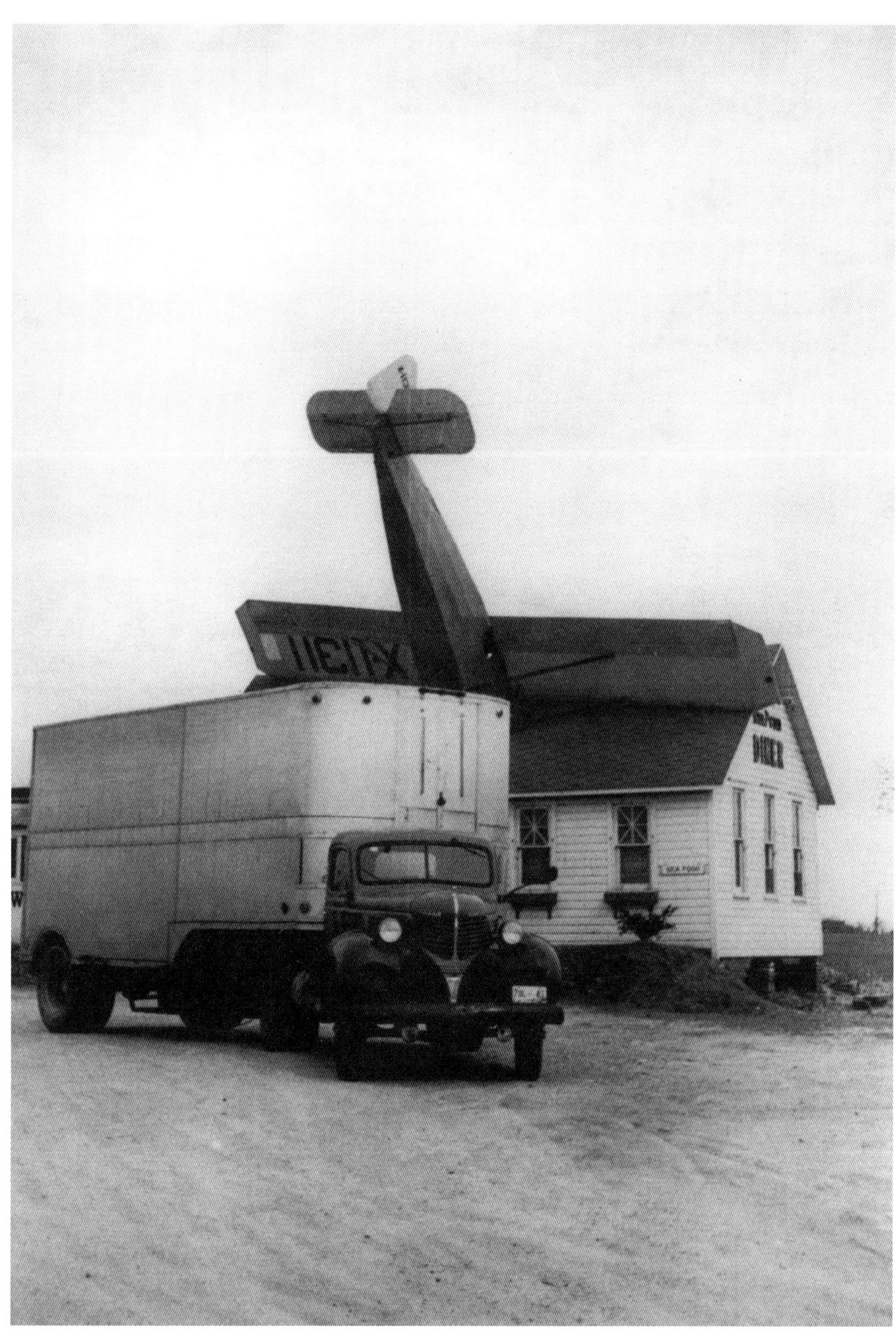

Warner Brothers executives accompany actress Bette Davis on board a special train in 1939. Davis and many other celebrities traveled to Wilmington during the 1930s and 1940s to promote their movies.

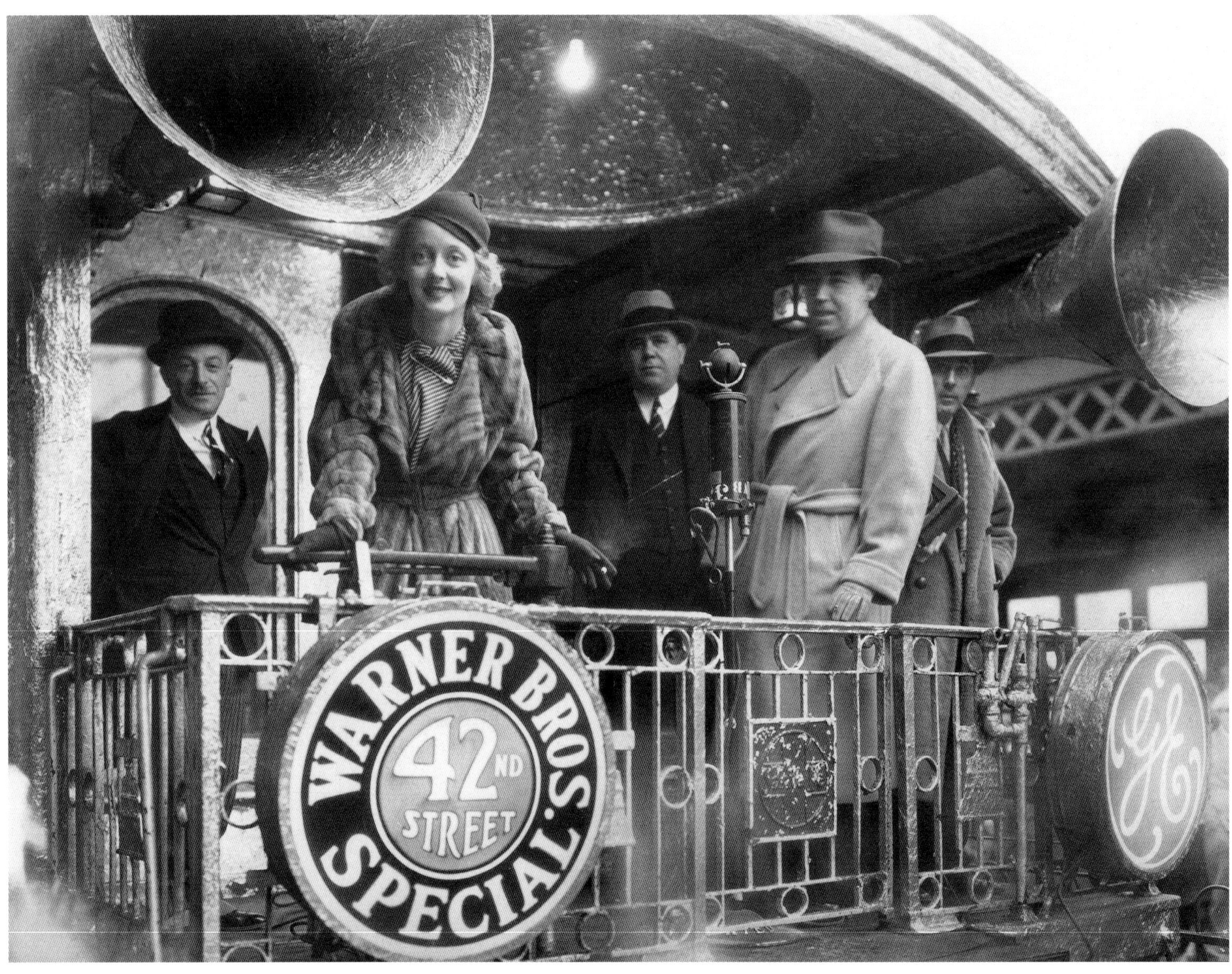

To help boost civic pride, fire fighters put on displays of their apparatus for the public. This display at Rodney Square probably drenched most of the people in attendance, including those gathered on the steps of the City-County Building.

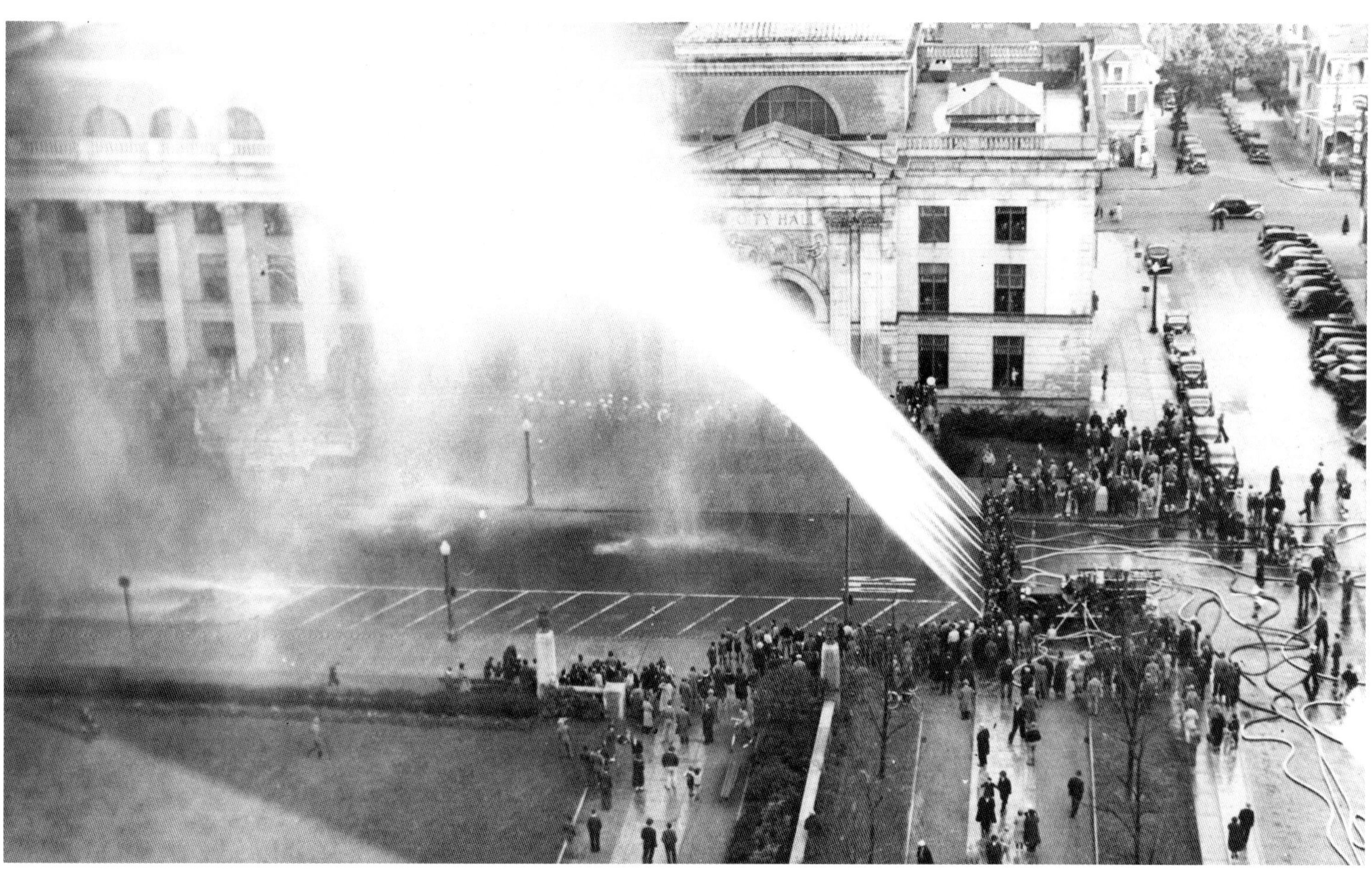

A view north along the 800 block of French Street past the facade of the National Theater. Before the desegregation of public facilities, the National was the only theater for African Americans in Wilmington. Owner John O. Hopkins rented out the upper floors for social events for the African American community.

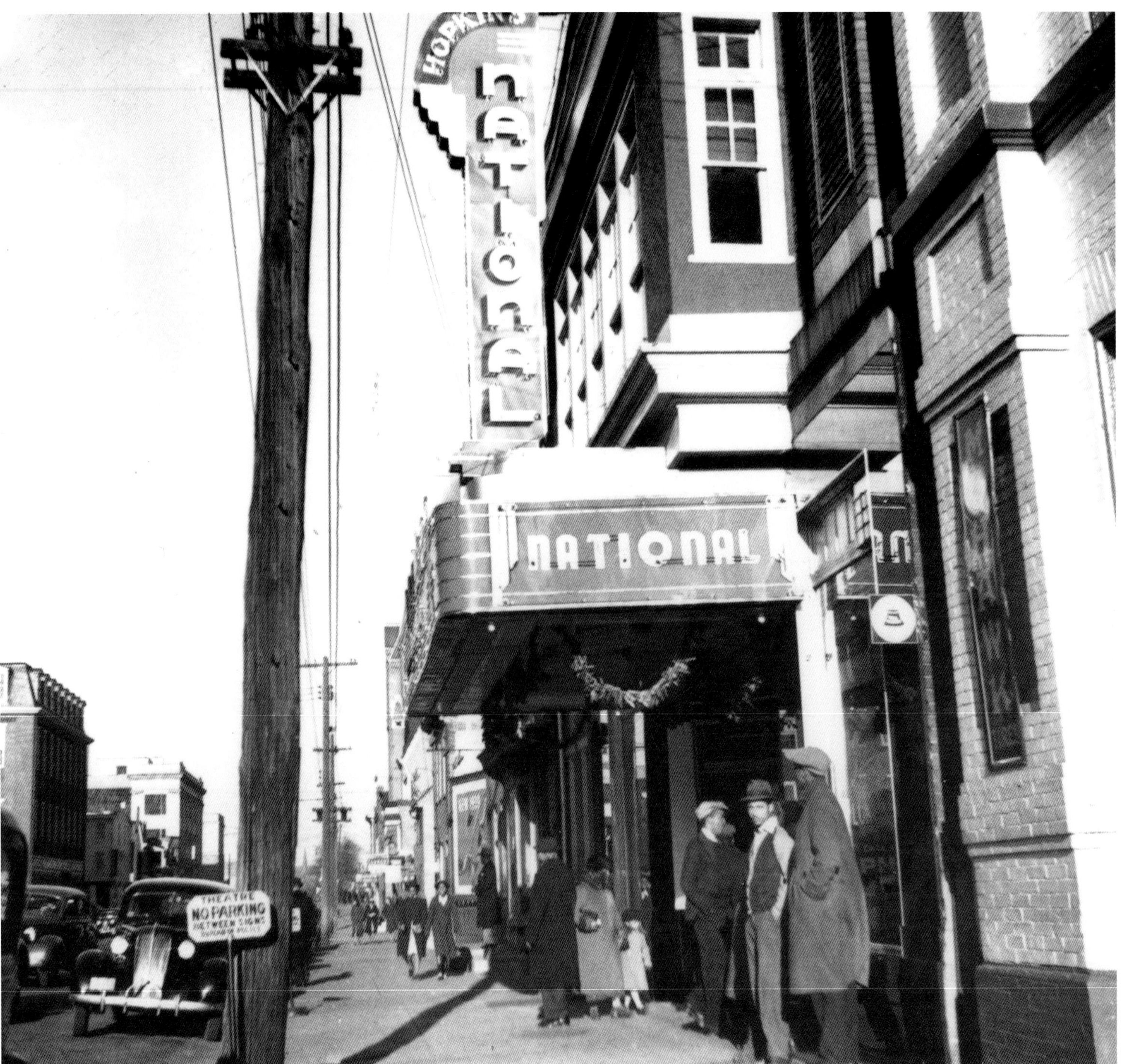

Wendell Willkie campaigned in Wilmington on October 31, 1940, during his bid for the presidency. To help boost his appeal, especially in the African American community, he recruited heavyweight boxing champion Joe Louis to campaign with him. Here Louis and Willkie address a crowd that has gathered along the 700 block of French Street.

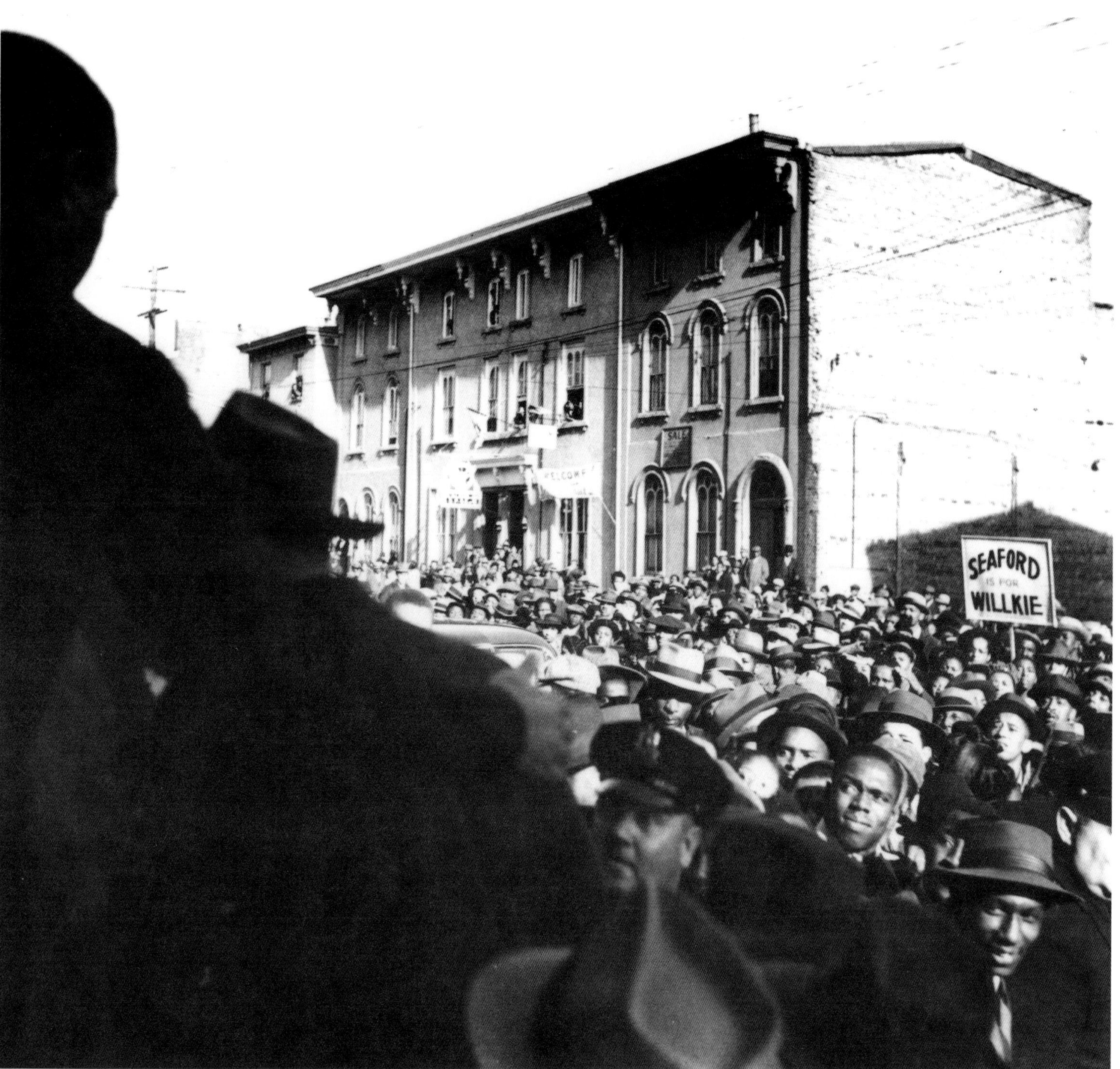

In 1940, trolley lines still mark the street in front of the Aldine Theatre, where Bela Lugosi is starring in *The Human Monster.* At this point in its history, the Grand Opera House next door had also become a movie theater.

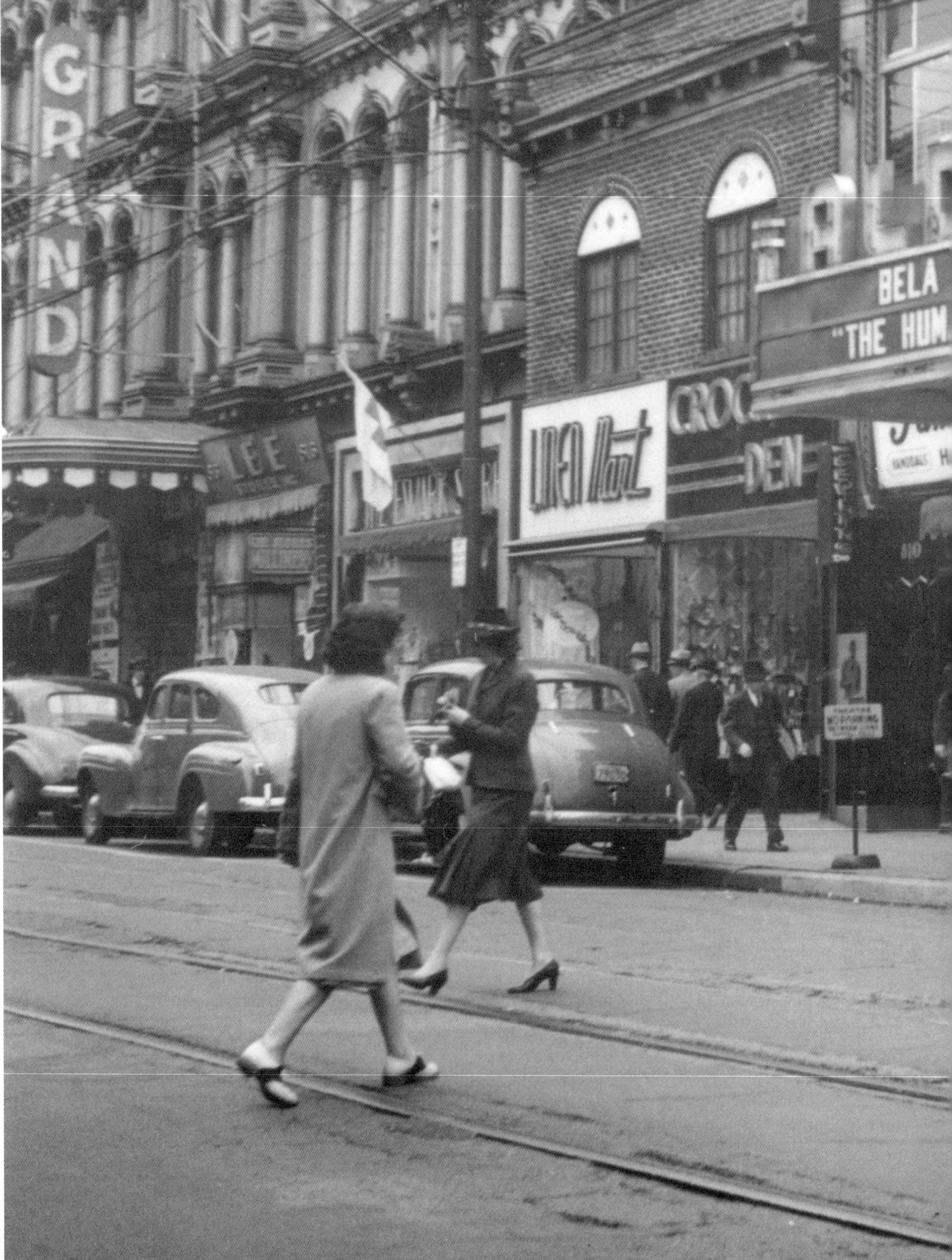

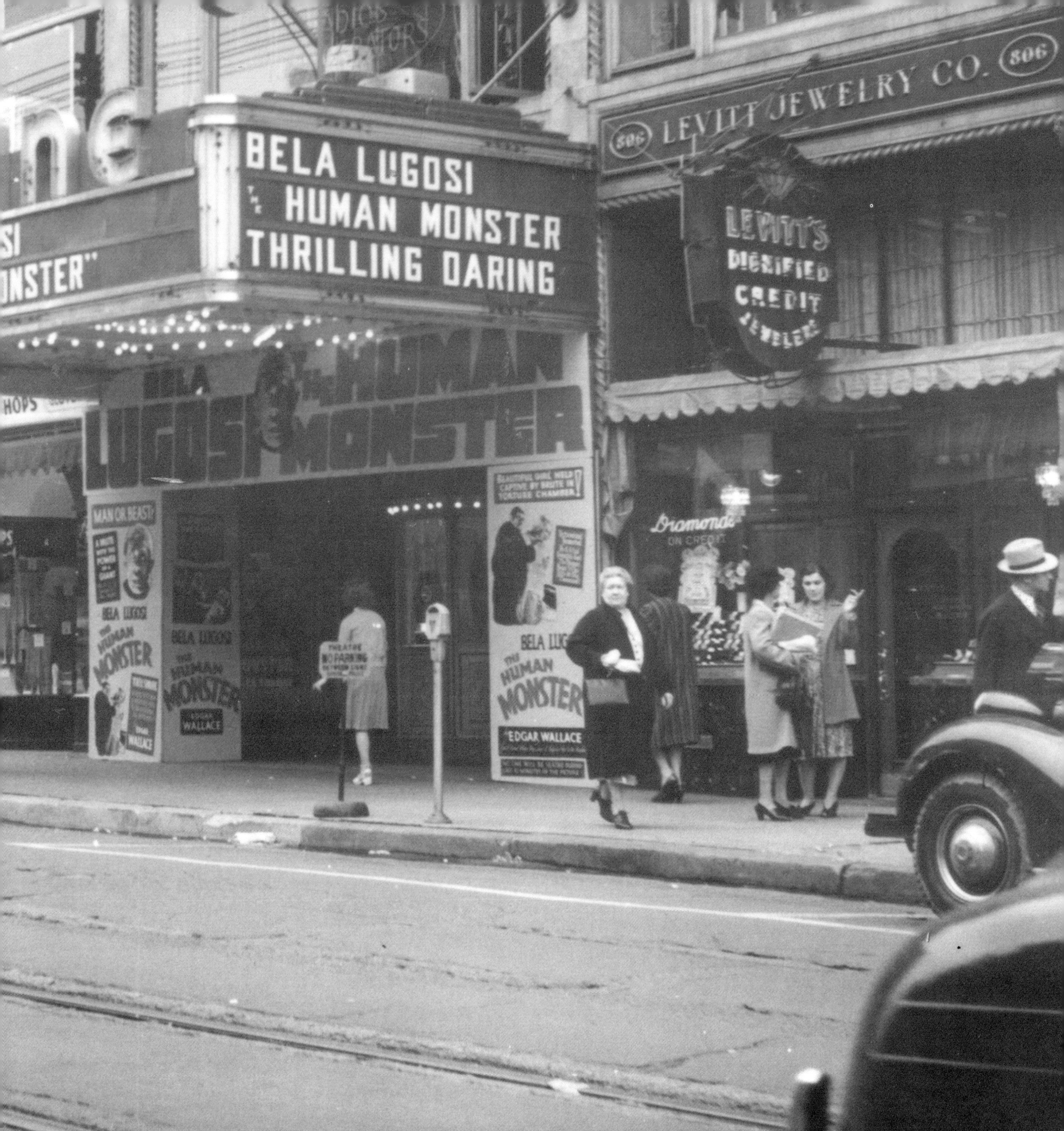

BELA LUGOSI
HUMAN MONSTER
THRILLING DARING
LEVITT JEWELRY CO.
806
806
LEVITT'S
DIGNIFIED
CREDIT
JEWELERS
BELA
LUGOSI
HUMAN
MONSTER
MAN OR BEAST
BELA LUGOSI
THE HUMAN MONSTER
BELA LUGOSI
THE HUMAN MONSTER
THEATRE
NO PARKING
BELA LUGOSI
THE HUMAN MONSTER
EDGAR WALLACE
Diamonds
ON CREDIT

The boardwalk of Bethany Beach is shown here on a hot and quiet day in the 1940s.

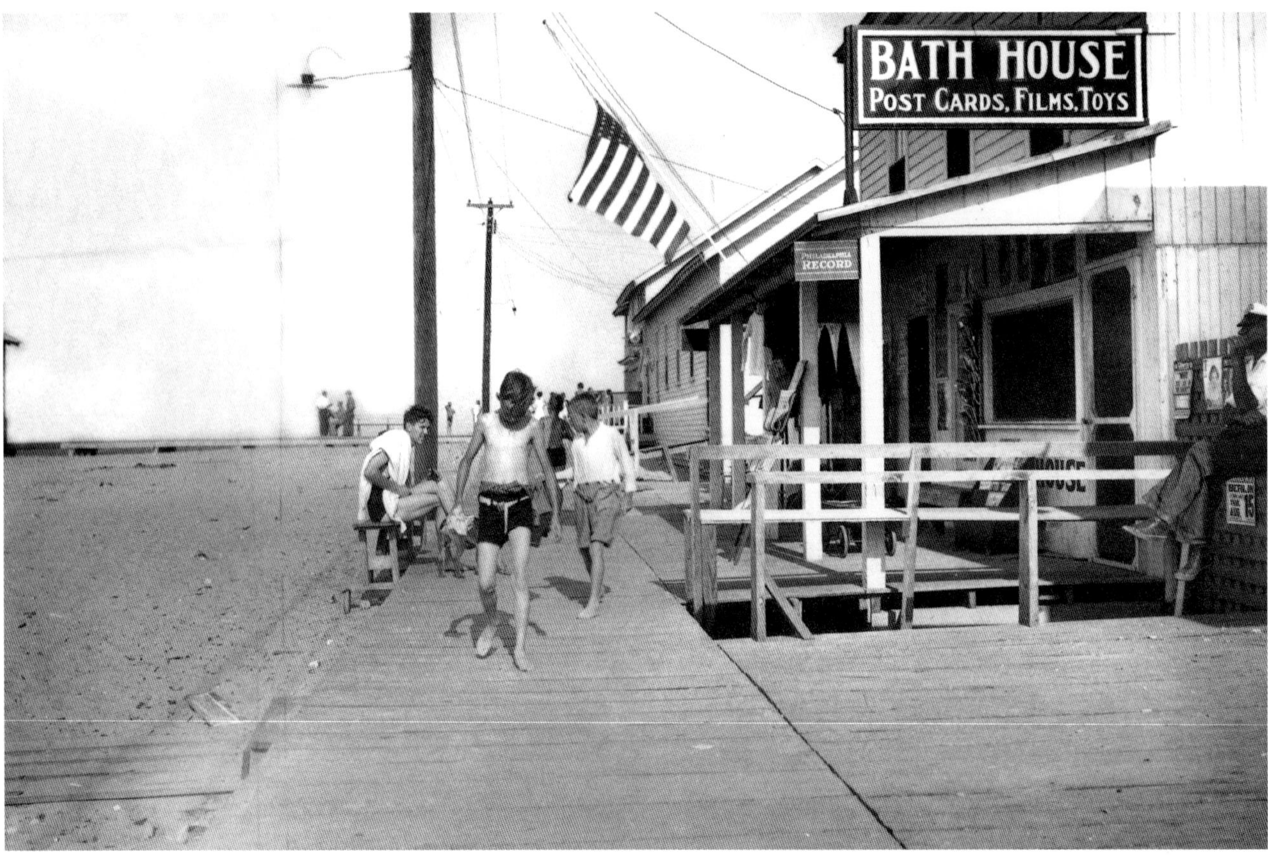

Airman Ralph "Lee" Minker poses in the cockpit of his B-17 bomber. He named his plane *Blue Hen Chick* for his home state. Just 17 when Pearl Harbor was bombed, Minker was quick to enlist when he came of age. He began his Army Air Corps training in early 1943, leaving as a captain in August 1945.

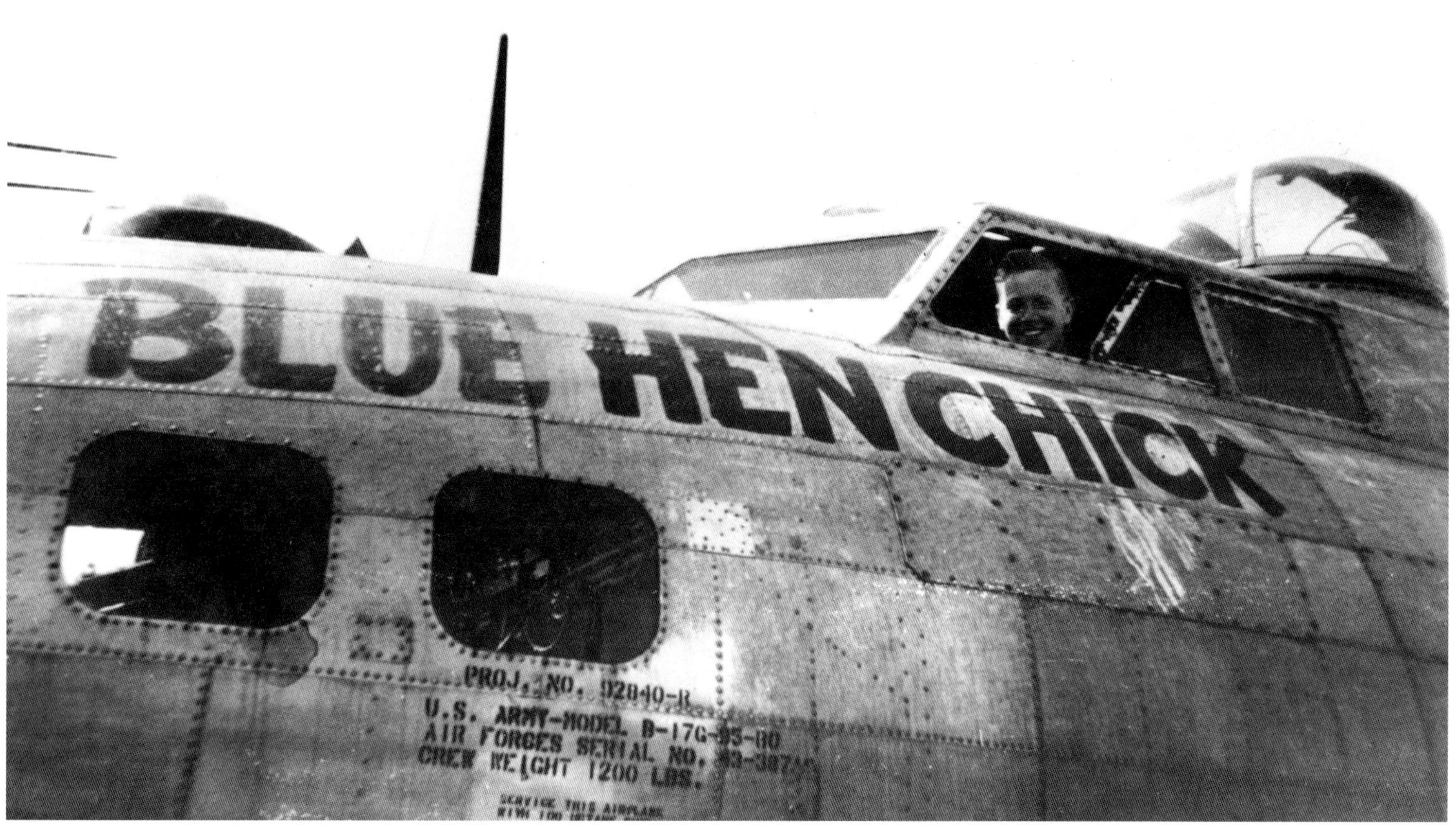

These men are scraping skins in the "beam house" of the Allied Kid Company located at 4th and Monroe streets in Wilmington on June 3, 1943. This job was heavy, messy, and hard. Wilmington was well known for its leather tanneries, some of which produced very fine kid leather. Allied was in business in Wilmington from 1930 to 1978.

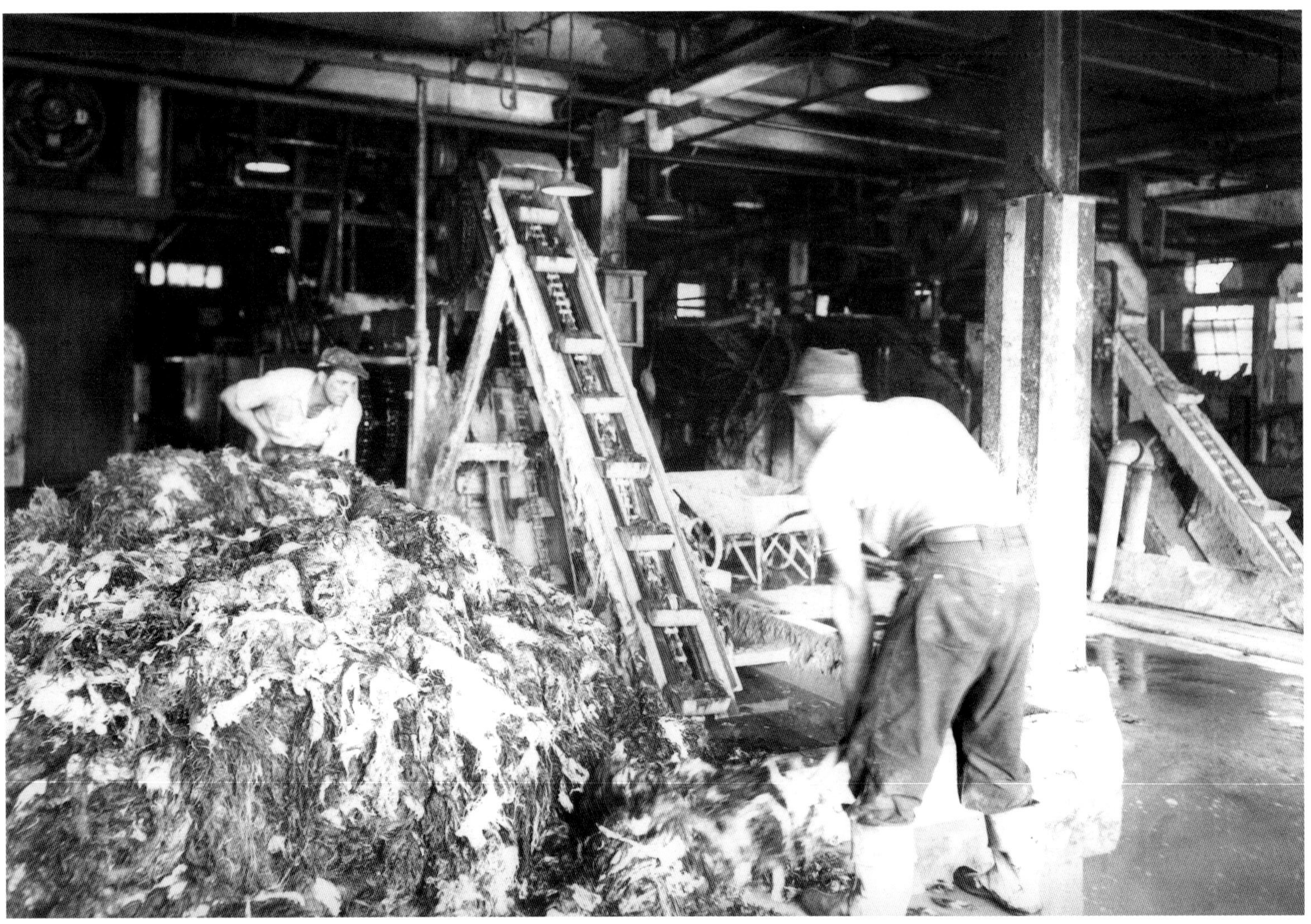

War bond sales ladies take a break beside a trackless trolley in Wilmington, where bond sales are under way. The trolley was parked outside the DuPont Building on Rodney Square.

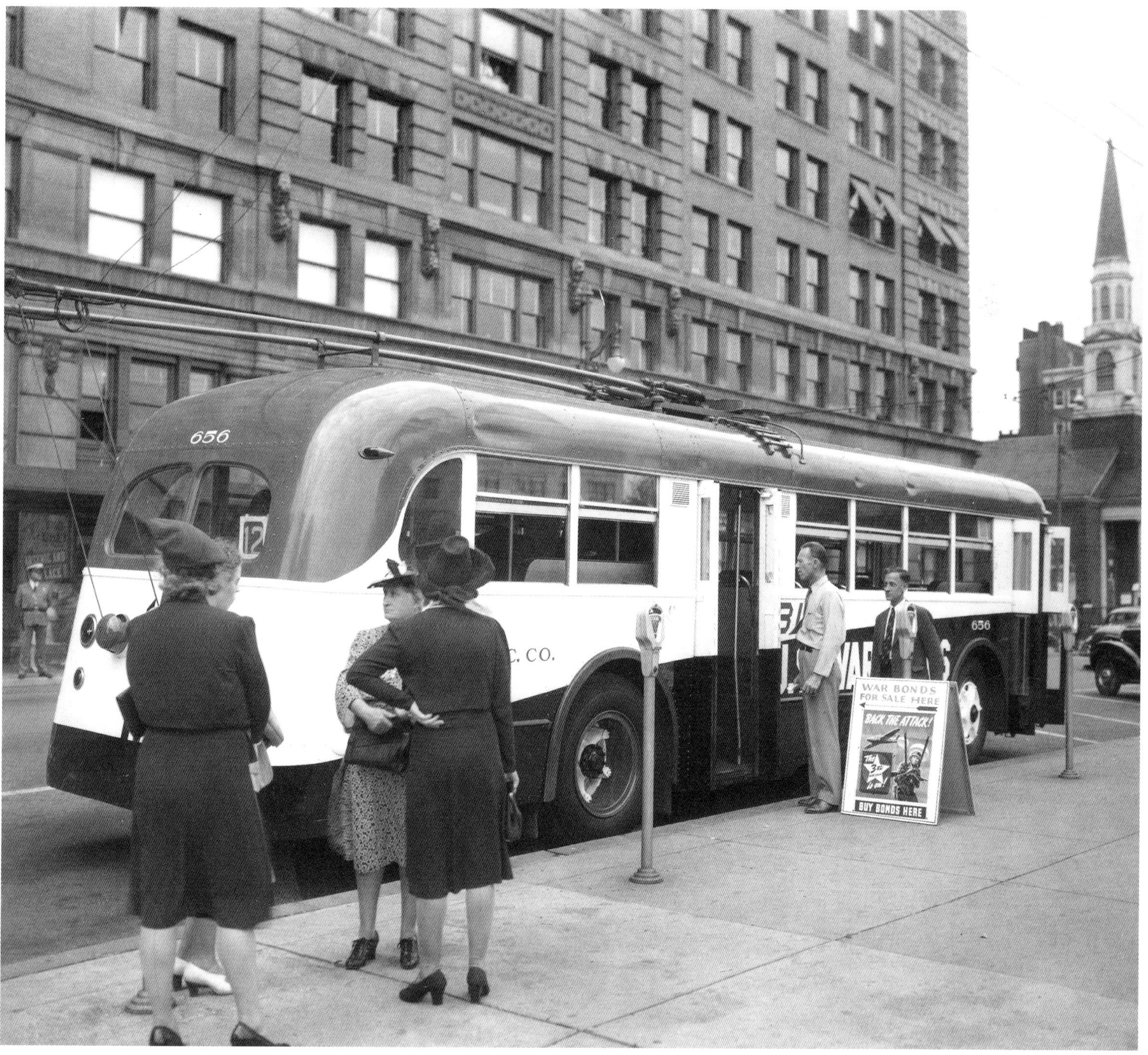

A cause for celebration and hope that the war would end, this launch might have been especially poignant as it took place at Dravo Shipyard during the holidays on December 23, 1944. Dravo opened a barge assembly and launch facility in Wilmington in 1927. It won wartime contracts to build gate vessels designed to raise and lower anti-submarine nets in harbors.

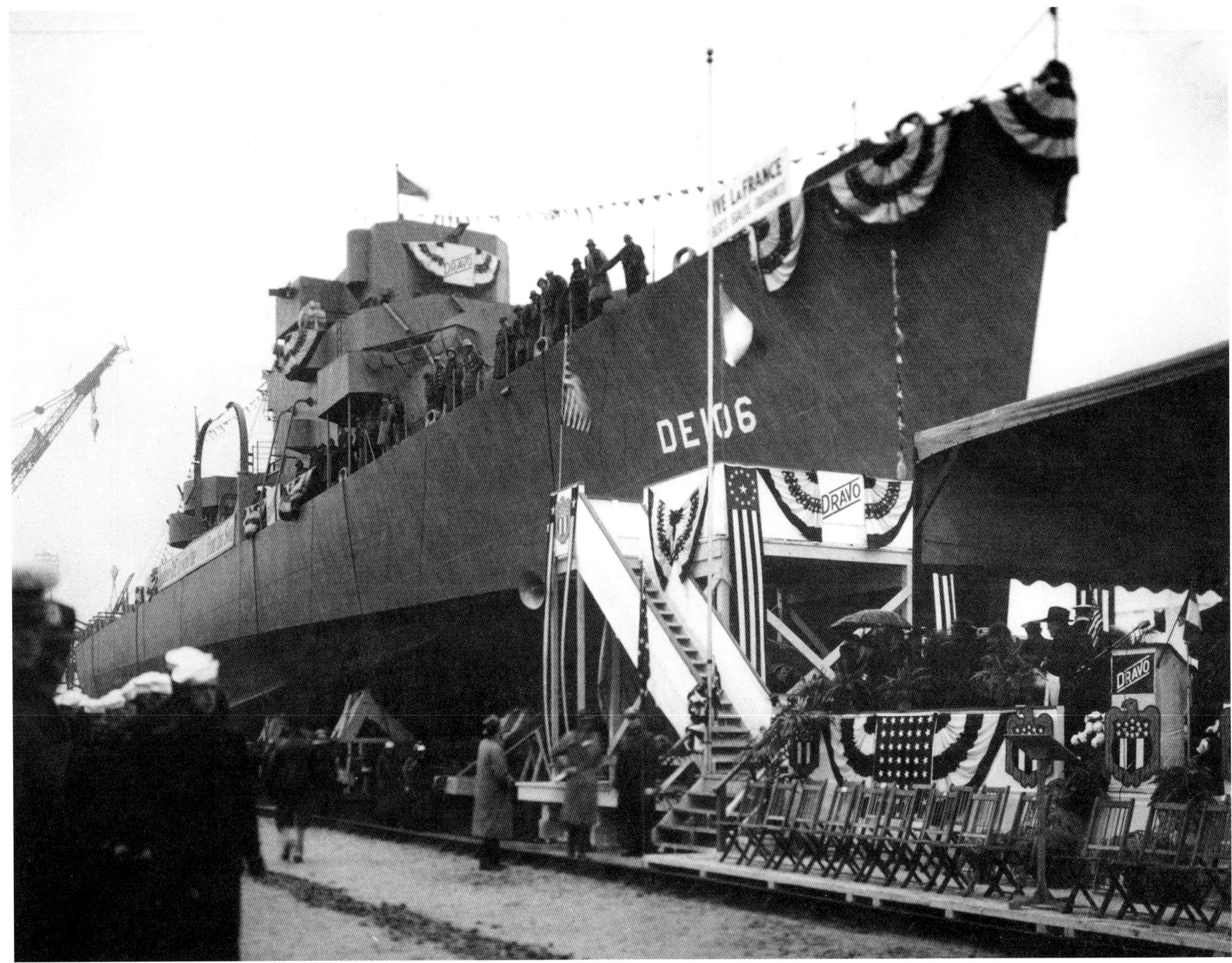

Three pilots walk along the tarmac at the New Castle County Army Air Force Base during World War II. These women were pilots for WASP (Women Air Force Service Pilots). The first women trained to fly U.S. military aircraft, they ferried planes from the factory to airfields and military bases. One of their bases was in New Castle.

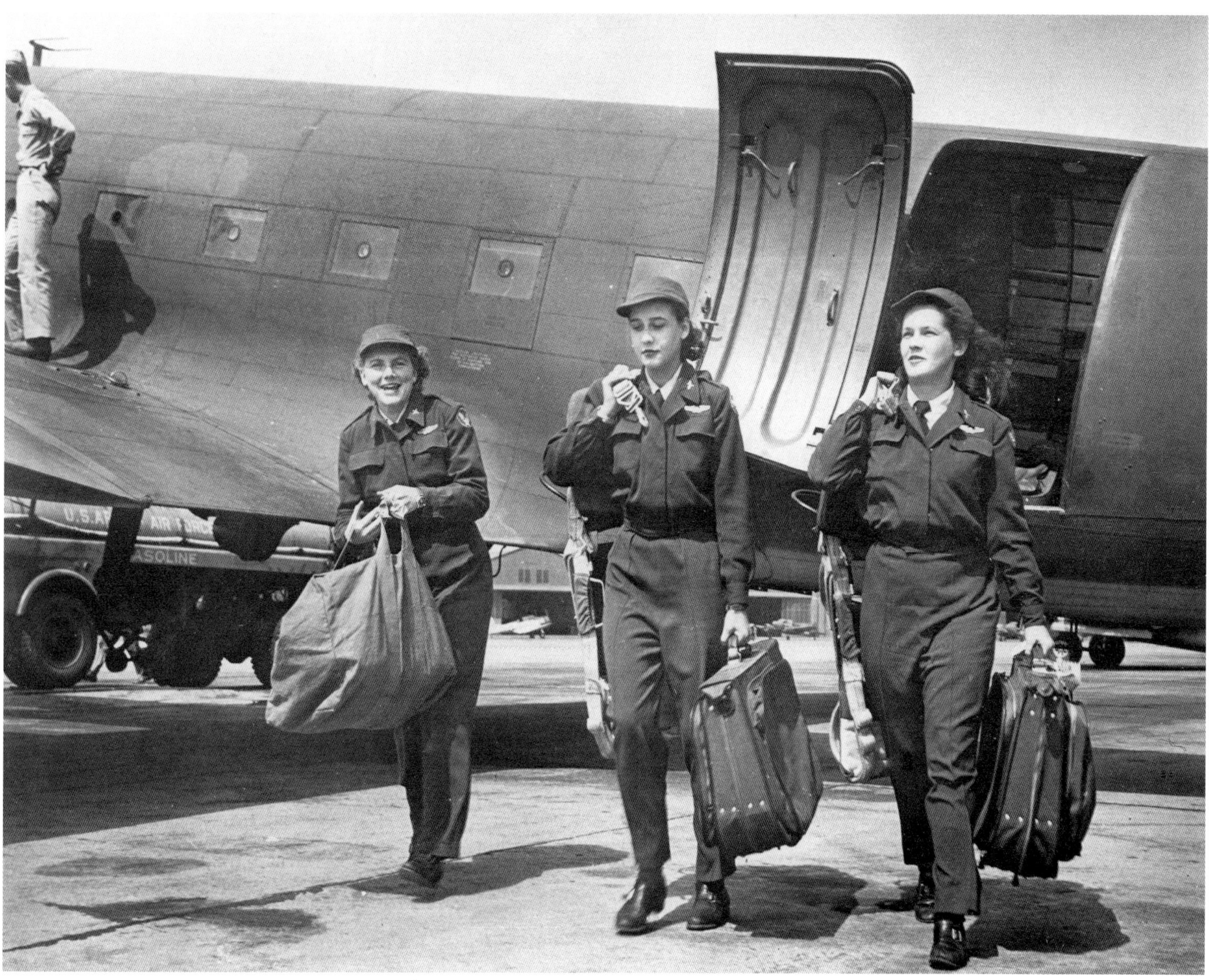

Everyone got involved in war bond sales. Pictured here is the family of Wilmington mayor Thomas Herlihy, Jr., in 1945. Pearl Herlihy stands at the booth with her sons, Thomas III and Jerome. The photograph was taken inside the City-County Building on Rodney Square.

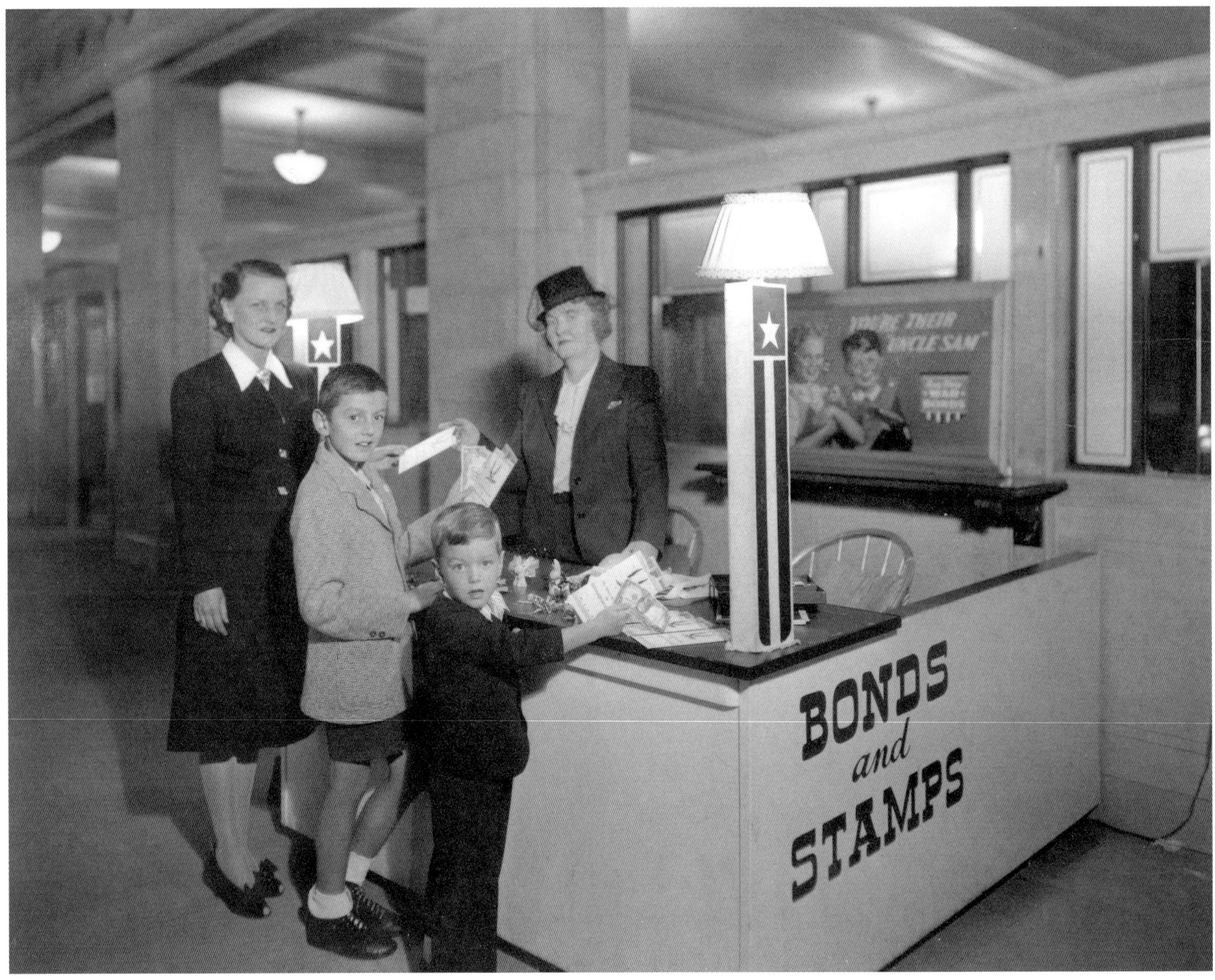

Here is an interior view of an air transport plane carrying wounded soldiers from France to the New Castle County Air Force Base.

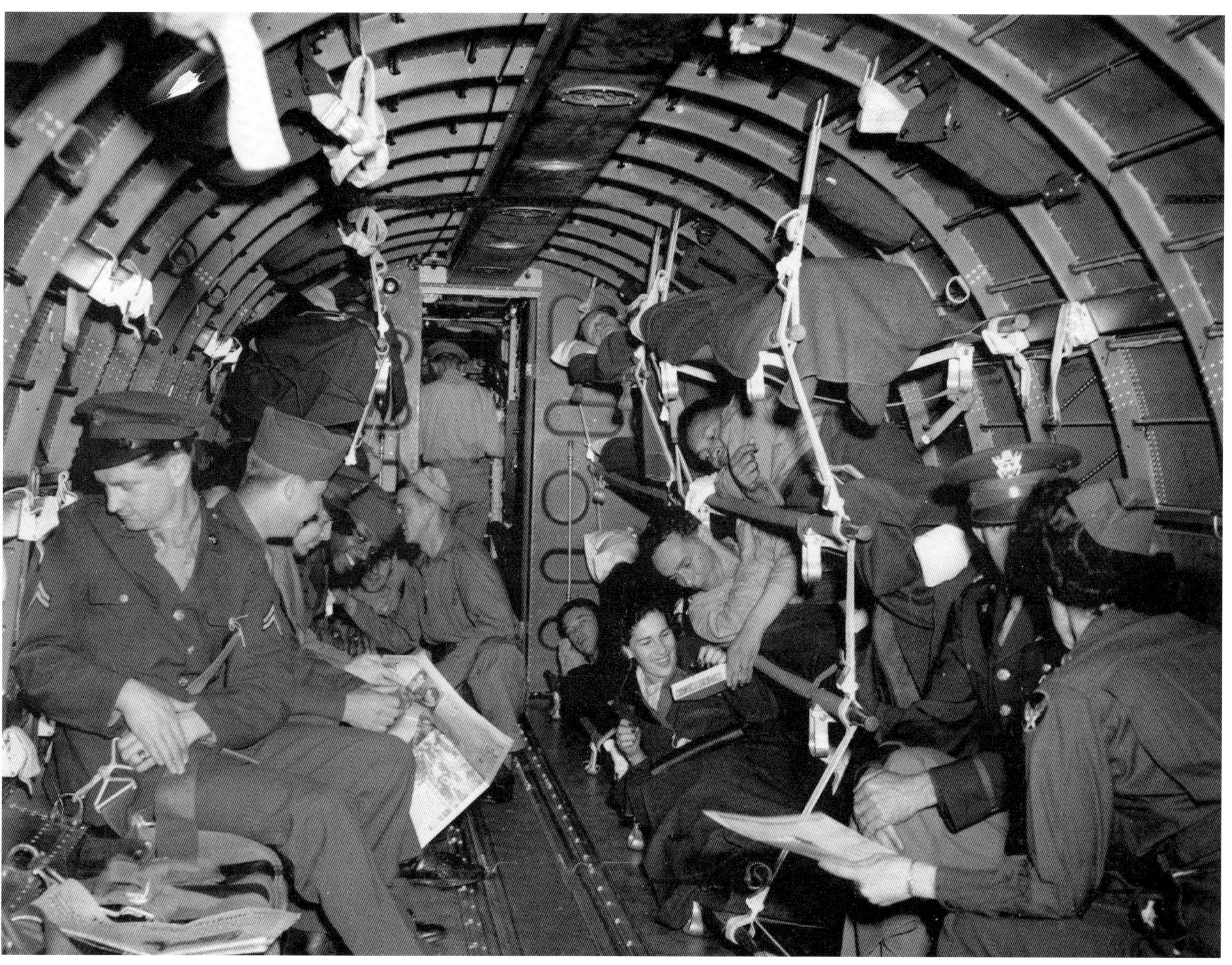

This hot, sunny day brought a boost to the local economy for years to come. This photograph was taken at the groundbreaking ceremonies for the General Motors Assembly Plant at Boxwood on August 28, 1945. One of two to move to Delaware, these assembly plants would change the local economy for the next 50 years.

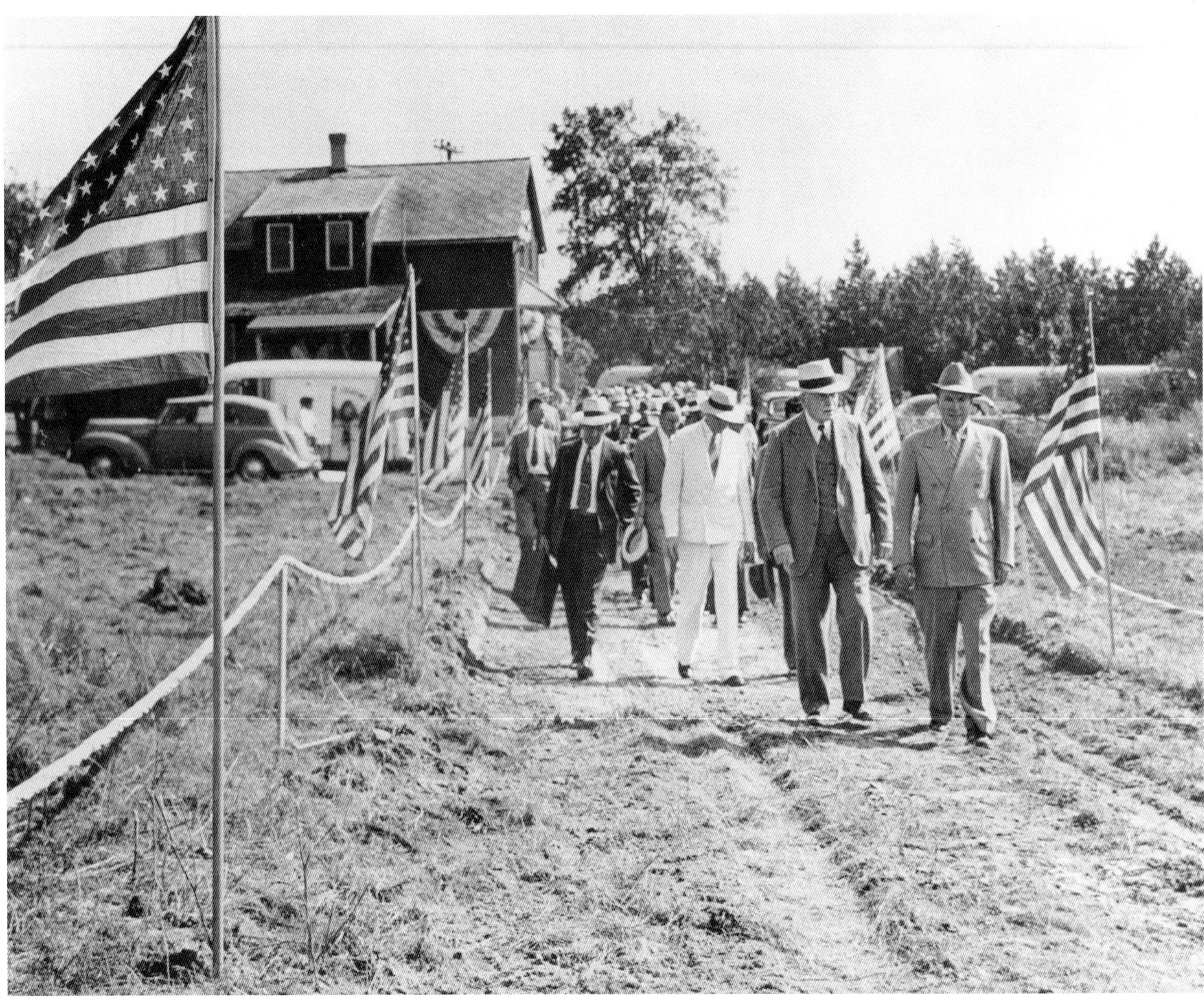

Photographer Roy Wall took this classic photograph of the Delaware State House on the Green in Dover. Originally commissioned to be built as the Kent County Court House, it was completed in 1791, but plans changed and it opened as the State House. For many years it housed the county court. One of the nation's oldest standing state houses, it was used until Legislative Hall opened in 1933. Today it is a museum.

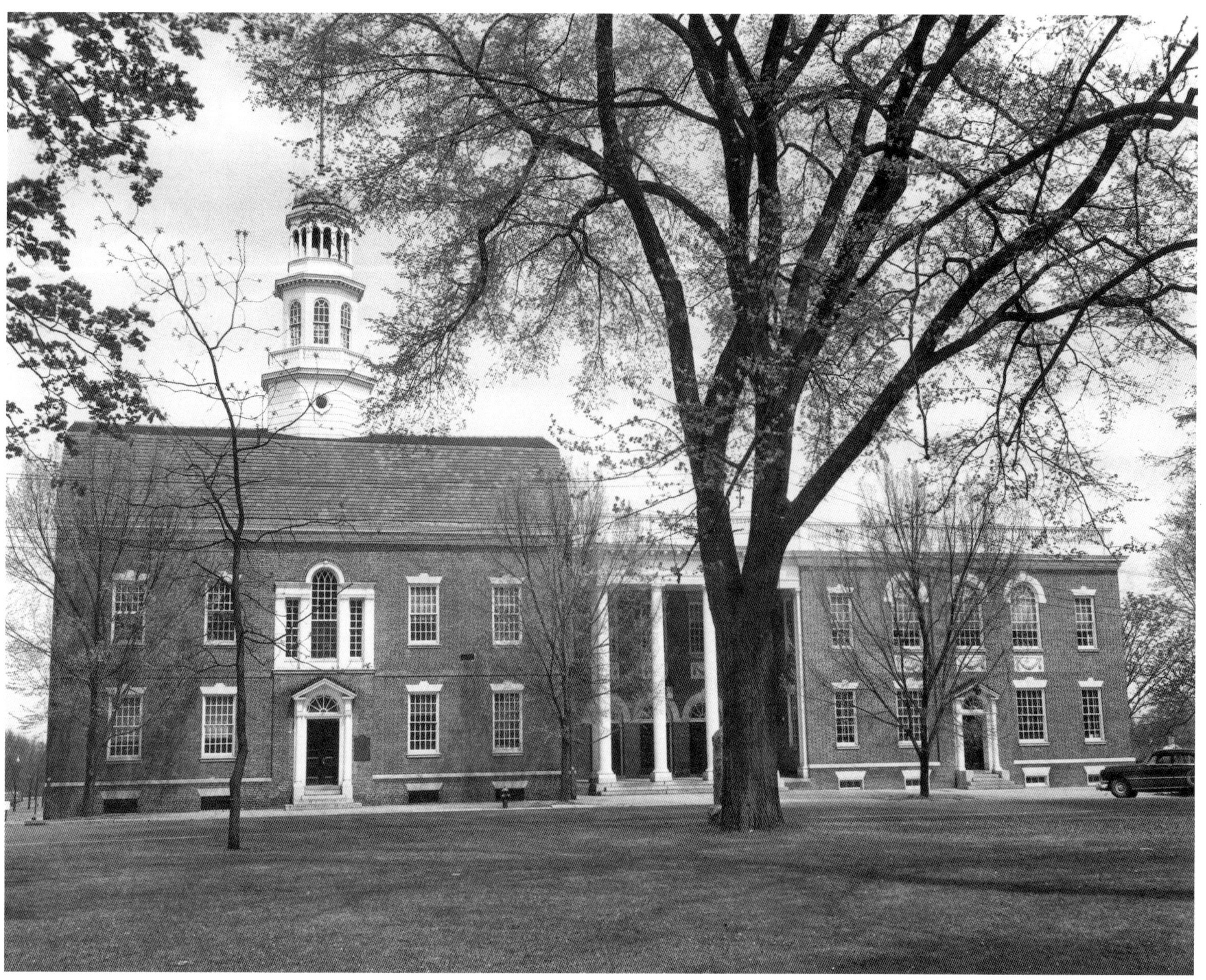

Two players for the Wilmington Blue Rocks give pitching advice to young players at Wilmington Ball Park in the 1940s. In 1940, R. R. M. Carpenter brought baseball to Delaware and from 1940 to 1944 Connie Mack owned the team. The "Rocks" played as a farm team for the Philadelphia A's from 1940 to 1952. In 1993 another farm team, also named the Blue Rocks, came to Delaware playing for the Kansas City Royals.

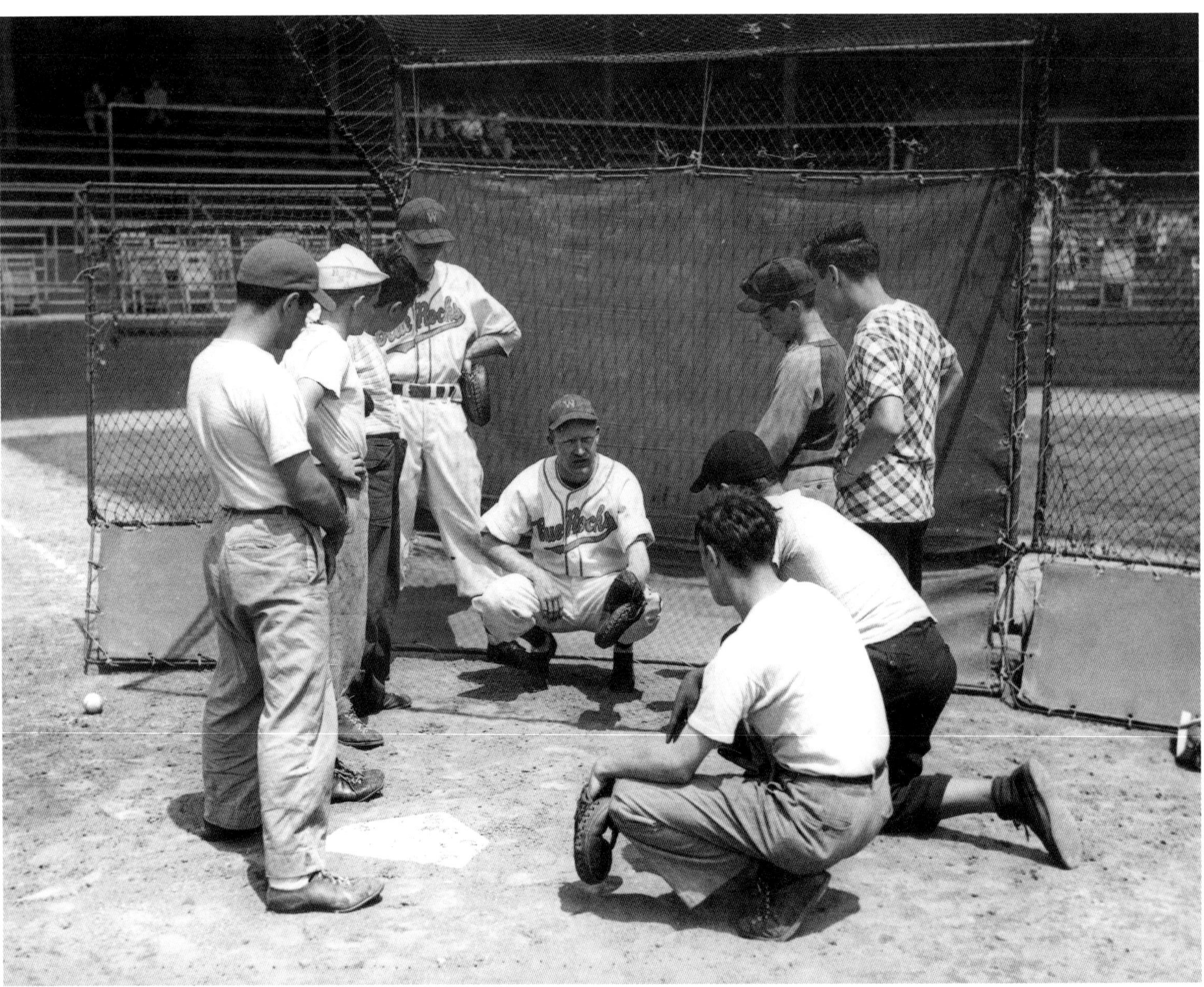

Delaware in the Postwar Era

(1946–1970s)

Great challenges and great opportunities characterized the postwar years. Delaware's population increased 19 percent in the 1940s, 40 percent in the 1950s, and 23 percent in the 1960s. By 1960, more than half the state's people lived in northern New Castle County. Most notable was the rise of the African American population in Wilmington. In 1952, the state supreme court ruled that segregated public schools were unconstitutional, a case that became part of the 1954 United States Supreme Court ruling, *Brown v. the Board of Education.* Other public facilities followed suit, the YMCA in 1951 and the Hotel DuPont in 1953. In 1961, the State Council on Human Relations was created to ameliorate race relations.

Suburbanization, with origins reaching as far back as the 1910s, became a significant force in the 1950s. A growing suburbia that left many old houses and historic neighborhoods to crumble, coupled with urban renewal, which destroyed them outright, changed the face of urban areas in the state.

Delaware's economy was able to provide most returning veterans with jobs while simultaneously returning to peacetime production. The state negotiated the relocation of a Getty Oil refinery to Delaware City. General Motors and Chrysler built plants in 1947 and 1950, respectively, while DuPont, Hercules, and Atlas continued rapid growth. National Cash Register in Millsboro, International Latex in Dover, and Leeds Travelwear in Clayton opened local plants. Sussex County agriculture and the broiler industry flourished. Delaware ranked fifth in the nation and Sussex County ranked first among counties in broiler production. Several agribusinesses also continued to prosper—Cannon's and Newton's in Bridgeville, and Townsend's in Eastern Sussex.

The development of the coastal resorts had a considerable economic effect on Eastern Sussex County. When depression relief workers improved land drainage and removed mosquitoes in the 1930s, they helped lay the groundwork for renewed prosperity. Prosperity brought more cars, more travel, and overburdened roadways as local railways discontinued passenger service. In the last decades of the century, Delawareans sought solutions to economic, cultural, and social problems as the state's economic forecast continued to improve.

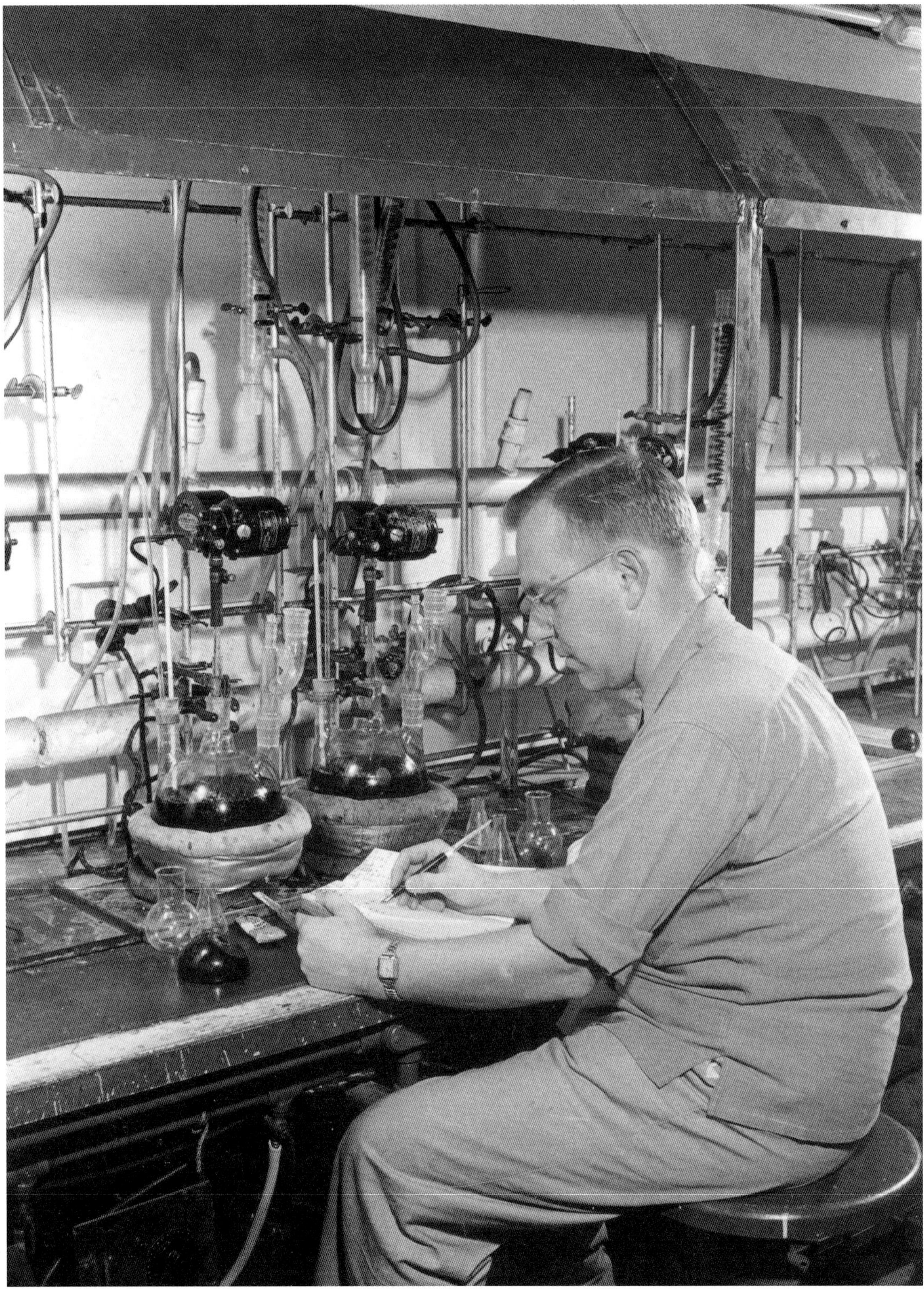

A scientist is at work in the Central Research Department of Atlas Chemical Company in 1954. Atlas Powder (later Chemical) Company was formed in 1912 when the DuPont Company lost a federal antitrust suit. In 1971, Imperial Chemical Industries (ICI) purchased Atlas to help expand its business into the United States.

Members of the National Guard pose with a giant ball on the grounds of Fort DuPont. Originally opened as Fort Reynolds, a battery at the entrance to the Chesapeake and Delaware Canal in 1864, the current buildings at the fort grounds were constructed in 1897. The fort was renamed Fort DuPont in honor of Rear Admiral Samuel Francis Du Pont. It served as the harbor command defense post until Fort Miles opened in 1942.

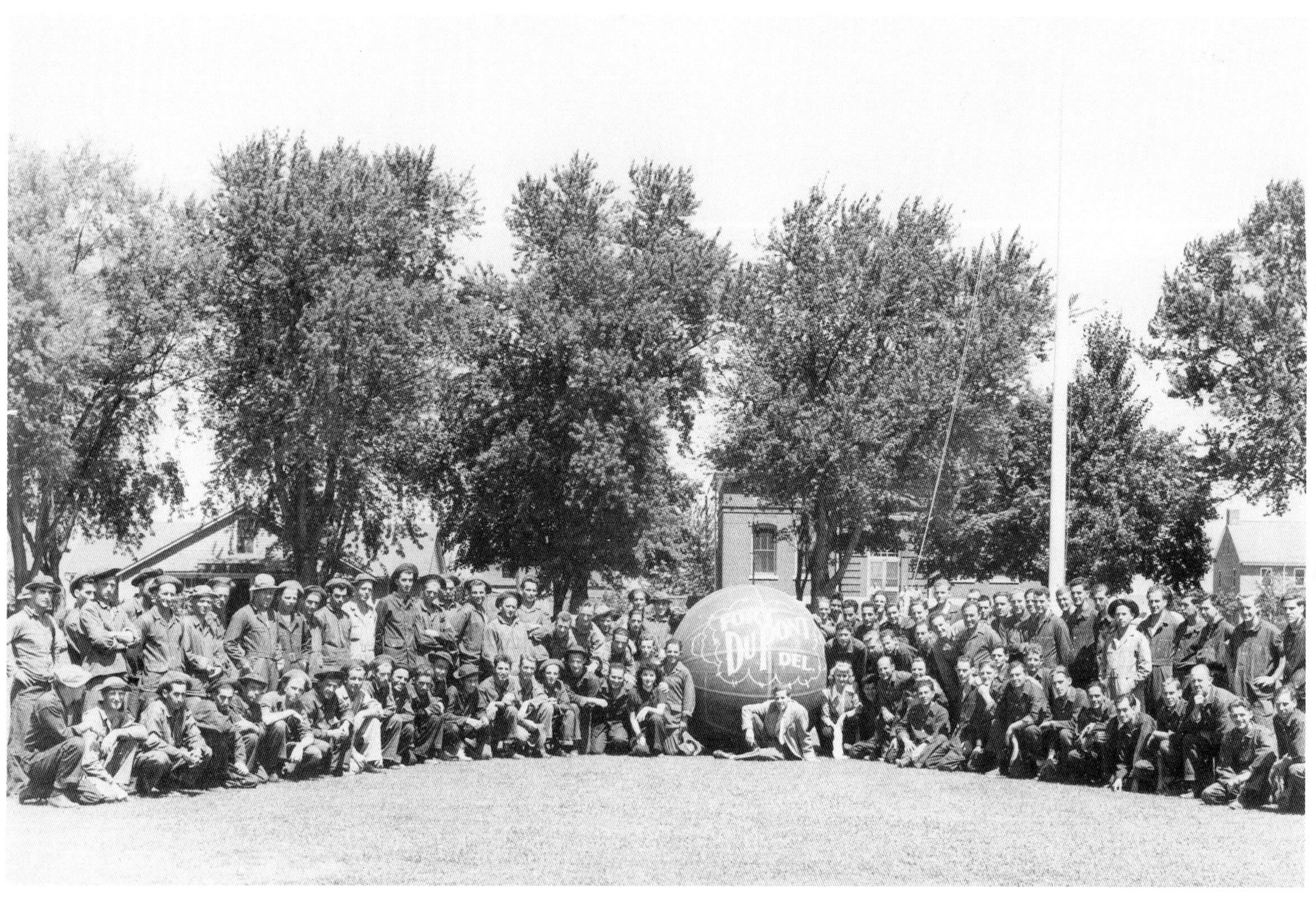

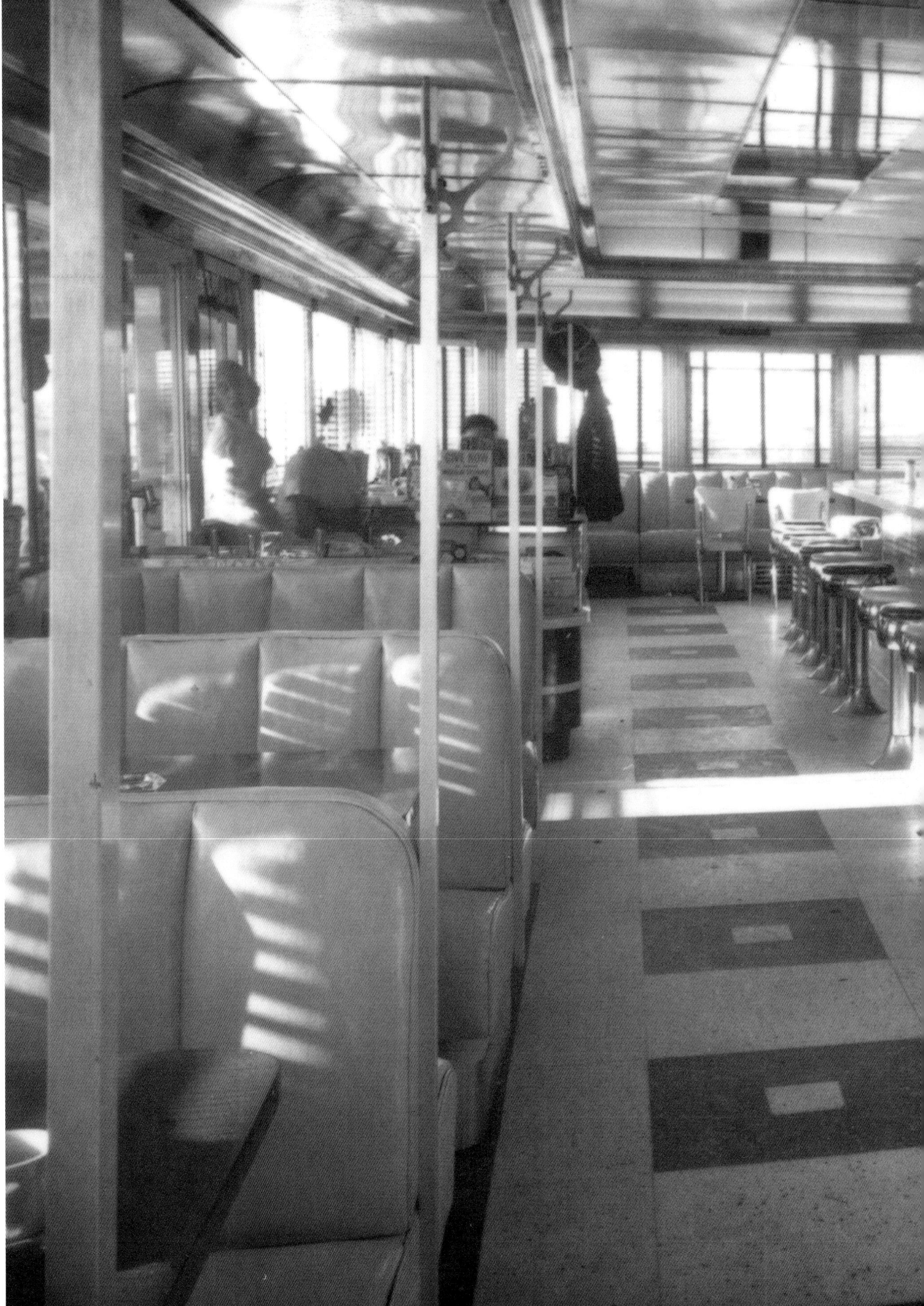

An interior view of the Hollywood Diner on Route 13 in Dover. The diner opened in 1955 and was one of five known as the Hollywood Diners of Delaware. The post–World War II period was the golden age of diners, when they were built of the newest and flashiest materials. This diner is still open 24 hours a day, 7 days a week.

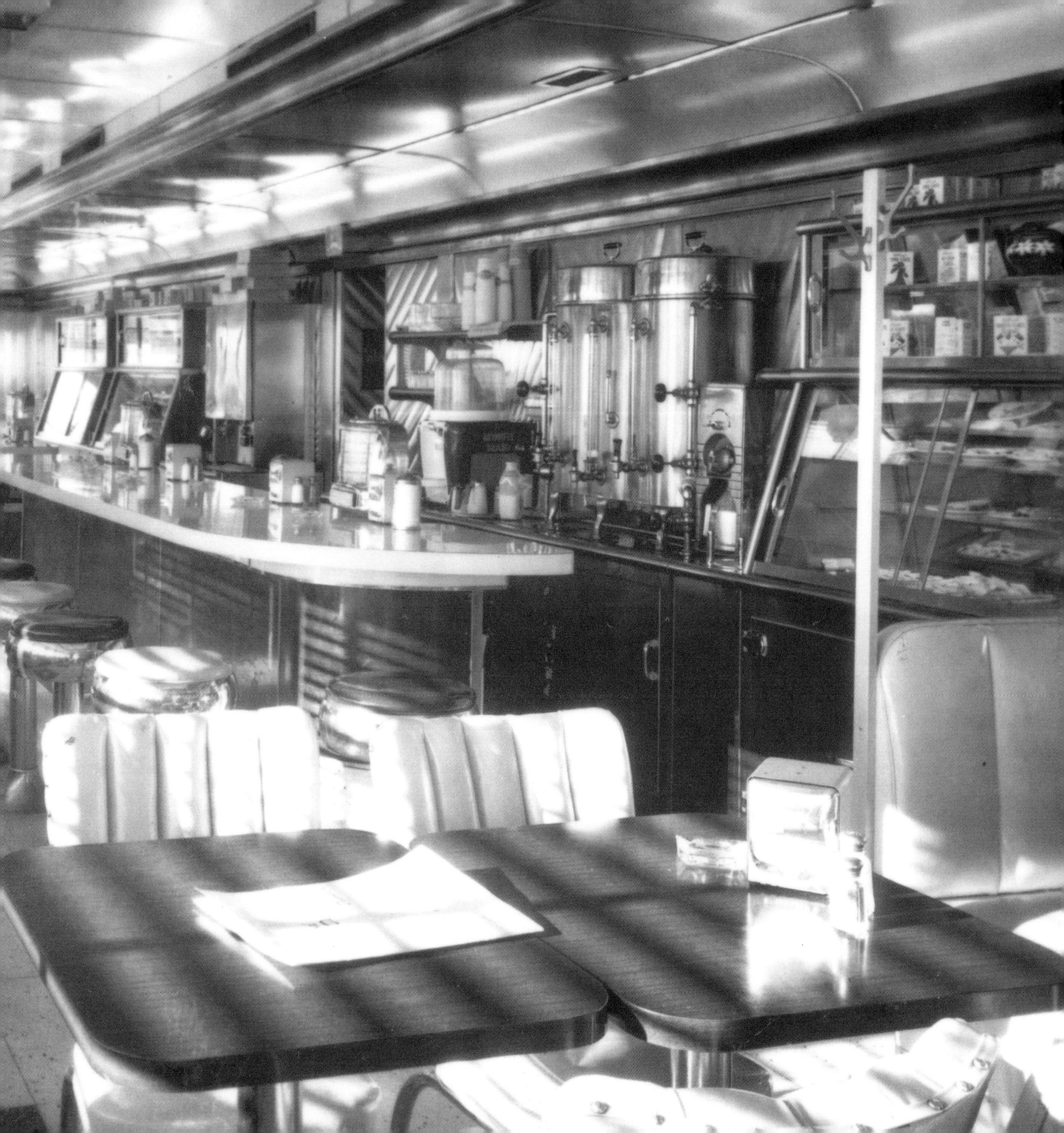

A crowd watches and waits for fried chicken at the Delmarva Chicken Festival. The enormous frying pan debuted in 1950, courtesy of Delmarva's poultry industry, which runs the festival. Made by the Mumford Sheet Metal Company of Selbyville, it is 10 feet in diameter and can fry 800 chicken quarters. One of the giant pans used at the festival is on permanent display in the Delaware History Museum.

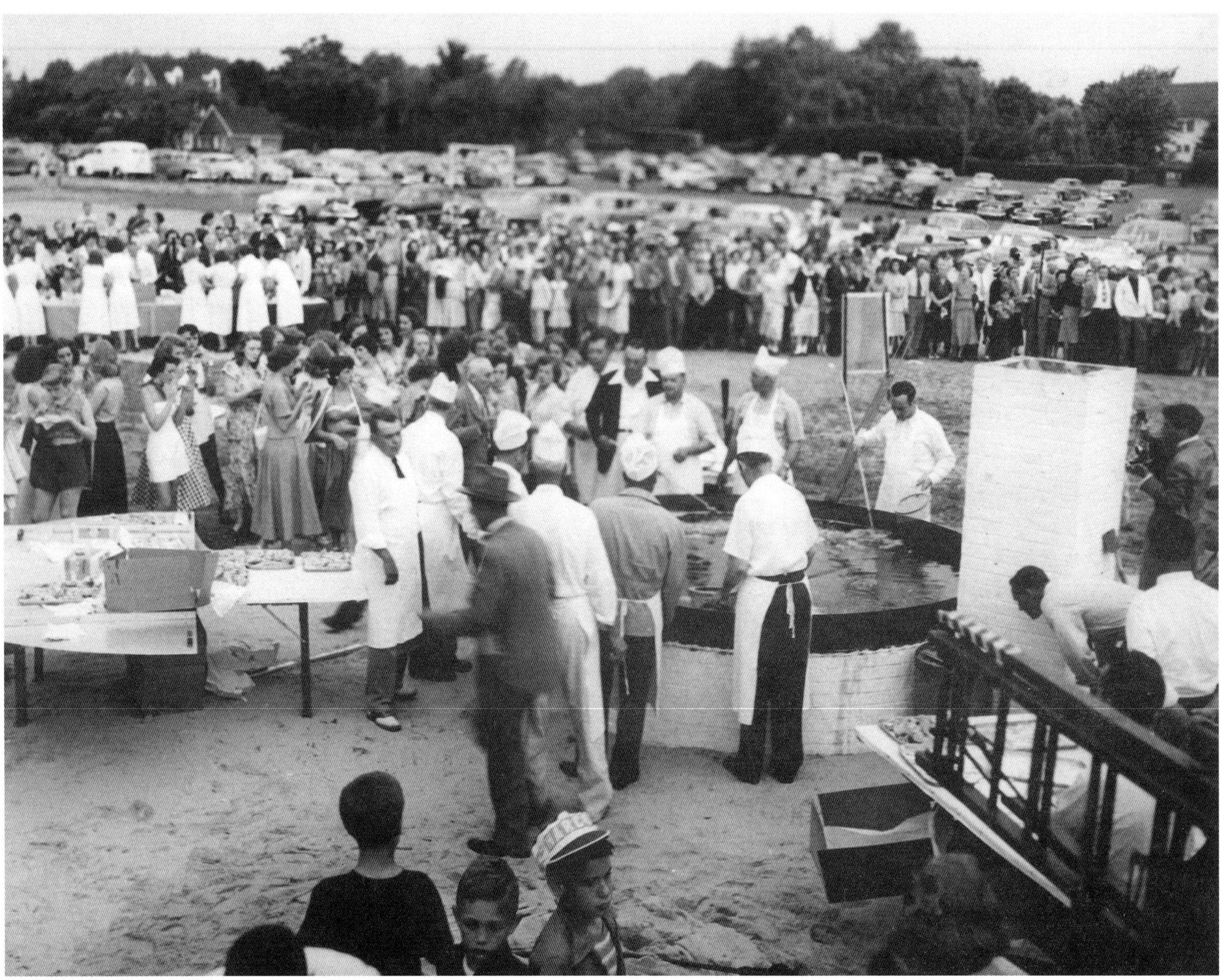

The USS *DuPont,* DD-941, was launched at Bath, Maine, on September 8, 1956. It had anti-aircraft, anti-submarine, and anti-surface defense capabilities. The ship was named for Admiral Samuel Francis du Pont, the naval hero of the Battle of Port Royal. He was instrumental in setting up the Naval Academy and was named a rear admiral. The USS *DuPont* was active for five years.

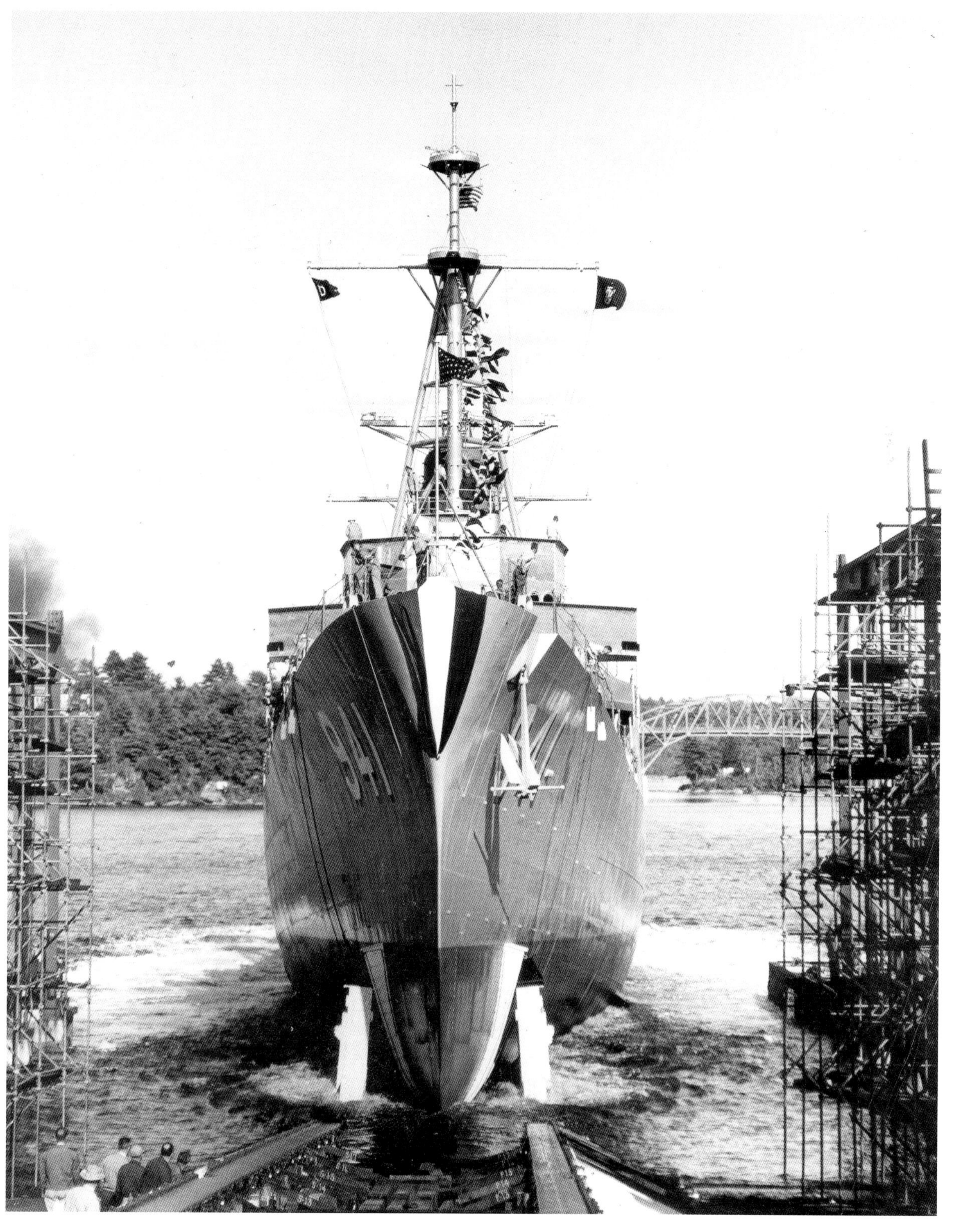

In the years of the cold war, people were well aware of the threat of nuclear bombs. Here missiles and rockets were the talk of the day at this public education event for civilian defense on July 20, 1954. Civil defense groups were started to help people prepare for a nuclear event. The organization was eventually reorganized into the Federal Emergency Management Agency.

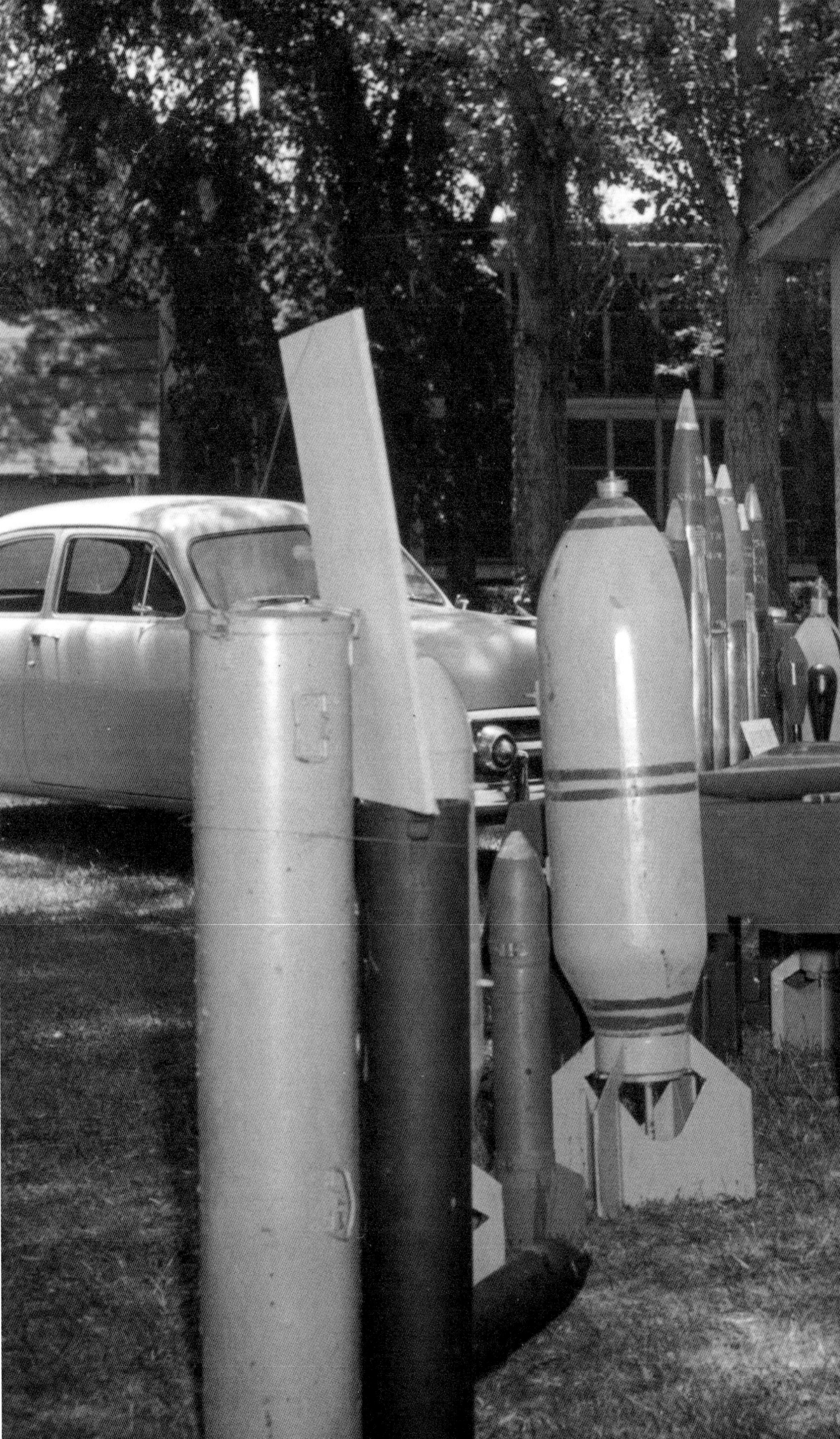

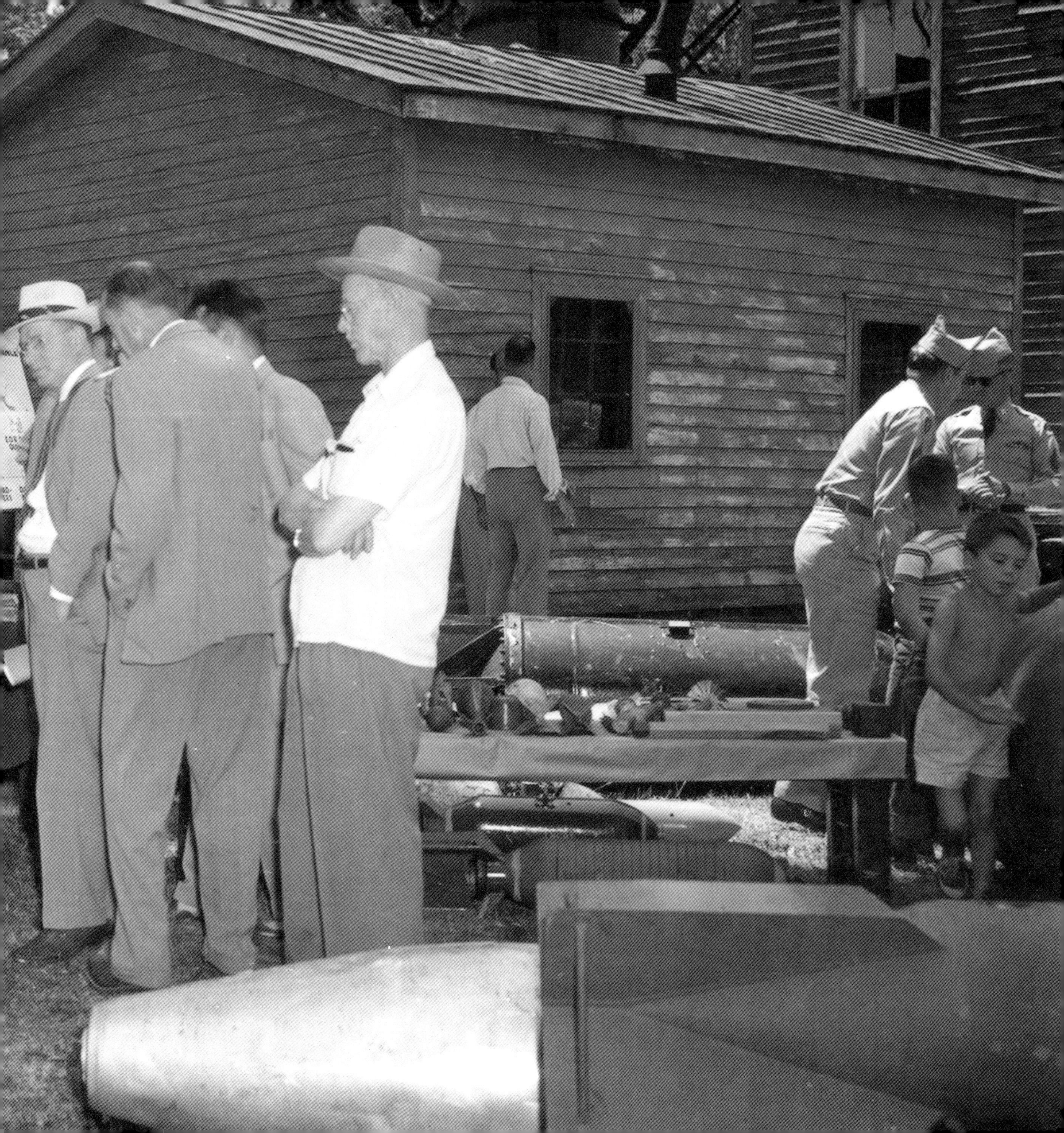

Civil Defense Demonstration Day on July 20, 1954, was well attended by people of all descriptions. It included speakers and hands-on demonstrations and provided information about bomb identification, shelters, and even human anatomy. Programs to help instruct and prepare civilians in military emergencies began in the 1920s but became widespread during the cold war years.

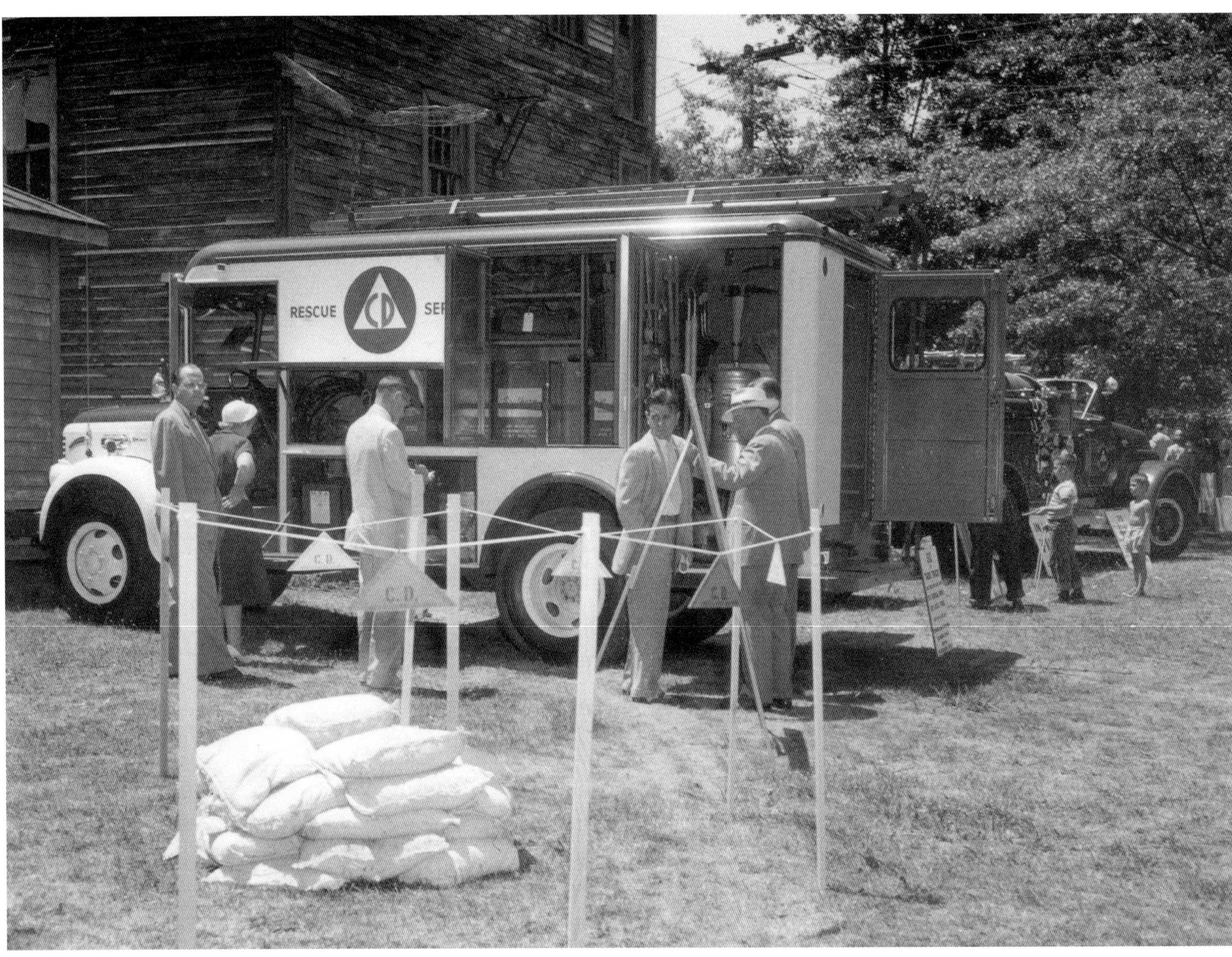

A Korean War soldier is mourned by family and friends outside the B&O railroad station at Shallcross and DuPont streets in Wilmington. Here the city treasurer, Alex R. Abrahams, greets the family and says a few words to those gathered. Delaware lost 66 soldiers in the conflict. This soldier was one of three men from Wilmington who were killed: Louis C. Hairsine, Leroy Shahan, and William P. Winnington, Jr.

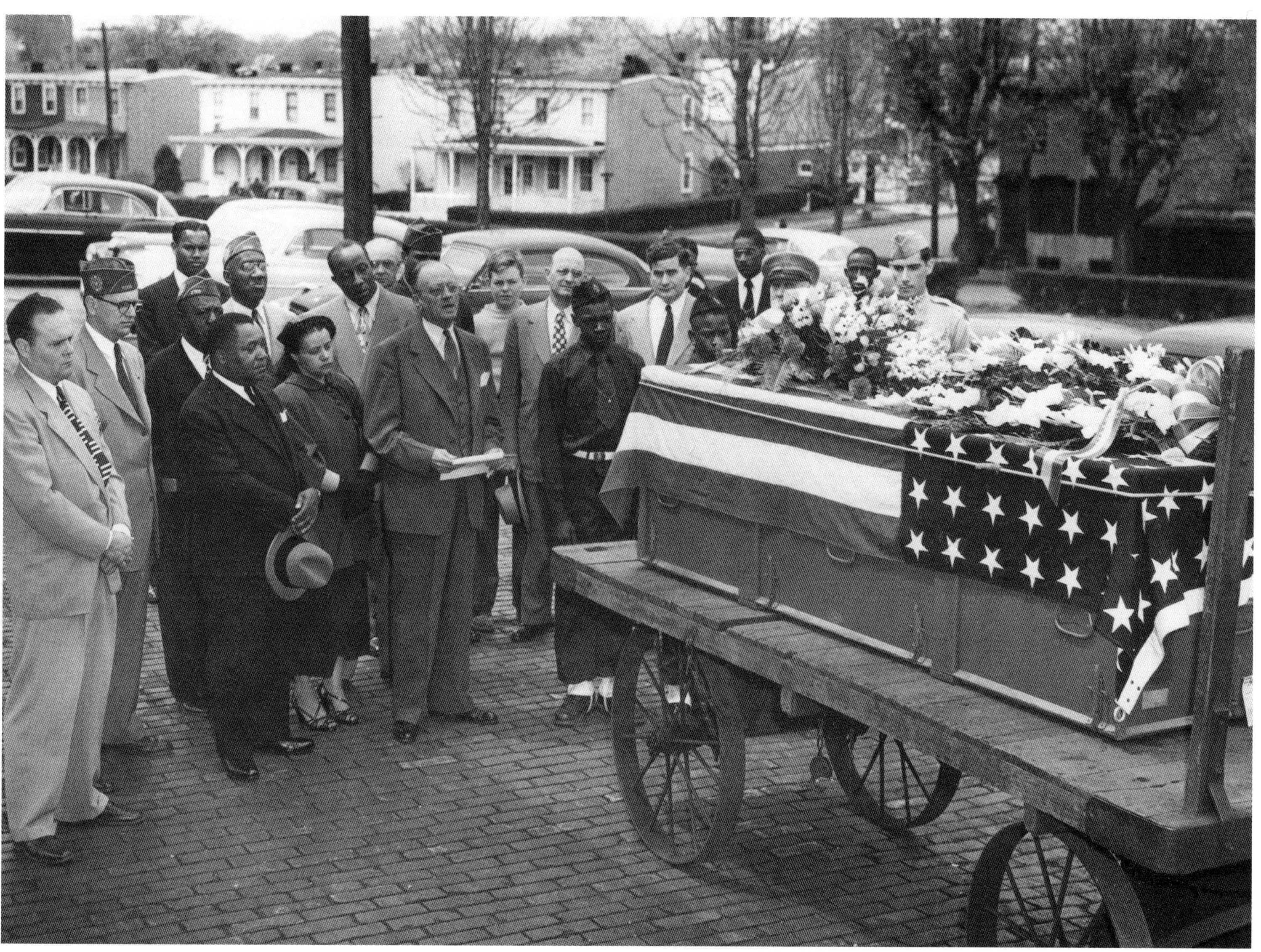

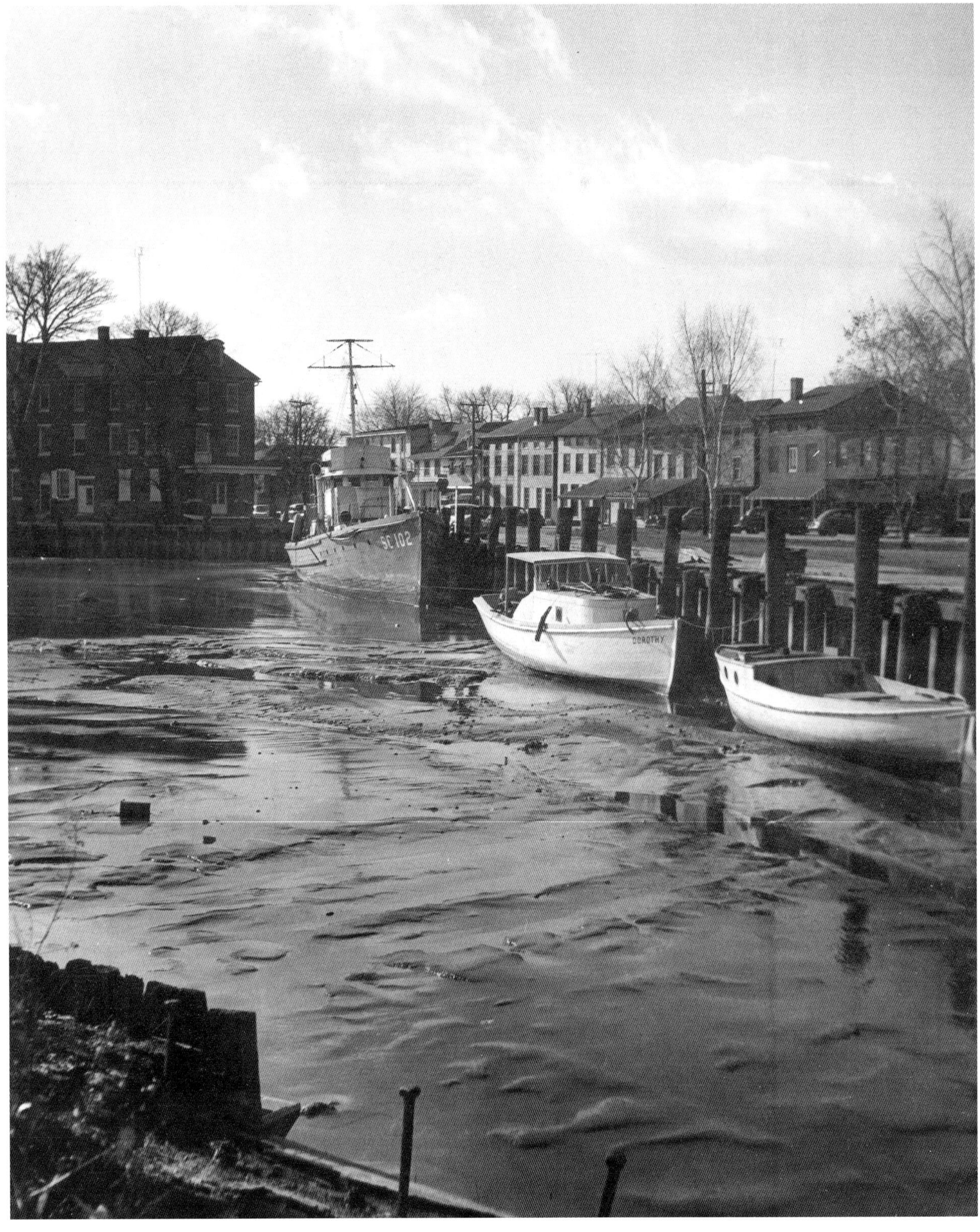

Boats are tied up along the canal in Delaware City during low tide. Today the main shipping entrance to the Chesapeake and Delaware Canal is at Reedy Point. The Delaware City entrance remains open to pleasure boats.

Photographer Orlando Wooten shot this view of the Laurel train station as it appeared in the 1950s.

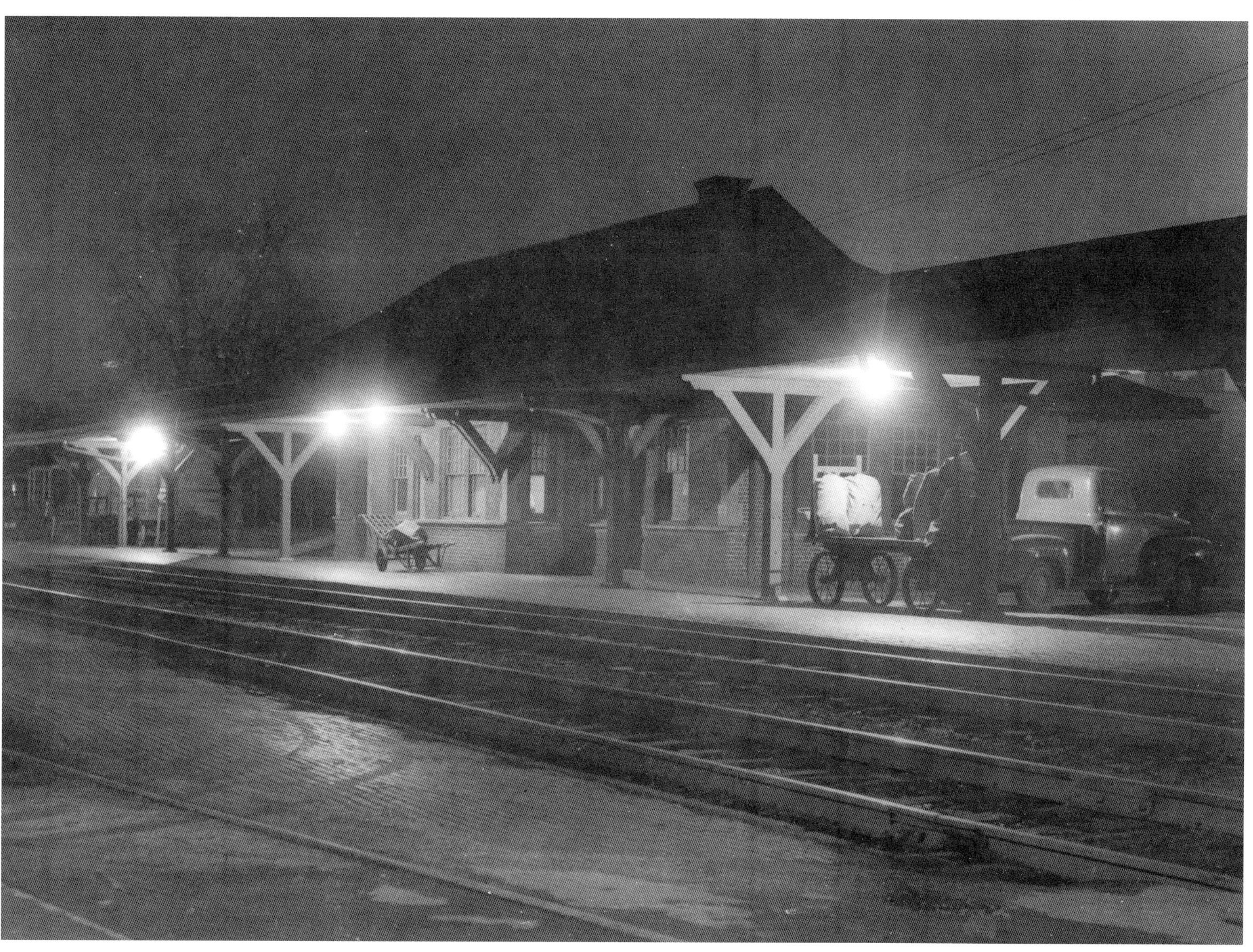

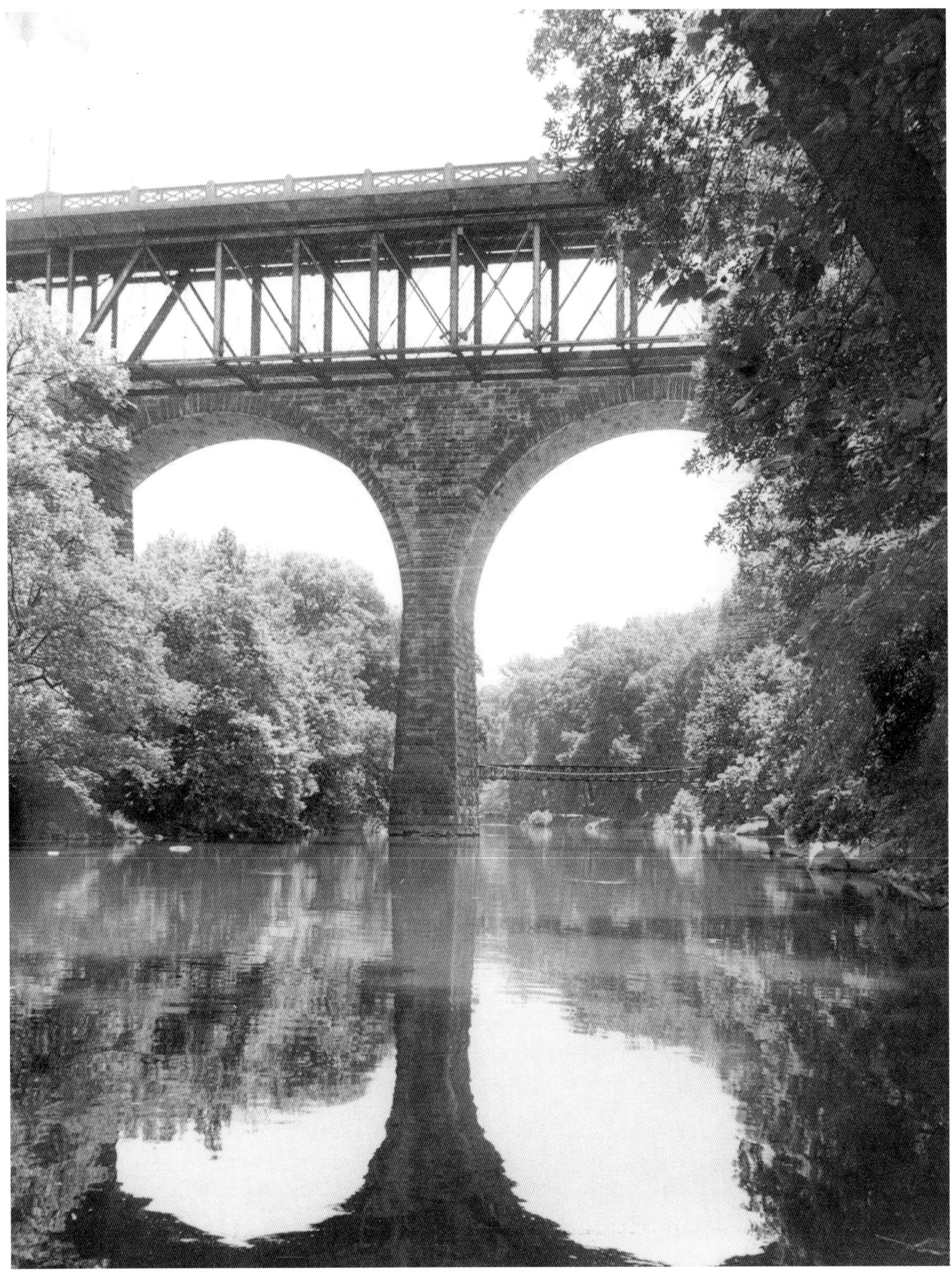

Shown here is the massive and stunning Baltimore & Ohio Railroad's arched stone bridge over the Brandywine River just west of downtown Wilmington. The bridge was built in 1909 to replace a steel truss bridge that could not handle newer, heavier trains. The truss bridge was rebuilt for use by automobile traffic. Seen below the B&O bridge is a smaller bridge for pedestrians.

This crew of men from the Virginia National Guard operates an M-7 Director at the South Range, Fort Miles, Bethany Beach on July 30, 1953. M-7 Directors were anti-aircraft sighting devices. The fort was envisioned after World War I, but construction was postponed during the Depression. It was meant to defend against the strongest German ships. World War II ended before the fort was completed, but it remained commissioned to train soldiers.

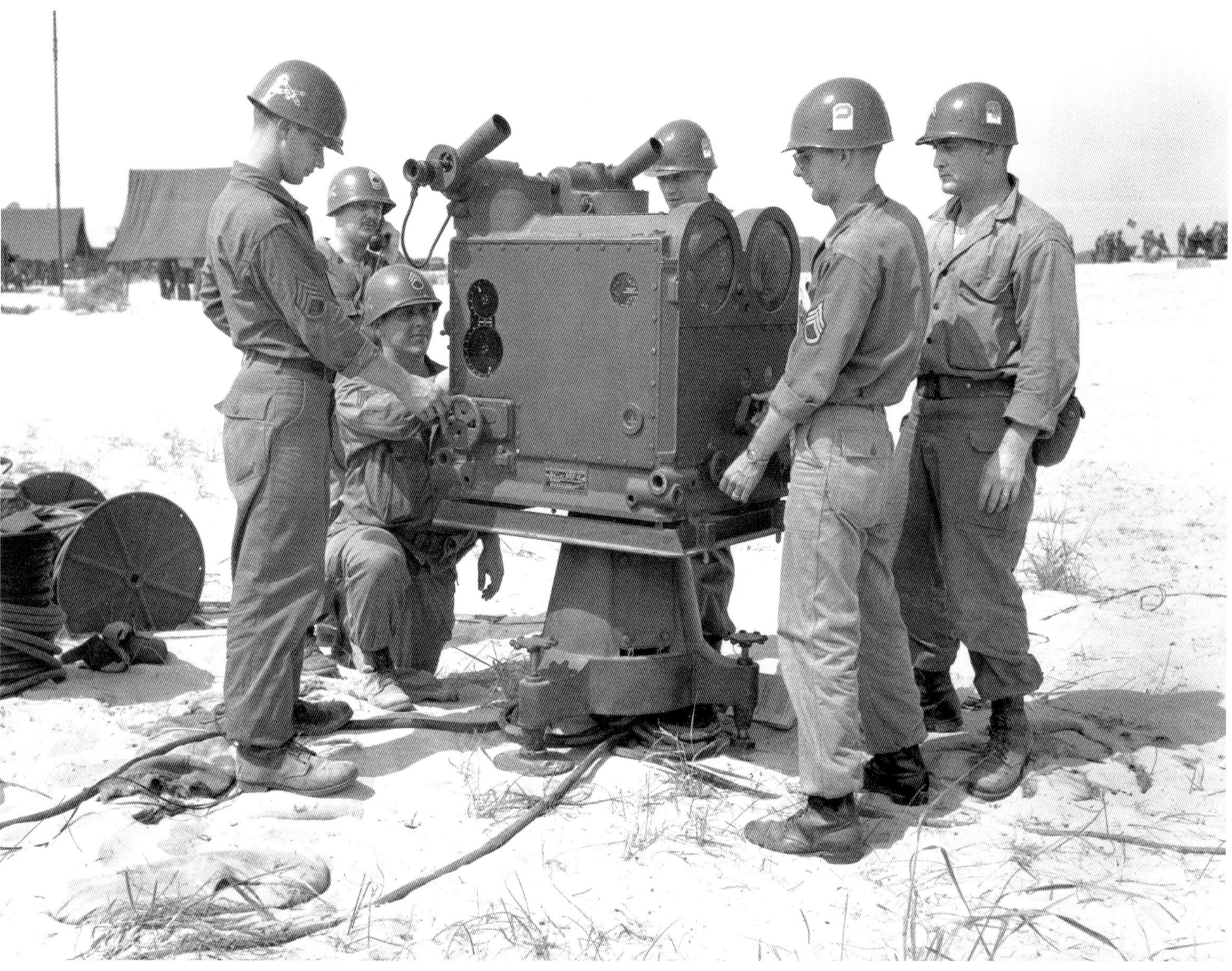

This panorama of the 313th Signal Battalion from Fort George Meade in Maryland on the north range of Bethany Beach was photographed on August 3, 1953. In the next two decades the fort became home to a secret underwater listening lab.

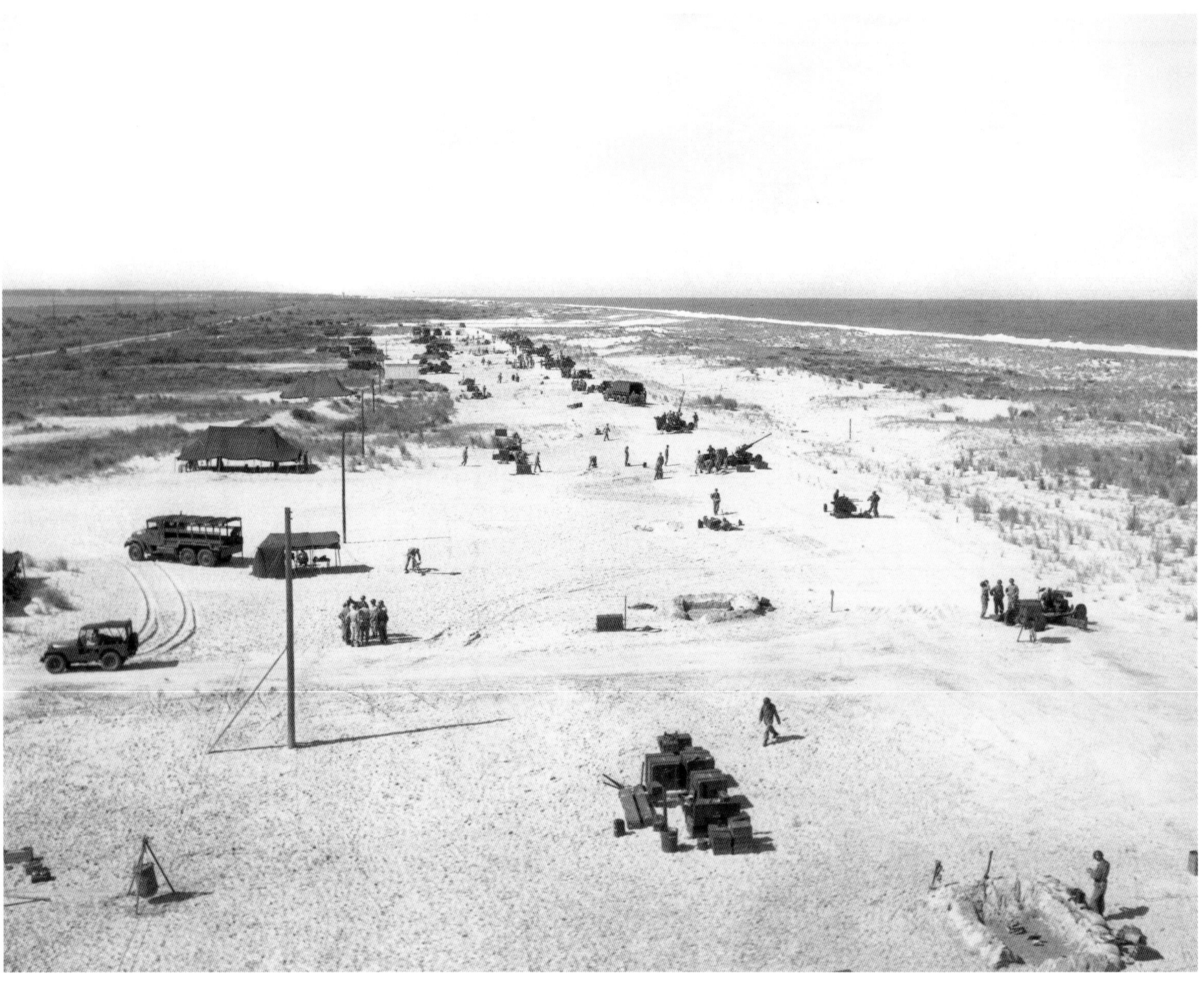

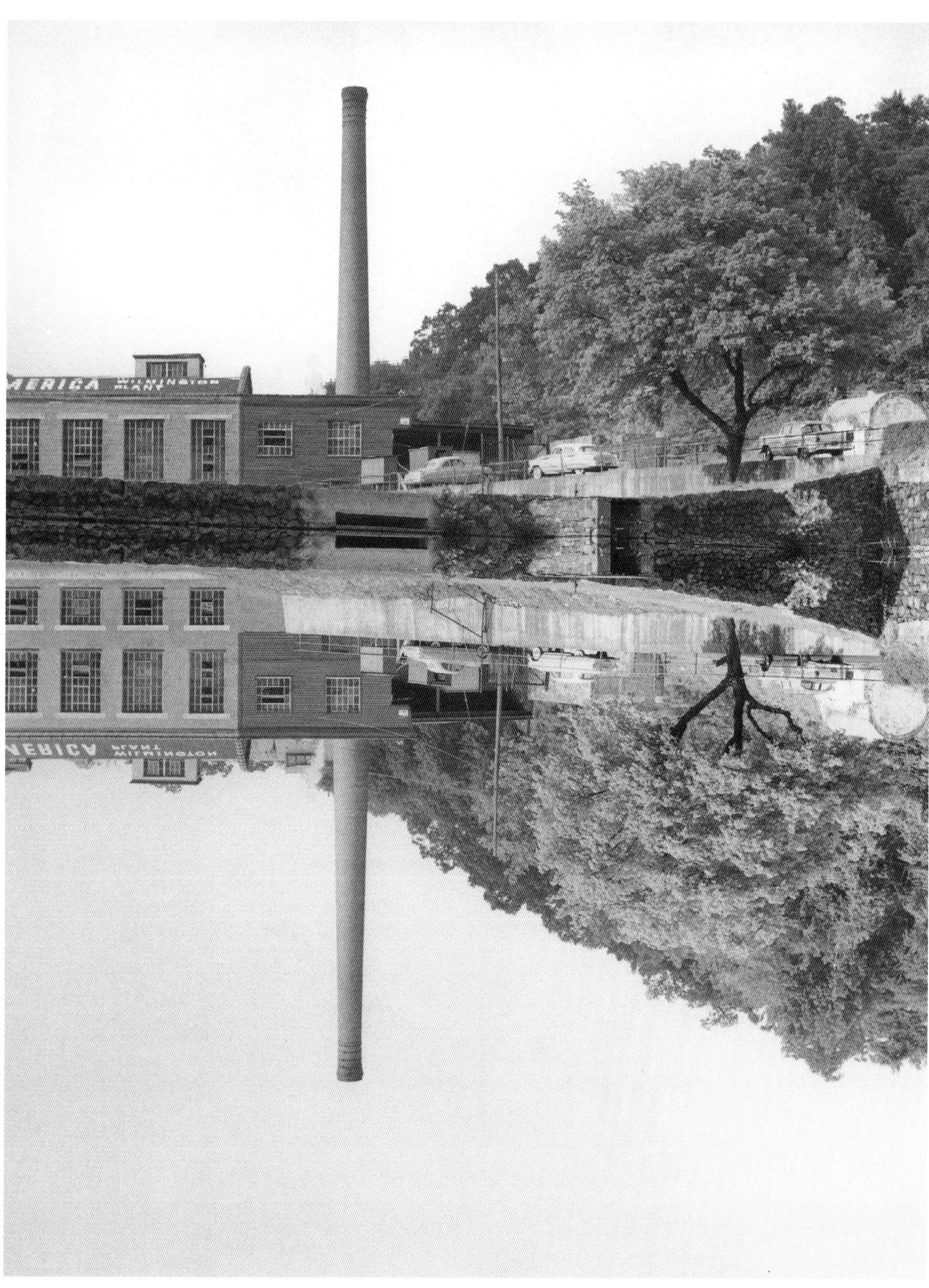

Photographer Cameron F. Jones recorded this view of Augustine Mills on the Brandywine on a placid day. Originally built by Jessup and Moore Paper Company, the buildings were later used by the Container Corporation of America. This mill produced magazine and textbook papers and pulp. The company grew to include the Rockland Mills before it closed in 1942.

This is a view of construction of the first span of the Delaware Memorial Bridge in February 1951. Workers are installing one of two 4,100-foot cables, each measuring 20 inches in diameter. Each cable was made of 19 strands, and each strand was made of 436 separate 3/16-inch diameter steel wires. In all, approximately 12,000 miles of wire were used in the bridge cables. The main cables are spun across the bridge's two 417-foot-tall towers and help suspend the roadway.

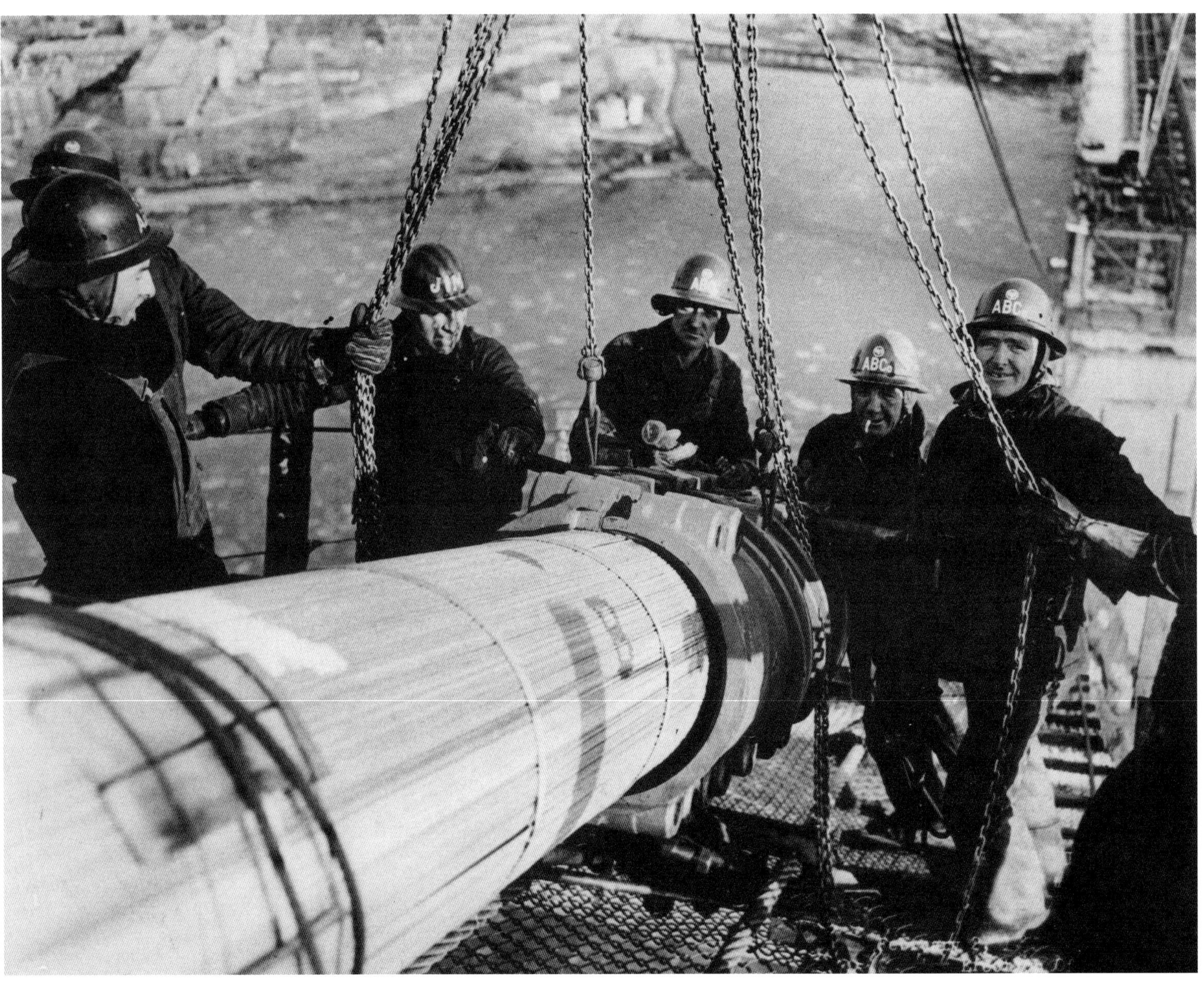

This view shows work on the first section of the west tower on the Delaware side of the Delaware Memorial Bridge one year into construction of the first span. The foundation, which measures 95 feet by 221 feet, dwarfs the construction workers, yet they are using their bodies to lean against the tower to position it perfectly within the base. Construction of this first span began in February 1949. The bridge opened in August 1951.

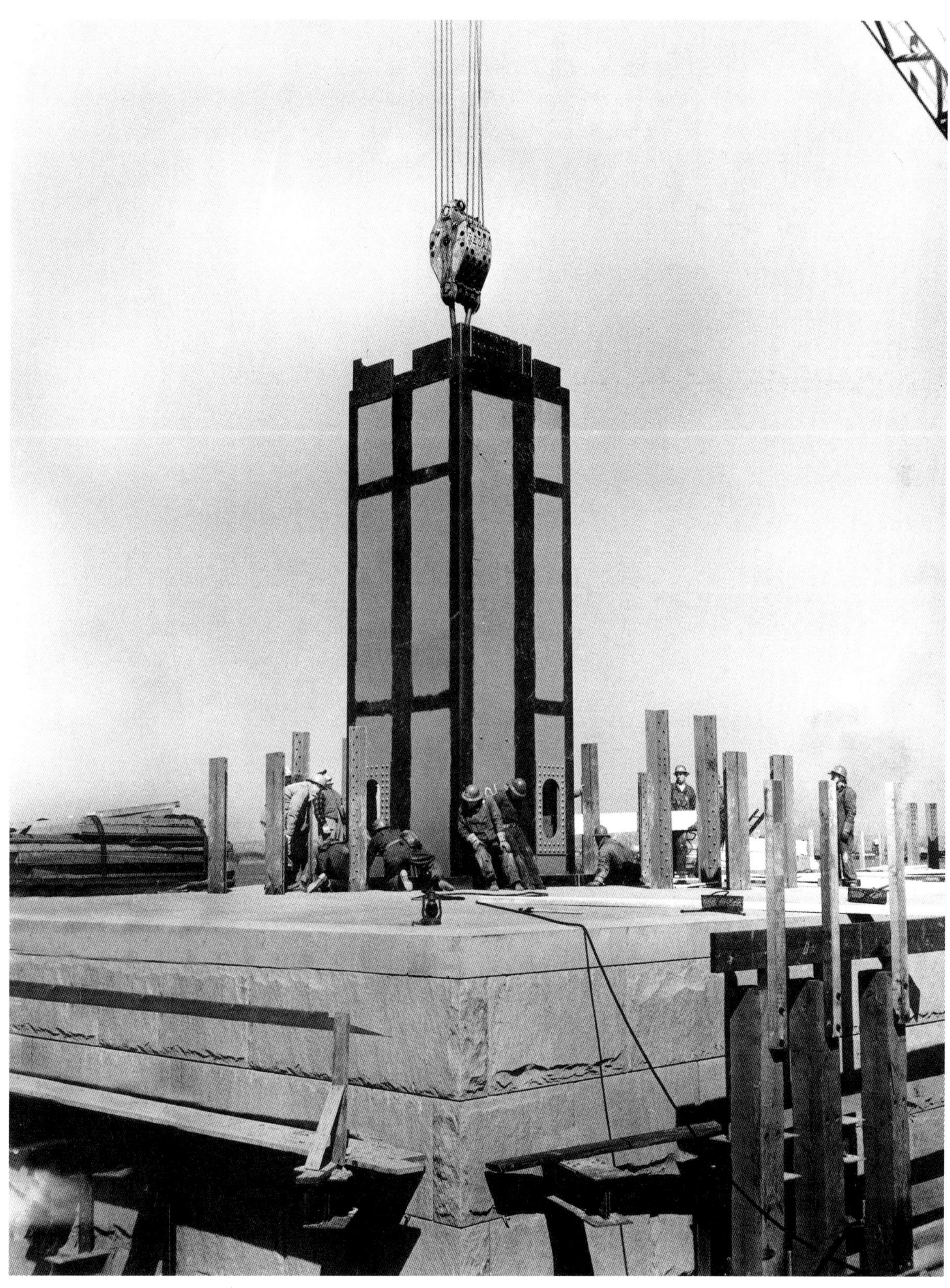

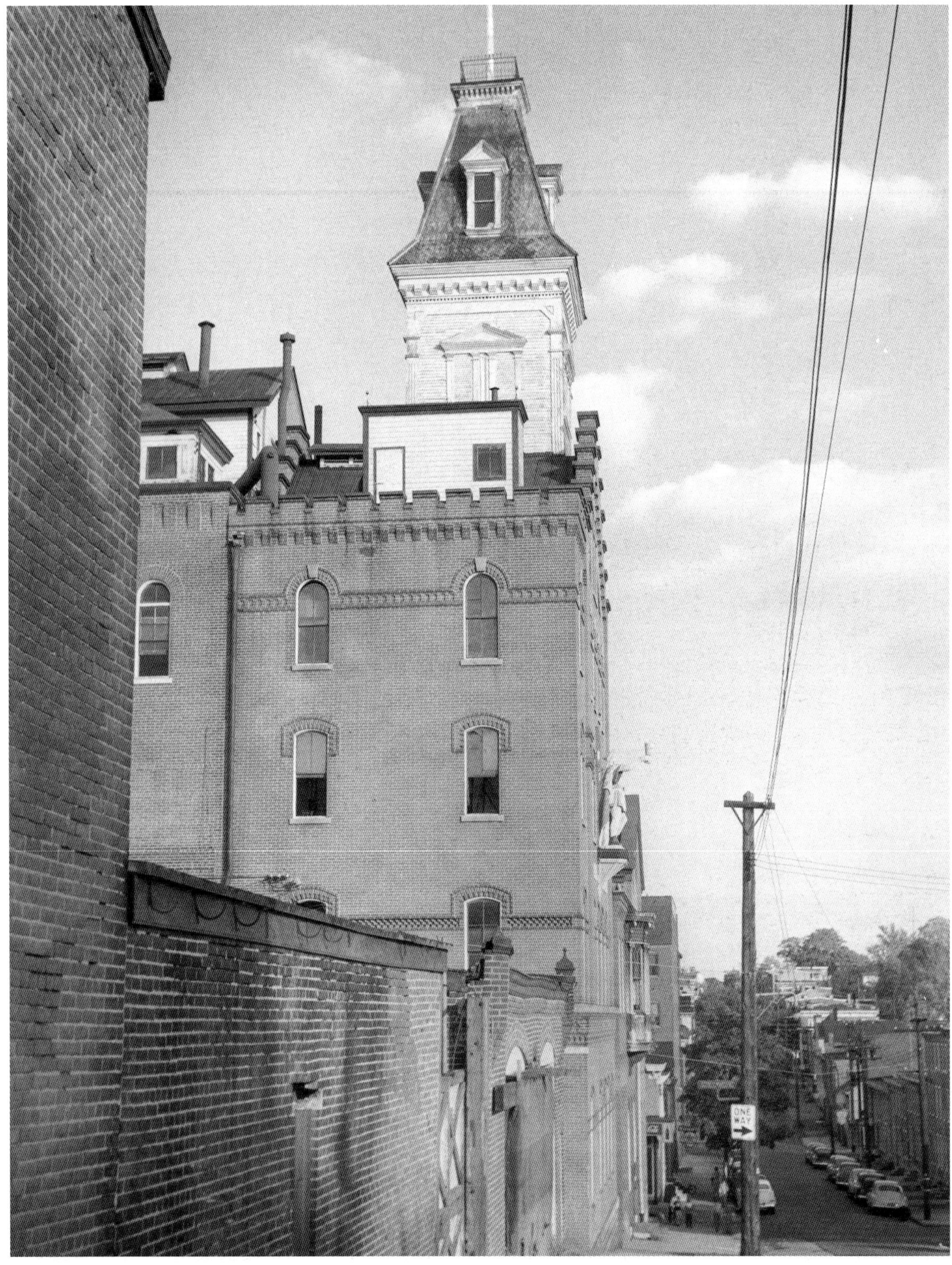

Begun as the Joseph Stoeckle Brewing Company, this business was later the Diamond State Brewery, located on 5th Street between Adams and Jackson streets in Wilmington. This photo was taken in October 1951 and shows the front facade, including the statue of King Gambrinus, known as the patron saint of beer. Statues of Gambrinus adorned many late-nineteenth-century breweries to honor the rich heritage of beer-making.

The first motorcade drove over the Chesapeake Bay Bridge on July 30, 1952. It is hard to overstate the importance of this bridge-tunnel to transportation in and around the Delmarva Peninsula. A feat of engineering, its opening day was one of great celebration attended by dignitaries from both states. Here Maryland governor Theodore McKeldin, former governor William Preston Lane, and Delaware governor Elbert Carvel stand at the edge to look out over the bay.

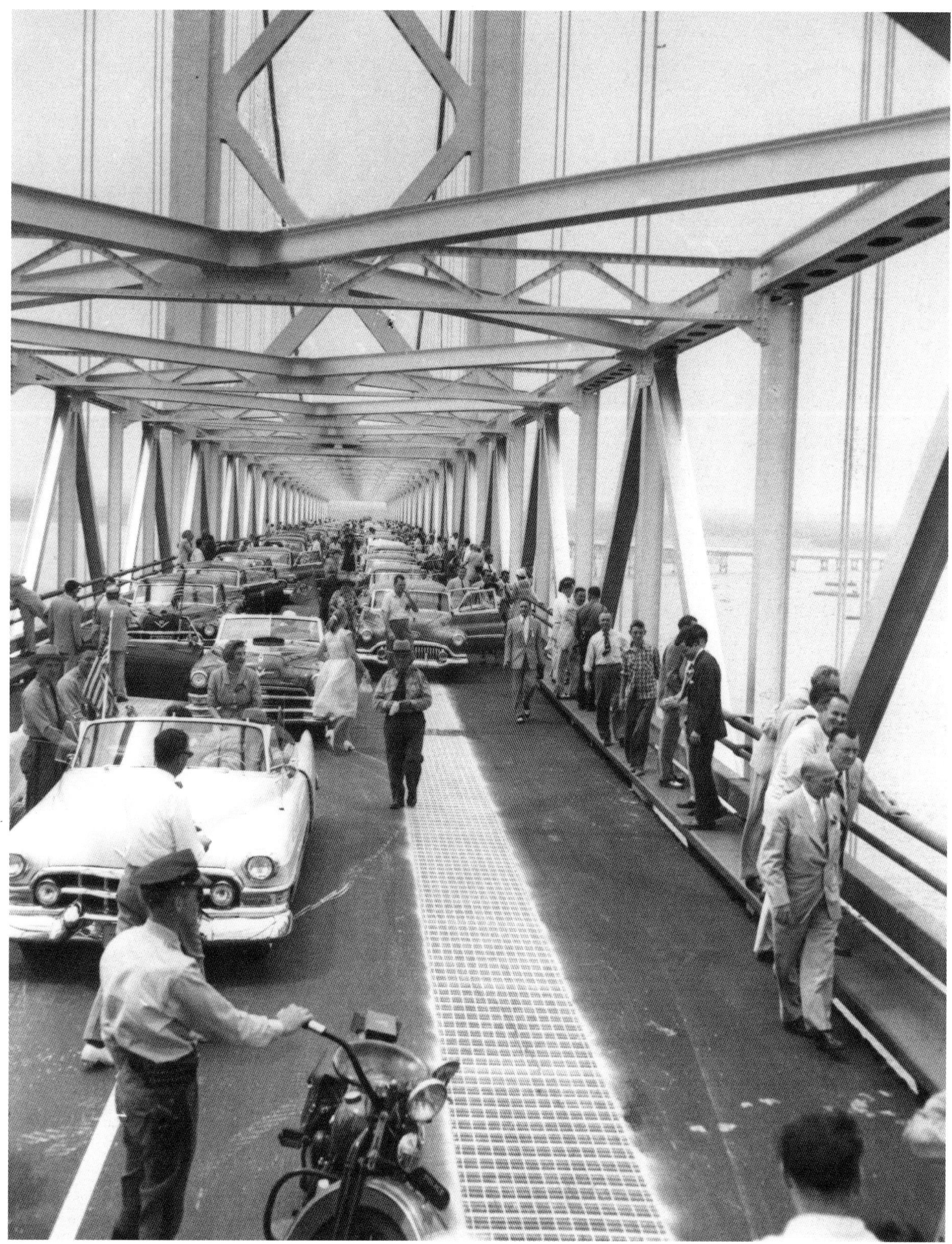

This view shows the completed first span of the Delaware Memorial Bridge, which opened August 16, 1951. The roadway was suspended 188 feet above the waterway in order to accommodate the tallest ships traveling to the ports of Philadelphia and Camden and the Philadelphia Navy Yard. The bridge was then the sixth longest main suspension span in the world. The American Institute of Steel Construction named it the most beautiful large steel span of the year.

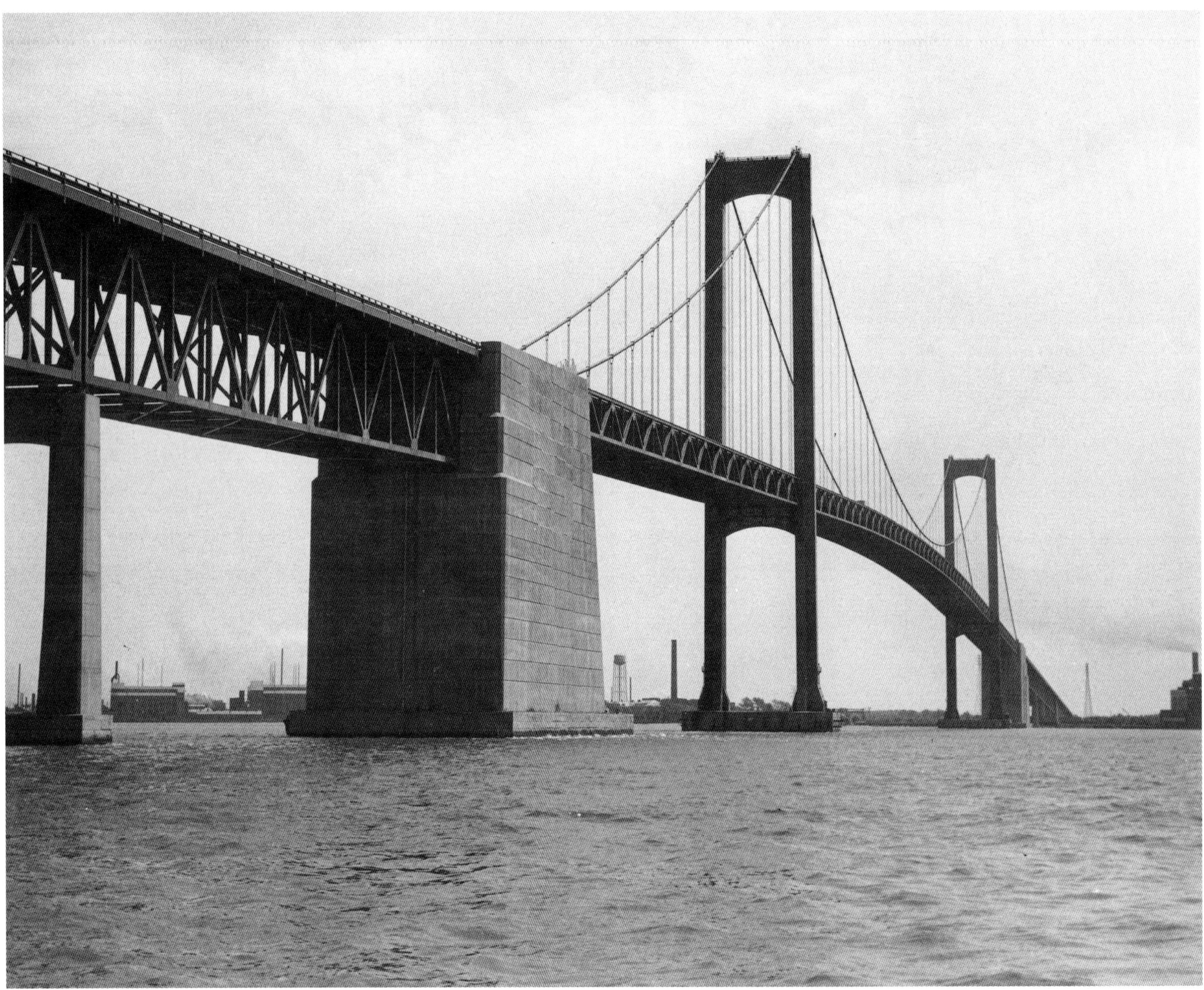

During the 1950s communications cables were added throughout the state as communications became increasingly sophisticated. Here workers are placing new wires at an unidentified location downstate.

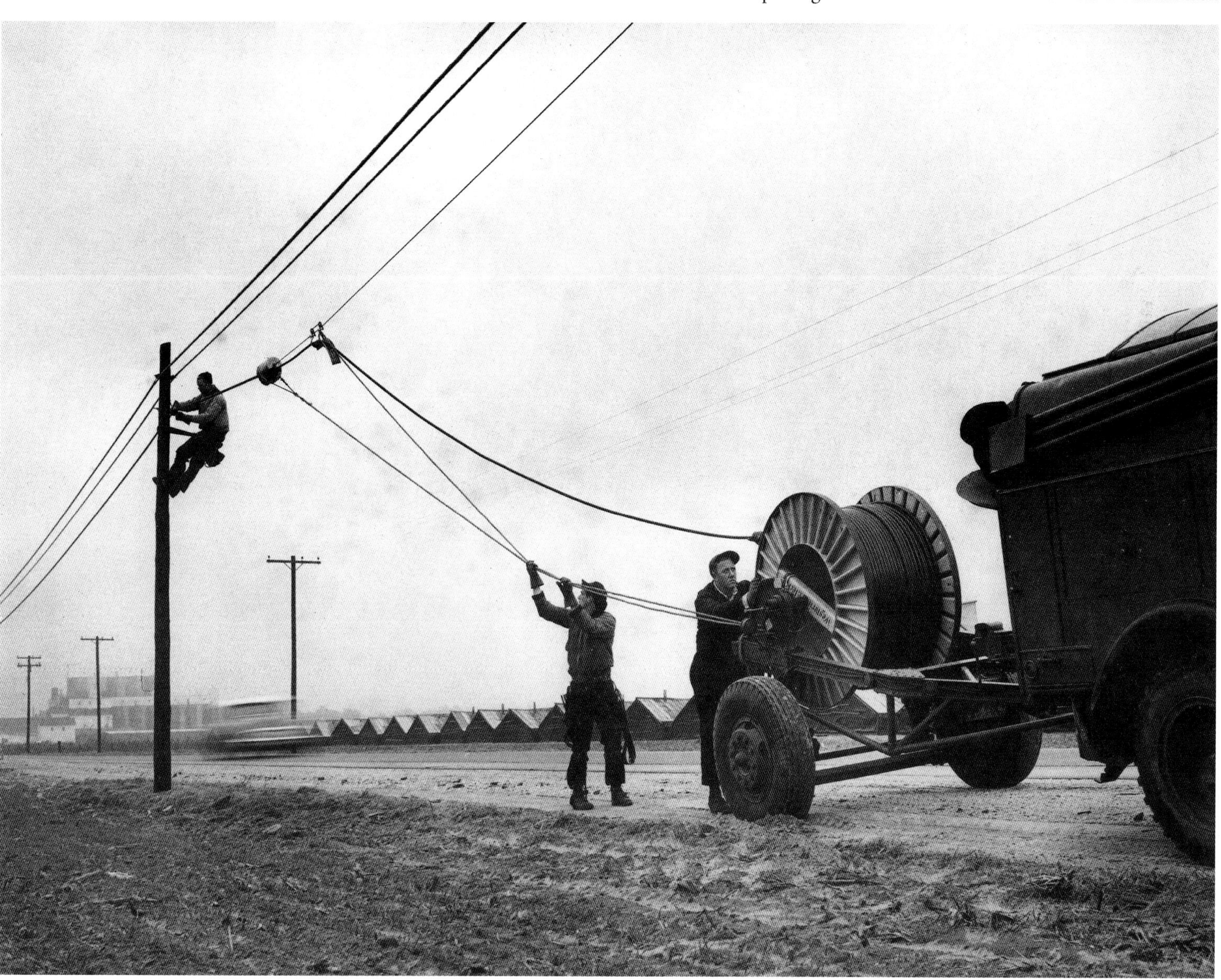

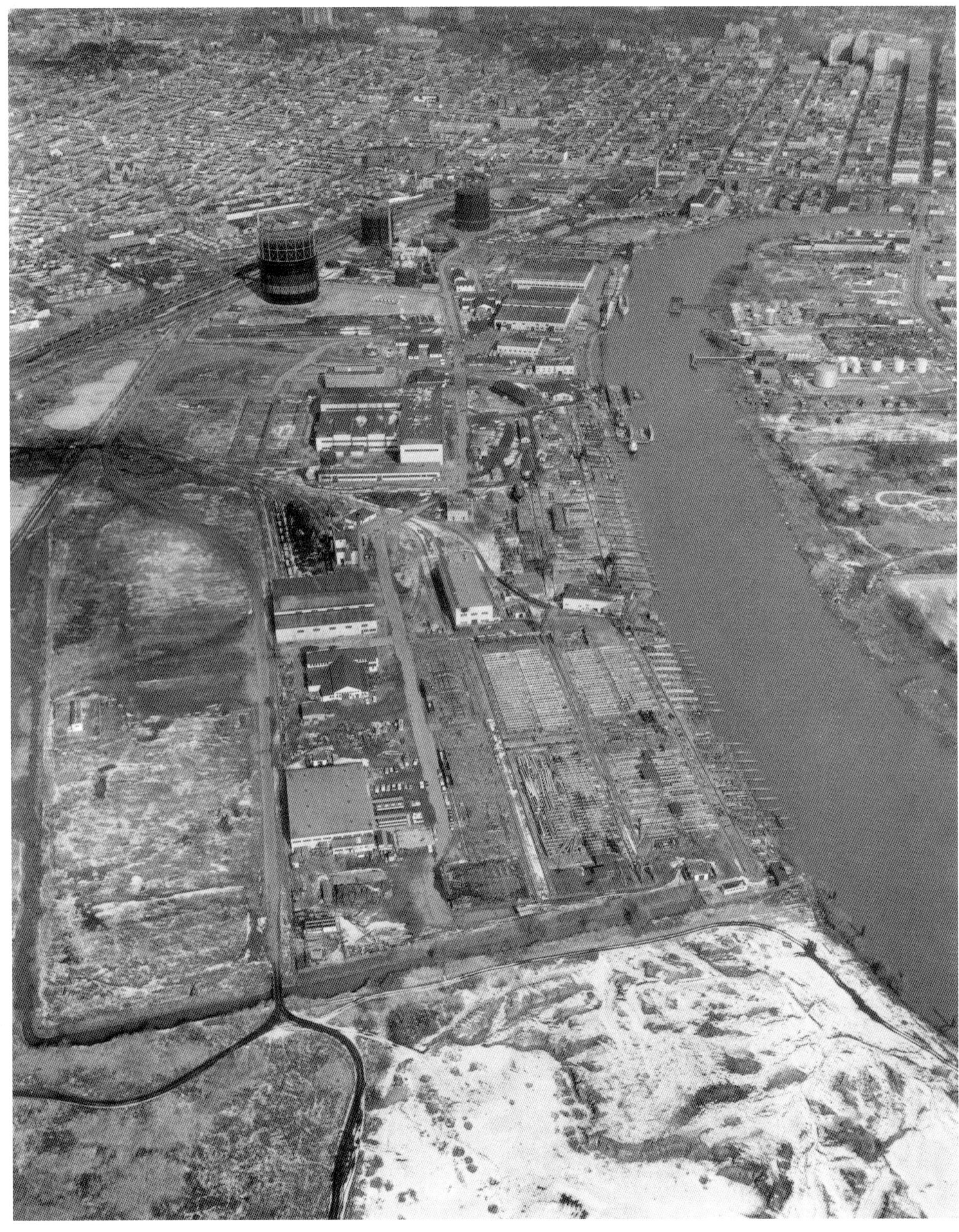

This aerial view shows the Dravo Shipyard property along the Christina River on January 24, 1961. In late 1940 the Navy first contracted with Dravo and later designated Wilmington as the lead shipyard for landing-ship and destroyer escort production. Navy funds were used to expand the yards, which reverted to government property after the war. In 1965, the company announced that it would close the yards and lay off the remaining 80 employees.

Members of the Motley family from Seaford prepare to board the bus for a civil rights rally in Washington, D.C. The March on Washington for Jobs and Freedom took place on August 28, 1963. It was the largest demonstration in Washington to date and the first with extensive television coverage.

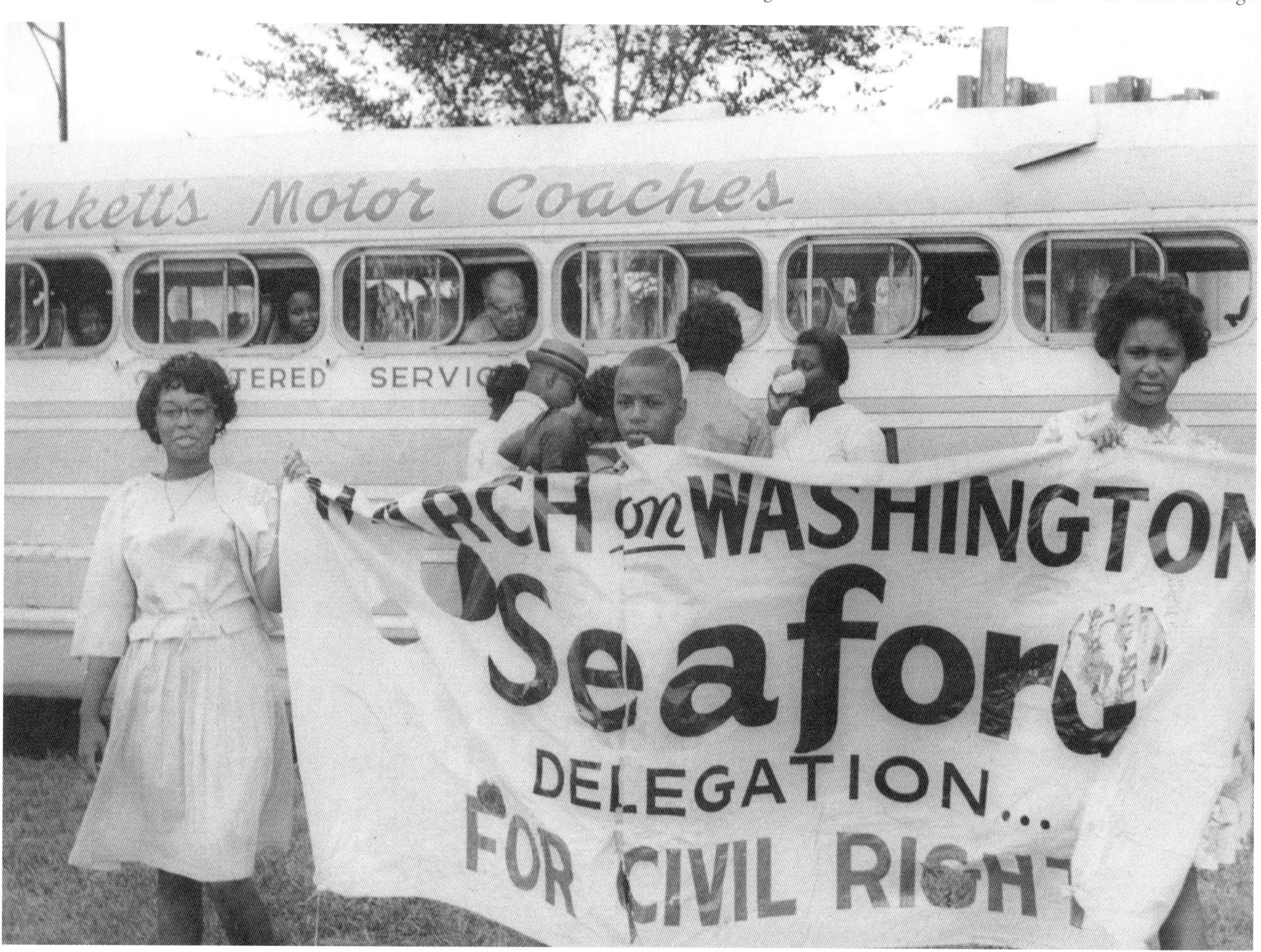

This graveyard is part of St. James Protestant Episcopal Church in Stanton. This site at St. James Church Road and Old Capital Trail has hosted church services since 1677. The building shown dates to 1823, when it was consecrated after a fire destroyed an earlier building. The earliest-known grave in the cemetery is that of John Armstrong, who died November 23, 1726.

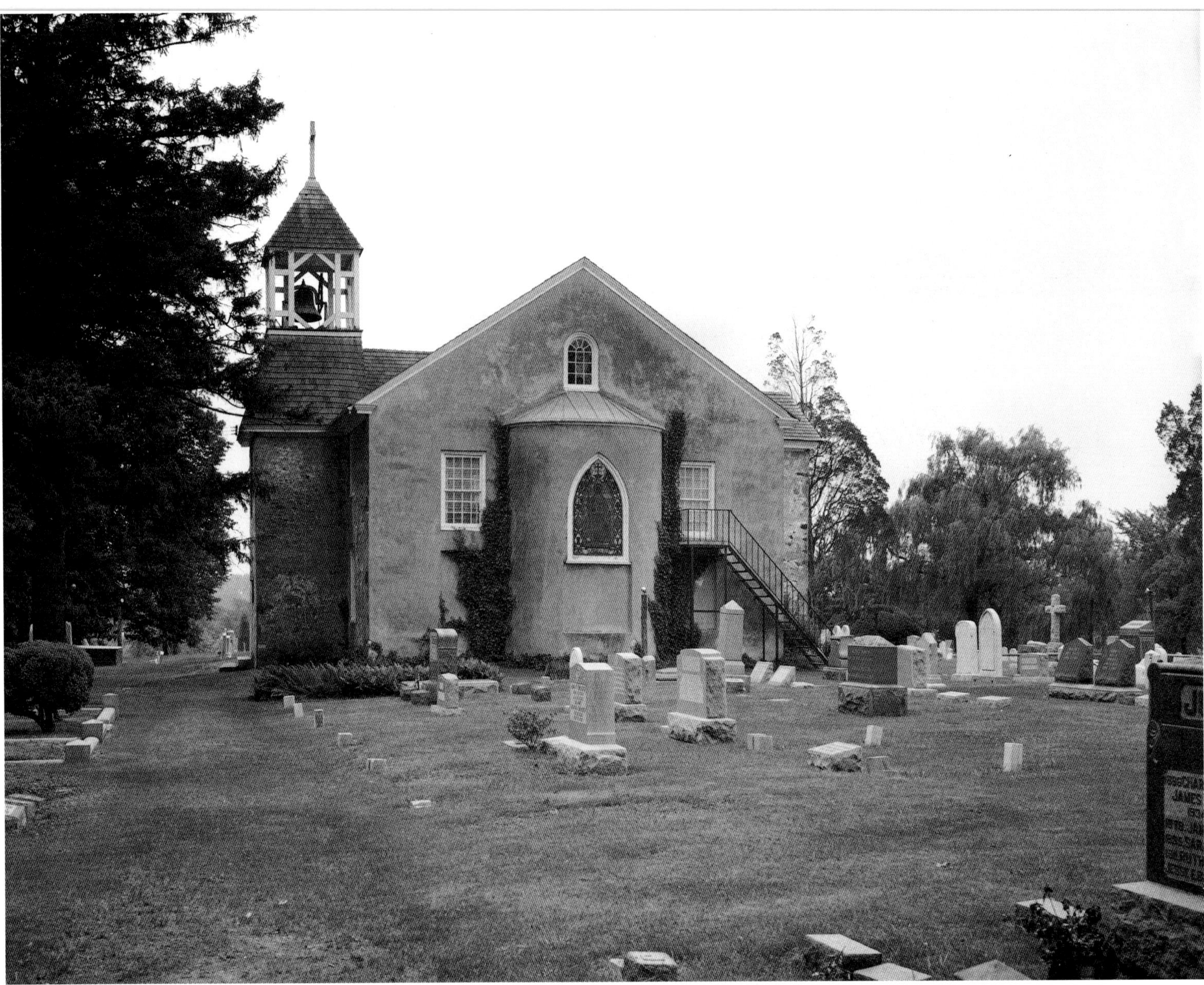

A farm typical of the many that dotted the landscape of rural Delaware in the 1950s and 1960s.

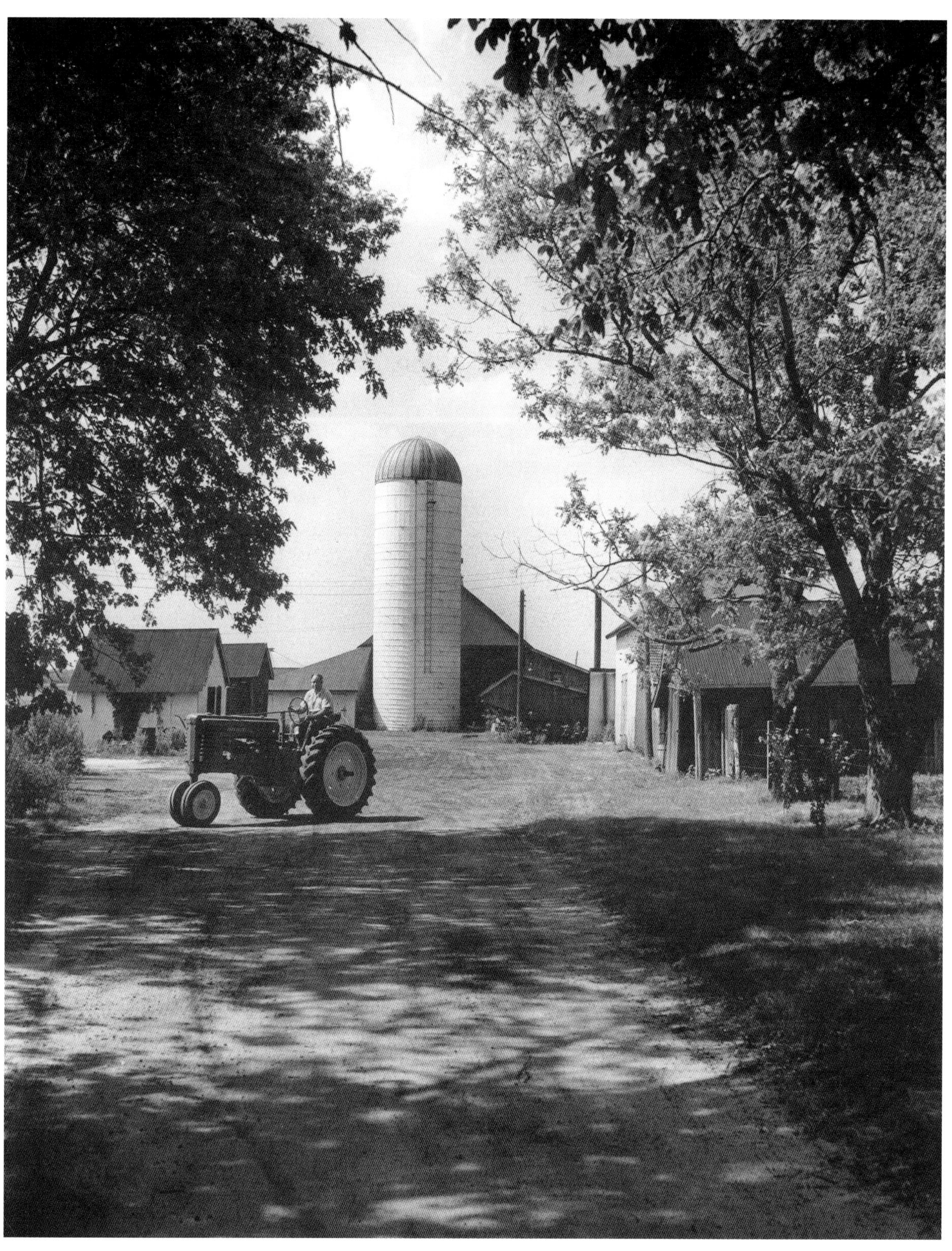

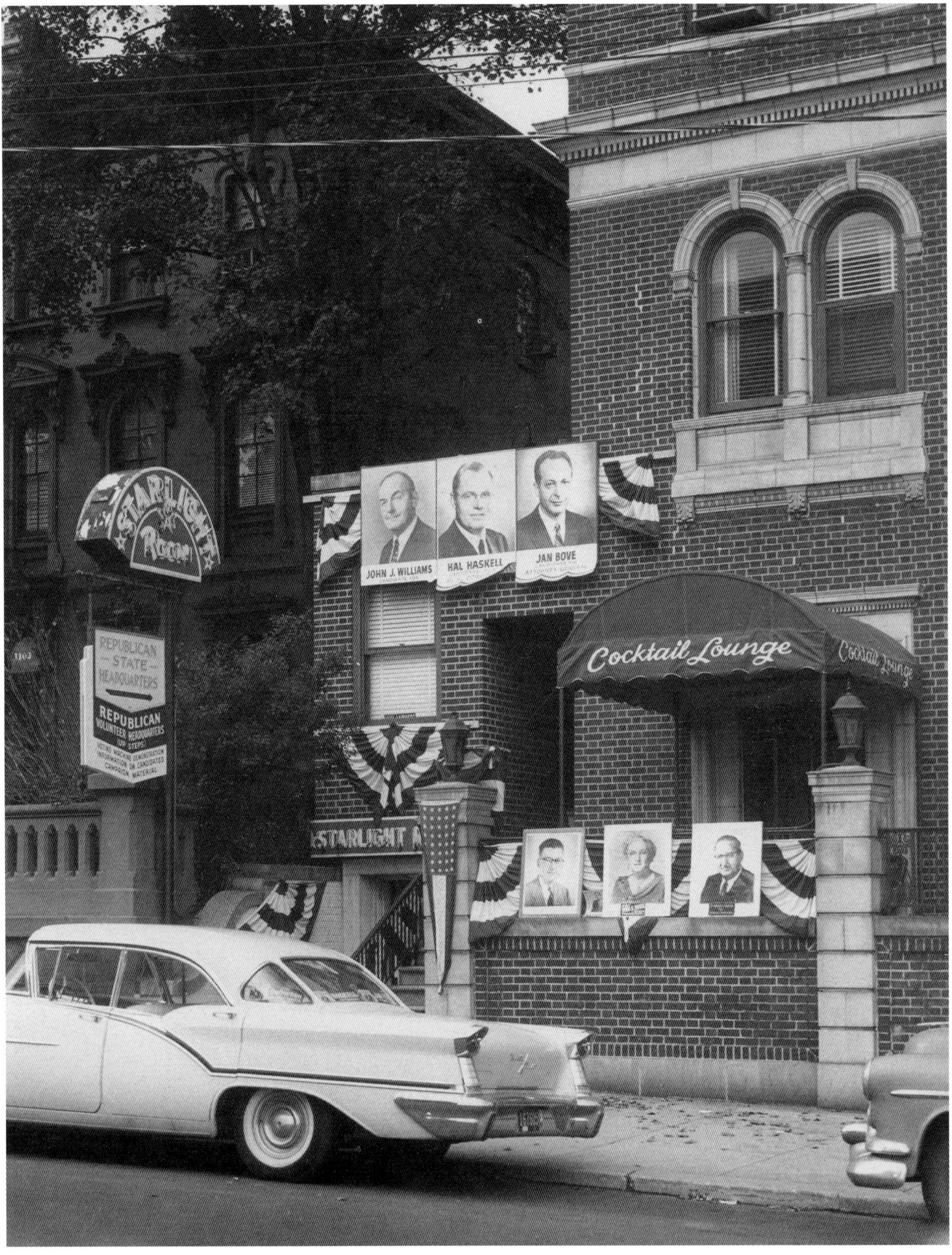

Campaign time in Wilmington finds the Republican State Headquarters open next door to the Starlight Room on October 28, 1958. The office was located in the Hotel Rodney at 1105 Market Street. The hotel, located next to the Wilmington Club (formerly the John Merrick house), has since been demolished. In the race, John Williams was reelected, but Hal Haskell would not win his bid for mayor for another decade.

This is a view of Rehoboth's boardwalk and crowded beach in the 1960s. After decades of tremendous growth in the 1930s and 1940s, including a large influx of Washington, D.C., visitors, Rehoboth took the name "Nation's Summer Capital." On March 6, 1962, a terrible storm pounded the beaches of Sussex County for three days as it stalled off the coast, causing tremendous damage to Rehoboth and surrounding communities.

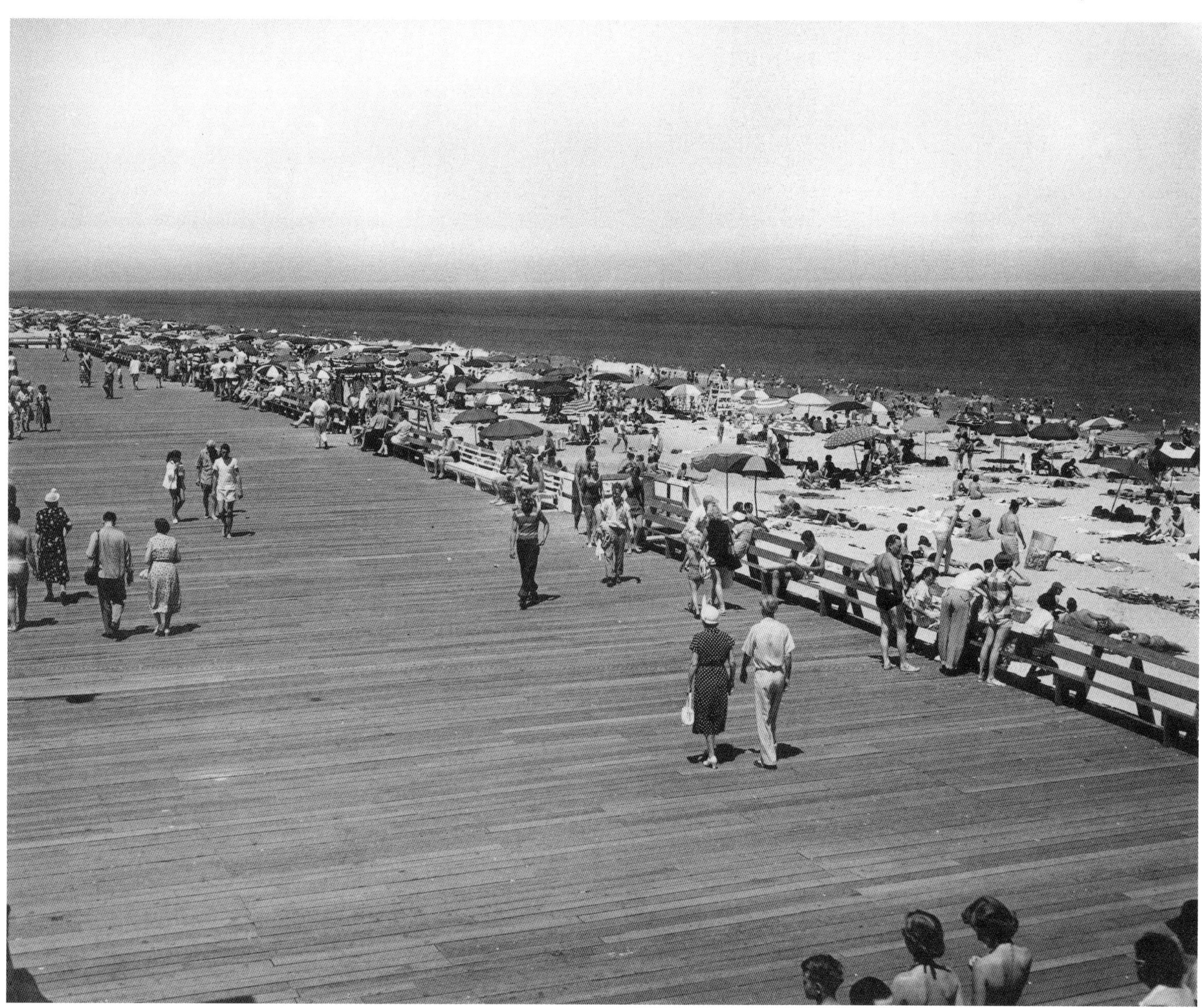

This scene is from a Blue-Gold game in the early 1960s. Bob Carpenter and Jim Williams, sports enthusiasts and parents of children with cognitive disabilities, inspired the first game played on August 25, 1936. Each year 36 players from Delaware's high schools play in this fund-raising and awareness-raising game in support of cognitive disabilities. The Blue team consists mostly of players from New Castle County, and the Gold team consists mostly of players from Kent and Sussex counties.

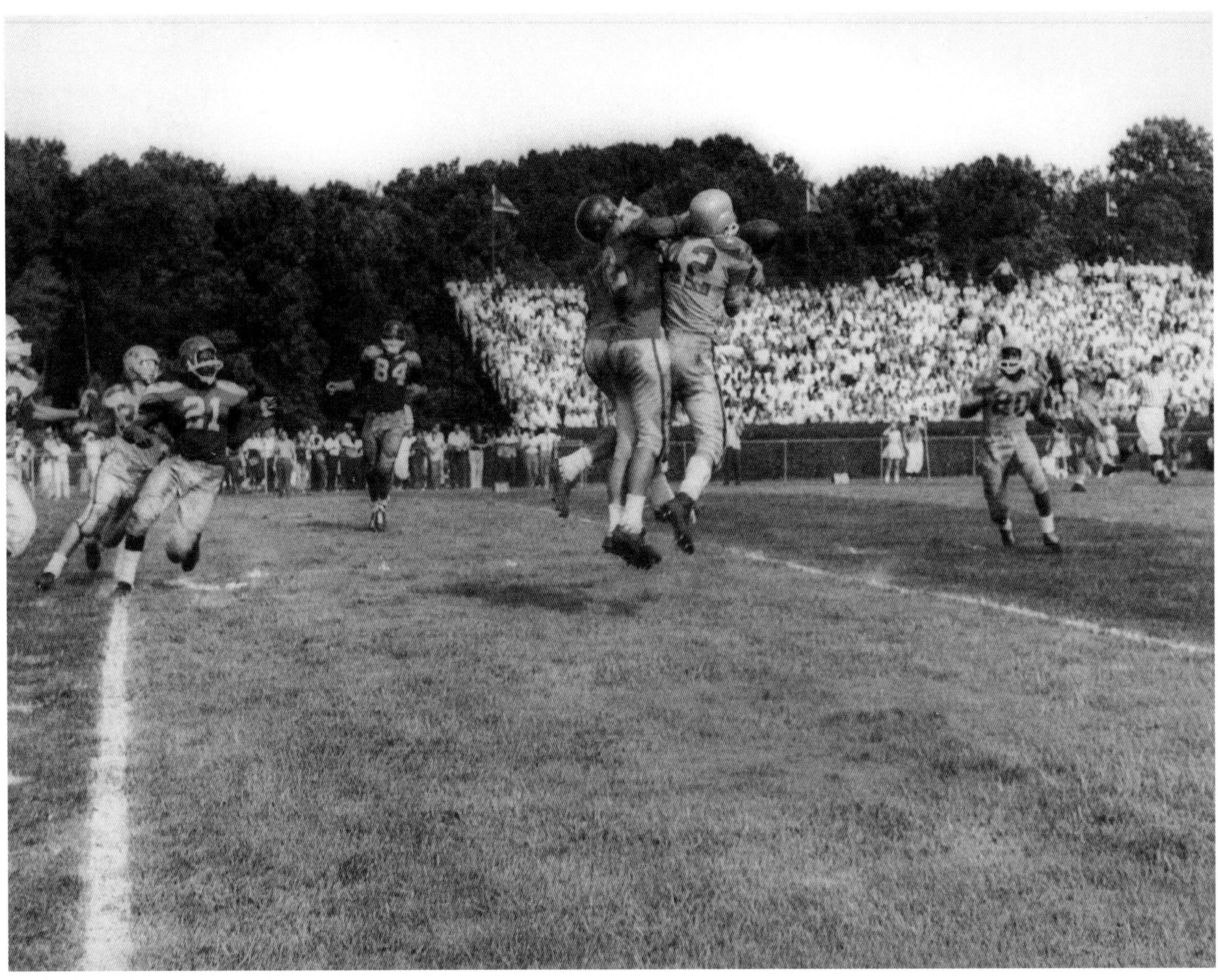

Democratic candidate John F. Kennedy addresses a large crowd gathered at the New Castle County Airport during the 1960 presidential race.

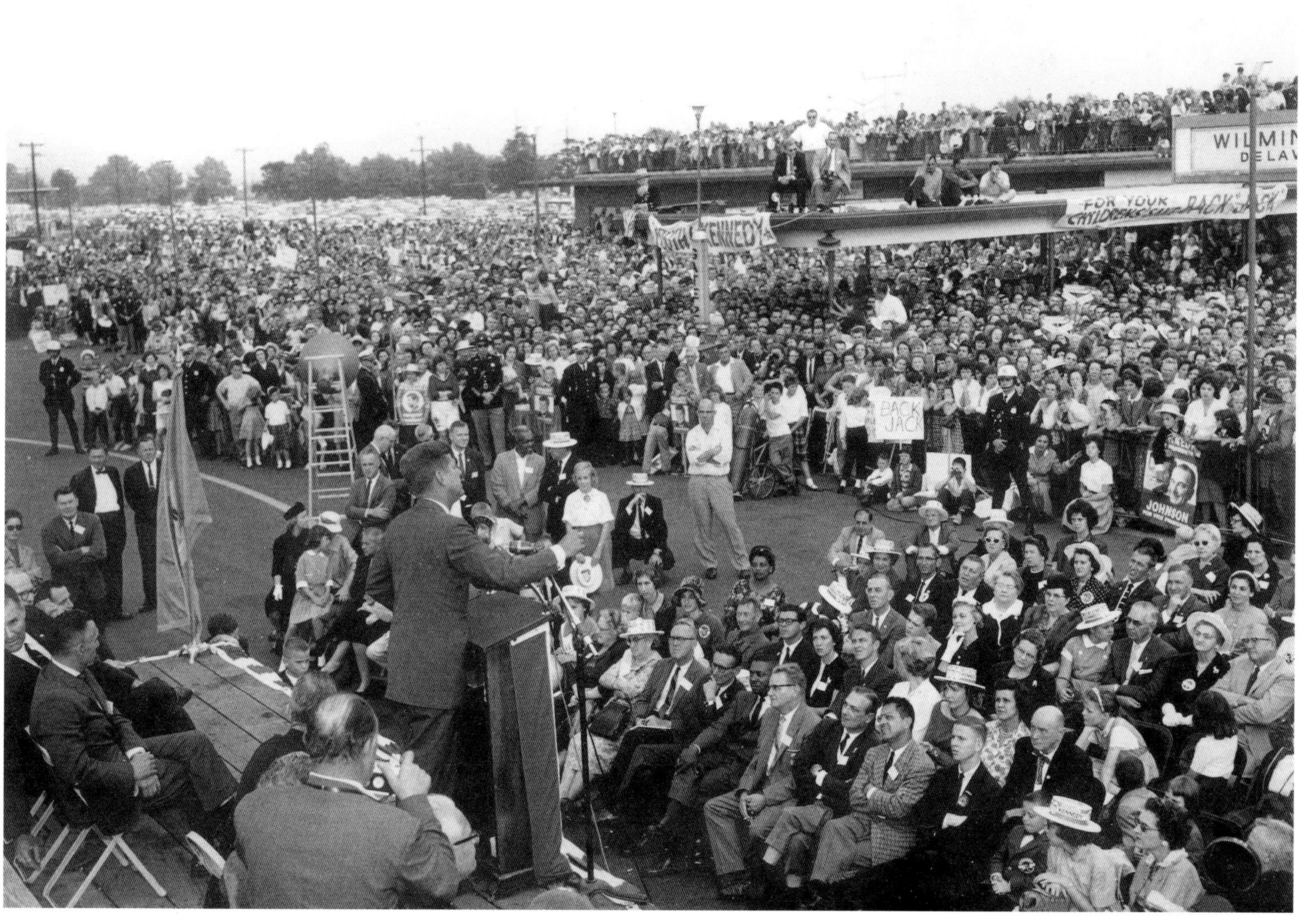

The Charles Meat Market at 7th and Jefferson streets in Wilmington was damaged during the race riots of April 9, 1968. After the assassination of Martin Luther King, Jr., riots erupted across the nation and in Wilmington. The Delaware National Guard quickly stemmed the violence. Using a strategy considered misguided today, the governor left the troops on city streets for nine months, making Wilmington the nation's longest-occupied city after the riots.

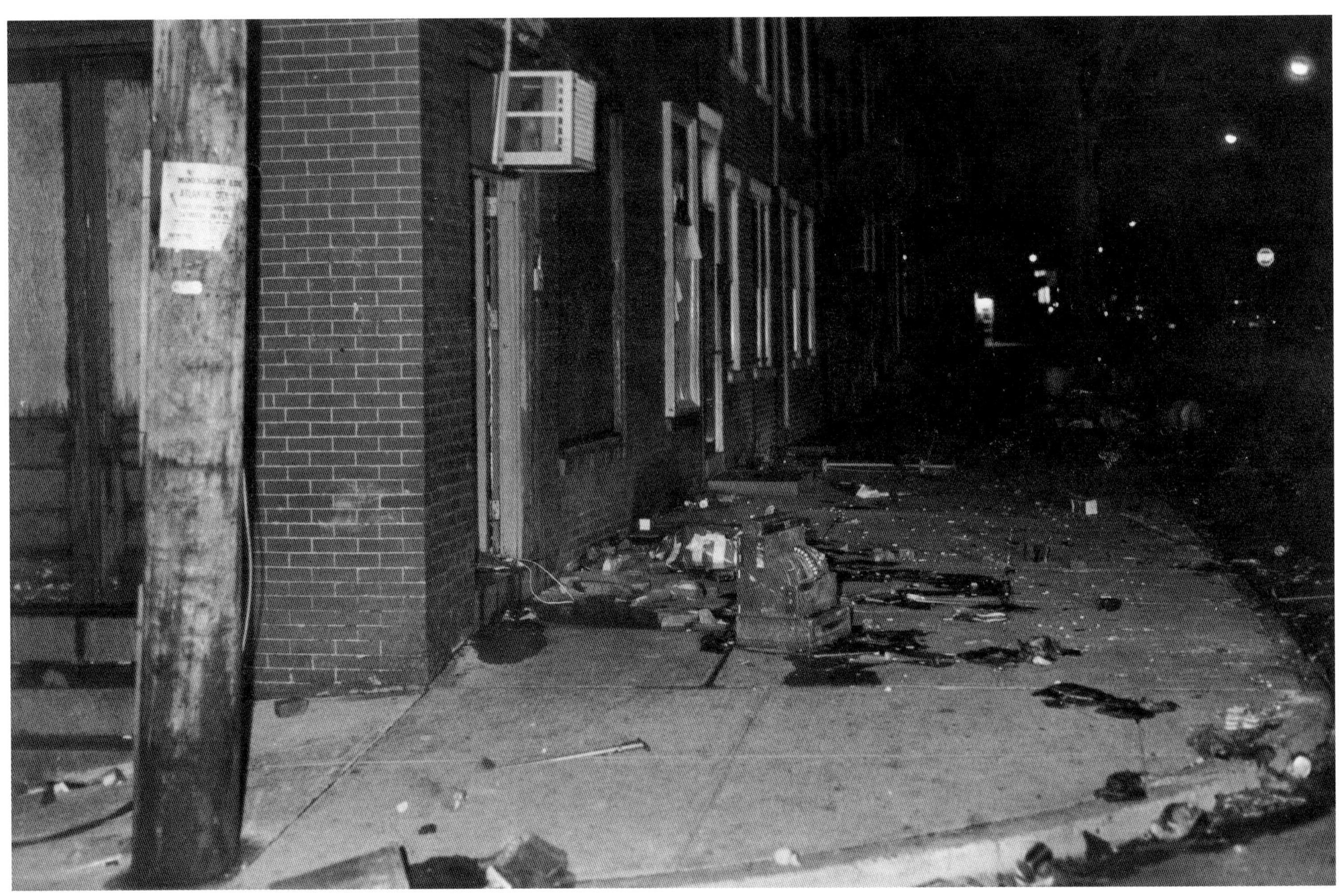

Young people demonstrate against the Vietnam War and President Nixon in favor of Chris Smith at the Democratic Convention in Dover in the early 1970s. Unsuccessful in his campaign, Smith ran on the peace platform.

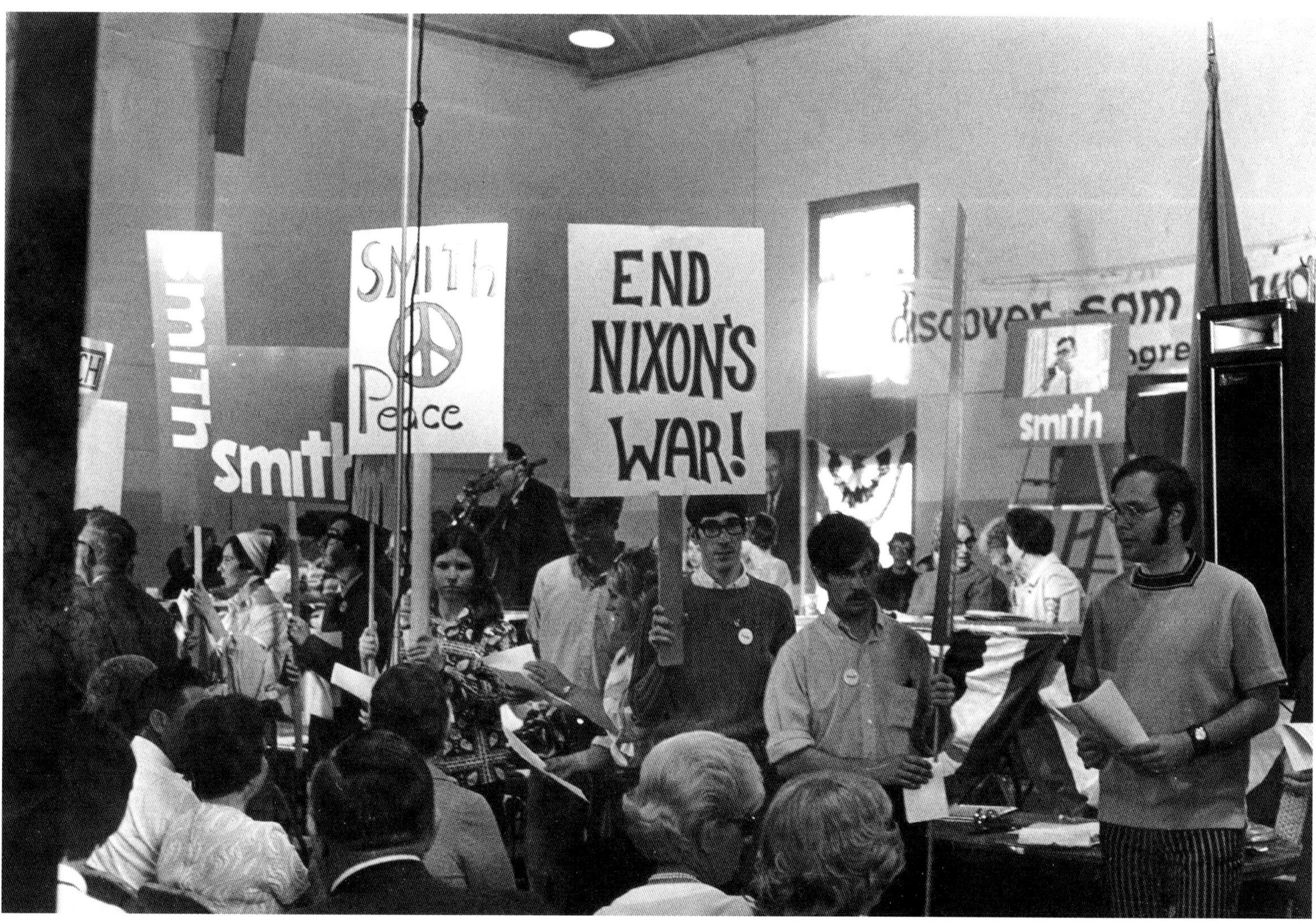

An open house at the Dover Air Force Base, late 1960s. The Army leased the Dover Municipal Airport 10 days after the bombing of Pearl Harbor. It was used for securing the coastline, as training grounds for P-47 Thunderbolt pilots, and as the site of secret rocket development. After the war, unlike the New Castle site which reverted to civilian use, the government retained possession of the base. In 1971 the base received its first C-5 Galaxy transport plane.

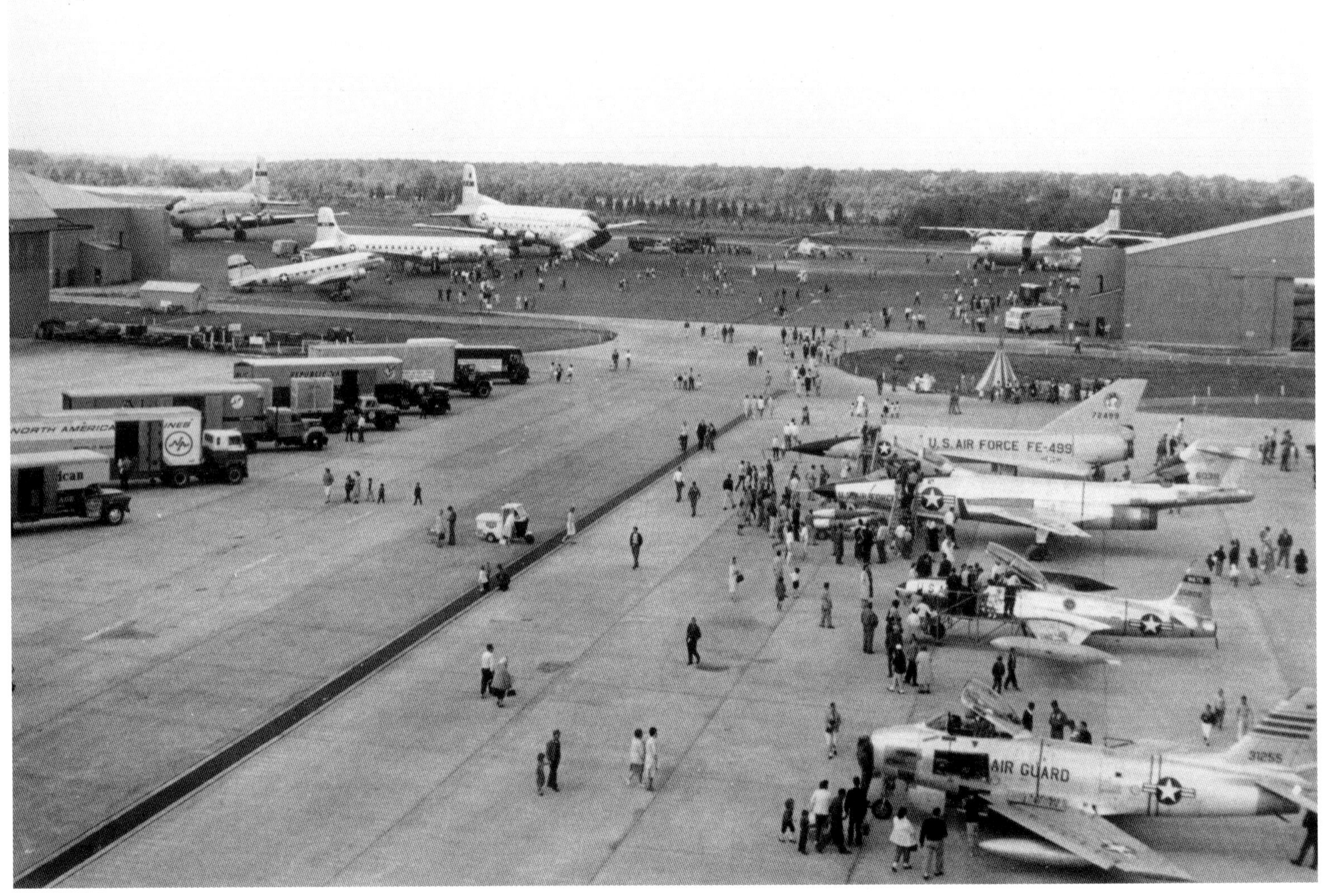

Twilight silhouettes the east-end lighthouse at the Delaware Breakwater, under almost perfectly calm conditions.

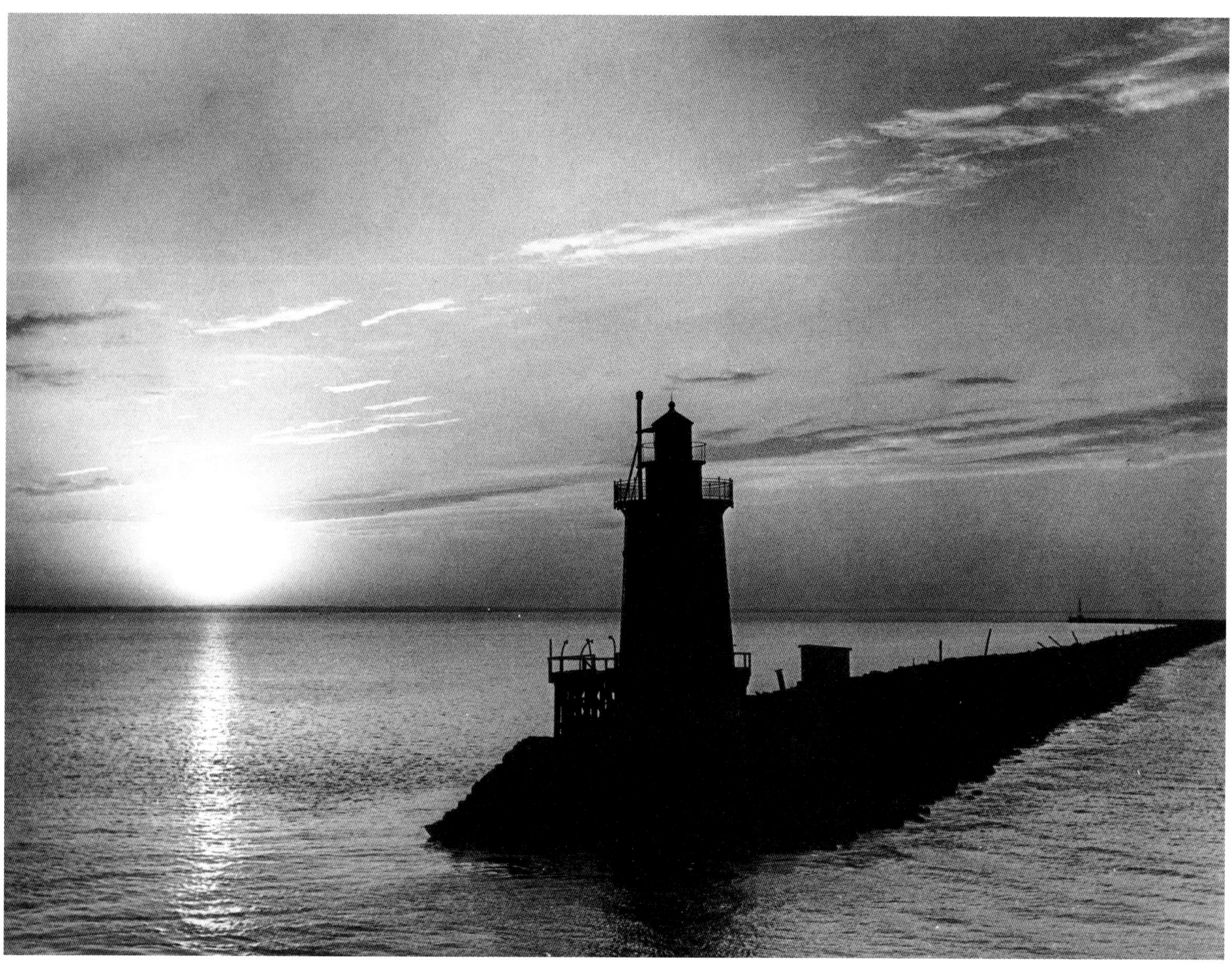

Notes on the Photographs

These notes, listed by page number, attempt to include all aspects known of the photographs. Each of the photographs is identified by the page number, photograph's title or description, photographer and collection, archive, and call or box number when applicable. Although every attempt was made to collect all available data, in some cases complete data was unavailable due to the age and condition of some of the photographs and records.

II **John J. Hagan Tug**
Library of Congress
lc-usz62-60484

VI **Taking a Break**
Library of Congress
lc-usz62-116752

X **Swedes Church**
Courtesy of the Delaware Historical Society
Stereocard 1998.21

3 **Grace Methodist**
Courtesy of the Delaware Historical Society
Stereocard 7

4 **Fort Delaware**
Courtesy of the Delaware Historical Society
Del122

5 **Market Street**
Library of Congress
09585u

6 **Tilton Hospital**
Courtesy of the Delaware Historical Society
Del141

7 **Soldiers**
Courtesy of the Delaware Historical Society
Del153

8 **Locomotive No. 1**
Courtesy of the Delaware Historical Society
Del192

9 **Leisurely Pose**
Courtesy of the Delaware Historical Society
Collins Beach stereocard

10 **New Castle**
Courtesy of the Delaware Historical Society
Stereocard_2002.46.13

11 **Limestone Kiln**
Courtesy of the Delaware Historical Society
Stereocard_41.76.104

12 **Work Force**
Library of Congress
87.17.4022

13 **Water Street**
Courtesy of the Delaware Historical Society
Del190

14 **Holly Tree Inn**
Courtesy of the Delaware Historical Society
Del138

15 **Aerial Truck**
Courtesy of the Delaware Historical Society
Del119

16 **Water Street Station**
Courtesy of the Delaware Historical Society
64.51.1

17 **Wooden Ship**
Courtesy of the Delaware Historical Society
Del209

18 **Humphries Haberdashery**
Courtesy of the Delaware Historical Society
Del065

19 **Grasshopper Engine**
Courtesy of the Delaware Historical Society
Stereocard 41.76.98

20 **Train Station**
Courtesy of the Delaware Historical Society
Newark Train station, ca. 1890

21 **Hebb's School**
Library of Congress
Misses Hebbs class of 89

22 **Breakwater**
Library of Congress
09096u

24 **5th Artillery**
Courtesy of the Delaware Historical Society
Del152

25 **Bicycle Club**
Courtesy of the Delaware Historical Society
Del113

26 **Covered Wagon**
Courtesy of the Delaware Historical Society
46.85.6

27 **Town and Country Store**
Courtesy of the Delaware Historical Society
Del230

28 Shipwrecked
Courtesy of the Delaware Historical Society
Del200

29 Hagley Museum
Courtesy of the Delaware Historical Society
Del172

30 Passenger Car
Courtesy of the Delaware Historical Society
Stereocard 41.76.87

31 Mill
Courtesy of the Delaware Historical Society
Del169

32 Annie Jump Cannon
Courtesy of the Delaware Historical Society
Del186

33 Christening
Courtesy of the Delaware Historical Society
Del067

34 Young Cyclists
Courtesy of the Delaware Historical Society
Del222

35 New Castle Courthouse
Courtesy of the Delaware Historical Society
Del100

36 Vendors
Courtesy of the Delaware Historical Society
Del069

37 Christ Church
Courtesy of the Delaware Historical Society
Del083

38 Lord Baltimore
Courtesy of the Delaware Historical Society
95.167

39 Clawson S. Hammitt
Courtesy of the Delaware Historical Society
86.33.12

40 Republican Invincibles
Courtesy of the Delaware Historical Society
Del111

41 Volunteer Yacht
Courtesy of the Delaware Historical Society
Del215

42 Rail Station
Courtesy of the Delaware Historical Society
Del196

43 Parade
Courtesy of the Delaware Historical Society
Del181

44 Claymont Brick Works
Courtesy of the Delaware Historical Society
Del144

47 Delaware City Hotel
Courtesy of the Delaware Historical Society
Del139

48 Christina River
Courtesy of the Delaware Historical Society
Del201

49 Small Tavern
Courtesy of the Delaware Historical Society
Del137

50 In the Stocks
Library of Congress
31931u

51 Torpedo Boat
Courtesy of the Delaware Historical Society
Del164

52 Children in a Tree
Courtesy of the Delaware Historical Society
Del102

53 Colonial Band
Courtesy of the Delaware Historical Society
Del179

54 Residential Street
Courtesy of the Delaware Historical Society
Nitrate postcard neg 95

56 Laying Sewage Lines
Courtesy of the Delaware Historical Society
85.36.27

57 Delivery Wagon
Courtesy of the Delaware Historical Society
Del076

58 White Brothers
Courtesy of the Delaware Historical Society
6.28 part 4

59 Silk Mill
Courtesy of the Delaware Historical Society
Del167

60 Operating Room
Courtesy of the Delaware Historical Society
Del134

61 Apprentices
Courtesy of the Delaware Historical Society
85.26.98

62 Vienna Bakery
Courtesy of the Delaware Historical Society
Del066

63 DuPont
Courtesy of the Delaware Historical Society
Del073

64 Charles Ottey
Courtesy of the Delaware Historical Society
Del064

65 Young Boys
Courtesy of the Delaware Historical Society
1997.15

66 Old Home Week
Courtesy of the Delaware Historical Society
Del177

67 Walnut Street
Library of Congress
3b36045u

68 Felton Store
Courtesy of the Delaware Historical Society
Del231

69 Harvey Buchanan
Library of Congress
03595u

70 Daisy Langford
Library of Congress
00796u

71 Delaware River
Courtesy of the Delaware
Historical Society
Del212

72 Joseph Severio
Library of Congress
03564u

73 Michael Mero
Library of Congress
03565u

74 Ice Cream Truck
Courtesy of the Delaware
Historical Society
Del055

75 Young Newsies
Library of Congress
03582u

76 Lillie Donohoe
Courtesy of the Delaware
Historical Society
Oversize 3.20-1 to -4

78 Buying Lunch
Library of Congress
03611u

79 Delaware Street
Courtesy of the Delaware
Historical Society
50.20.122

80 Charles Rumford
Courtesy of the Delaware
Historical Society
Rumford Alb A No 17

82 Young Street Vendor
Library of Congress
03573u

83 Hoisted Train
Courtesy of the Delaware
Historical Society
Del095

84 Hulling Strawberries
Library of Congress
00788u

85 Electric Trolley
Courtesy of the Delaware
Historical Society
Del195

86 James Lequlla
Library of Congress
03563u

87 Laying the Cornerstone
Courtesy of the Delaware
Historical Society
50.20.46

88 Churchyard
Courtesy of the Delaware
Historical Society
Del085

89 Dapper Crowd
Courtesy of the Delaware
Historical Society
DuPont Col 2000.124.88

90 Lighthouse
Courtesy of the Delaware
Historical Society
Oversize 6.7

91 Du Pont Party
Courtesy of the Delaware
Historical Society
duPont Col 2000.124.112

92 National Guard
Library of Congress
6a32806u

93 Police Patrol
Courtesy of the Delaware
Historical Society
Del124

94 Race Car
Courtesy of the Delaware
Historical Society
Del226

95 Millinery
Courtesy of the Delaware
Historical Society
Del052

96 Little Creek
Courtesy of the Delaware
Historical Society
Del097

97 Public Building
Courtesy of the Delaware
Historical Society
50.20.83

98 WWI Parade
Courtesy of the Delaware
Historical Society
Del182

99 Armistice Day
Courtesy of the Delaware
Historical Society
Del163

100 Fort Delaware
Courtesy of the Delaware
Historical Society
Del123

101 Red Cross
Courtesy of the Delaware
Historical Society
Del132

102 Helen Jones
Courtesy of the Delaware
Historical Society
HelenJones 2

104 Absecon
Library of Congress
3a44413u

105 Tobin's Market
Courtesy of the Delaware
Historical Society
Del229

106 Aerial
Courtesy of the Delaware
Historical Society
Del216

107 Plate Mill Table
Courtesy of the Delaware
Historical Society
Del142

108 Farmers Market
Courtesy of the Delaware
Historical Society
Del068

109 Engine No. 6
Courtesy of the Delaware
Historical Society
Del118

110 DuPont Company
Courtesy of the Delaware
Historical Society
Del107

111 Gild Hall
Courtesy of the Delaware
Historical Society
Del086

112 State Road
Courtesy of the Delaware
Historical Society
Eckman Coll- duPont Hwy-2

113 Bellanca Airfield
Courtesy of the Delaware Historical Society
86.19.15

114 Spirit of St. Louis
Courtesy of the Delaware Historical Society
62.24b

115 At the Beach
Courtesy of the Delaware Historical Society
Del028

116 White Brothers
Courtesy of the Delaware Historical Society
81.07

117 Synagogue
Courtesy of the Delaware Historical Society
87.17.230

118 Train Station
Courtesy of the Delaware Historical Society
Del092

119 Parade
Courtesy of the Delaware Historical Society
Del178

120 Queen Anne Pier
Courtesy of the Delaware Historical Society
Del199

121 Brewing Company
Courtesy of the Delaware Historical Society
Del060

122 Savoy Theater
Courtesy of the Delaware Historical Society
Del234

123 Spot Cafe
Courtesy of the Delaware Historical Society
Szynmanski 2003.15.228

124 Caterpillar Tractor
Courtesy of the Delaware Historical Society
3165

126 Old Academy Building
Library of Congress
031742pu

127 Delaware Hospital
Courtesy of the Delaware Historical Society
Del133

128 Lea Mills Fire
Courtesy of the Delaware Historical Society
Del170

129 Ushers
Courtesy of the Delaware Historical Society
Del235

130 French Street
Courtesy of the Delaware Historical Society
Szymanski 2003.15.169

131 H. P. Cannon
Courtesy of the Delaware Historical Society
Del003

132 Wilmington
Courtesy of the Delaware Historical Society
Frank 85.4.222

134 Race Contestants
Courtesy of the Delaware Historical Society
Del227

135 Ferry
Courtesy of the Delaware Historical Society
Del109

136 Maypole
Courtesy of the Delaware Historical Society
Del116

137 Middletown
Courtesy of the Delaware Historical Society
Del099

138 Army Ship
Courtesy of the Delaware Historical Society
Del143

139 Barbers
Courtesy of the Delaware Historical Society
Szymanski 2003.15.102

140 Farmers with Crops
Courtesy of the Delaware Historical Society
Del007

141 Cannery
Courtesy of the Delaware Historical Society
1998_69.7

142 Governor Buck
Courtesy of the Delaware Historical Society
85.4.288

143 Nursery School
Courtesy of the Delaware Historical Society
2002.17

144 Estella Hodges
Courtesy of the Delaware Historical Society
Szymanski 2003.15.123

145 Floodwaters
Courtesy of the Delaware Historical Society
Del176

146 School Bell Colonial
Courtesy of the Delaware Historical Society
Del136

147 Perfect Landing
Library of Congress
131051

148 Bette Davis
Courtesy of the Delaware Historical Society
Del232

149 Hose Demonstration
Courtesy of the Delaware Historical Society
Del120

150 French Street
Courtesy of the Delaware Historical Society
Szymanski 2003.15.24

151 WENDELL WILLKIE
Courtesy of the Delaware Historical Society
Szymanski 2003.15.268

152 TROLLEY LINES
Courtesy of the Delaware Historical Society
Szymanski 2003.15.230

154 BOARDWALK
Courtesy of the Delaware Historical Society
Del087

155 BLUE HEN CHICK
Courtesy of the Delaware Historical Society
1998.76

156 BEAM HOUSE
Courtesy of the Delaware Historical Society
87.17.377

157 BOND SALESWOMEN
Courtesy of the Delaware Historical Society
85.4.129

158 DRAVO SHIPYARD
Courtesy of the Delaware Historical Society
Del074

159 PILOTS
Courtesy of the Delaware Historical Society
Del161

160 BOND SALES DESK
Courtesy of the Delaware Historical Society
Del158

161 TRANSPORT PLANE
Courtesy of the Delaware Historical Society
Del159

162 GM GROUNDBREAKING
Courtesy of the Delaware Historical Society
Del146

163 DELAWARE STATE
Courtesy of the Delaware Historical Society
86.33.3

164 BLUE ROCKS
Courtesy of the Delaware Historical Society
Del223

166 SCIENTIST
Courtesy of the Delaware Historical Society
Bungarz 5498

167 NATIONAL GUARD
Courtesy of the Delaware Historical Society
Del121

168 HOLLYWOOD DINER
Courtesy of the Delaware Historical Society
Bungarz 60 275

170 CHICKEN FESTIVAL
Courtesy of the Delaware Historical Society
85.4.236

171 USS DUPONT
Courtesy of the Delaware Historical Society
duPont launching, duPont c

172 ROCKETS AND MISSILES
Courtesy of the Delaware Historical Society
Bungarz 8447

174 CIVIL DEFENSE
Courtesy of the Delaware Historical Society
Bungarz 8429

175 DRAVO SHIPYARD
Courtesy of the Delaware Historical Society
Bungarz 62-2345-6

176 CANAL
Courtesy of the Delaware Historical Society
85.4.255

177 TRAIN STATION
Courtesy of the Delaware Historical Society
Del189

178 STONE BRIDGE
Courtesy of the Delaware Historical Society
Del20

179 VIRGINIA NATIONAL GUARD
Courtesy of the Delaware Historical Society
Del156

180 BETHANY BEACH
Courtesy of the Delaware Historical Society
Del155

181 AUGUSTINE MILLS
Courtesy of the Delaware Historical Society
Del174

182 CONSTRUCTION CREW
Courtesy of the Delaware Historical Society
Del039

183 MEMORIAL BRIDGE
Courtesy of the Delaware Historical Society
Del037

184 BREWING COMPANY
Courtesy of the Delaware Historical Society
Del056

185 MOTORCADE
Courtesy of the Delaware Historical Society
Del041

186 MEMORIAL BRIDGE
Courtesy of the Delaware Historical Society
Del038

187 INSTALLING CABLES
Courtesy of the Delaware Historical Society
Del057

188 KOREAN WAR FUNERAL
Courtesy of the Delaware Historical Society
85.4.3

189 CIVIL RIGHTS ACTIVISTS
Courtesy of the Delaware Historical Society
Del185

190 GRAVEYARD
Library of Congress
304879pu-1

191 Farm
Courtesy of the Delaware Historical Society
Del015

192 Republican Headquarters
Courtesy of the Delaware Historical Society
96.107.200

193 Boardwalk
Courtesy of the Delaware Historical Society
Del026

194 Blue-Gold Game
Courtesy of the Delaware Historical Society
Del220

195 JFK
Courtesy of the Delaware Historical Society
Del187

196 Race Riot
Courtesy of the Delaware Historical Society
Del125

197 Vietnam Protesters
Courtesy of the Delaware Historical Society
86.33.28

198 Municipal Airport
Courtesy of the Delaware Historical Society
Del150

199 East End Lighthouse
Courtesy of the Delaware Historical Society
Del149